Ballington Unkorked

The autobiography of a World Champion Road Racer

REDLINE BOOKS

For Craig and Jake; without them life would not be as much fun.

Stan Shenton did three big things for this autobiography. He introduced the manuscript to Redline Books, he wrote a treasured foreword and he came up with the title. My original title had been 'Place of Dreams'. I was never happy with this but could not come up with anything better. Then Stan had a brainwave. He rang me and said, 'I think I have the perfect title for your autbiography. Hence, 'Ballington Unkorked'.

Thanks Stan, for your interest, kind words and ingenuity!

Kork Ballington.

ISBN: 978 0 9544357 5 2

Printed in Italy by Printer Trento

REDLINE BOOKS

Designed and published by Redline Books. **www.redlinebooks.co.uk**

Contents

Part 1: Background

Part 2: In at the Deep End

Ballington Unkorked

Ballington Unkorked

Kenny Roberts

It is great that Kork has written this book. It reminds us of what we were all doing more than twenty years ago, how some things were good and some things weren't.

Racing was a whole lot different then. There weren't the big teams and the money that we have in GP racing now. What hasn't changed is the fact that a rider who is as complete as Kork was, will get to the top.

To me that was Kork; the complete rider, he could get it right more often than the other guys he was racing with. It didn't mean he was the best at any particular area but he was good at them all and good all the time.

Of course he was racing a lot with Gregg Hansford and Gregg was one of the all-time great brakers. I was probably a bit more aggressive with the throttle and exit of the corners. Kork didn't have to be quite as crazy as Gregg on the brakes or push the limit as hard as I did on the throttle. Because he knew that if he lost a fraction to Gregg or me there, he was going to make it up somewhere else, over all he had it working for him.

He and his brother Dozy had something special worked out so that the motorcycle was the best it could be and Kork was getting the best out of it on the racetrack. They had it right... that was the way Kork went racing, he had it right, he made it work for him.

And that's the way he's done this book too, he's done it right, it's all there...

No1. Kenny Roberts, one of the all time great GP competitors.

Stan Shenton

I first met Kork in 1973 through a South African mechanic who was working for me at that time and came from Kork's home town. In 1974 when I became Kawasaki Team Manager and formed the UK Kawasaki team I saw him more often at race meetings, so when I was looking for a rider to partner Barry Ditchburn for the 500 mile race at Thruxton I offered it to Kork. He jumped at the chance.

In the event they won the race in spite of the fact that the gear change lever was on the wrong side for Kork.

At the end of 1977 the Japanese directors of Kawasaki decided that they wanted a new rider for the 1978 season and asked me who did I think could win a World Championship for them as they were sure that their machines were good enough to do it.

I suggested Kork and they agreed so Kork joined the team at the start of 1978 together with his brother 'Dozy'. The rest is history, and very well documented in this book.

Kork grabbed the opportunity with both hands, as I knew he would and finished the year with not one, but two World Championships.

His record was impressive, he finished every race in the series except two and these from electrical faults not rider error. Not one crash in spite of tough opposition from Kenny Roberts and Gregg Hansford to name but two.

He was the finest rider that I was ever involved with, having a pin-sharp racing brain he reacted instantly to signals and was an exceptionally talented rider.

I am proud to have been associated with him.

Team Kawasaki Manager

Scott Iwasaki

Back in 1977, Kawasaki signed on a new professional rider to help strengthen the company's racing activities in the FIM World GP Series. The rider was Mr. Hugh Neville Ballington, popularly known as Kork Ballington.

For manufacturers like Kawasaki selling motorcycles around the world, there is more than a single objective when hiring professional roadracers. Firstly, the manufacturers can use the rider's expert skills to compete with the other manufacturer's racers. The rider's skill, therefore, primarily represents his commanding use of the capabilities of the machines built with the latest technology by the factory, on a variety of circuits over the course of a year under differing conditions. Each circuit presents the challenge of riding around a complex of curves and straights on changing surfaces, at very high speeds, in all weather conditions.

Mr. Ballington is the only rider I know who has consistently utilized the machine's capabilities to great extent yet without compromising safety. He did this through courage, grim determination and dogged perseverance under the toughest adversity in the fierce competition. Kork did not seem to have the word 'Retire' or 'Quit' in his lexicon. He raced tenaciously to the finish line, hence offering a great deal of useful data for the development engineers.

Secondly, by winning on the track, the manufacturer can prove the superiority of its engineering and convince customers of the superiority of its production technology. Riding Kawasaki, Mr. Ballington made this more than feasible by winning and holding the FIM World GP Championship in 250cc and 350cc classes for the two consecutive seasons beginning in 1978. Kawasaki owes Kork a great deal for his contribution to Kawasaki's brand image all over the world.

What surprises me was that his talent went well beyond his riding techniques. He was extremely well-read and his exceptional writing ability produced excellent reports for effective communication with our Japanese engineers, who tend to get uncomfortable with oral communication.

Amazingly, there was a big contrast between the rider and the man himself. Before and after wearing his helmet, he was very peaceful and did not seem to have the aggressive spirit he displayed while racing. In this book, he does not hesitate to admit that he was shy. His sportsmanship and his truly humble character add an unspoken glow to his success.

Perhaps the most important achievement so far in his life may be the inspiration he has given to younger motorcycle riders who have chosen a motorcycle as the easiest and most economical way to enter into the world of motorization. They can learn from such an outstanding leader like Kork that there is much more to riding a motorcycle than pursuing speed, and there are ways to be successful.

I sincerely hope that readers of this autobiography will get a flavour of the style and skill that spectators witnessed seeing Kork in action.

Shigeki Iwasaki
Former Senior Manager, Motor Sports Dept.,
Planning and Control Office,
Consumer Products Group
Kawasaki Heavy Industries, Ltd.
Akashi, Japan.

Prologue

It was a cold windy wet December day in 1972, not typical weather for this time of year in the Natal Midlands. The cream of South Africa's roadracers were assembled on the grid of the Roy Hesketh circuit just outside Pietermaritzburg, the capital of Natal. The tension was at fever pitch. There was a buzz of anticipation around the picturesque circuit where a larger number of spectators than usual ignored poor conditions to watch the battle. The riders, clad in black leathers, sat nervously on their motorbikes while the mechanics made last minute adjustments and checks. The stakes were much higher than usual. The occasion was the first (and last) 'Mercury Race of Champions' event, a race of twenty-one laps, open to all classes.

The event was conceived by Jimmy McMillan the editor of the Durban based 'Natal Mercury' daily newspaper, and orchestrated by Joe Mulraney, the enthusiastic motoring editor. There were two prizes, each consisting of one air ticket to Europe, sea freight for two bikes and R400 cash towards expenses. The format: Competitors eligible for each prize would be the first Natal rider across the line and one other, chosen by a selection committee as a deserving candidate, regardless of finishing position or province of origin.

In those days South Africa had a vibrant road race series, thanks mainly to Yamaha's TD and TR production racers, as well as a strong economy and a strong currency. The Roy Hesketh circuit, 2.901km in length, was one of the finest short circuits that I have ridden on. It was situated on a hilltop outside 'Sleepy Hollow' Pietermaritzburg, 80km inland from the port of Durban in the province of Natal. All of South Africa's many world class riders and the bulk of the national champions came from Natal. One of the reasons for this provincial record was that this circuit demanded fine skill and we had free access to it seven days a week for unrestricted practice. In the entry list at Roy Hesketh on this day, were at least ten aces including current and former South African champions capable of winning the race. I was the reigning national Unlimited Class champion (racing bikes up to 1000cc), a title I took on a 1970 H1R Kawasaki 500 after a hard season against former South African champion, Les Van Breda from the Transvaal, on a TR500 Suzuki.

It is funny how things turn out. Certain things happen at certain times which can have a huge impact on the rest of our lives by creating a link to another chapter in our life's journey. Opportunities offered, such as the Race of Champions, and decisions made have such influence on events further along on our journey.

One such decision was made after we won the 1972 SA Championship. My father Johnno, as he was known to all, team leader and sponsor, brother Dozy, co-sponsor and chief tech, and I decided that for the 1973 Championship we would need to improve the H1R in order to remain competitive in the unlimited class and defend the crown. A new bike was out of the question as the budget would not stretch to it. What we could afford was something from the renowned workshop of British chassis constructor, Colin Seeley, a beautiful chassis which he had produced to take the 500 or 750 Kawasaki three cylinder

On the way to winning the 'Race of Champions' at Hesketh in December 1972 on the Seeley H1R.

Race of Champions. On bike 72, I go grass-tracking to avoid a pile-up on lap one. 43 is Mike Fogg, 77 Les Van Breda, 42 Johan Boshoff.

motor. Ace British rider, Paul Smart had been riding a 750 version in the USA with success. We ordered one and had it airfreighted to South Africa. The large wooden box with the chassis inside arrived a few days before the Race of Champions. Opening the box was a big event for all except my mother. She always thought we were nuts. I think she used to quantify racing parts as potatoes and cabbages, but never said so and always gave us support. She came out to the circuit to watch me in the early days when I was racing 50cc. Unfortunately I crashed right in front of her and her sister, Doreen, at high speed one day. After that the pair of them were seldom seen at the track and certainly never went near the corners again!

After working around the clock, the motor was fitted into the beautifully constructed nickel-plated frame with, luxury of luxuries, hydraulic disc brakes front and rear. Plumbing the three big expansion chambers into the low Seeley chassis was a nightmare but with everything bolted in place we set off to try it out. What a lovely ride! Roy Hesketh circuit had a couple of sections which were difficult even after we had made a lot of improvements on the old H1R. These were high speed sections on which you had to be very careful on the old H1R. The Seeley was on rails. It was magnificent!

I had to curtail my practice laps because the bike had arrived with the latest Dunlop tyres, which, judging by the rapid wear and excellent grip, appeared to be of a softer compound than was normally available to us. To save the tyres, I only did enough to get the feel of the Seeley and make adjustments before parking it for official practice the next day.

As I already said, It is funny how things turn out in life. As it happened, the soft compound tyres were to be the 'ace up my sleeve.' Race day dawned, heavily overcast and cool with a persistent precipitation. During official practice on the morning of race day I was astounded by the amount of grip the new Dunlops gave in the wet conditions. It felt like I was leaning over five degrees more than usual and up Beacon Hill, an excellent third/fourth gear uphill right-hander, I was getting the back to drift controllably under power. This was not possible on the tyres I usually used on the old H1R. The cool weather also helped the motor keep some of its torque, which usually disappeared after two or three laps in hot conditions. This would help a lot on a wet circuit by allowing me to use lower rpm coming out of the corners, thus avoiding wheelspin and ensuring a faster and smoother exit from the bends.

During the race I took the lead in the early stages and won by a fair margin. Had the race been in dry, hot weather I might not have been able to beat the TR2B 350s with the tired H1R motor and I believe the tyres would have overheated and lost grip. Had I not won I doubt if I would have been the other 'most deserving' rider. I believe that tag had Mike Fogg's name on it before the event in case he was not the first Natal rider across the line. As reigning 250 and 350 South African champion, Mike obviously had a great deal of talent and was certainly a deserving candidate for the prize. Had I not won, I would not have been packing my toolbox and heading for the most exciting and awesome experience of my life.

I strongly doubt that we would ever have organized an independent European excursion, simply because our finances would never have allowed it. Had I not won this race and gone to compete in Europe, I would not have become multiple World Champion. Someone else's name would have been in the record books for the 1978 and 1979 250 and 350 World Championships. The one and only Race of Champions event, the rain, the ace Dunlop tyres, they all seemed to come together for my exclusive benefit.

Once the far-reaching ramifications of this win sank in and the euphoria had subsided leaving the cold hard facts about the situation, my next thoughts were, 'Oh shit, what are we going to do now?'

These were the hard facts: We did not have the kind of money to launch a professional campaign in Europe. Basically sponsorship of the nature required for such a campaign was just not around. Finding sponsorship for local racing where a sponsor could at least see some benefit was hard enough, so raising money for something taking place on the other side of the globe was not going to happen. My 500, although now with a competitive chassis had a well-used two plus year old motor that was battling to pull the skin off a rice pudding and my second bike, a 250cc TD2B Yamaha of 1971 vintage, was now well over one season old. It would not be competitive against the water-cooled TZ250 Yamaha due for introduction in 1973. Neither bike was likely to be competitive in South Africa in 1973. What chance would I stand with outdated machinery and no money in Europe, the centre of the universe for road racing? Nevertheless, we decided that we might as well have a go, so we made our plans.

Part 1: Background

The beginning

Me at one year old in 1952.

I was born on April 10th 1951 in Salisbury, Rhodesia, now Harare in Zimbabwe, the third child of John and Joan Ballington. At the time my parents, both South African, were in Rhodesia because my father, a printer by trade, was there on contract as Workshop Manager at the Rhodesian Herald. I was never christened, but named Hugh Neville. The nickname Kork happened later, don't ask how or why. My folks lived in Salisbury until I was about 3 years old, when they returned to South Africa with Deryck, 9, Lynn, 6 and myself. I have a few hazy memories of Rhodesia, one of which was riding with my father on his little two-stroke Corgi scooter. It was a tough little fold-up machine for military use designed to be dropped by parachute. It had a low flat tank and high handlebars and I used to stand on the tank and hold onto the bars. I have clearer memories from the age of about 4 or 5 years old. We lived in a suburb outside Durban called Cowies Hill. In those days it was very undeveloped. Most of the roads were dirt and there was a lot of dense bush. The gardener was always bringing dead snakes hanging off the end of his rake to show us. This would get us excited which was probably his objective. We lived in a small house, which my father built himself, in a quiet street. I don't remember much about our home but remember our car quite well. We had a black Citroen with sweeping front wheel arches and a wooden dashboard that had the gear lever located in the middle of it. It was Johnno's pride and joy. I loved watching the speedometer indicator arm moving to bigger numbers as we went faster which was exciting. I couldn't wait to grow big enough to see over the dashboard and reach the pedals so I could have a go at driving.

My father worked for the main daily newspaper in Durban and in those days most families had only one car. My mother would drop him at the bus stop on the main Pinetown to Durban road and he would go to work in the city, with a lot of other dads, and return later by bus. Mom and I would drop Dozy and Lynn at school. Most mothers in those days did not work, the house itself was a full time occupation. My mother was busy all day with few modern conveniences to help. We had a washing machine that used to slosh the clothes around inside but to get the water out of them they had to be fed into a hand operated mangle one by one, minding not to pop buttons off, before being put on the line to dry. I remember watching her stringing and chopping the fresh beans or popping peas out of the pods. Most foodstuff needed some kind of extra preparation to get it into an edible state. Even the chicken used to come with its head and legs attached!

Life was very uncomplicated. You did not have a special pair of sport shoes for every application, a pair of Dunlop plimsolls was used for nearly all sports. Gradually marketing, global communications, and consumerism have changed all of this and created the huge pressures of today's society. Growth became the catchword, growth for prosperity, growth for a high flying lifestyle, growth to fund a bigger house and overseas trips... uncontrolled growth to knock a hole in the ozone layer and cook us all! When I compare the state of the world and lifestyle of

Me and Dozy with the old Citroen in the Rhodesian bush.

today's kids with those days of my youth in South Africa I feel lucky to have been raised in such seemingly uncomplicated times. Fortunately we did not have thousands of dollars worth of video games designed to be obsolete by next Christmas, to preoccupy us and keep us indoors. We could get on with being kids, having to make up games to keep busy using our imaginations, developing practical skills. I learnt to make up games to amuse and keep me busy until Dozy and Lynn came home, although that did not really guarantee either of them would play with me. Baby brother was often treated as if he had a contageous disease!

I recall spending a lot of time with a kid from the neighbourhood. He had an old metal pedal car with skinny wheels and a steering wheel. I was not interested in the pedals because you could never get up to a speed worth mentioning by pedalling. We used to push it up one of the steep hills nearby and take turns freewheeling down. I would have given anything for a pedal car to race against the neighbour but the folks could not stretch to it at that stage.

Mom and Dad at their wedding in 1944.

Posing with Dozy and Lynn, in 1952.

The soapbox cart

The year I started school, when I was 6 years old, we moved from Cowies Hill to nearby Pinetown. I think Johnno's aim was eventually to shake off the printing job so he took the lease of a trading store which sold everything from bicycle parts to bread. Above the store was a two bedroom apartment with a big covered veranda over the front of the shop. The shortage of rooms meant that Dozy and I slept on the veranda which was very exciting, like camping every night only in a real bed. It was so cosy watching a storm or looking at the stars from a comfortable bed. Johnno went to work at the Natal Mercury newspaper every evening and came home very late so mom ran the store in the morning while he slept and he would help in the afternoons before going off to his night shift in Durban.

I loved the new location. It had a huge piece of ground with a good selection of trees to climb and build a treehouse. It was also on the old main road to Pinetown so there was a fair amount of traffic coming past. It was far more interesting than Cowies Hill. Two of my favourite commuters were Dr. Savage who drove a

Dozy and I loved creating!

Mom, Dad and kids circa 1954.

blood red Alfa Romeo Sprint Veloce and Mrs MacDonald who had the ultimate vehicle, also blood red, an E type Jaguar. Dr. Savage used to come back and forth like clockwork so I knew when to look out for him but Mrs MacDonald was more elusive, a glimpse of the Jag was a rare treat.

Dozy was a skinny, studious-looking kid with glasses and a brace to control his buck teeth. At about 14 yrs old he was mending old radios, messing with anything electronic and doing all kinds of experiments with his chemistry set. We had a great treehouse thanks to him. We used to get the Beano and Dandy comics through the post, I think it was once a week. I would help myself to some sweets from the handy confectionery section of the store and retreat to the luxurious seclusion of the treehouse to read the comics. One day Dozy scrounged some wheels and a bunch of wood to build a soapbox cart. His cart was revolutionary. Instead of steering with rope he designed a system with wire wound around a broom handle and attached to the front axle via two pulleys. On the end of the broom handle was fixed an old car fan belt pulley, perfect as a steering wheel. When turning the belt pulley one way or the other the broom handle would wind up the wire one side and let it out the other, thus turning the front axle. It worked perfectly. His aesthetics were totally functional. The main plank, or disselboom, to use Voortrekker terminology, was on top of the axles so it had a high centre of gravity. We had hours of fun with it but Dozy was never a racer. One day he had a major crash down one of the dirt roads nearby, lost some skin and perhaps his nerve! On the day it happened I was placed on the best corner halfway down the hill as a traffic marshal. The roads were seldom used, but if a car came along I would wave and jump up and down to warn Dozy to pull over. He had started from higher up the hill than his last run to get more speed. The all-steel rear wheelbarrow wheels sounded like distant thunder as he picked up speed, fast approaching the bend. All was clear. He turned into the bend at great speed. The cart began to drift. He corrected the slide but it got bigger. Next moment the whole thing tipped up and rolled over three or four times. Dozy was thrown out and received minor abrasions and a major fright. I inherited the cart and set about remodelling it to look more like a racing car. I figured it rolled because it was too high, so I placed the disselboom under the axles which lowered it by a couple of inches. I built a small seat with low sides and added a neat racing type rear to the cart. It looked hot and went beautifully. On its maiden voyage which was down the neighbour's steep driveway and onto the shop forecourt, I lost control completely but the cart just spun around and came to a dusty stop facing back the way we came. My design worked. The low centre of gravity prevented it from tipping. I had such fun with the cart. The steel back wheels with poor grip were indestructible, perfect for learning skid control and taught me the value of smooth driving because driving the cart was a constant balancing act to keep momentum while trying not to slide too much.

At one time Dozy and I built an underground hideout on the empty acreage next door by digging a hole in the ground about two metres square and one metre deep. Over it we laid poles and on top of that branches, planks and whatever we could find to make a roof. One day we 'borrowed' a packet of cigarettes from the store and together with Lynn sat in the hideout for a serious session of chain smoking. Mom was not stupid. She knew what we were up to and in any case the smoke pouring out of the ground was a dead give-away. She merely observed and waited. Sure enough, we emerged a while later not feeling too good. I am not sure about the other two, but I was violently ill, much to the amusement of mom who smiled sweetly and asked if we had enjoyed smoking!

When I was about nine or ten, I got a shining new Raleigh three speed bicycle for my birthday. It was my pride and joy, the best thing I would ever get. I was now at junior school in Pinetown, about three miles away, so the bicycle was intended as my transport to and from school. What a buzz riding the spanking new bike into the main gate to park in a rack alongside the other bicycles. Not many had a Sturmey Archer three speed gear system. I was floating on clouds that day. The only thing that needed changing on that bike was the handlebars which were high and swept back into a very sedate position. I removed them and replaced them upside down, transforming them into a semi-racing style, perfect! Everywhere I went I was in a semi racing crouch, cutting under the wind at full speed.

Playing golf with dad in 1960.

I get hooked on speed

Around that time a new Grand Prix racing circuit was built just outside Pinetown in an area called Westmead. It was a superb, world class facility. One of the first international races that took place there was in 1962. I rode there on my Raleigh three speed and found a good place to watch on the exit of a bend called Club Corner. I could see the bikes coming past the pits and control tower, under the Dunlop bridge at speed and then slow down and heel over for Club Corner. I could see every wiggle and twitch of the bikes and the body movements of the riders as they worked at the handlebars, opening the throttle on the exit of the bend and simultaneously flicking the clutch and gear lever each time they shifted gear as they sped towards the next bend. It was the first time I saw a motorcycle race and I was totally blown away. There was the addictive smell of Castrol R racing oil and the sound of the open exhausts cracking out a tune while the rider in tightly fitting black leather racing suit shifted through the close ratio gears with a crisp precision as man and machine sped from one corner to the next. There he would again lean over at an impossible angle, sparks occasionally flying as an exhaust or footpeg scraped the track. Then someone would overdo it, leaning over beyond the grip capabilities of the tyres and slide off, the bike spinning along on its side and the rider sliding and tumbling along with a new urgency in his body language off into the dusty edge of the circuit to pick himself up and limp to safety. The flag marshals immediately began waving yellow flags to warn others of the hazard until crash marshals picked up the bike and moved it out of the way. The noise, the action, the bike and rider leaning over

Losing the front end of my three-speed Raleigh.

Me and Dozy in 1960.

With Douglas the handyman and Biff the bulldog circa 1960.

at seemingly impossible angles pushing skill and equipment to the limit, the crash being the consequence of overexuberence, the penalty for misjudgement. This was the best thing I ever saw and I was hooked. I rode all the way home at full speed dreaming that I was one of those mysterious black-suited heroes and rode every bend to the limit of the skinny bicycle tyres.

I still have the programme from that meeting, 20th January 1962. Amongst the mysterious heroes I was watching, although I had no idea as to their importance at the time, were Jim Redman, Phil Read, Gary Hocking and Paddy Driver. No wonder I was hooked! It is amazing to think that one day I would know Jim, Paddy and Phil well and actually race against Phil! Ironically, Gary Hocking, the popular Rhodesian and 1961 350 and 500 World Champion with MV Agusta, changed to Formula 1 cars and was tragically killed in a high speed crash at Westmead in December 1962 practising for the Natal Grand Prix.

At this stage I was doing well at school academically, running in the top ten of about thirty-five pupils in class. Pinetown Junior School was a mixed bag. It was a large government, co-ed, dual medium school catering for English and Afrikaans speaking kids. The English and Afrikaaners did mix with each other but mostly it was them and us. Sometimes we would get into arguments and our favourite, most harmful retort would be to call them 'Afrikaaner vrot banana'... vrot meaning rotten! They would call us verdomde rooinekke or soutpiele, the former meaning damned rednecks, the latter, saltcocks. The Afrikaaners said that English speaking South Africans had one leg in England, one leg in South Africa and that left their cocks hanging in the salty Atlantic ocean.

I excelled in sport without trying. I was blessed with good balance, judgement, co-ordination and natural fitness, so proved to be a very good all-rounder. The South African sport-crazy outdoor lifestyle and system whereby sporting activities were compulsory at school nurtured and encouraged my natural skills. Without exception every child had to take part in the team sport of the season. You would have to be at death's door to get excused from sport practices which took place every afternoon after class. Success at any extra-mural activity was rewarded with recognition, usually during morning assembly but the recipients were expected to remain modest. Discipline at school was totalitarian. If you stepped out of line you were in trouble and disobedience was hammered, usually with the cane. The system didn't exactly encourage shy introverts out of their shells. Children at that time were wary of having their say in adult company and not encouraged to do so.

We lived in the little apartment above the trading store until I was about eleven, at which stage Johnno decided to sell the store to concentrate on a home-building venture. Building was one of his passions and he built two of the homes we had lived in. He sold vacant land that he owned in Cowies Hill and bought land in Pinetown to start building speculatively. We moved out of the shop into a wonderful old traditional South African homestead with corrugated tin roof, verandas on every side, high ceilings and wooden floors. It was situated on a large and interesting bushy piece of ground across the road from the trading store.

On the carrier of a friend's Sachs, with Dozy, late 1950s.

Junior and High School days.

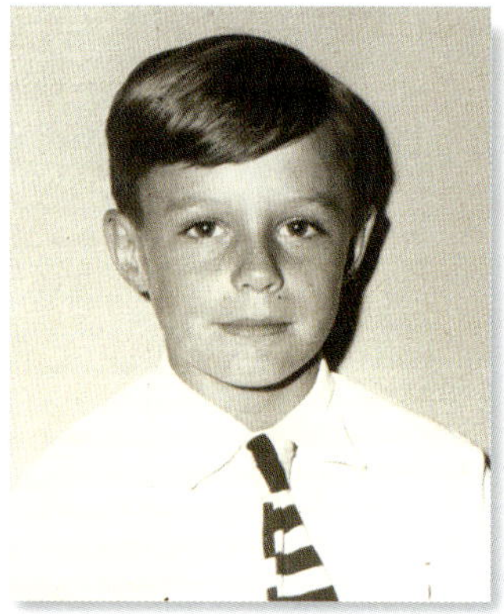

The Maz and The Circuit del la Casa

Around the time we moved into the homestead, Dozy turned sixteen, the magic age at which he was old enough to get a learner's licence for a 50cc motorcycle and consequently Johnno bought him an old Maserati T2SS 50cc three speed two stroke. It was beautifully styled, with a sport style fuel tank and seat, a neat tube frame and clip-on racing handlebars. On each side of the seat at the rear were two round white plates which would normally take a racing number. I was over the moon with this magnificent two-wheeled masterpiece. He often took me on the back, sometimes as far as the public swimming pool, which was a heavenly ride. Lifting on a 50cc motorcycle was illegal, so to try and dodge the cops, Dozy took the back roads with all the corners and I used to love leaning over with him as we went around them. He was not a hooligan or bad rider, the two bad accidents that he had within months of getting the Maz were not his fault. Both times drivers had turned across his path and both times he went flying over the bonnet of the cars, fortunately without serious injury. This must have been about when mom started turning grey.

She did not know it but she was in for a nerve-wracking time from here on! About a year later the Maz was totally worn out so it was replaced by a second-hand Honda 50 C110 four stroke with four gears. These recently launched Japanese 50cc bikes were eclipsing the Italian ones technologically, although the styling lacked the Italian flair. The Maz was not sold but left in the shed with the motor in pieces. I spied this lot and started trying to piece it together. I enjoyed technical problem-solving and worked out how to reassemble the motor then set it back in the frame. The biggest surprise was the day I put fuel in the tank and gave it a push. It started! Our garden had the perfect layout for a race track including a jump up the bank in the front yard. There were a lot of trees, fences and hedges with which to demarcate a circuit. Thus I began what was to be a long and passionate association with two wheels.

The lawn suffered, but Johnno was very laid back. He never tried to put a stop to proceedings. He simply watched with interest. He was a man of few words until it came to our sporting activities, then he was full of good advice and helpful tips. One of his favourite sayings was, ' A winner never quits and quitters never win.' Johnno's folks died when he was a toddler and he was placed in an orphanage in Durban. According to him, the only way to escape from the miserable life in the orphanage was by getting a job and the only job available at the time was a printer's apprenticeship so he took it at the age of fourteen! Perhaps the draconian upbringing of the orphanage led him to be very soft on us or perhaps it was the lack of parental guidance which caused him to be too laid back with our upbringing. Whatever the reason, there was seldom any discipline from him and perhaps we were allowed too much freedom.

He had been a world class long-distance runner and won five gold medals in the Durban to Pietermaritzburg 90km Comrades Marathon, because of severe elevation changes,a race reputed by experts to be one of the world's toughest long-distance events. In the early days it attracted a few hundred entrants. In the year 2000, the event attracted over 25,000 entrants, many from overseas. Gold medals go to the first seven finishers and out of five starts he had five gold, his best finishing position being second. His brother Hardy was a legend, holding world long-distance records in 100 mile and 50 mile races in England. Hardy won the Comrades an amazing five times so there were competitive genes in the family. Many years later my sister Lynn's first child, Lan Bale became a highly acclaimed Junior Springbok tennis player and went on to play professional tennis all over the globe.

I am not sure if poor old mother gave my father harsh words about what I was up to but I somehow don't think so. I think she might have given up by then. I was most fortunate that he had this laid back attitude which allowed me the freedom to develop along my chosen path. Little did we know it, in these early years with the soapbox cart, with my bicycle, with the tired Maserati and then the big AJS on the garden race track I was developing extraordinary skills that were going to be amongst the best in the world many years later. Without knowing it, through trial and error and a lot of practice, I was gradually improving my ability related to smoothness, judgement, balance, powers of concentration and focus and parallel to these I was developing confidence and a belief in my ability to ride fast and safe. I can still conjure up images and feelings as clear as crystal of steering the cart to the limit, or riding the Maserati with both tyres sliding so slightly and drifting the Ajay on the dirt track around the house. I was indeed fortunate that mom did not interfere and that Johnno was not the type of person to hit this on the head and say that there was to be none of this dangerous nonsense going on in his back yard.

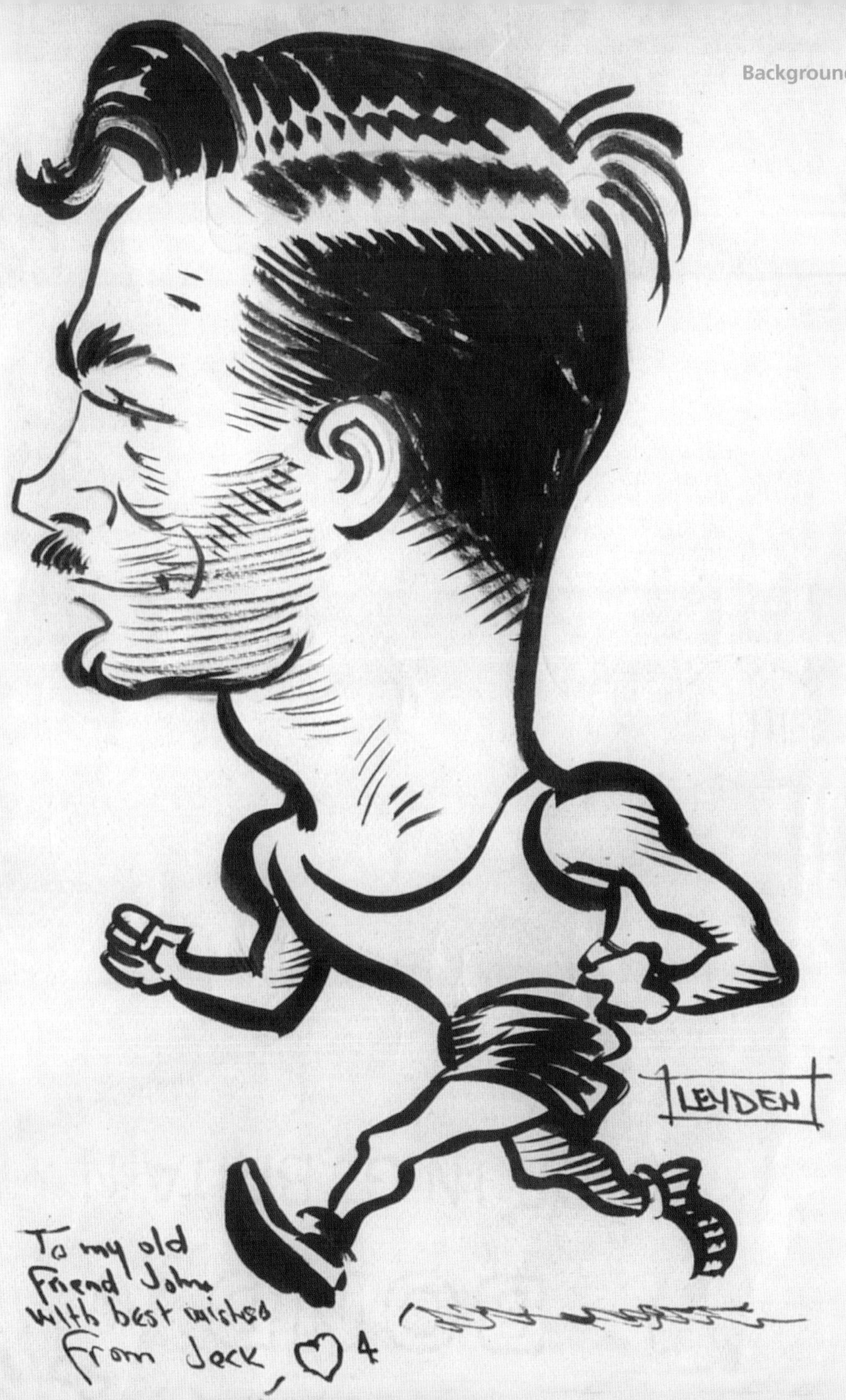

A Jock Leyden caricature of Johnno running.

The 350 Ajay, new lessons

In about 1963, Dozy, the lucky devil, finished high school. We did not call it graduating in those days and there were no fancy ceremonies. You simply finished twelth year and got the hell out of it as fast as your legs could carry you. He got a good job with National Cash Registers in Durban working as a technician. This heralded a new era of prosperity as he was being paid fairly handsomely. As soon as he saved some money, Dozy bought a burnt-out Matchless 500 which he spent weeks restoring to perfection. It was a powerful brute and a ride on the back under full acceleration was a new realm of sensation. The brute simply carried on and on accelerating through the gears until the world was flashing by at an alarming rate. Next Dozy bought an AJS 350 as scrap to rebuild as a dirt tracker to ride around the 'Circuit del la Casa'.

Being the great brother that he was, he let me ride it... if I could start it. This was a major problem because I was a skinny short twelve year old. With starting the Ajay, the word determination took on a new meaning for me. I would come home from school just itching to get on this immense 350 single cylinder and lap the house, the only hurdle between me and absolute pleasure was the task of getting it going. To start with I could not touch the ground when sitting astride it and it was a heavy beast. I would wrestle it from the shed and lean it against the back step with the left foot peg on the step because the dreaded kick-start lever was on the right side. Starting these old British singles was an art. You had to prime the float bowl just right to make sure there was enough petrol in it and set the choke to a certain setting which was easy enough. The next step was to put weight on the kick start lever until the huge single piston got just over the top of the compression stroke. Then you had to grit your teeth and jump on the kick start with all of your might to get that old piston going fast enough to gain momentum that would carry it over the next compression cycle when, hopefully, the engine would start. People have been known to sustain serious leg injuries if the bike backfires on the compression stroke thus sending the piston back in reverse at great speed. This would punch the kick start lever immediately right back up so if you were still standing on it and if your leg was still straight you could get launched right over the handlebars. I went through all sorts of gymnastic manoeuvres starting the Ajay and always succeeded. It took a number of attempts, but once going it was total heaven. The bike had an open exhaust so made a great crackling noise. There were no neighbours close by so I was able to indulge myself on most afternoons without irritating anyone, perhaps with the exception of my mother and my sister.

With this powerful 350 came new lessons. Driving and riding techniques with the cart, bicycle and weak Maserati were very much based on powerless or low power riding techniques which entailed maintaining high rolling speed in bends with almost no sliding if possible. The trick to fast laps of the house on the Maserati was to learn to be able to take the tyres to the limit of adhesion, and keep it on that fine edge, without breaking that adhesion. Sliding causes friction at the tyre which in turn arrests the forward motion of the vehicle.

Unless the motor has enough power to keep the forward momentum going while the slide is being controlled, the vehicle will lose speed, which is undesirable.... not the object of the exercise. On the Ajay, feeling like a tick on an elephant's back, I learnt the immensely pleasurable art of throttle control and using the power of the motor to steer the bike. I realised that I was not strong enough to wrestle my way out of problem situations so conducted the familiarisation period with the Ajay with extreme caution. I also knew that if I was to crash and get hurt on this bike, mom would definitely ban proceedings.

With this in mind I started slowly and cautiously, gradually building up speed and learning from the bike what I could and could not do. This approach stayed with me throughout my racing days and undoubtedly saved a lot of skin. The riding sessions were never long, twenty or thirty laps at a time when I got home, often late in the afternoon after sport training. It did not take long before I was comfortably power sliding the Ajay around the bends, opening the throttle progressively in the bend until the rear wheel would start sliding at which stage the throttle needed to be feathered then opened the right amount to keep the drift going smoothly, at the same time increasing speed on the exit of the corner. It was a continual balance of the right amount of throttle at the right time to suit the circumstances. Racing lines would differ between the two riding techniques. With the high maintenance of rolling speed technique as with low or no powered vehicles, I had to use all the road, or in the case of the garden all the space that I mentally demarked or was indicated by shrubs or walls as the race track. For example in the case of Kitchen Corner, a ninety degree left hander, I would approach it past Lynn's bedroom right up against the thorny hedge, slow down to the right speed and peel smoothly into Kitchen maintaining exactly the right pace. At the apex of Kitchen I would be right on the inside of the bend and without changing the angle of lean of the Maz, or my bicycle, sweep on through the bend, effectively freewheeling until after the apex when power or pedal could be gently reapplied and we would end up right on the very outside edge of the track on the exit of Kitchen before opening the throttle wide or pumping those pedals. That was the fastest racing line through there on low powered vehicles. Options increased with power. On the Ajay I could use the classical, sweeping, rolling speed racing line or slow down a little extra on the entrance to Kitchen Corner, peel in sooner to the apex, lay the bike over and at the same time ease the throttle open to get the rear wheel sliding a little, not too much, lift the bike upright a couple of degrees, maintain the slide while accelerating all the way out of the bend and hit the straight at good pace. I was a logical thinker and could work out how to do it without anyone to teach me the techniques involved. Everything I did as a kid regarding racing around corners simply seemed the right way to go, the lines, the throttle control and so on, all happened naturally. I simply let my body and mind do what seemed right.

It was around this time that I had grown enough to reach the pedals and see over the dashboard of the Citroen. Johnno was a good sport and agreed to let me do a few laps of the house in it provided I did not try any speeding! It was great fun, but not in the same league as cranking a bike around. I might have been a quiet kid but I was no angel. One day I was alone at home and decided to try and drive around the house in the old VW Combi that Johnno recently bought for carrying building material. One lap was fun, then two... eventually I was getting up quite a pace in second gear and actually getting the back of the Combi to slide on the hard sand around Kitchen Corner. I finally got too brave and took Kitchen too fast. The high narrow Combi got very sideways and without warning went up on two wheels. It hovered there as if deciding which way to go while I clutched the steering wheel, white-knuckled, and stomach churning. Much to my relief it came back down. I parked it smartly. I would have been very unpopular if mom and dad had come home to find the Combi on its roof in front of the kitchen!

A short circuit racer starts to take shape

Around 1965 when I was in ninth grade, my schoolwork started going downhill. Between the bikes and to a far lesser degree, the babes, the academic pursuits suffered badly. Pinetown High School was co-ed so we had to look at these mysteriously appealing, interestingly shaped creatures, all day. I was way too shy, and when I fancied a girl I was unable to approach her. If she ignored me I would take it as rejection and give up. If a girl gave a sign or a message that she liked me, only then would I have the courage to plan an approach. It might be to meet at the Gaiety Cinema in central Pinetown on Saturday afternoon for movies, or at a social event at the civic centre on a Saturday night. I was hopeless at courting and had terrible trouble trying to find the courage even to hold her hand or ask for a dance. Perhaps shyness was my good fortune. Some of my friends had lost interest in their bicycles and were becoming strangely obsessed with girls, preferring to spend the afternoons and weekends with their girlfriend rather than messing around on two wheels. I thought this was crazy and stuck to my two wheeled companions. After all, I didn't have to talk to them!

It was around this time that I had my first encounter with alcohol. One Friday night my best friend, Nico Venter and I, rode to the Imperial Hotel in Pinetown to watch Dozy and his mates playing snooker. We were not allowed in the licensed area so watched with interest through the window which opened onto the parking lot behind the hotel. The next thing two Lion Ales were placed in front of us by Dozy and his grinning mates. I had occasionally had a sip of old dad's beer and liked the flavour very much so a whole bottle was an interesting notion. Nico and I eagerly accepted the brown bottles and retreated into the shadows of the car park. Shortly after we finished our ales a strange light and carefree feeling came over us which led us to ride around the car park doing wheelies and huge broadside skids, now entertaining the creators of our mirth. The more Dozy and his friends laughed at us as they watched through the snooker room windows the more ridiculous we got. We survived and the next day there were a few cuts and abrasions and perhaps a headache, to bear testimony to the encounter with the brew!

I played for the A teams in rugby and cricket and also represented the school in athletics in the 880 yards race. My opposition in the 880 at school was Louis Grobler from the Afrikaans segment of PHS. We were a total contrast. Louis was very tall and I was the second shortest guy in our grade. In every event I would challenge Louis all the way to the final straight when his long legs would help him inch ahead. We always finished thus. I was an excellent long distance runner where stamina counted most and finishing speed was not as important as in the 880.

Johnno still went for reasonably long jogs on Sundays and I would go with him. One particular year when still classified as a junior I was in superb shape from training with Johnno and heaps of bicycle riding, I went out and won the annual school cross country event held over a distance of about 5km, beating all the senior pupils as well. I remember starting out slowly as Johnno had advised, to get my rhythm going, then gradually increasing my pace to cut through the field of fast starters. By halfway I was

Competing in the 880 yards for my High School, 1965.

flying and not in the least tired. Johnno was there with water and a sponge and jogged next to me for a few metres, dousing me with the sponge to freshen me up. I remember passing Louis Grobler which gave me immense pleasure. I also remember passing the last of the seniors, who was leading the race, on the way up the Old Main Road within half a km of the school gates. He stepped up his pace to try and stay with me but I was not even panting and left him. It was a big surprise to everybody when little Ballington sprinted through the main gates and down the steep tarmac descent onto the field to complete one lap of the athletics track to the ribbon, hardly out of breath. Not believing a junior could accomplish this with such apparent ease, the headmaster ordered an investigation to find out whether I had taken a short cut. Other competitors were asked if they had seen me all the way around the course which was naturally affirmative, so the matter was laid to rest. I obviously had what it took to run distances, which was in keeping with the family tradition, but it did not excite me. Training for long distance was tedious so I never got serious about it, preferring to jog a few km now and then simply to keep fit for rugby or athletics.

I was so desperate to watch motor racing that one weekend when an important race meeting was on at Roy Hesketh, 70 km from Pinetown two mates and I did the 140km round trip on our bicycles simply to watch a few races! Riding there was a mission so on most occasions I would hitch-hike to Pietermaritzburg on race day and hitch back to Pinetown after the last race was run. Around the time the Westmead Grand Prix circuit was built, a go-kart track was also laid out on the hill in the loop of the main circuit formed by Club Corner, The Draai and The Rise. It was becoming a meeting place of Pinetown's Buzzy Boys, the guys with road going 50s who were racing converts. (50s were popularly known as Buzz-bikes for obvious reasons.) They would meet there at weekends to compare notes and do laps. I would ride out on my bicycle and observe proceedings. At this stage the best bikes were the Honda C110, the Yamaha YF1 and the sleek Suzuki 50. They were fairly evenly matched in standard trim so lap times of the fast guys were similar. In the corners each bike looked different. The Suzuki appeared the most stable, the Yamaha wallowed a little as if the suspension and shock absorbers were too soft. The Honda's front wheel, with its strange leading link front suspension, pattered mildly. I would sit and watch the guys having such fun, pondering how I was going to get to utilise this splendid race track before turning sixteen, the legal age for a 50cc licence. I mean, I did not actually need a licence simply to do laps at weekends but I would need a reasonable bike and I would need to get it the 8 km from home to the circuit.

I decided on a plan, I would take the dead Maserati motor out of the frame and look for a newer Japanese 50cc motor to try and fit into the Maz frame. With this goal in mind I embarked on stage one, preparing the frame. I modelled a fibreglass tank extension to make the tank look like a racing one. I built a crude little racing seat and through friends with welding and other engineering facilities had a set of neat racing footpegs made.

The finish left a lot to be desired because we had few tools with which to do it properly but it looked like a racer and it felt like a racer. Unfortunately it did not go like a racer because it had no motor! I was so desperate to experience fast forward motion on my creation that I used to freewheel it down Stapleton Road lying flat on the extended tank in a racing crouch, dressed in my usual attire of shorts, t-shirt and no shoes, attracting concerned stares from passing motorists. We used to get up to quite a lick by the time I would have to brake hard and crank it right over into a side street. It would have taken some explaining if a cop had driven by during these strange excursions. If I had carried on down Stapleton without turning off I could have freewheeled onto the main freeway to Durban which would have been a laugh, this young shoeless maniac with a glint in his eye on a motorless motorcycle wearing shorts and t-shirt freewheeling down the high speed freeway to Durban!

Eventually an old C110 motor materialised very cheaply via Colin from Pinetown. (We won't use his last name!!) Colin used to be able to procure almost any part you wanted quickly and cheaply. We admired him for his enterprise and good service and could not understand how he did it. If you needed a wheel, one call to Colin and two days later the wheel turned up. The cops were also very interested. They eventually caught him stealing a bike which was no doubt destined to be stripped for spares. The cops descended on his house and found a graveyard of buried bike parts in his yard! Although we reported that we had bought it from Colin, the 'hot' motor was not reclaimed by the cops so was fitted into the Maz frame.

It all worked out and the Honda/Maz started and went. The first stage of my plan was complete. Johnno was reluctant to take me to Westmead though. It would have been so easy to stick the bike in the back of the Combi and head off to the track but he refused. I decided the only way would be to ride it there which was a pretty stupid idea. The track was on the other side of town and the Pinetown traffic cops were a prolific and stern bunch. I thought, okay, I would ride it down the back roads and then push it through town and remount when back in the quieter areas. Johnno explained later that he expected this racing thing was a passing fad and observed proceedings without becoming too involved. When I asked him if I could push the bike out to Westmead he realised it was time to get involved. The seats came out of the Combi and the Honda/Maz went in. So the first team trip to the track took place some time in 1966 and it was heady stuff indeed. Although the bike did not steer too well and did not go too well and the tyres were old and worn, it was glorious out there on the little go-kart circuit. I had finally made it. From then on Johnno and Dozy took more of an interest. We even did a trip to Pietermaritzburg one Sunday to try the legendary Roy Hesketh circuit. This was an exciting outing. For days afterwards I would mentally go over the circuit layout, doing laps in my mind and visualising how Quarry Curve should be taken or the best way around Angels Angle and recall the sweet sound of the little four stroke Honda engine buzzing along down the long main straight, singing to me as I listened intensely to every note.

Action on our C110 Honda.

The team builds a real racer

By 1966 a lot of organized go-kart and 50cc racing was taking place at the track with the two branches of the sport becoming amalgamated under the same umbrella. All racing events were organized under the auspices of the Natal Motorcycle and Car Club. Racing was well supported in both karts and bikes and there was intense inter-city rivalry at the races between Durban/Pinetown NMCC members and the guys from the Pietermaritzburg club, Maritzburg Motorcycle and Car Club.

I was about eight months from my 16th birthday when I would be eligible for a road licence. This would allow me to get a competition licence. In the meantime things had taken a dramatic turn at home. Dozy's C110 Honda fifty road bike had not yet been sold. It was agreed that we would scrap the Honda/Maz and turn the C110 into a racer. Life had indeed taken on a rosy hue. By dogged perseverance I had enlisted the help of the people who meant the most to me. We could only go forward from here and so the project began. I was the happiest, luckiest kid alive. We stripped the C110 completely and shelved all parts not needed for racing. The fuel tank was extended to race status. The Honda frame, a pressed steel affair, underwent major surgery as all unnecessary bits were cut off to lighten it. Racing handlebars and seat were manufactured by me and welded by a friend. The motor was stripped by Dozy to receive some horsepower attention. I gave the frame parts a coat of aerosol orange and the tank gloss black. The colour scheme was a copy of one of the riders I liked to watch at Hesketh, a guy by the name of Ophie Howard. He was as smooth as silk and the preparation of his 500 Matchless G50 was superb. It was painted orange and black and always looked highly polished. His racing number was 72 so I decided to use this as my first number and to emulate his standard of preparation.

To increase the power of the motor Dozy bought a race kit from the Honda dealer in Durban. It was the first time I saw such shiny new parts, and they were racing parts to boot, all the way from Japan, that mysterious place that young racers held in awe. We had the utmost admiration for the Japanese because of the superb

My first race, Roy Hesketh in 1967. Honda 50cc C110. I finished third. Trevor Tilbury, later to wield spanners for the likes of Kenny Roberts, looks on.

The 'Real Racer' hot C110 Honda at Westmead in 1967.

road bikes and exotic multi-cylinder, high revving, feats of racing ingenuity that they seemed to produce so effortlessly. These bikes were beginning to dominate the world of motorcycles, both on the roads and racetracks. In our kit from Japan was a high compression piston, lightweight pushrods and special valve springs. Gabby Galbraith, my jovial older cousin, a highly skilled car mechanic and a race enthusiast, had contacts all over Durban in motor racing. One of his friends ported the head, neatly shaping the inlet and exhaust ports for improved gas flow and therefore better breathing efficiency. Another of his connections at an engineering shop cut the cam to some Cosworth profile. We had the cylinder honed and assembled the motor with all the hot goods. We also bought a tuned megaphone designed to enhance the performance of the kitted motor. This was such exciting stuff and completely took over my body, mind and soul.

I polished all metal bits to a mirror finish, the paint job was high gloss and smooth so when the whole package was assembled and stood on the veranda it was beautiful. We started it for the first time and it fired into song, making that crisp crackling roar that can only be made by a hot four stroke with a megaphone extracting and amplifying the explosion created by the complex process taking place in the cylinder head. Race-tuned four strokes such as our little C110 are technically marvellous. With the high lift cam, shaped inlet ports and high compression piston, special valve springs and light pushrods, plus some of Dozy's own touches, it became far more efficient and powerful and with the help of the megaphone, made that wonderful sound created by the four stroke process. As the piston goes down the inlet valve opens and a mixture of high octane racing fuel and air is sucked in via the carburettor, through the specially shaped and polished inlet tract, past the inlet valve, now lifting slightly higher and staying open slightly longer because of the special cam. As the tiny piston starts ascending, the inlet valve closes. The gas, now more of it than there would be in a standard motor, is trapped in the cylinder. The high compression racing piston with its higher crown compresses the fuel-air mix more than normal because the space in the cylinder head is less than standard so that when the spark plug fires near the top of the pistons compression stroke, the mix explodes with far more ferocity than normal. This blows the piston down with more thrust giving the motor more power. On the next up stroke, the exhaust valve opens wider than standard to cope with clearing the greater amount of burnt gas through the shaped port. The shape of the megaphone creates a pulse that helps pull the burnt gas out as well as emit the noise, the result of the fuel/air mix exploding at up to one hundred times a second at peak rpm, the wonderful melodious howl that characterises a racing four stroke.

Not only did our creation look and sound superb but it went superbly. It pulled well on the straights, the brakes worked well and it handled nicely in the corners. This being my first meaningful hard surface circuit experience, I started out taking it easy and slowly built up confidence in myself, the machine and the circuit. I had the distinct advantage of my extensive experience at the 'Circuit de la Casa' and even from things learnt in the soap box cart and on my bicycle but most importantly, I had the great passion which I felt about this thing I was doing. The passion led to the skills that I had already nurtured, making it all so much easier. It did not take long before I was braking hard and late and leaning over steeply through the bends and turning excellent lap times, the equivalent of some of the guys who already had extensive racing experience. Westmead go-kart circuit turned out to be the primary school of my road racing career. It was an excellent track to start on, being safe with wide crash areas. It was technically demanding with slow and fast corners, was not fast enough to be hazardous and it had a good surface on which we could confidently lean over low. A story related to me recently by one of the old NMCC officials was that the legendary British roadracer, Mike Hailwood, who lived in Westville near Durban at the time, was watching us kids racing at Westmead one Sunday and had commented that the stuff world champions are made of could be produced from such an environment!

All of us at Hesketh with my magic C110 Honda.

The start of great things

At the age of sixteen, now armed with a suitable machine and a competition licence for 50cc racing, I entered my first meeting. It was on 7th May 1967 and was a five lap race on the Roy Hesketh main circuit. I came third and according to my records got R2.00 prize money! (At the time worth about £1.00) The race was won by a very talented rider from Maritzburg, also on a C110 Honda. His name was Mike Grant. Mike was one of the best riders produced in South Africa. His injury in Europe during his tour in 1972 prevented him from achieving great things overseas. He was another talented product of the vibrant 50cc racing scene on the go-kart tracks of Natal.

By the end of the year I had ridden at nine meetings at five different circuits in Natal. Three of them were go-kart tracks like Westmead, one was my first race, on the Roy Hesketh big track and the other was my first taste of racing on a road circuit. The event was at the small town of Eshowe in Zululand. The course ran partly in a suburb and partly through the park complete with trees, kerbs, poles and straw bales, much like a miniature Montjuich Park where I won my first GP. At each of these events there would be three or four short races which enabled the riders to concentrate on improving performance and rectifying previous mistakes. It was an excellent school. Races were well subscribed with ten to fifteen starters. Competition on the tight, narrow go-kart tracks was fast and furious, reminiscent of British short circuit racing with not an inch given away. At my second race meeting which was at my temple, Westmead, I had my first taste of being in the lead, but coasted to a silent halt with a broken coil wire. It was at my third meeting that I had my first sweet, sweet taste of victory. This was at the BP Bend link go-kart track, a part of the Roy Hesketh circuit. Of four races I rode that day, I won two and was second and fourth in the others. I received a small egg cup sized silver-plated trophy for the effort. It stands proudly amongst my huge collection of trophies from all over the world and still means a great deal to me. The race that I finished fourth in was a handicap race. These handicap races were significant, in that the fastest rider of the day would start last by the time he was estimated to be faster than the slower competitors. I was always with the fastest riders at the back and these races were excellent track craft practice because we would have to cut through from the back overtaking as many riders as possible to try and win. I ended the season with five race wins under my belt from nine meetings. We had a few silly breakdowns from poor preparation and I had a few minor crashes while trying too hard or exploring the limits, all part of the broader experience.

In 1967 I began realising my childhood dreams. I would be on the clouds after a race weekend. I was also becoming a mini hero at school but was too shy and modest to capitalise. After a winning weekend the young ladies would point and whisper, which was flattering, but still did not build enough courage in me to take the bull by the horns! School work was the biggest victim of my weekend activities. I sat through classes dreaming and planning what we would do at the next race and consequently was hovering around the bottom of the class, much to mom's dismay. Johnno, maybe because of his orphan background held different views about education, never put any pressure on me to study and was now 100% behind the racing which he enjoyed thoroughly. He was there with his stop watch and checklist... petrol in, tyre pressures right, chain tension right and so on. Dozy did not come to all of the races but was essentially the technical and part financial help of the team. His circle of friends was into playing snooker at the Imperial Hotel, going to the beach, ogling chics and modifying their cars. At one stage Dozy decided that he wanted to have a go at racing. We had enough parts to build two Honda 50 racers which we did

Racing 50s at Eshowe in Kwa-Zulu Natal. I am number 4.

painting them identically, even our helmets were painted the same. His debut was at Eshowe but Dozy was not destined to be a racer. He had his first crash pulling into the dirt surfaced pits at the end of practice when he pulled the front brakes on too hard, locked the wheel and went down. Next crash came during the first race when he politely moved over in a bend to allow a faster rider to pass him. He ran into some gravel on the outside and went down. The final straw came in his next and last race when the front brake cable jumped out of its holder while braking for a corner and he went straight on into the straw bales and fell. Lynn enjoyed the buzz at the races and being associated with the successful team. She became my greatest supporter. Mom came to the nearby meetings on the small go-kart tracks. She was a quiet level-headed person so I can only imagine that she must have been somewhat baffled, possibly stunned by proceedings, but in view of what had been going on in her garden for so long was probably not totally surprised. Because our family was not well off, she undoubtedly did without certain

Bronnie at two years (left, four years), ain't she gorgeous!

luxuries because of the racing, something I would only appreciate many years later. The racing, not only for the Ballingtons but most other competitors, was a family affair. At every event were the parents and brothers and sisters of the riders, there to support what they were doing and pull together as a team. The racing circle became a mini society of people who laughed, raced, argued a lot and grew as individuals together.

The end of year exams came and went and I scraped through by a gnat's knacker to head into the last lap of my academic career, the final year. At the end of 1967 Johnno was offered a partnership and position as the manager of a tomato farming project with friends of his. This meant moving to Thornville, a small farming community abut 20km from Pietermaritzburg. I would have to do my final year in Pietermaritzburg at Alexandra High School.

Once again fate played into my hands. The move closer to Maritzburg proved to be vital to advancing my motorcycle racing aspirations. I would meet some key people in Maritzburg and I would have convenient access to Roy Hesketh circuit, the high school and university of my racing world. This was to play a crucial part in my development as a rider and with regard to setting up chassis and suspension and the complex task of the tuning of race motors. Another significant event to take place that year, 1968, in Maritzburg was the first contact with the person who would become my biggest buddy, fan, lover and mother of our children, Bronwyn Randles, the prettiest girl I ever saw. She had sparkling blue eyes and big smile. It was love at first sight but of course I did not have the courage to let it show!

1968 started well for us with wins at the first two events. Significant at this time was that two strokes were becoming faster as one or two thinkers got to grips with the art and science of two stroke tuning. In the second and third events I was beaten by a guy I used to race against on bicycles at a bush bicycle track we frequented at Pinelands near Pinetown, George Cummings. George had an amazing Bridgestone 50 with a race kit which included close ratio gears, high performance cylinder, piston, head and exhaust system. When it went it was very fast and George beat me in two Natal Championship races in a row. Meanwhile, to keep pace we acquired a used Yamaha YF1 motor and I began putting together a 'bitsa' from a collection of parts, building what I thought was going to be a seriously wicked racer. I was leading the Natal 50cc Championship by a slim margin from Mike Grant but would need a faster steed to keep the title hopes alive!

I was immensely satisfied with my 'bitsa'. The object of the exercise was to produce a bike that handled well, but only using up the spare bits and pieces lying around the shed. I fitted the Yamaha motor to our spare Honda frame by making special mounting brackets and moved it forward in the chassis by about two inches which I thought would improve stability. I acquired a set of Suzuki front forks because I thought they had the most efficient damping and fitted them to the Honda frame. We did a little work on the motor and took it to its first race and won, beating George in the process. My creation handled like a dream. The Suzuki front fork worked way better than the Honda type

My hot 'bitsa', Honda frame, Yamaha 50cc YF1 engine and Suzuki forks.

Street racing on 50cc was an excellent school. Here I am, number 1, on the YF1 Yamaha.

leading link front fork that I had become used to and the bike was very stable as I had hoped, which gave me more confidence. This excellent little creation was to serve faithfully until 1971 when I built a lightweight tube frame for the motor.

By now, the middle of 1968, the farming project was not working so Johnno moved us into Maritzburg and resumed speculative home building. At the same time Dozy got a transfer to work in Maritzburg and was living at home again. We were now only minutes from the track which was always open and cost nothing to use, so it was very convenient to go there with the stopwatch to try any modifications or simply to do laps. On some weekends we would test early in the morning, rush back to our tiny workshop where Dozy would modify the cylinder, rotary valve, head or such and then rush back to the track to see if the lap time was better. It was such a learning curve and such fun especially when after a modification the lap times improved. I learned to detect minor differences in motor performance and power characteristics and analyse such things quickly. I still have detailed notes of modifications and the results of them in terms of lap times on the big track. This kind of practical test was far better than any dynamometer testing could be. Big horse power can be achieved using a dynamometer which can be simply described as an expensive horsepower testing machine, but often dyno power does not translate into fast lap times. Dozy and I learned an enormous amount from this backyard R&D. To start with, the Yamaha, with minor modifications, lapped Hesketh at just under two minutes at an average speed of 88kph. By June 1972 we had found a lot more power by

1968, action on the fifty at Roy Hesketh.

The Alpet Motors Suzuki AS50 at Roy Hesketh in 1968.

experimentation and ingenuity and were lapping at 1min 38secs, an astounding average speed of 107kph, still with only four gears. The very expensive five speed close ratio factory Kreidlers from Johannesburg, that used to come to Hesketh from time to time could not match such a lap time. The officials often impounded our little Yam after a race for stripping because other competitors kept protesting that there was no way a fifty could go that fast, that it had to be an oversize motor. The bike was regularly stripped and inspected and was always legal in every respect, the protesters ambling off muttering and shaking their heads in disbelief.

I was now winning most of the races and on the road to becoming Natal 50cc Champion. By August I received a letter from Yamaha Racing Division in Japan. I had written to them a few months earlier asking if they had any tuning tips for our YF1. I did not expect a reply but those decent guys in Japan sent me a full spec sheet on modifying the motor with dimensions for an expansion chamber to go with the modifications. We

The Alpet Motors Suzuki AS50 at Roy Hesketh with 'Sleepy Hollow' in the background.

Grr Baby.

Bronnie and Lynn at Westmead in 1969.

The Alpet Motors Suzuki AS50 with beautiful Syd Stacey frame.

1972, action on the fifty at Roy Hesketh.

At Drakensberg Gardens Hotel chasing Mike Grant.

immediately implemented the specs and the result was amazing. Our Yam now had a lot more power, pulled better at low rpm and revved higher. It was a jet and at our first race with the new specs at Westmead, I became the first rider to lap under forty seconds with an astounding 39.4 second lap and as my notes state, 'trounced the opposition and took three trophies home.' Team Ballington had lots to celebrate because we took the Natal 50cc Championship which was a pretty good effort considering it was our first full season, something to be really satisfied and proud of. We were a complete team, dad, Dozy, Lynn, Mom and me and by then I had built the courage to sweet-talk Bronnie into coming to the races so there was a little romance brewing. The tally at the end of 1968 was fifteen race meetings entered with eighteen race wins and a rather gorgeous steady girlfriend!

Fifty racing in Natal was hotting up with good entries and factory race kits for the two strokes becoming available. Gerald 'Baldy' Alexander of Alpet Suzuki in Durban became our first full sponsor when he invited me to race his superb factory-kitted Suzuki AS50 five speed which he bought from the importers in gold rich Johannesburg. On the track it was no quicker than my Yamaha, in fact had a far narrower power band, but an expense paid ride was big cheese. I rode it in the last few races of the year and it was interesting but was not an ideal set-up for me. Baldy's mechanic from his dealership would bring the bike to practice and the race and then take it away again so I had nothing to do with the preparation, therefore could not keep my finger on the pulse. I rode it until the end of March '69 winning a lot of races on it before Gerald decided to stop racing so I went back to my magic YF1 which was standing by.

At Westmead in 1969 ahead of Trevor Tilbury.

My first leathers, a beautiful set of Lewis that Uncle Hardy brought back from a UK trip.

Mike Hailwood on the 297cc Honda Six

Life in Sleepy Hollow

The move to Maritzburg led to a new circle of friends, most of them involved in racing. Maritzburg was a great place for teenagers and we had an excellent social life there. Everybody knew each other so if there was a party happening we would hear about it.

One of the biggest efforts that I have ever put into anything went into the last minute studying for year twelve final exams which I somehow passed. Something which spurred me on to study hard was the comment of our maths teacher. After trial examinations he suggested I go back to primary school and start again. I wish I could remember his name because he deserves some appreciation for not giving up on us. He made me and some other maths failures do extra classes after school. It did the trick and I ended up with a C in maths. It was one of the best days of my life when I walked out of the gates of Alexandra High for the last time on break-up day. When I think about it, I can still feel the relief and freedom that I felt at that moment. The ensuing celebration lasted for a long long time.

I recall the headmaster's words near the end of year twelve when I was hauled up for something, probably speeding or scraping my footpegs coming through the main gate. 'Ballington will never amount to much.' Academically he was dead right. I hope he remembered his words and noticed that I became one of South Africa's most successful international sportsmen of all time. Many years later I was invited to the school for the Founders Day celebration as guest speaker to address 750 pupils. I was introduced as the most successful student to have been produced by Alexandra High!

During 1968 I had the immense privilege of seeing Mike Hailwood on the 297cc six cylinder Grand Prix Honda.1968 was the year that Honda Racing Team pulled out of the World Championship series and paid Hailwood not to ride for another team. Mike spent 1968 doing international races and demo rides such as at Hesketh, on the awesome Honda six cylinder Grand Prix thoroughbred. We had inside information as to when he was going to practise and waited for hours on the outside of Angels for the moment. When it happened it was unbelievable and unforgettable. We heard the Honda fire up in pit lane. The noise of the six open megaphones magnifying the sound of the motor is hard to describe. From Angels we could see Hailwood flash by under the Dunlop Bridge and hear the shriek of the Honda as he changed back two gears for The Sweep. He then disappeared into the dip in the middle of The Sweep. When he emerged from The Sweep he was cranked over as low as you can go. My heart leapt into my throat and this was only his warm up lap! On this section you had to lose speed while leaning right over,

Dicing at the BP Link circuit in 1969.

Shimwells Racing Team, 1969. Syd Stacey (centre) Mike Grant (right).

braking and changing down at the same time. Without so much as changing his angle of lean or racing line he braked went down two gears and as smooth as silk negotiated Angels at a frightening angle of lean. At the apex he started getting the power back on to accelerate down the main straight. At peak revs, in excess of 18,000rpm, the sound was mind-blowing. The legendary man, four times 500cc, twice 350cc and twice 250cc World Champion, the legendary 297cc six and the legendary sound caused by over 800 tiny explosions taking place in the combustion chambers each second. I still remember the sounds and images as if they were yesterday.

Around this time I met Syd Stacey, a brilliant engineer and racer. Syd, the 1963 South African 250 champion, was workshop foreman at Shimwells, the Honda, BSA and Triumph dealer in Maritzburg. He was such a wealth of technical and racing knowledge. Shimwells were about to embark on a production class racing programme headed by Syd. I was offered a fully sponsored ride on their CB175 Honda, Mike Grant a ride on a CB350 and they were looking for a candidate to try the infamous CB450 black bomber, an ill-handling beast. After it threw the first two candidates off there were no more takers so Syd had to come out of retirement to tame it, which he did. This turned out to be such a professional set-up with Syd at the helm. Everything looked smart and the preparation of the bikes was impeccable. I learned a great deal from the association about preparation and presentation and a lot more besides. With the ride came position of motorcycle salesman for me for R160 a month plus commission. It was my first and only job in the conventional sense of the word and I hated selling with as much passion as I loved racing!

Thus I started 1969 with sponsored rides in the 50cc class on the Alpet Suzuki AS50 and the 175cc production class on the Shimwells Honda CB175. Life was great. I was learning a lot from Syd on the technical front and the whole family was together and settled into the laid back lifestyle of 'Sleepy Hollow' Pietermaritzburg. The race circuit dominated our lives. It was situated just beyond the eastern suburbs on top of a hill overlooking the city, like a sacred citadel.

The CB175 was an amazing bike. Slippery Syd, as Syd Stacey came to be known for his expertise at tuning production bikes, expertly cleaned the inlet and exhaust ports of its cylinder head as the rules said you could. This transformed it into a jet, increasing peak rpm substantially. The production class was split into about five classes with the CB175 slotted into the class for motorcycles up to 200cc. After a few races when I learned the bikes limits, I could keep up with the slower 350s. They would

On the CB350 Honda dicing with the legendary Johan Boshoff on his TR350 Yamaha.

Young love!

Sportrait

"KORK" BALLINGTON

THE 18-year-old lad with the strange nick-name was christened Hugh Neville Ballington. His father, John, and uncle, Hardy, were great marathon runners, Hardy winning the Comrades five times and seven Gold Medals, and John finishing second once, and gaining five gold medals.

Not unnaturally, Kork had a go himself and succeeded in winning the Pinetown High School cross country championship while still a junior.

But once he got the whiff of racing oil smoke in his nostrils, watching Hocking, Redman and company on the Westmead Grand Prix Circuit, he had only one ambition — to race a motorcycle. He turned 16 in April, 1967, and got a 50c.c. Honda. Two months later he raced at Hesketh, finishing third.

Thereafter he appeared regularly on the Westmead small track, and, at the end of the year, was runner-up in the championship ratings, going on to win the 50c.c. Natal Title in 1968. This year he has raced 175, 250 and 350 as well, and is leading the championship ratings in the 50 and 175 classes at this stage.

In the recent three-hour production race at Bloemfontein, his 175 was second in its class, eighth on index, and 11th overall.

CB175 at Angel's Angle.

leave me a little down the straight but I would catch and pass them in the corners and beat them to the line. This embarrassed some and raised many eyebrows. During the year the CB175 became the target of an official protest because of the way Syd got it to perform and the incredible lap times I could do on it. It was stripped and inspected with the camshafts, head and other parts taken away for measurement. Naturally everything was within the regulations so the protest was squashed. I loved it when our opposition protested. I considered it as a form of flattery. It meant we were good!

I won every 200cc class race effortlessly except for one when I fell off. I lost it on BP Bend during a race and fell heavily. I wanted to finish the race to score points in the championship so picked the bike up with a lot of pain from my left shoulder, got it started and continued, but my left arm was very weak and I rode the remaining few laps with very little help from it. After the race somebody noticed my left shoulder sagging. He remarked that he thought my left collarbone was broken. A trip to the medics to confirm a clean break was followed by a trip to the local hospital to strap it up! Despite missing a couple of races I had amassed enough points to win the Natal Championship for the class. The fifty was going great guns and I again won the Natal 50cc Championship. The season's tally was twenty race meetings entered and twenty-six race wins achieved. Syd and Mike won their classes as well so it was a clean sweep for Shimwells Racing Team.

Jock Leyden's caricature done in 1969. You knew you were doing something right when Jock turned up with his pencil and pad.

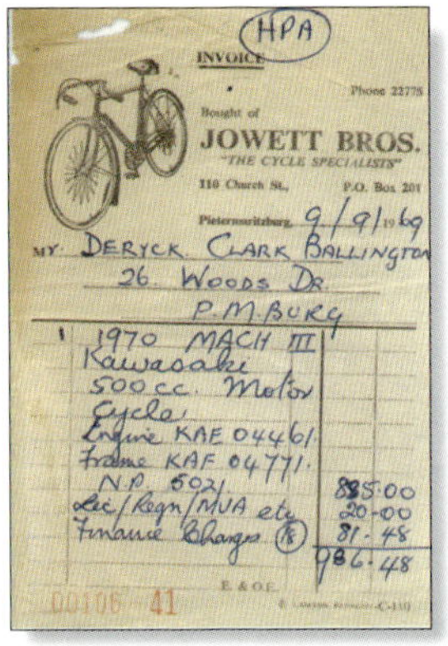

HPA

INVOICE

Phone 22775

Bought of

JOWETT BROS.

"THE CYCLE SPECIALISTS"

110 Church St., P.O. Box 201

Pietermaritzburg, 9/9/1969

Mr. DERYCK CLARK BALLINGTON
26. WOODS DR.
P.M.BURG

1	1970 MACH III Kawasaki 500cc. Motor Cycle. Engine KAE 04461. Frame KAF 04771. N.P. 5021.	885.00
	Lic/Regn/MVA etc	20.00
	Finance Charges	81.48
		986.48

E. & O.E.

00106 41

Preparations for 1970

In September of '69, Dozy splashed out and bought one of the new breed of superbikes for us to race in 1970 in the 500cc Production class. It was the first of the three cylinder high powered bikes from Kawasaki and it was amazing. Out of the box it was also amazingly dangerous. The tiny front drum brake was way short of the speed of the bike, as were the front forks, frame, rear suspension and wheels! The only thing right about it was the price. At R986 on the road, it was the cheapest, fastest bike around. The ultimate was the four cylinder Honda CB750, complete with disc brakes, but it cost too much. Anyhow we knew we could make it handle and make it stop, no question! It nearly caught me out on my first street test ride though. I was accelerating hard on a bumpy section of road which caused the inadequate front forks to start flexing violently in what is known as a tank slapper. The 1940s style friction steering damper which is supposed to help arrest such events, was totally ineffective. This was a tank slapper to write home about. Closing the throttle did not settle it, so I put the power back on and this did not help either. As I motored on down the road wrestling the beast, I was resigning myself to the fact that my scantily clad body with only shorts and t-shirt on, was about to sustain severe injuries from the inevitable smash. Then the wobble subsided.

The sneaky H1 caught Dozy though. He decided to show the queue of people buying tickets at the local movie house how his bike could go. He accelerated hard past them. The front wheel became light and developed a terminal tank slapper. Dozy lost it. He and the bike skidded down the road in front of dozens of onlookers. It was a mean beast.

Racing the 'Dynamic' 1969 H1 Kawasaki 500cc 3 cylinder in 1970.

Racing the 'Dynamic' 1969 H1 Kawasaki 500cc 3 cylinder in 1970.

Shimwells were not going to continue racing in 1970 so we were back to the old team with a new Kawasaki H1 500cc Mach III and the Yam YF1 now lighter and lower, with a smart home-made tube frame. Around this time I received my call-up papers to do compulsory military training. I was due to start at the Air Force training camp which by some joke was called Valhalla, near Pretoria in July for an eleven month stint serving my country. Hip bloody hip hooray! This would effectively spoil two years racing with the termination date sometime in June 1971. It was compulsory for all white South African males so there was no use bitching. In those days there was still some sense of patriotic loyalty to the country, and the idea that we would be proud to die protecting it from the communist enemy.

I was no longer selling bikes for Shimwells. Selling was something I was no good at and once I sold bikes to a few friends I never managed to sell another. I retired from selling and joined Johnno in the speculative home building game. It was good hard work which did not involve working with the public. It was fun to watch the neat little houses creep up day by day until completed. We would then move off to the next lot and start again.

The year turned out to be most interesting, starting with setting the Kawasaki up for racing. The first time I practised on it everything scraped on the deck. The suspension, springing and damping was too soft. The ride height was too low. It had no hydraulic steering damper, wobbled badly on the main straight and the front brake suffered badly from overheating, only working properly once per race which was at the first corner! After much modification, including re-calibrating the front fork

The awesome sounding race kitted CB350 Honda.

Limping home after a rare crash on the H1 at Roy Hesketh.

damping control holes and a major change of riding style, I started circulating in good times. Another innovation concerned the front springs. It became impossible to find ones of the right firmness until we found out that air rifle springs fitted perfectly down the inside of the standard springs. Thus we were able to get the spring tension at the front perfect. By fitting air scoops and experimenting with linings, until we found the most suitable, we improved the front brake to where, at best, it was just good enough. I also had to get used to the speed of it. Compared to the 500, the CB175 was a kitten. The H1 was capable of reaching 100kph in 4.2 secs and covering a standing start quarter mile in 12.4 secs. During the year it was clocked at 201kph on the short main straight. These figures are not bad for an air-cooled 500 in 1969. In the foreword of our original rider's manual, the bike is described as 'your dynamic partner', a very apt description. Our decision to race the 'dynamic partner' turned out to be good. We did get it to handle and stop acceptably as promised and I was immediately competitive. Although we firmed up the front and rear suspension and raised the ride height as high as it could go, the pegs and the pipes still scraped on the track. I had to adopt a spectacular 'hang off the side' riding style to get the most out of the bike on the corners. I won second time out on it at Hesketh. The sheer spectacle of the bike, which used to slide and wobble and my hairy looking riding style generated very good press coverage and spectator appeal.

On that same day I also won the 50cc race. Getting off one bike onto another was an experience. The lap time differential was about twenty seconds and the riding styles totally different. Nobody could ever say I was not versatile. Syd Stacey had prepared a CB350 Honda in a lightweight frame with a CR kit on it. I rode it at this meeting and it was very impressive, not far behind the TR350 Yamahas on speed and I got third behind two TRs. Unfortunately I only rode the Honda once more. I had to rev it to 12,500rpm all the time to stay near the TRs and it dropped a valve so the project stalled. It was a beautiful sounding bike with two open megaphones each howling out a magnificent tune, albeit not a patch on the sound of a Grand Prix six cylinder Honda. A big moment for me was in January after my first ride on the H1 at Hesketh. It was in a supporting race at the first South African TT, an international event won by Phil Read. I got third place in the production race. At the prize giving that night I was thrilled to be presented with the third place trophy by Mike Hailwood, the guest of honour.

Life was very exciting. In the space of three years I came from rookie on a little Honda 50 to someone who could get an impressive lap time out of anything that crossed my path. By the time I needed to pack my suitcase for a year in the Air Force in July to do my military training, I was leading the Natal Proddie and 50cc championships.

In action on the race kitted CB350 Honda.

I serve my country

July is winter in South Africa. I had never been, or wanted to be in chilly Pretoria at that time of year. The Government had different ideas though. Together with a few hundred other conscripts, we boarded a special train in Maritzburg for the overnight trip to Pretoria, each clutching a bottle of our favourite grog for the traditional last bash before being confined to barracks. The trip was memorable with about two hundred drunks singing and toasting whatever came to mind as the sandy brown South African railway carriages clickety-clicked through the night. Overindulgence and the motion of the rocking train turned a lot of the singing into heavy duty yodelling as the night wore on!

We had all heard about how tough military training was, so were not surprised when, from the moment our wobbly legs touched the platform in Pretoria station we had a barrage of verbal abuse hurled at us by the Gestapo-like soldiers who formed the 'unwelcoming' committee. They had zero regard for two hundred throbbing heads and we were herded into army trucks and taken on the roughest possible ride to our new home, the dreaded Valhalla. I was a bit shell-shocked by it all. As a winning racer in little old Maritzburg I was becoming used to a certain amount of respect and privilege around town. Now I felt I was being treated like a piece of shit. Thank goodness I had enough sense not to try and tell them my position in life and demand some respect. The few cheeky guys who dared to so much as utter one word of complaint suffered severely. There were a variety of punishments most of which involved some form of torturous physical exercise that never ended, like 1,000 push-ups. If you collapsed in the early stages you would get an order such as 'Jou sleg clomp kak. Sien jy daai boom....is jy al terug.' ('You horrible piece of shit. Do you see that tree... are you back yet') You would have to run to the tree as fast as you could. It might be a hundred metres or a mile away and even if you did it in superb Olympic style, it was never good enough for the Corporal. You would have to do it again or revert to the press-ups or bunny-hops or whatever form of sadistic amusement came into his mind. A lot of tough guys were reduced to tears by the severity and futility of the punishment. We learnt very quickly to shut up and do whatever these guys wanted and do it immediately with a 'Ja Korporal. Nee Korporal. Kan ek you gat soen (can I kiss your arse) Korporal.'

The first thing that happened at camp was that we lined up outside the barber shop and in quick succession were shaved almost bald. Some smart ass asked for a perm and spent the next twenty minutes doing the running and hopping bit. Obviously a sense of humour wasn't going to help.The Permanent Force Corporals who were in charge of us were all Afrikaans and never used English except when they could make fun of someone 'Ag shame, is the little English boy missing his mommy!' Another favourite of theirs was when you did something they did not like. He would say 'Is jy Engels of Afrikaans?' knowing full well you were English speaking. When you replied 'English Korporaal' They would say in heavily accented English 'No wonder you are so stupid.' The first three weeks of basic training were hell. The morning would start at about five o'clock with bungalow inspection. Our beds had to be very neat with perfect square edges, no ripples in the blankets and not a piece of fluff in sight. In fact most of us slept on the floor next to our beds so we could have a half hour extra sleep rather than get up at 4 am to make the bed. The floor had to be so shiny that you could use it as a mirror. Everything had to be as neat as a pin.

Once through the inspection we would assemble in our thin powder-blue denim overalls on the parade ground in perfect silent lines. The only noise apart from the ranting of the corporals was the crunching of the heavy frost under their boots as they paced backward and forward explaining to us what useless turkeys we were. We would be left standing perfectly still and

Airforce photos at Valhalla.

In khaki drag at Valhalla.

silent from 5.30 am for at least an hour until the sun came up. We were frozen with just the thin overalls on. I am not sure if it was psychological but as the sun rose it seemed to get colder until you lost all feeling in your fingers, toes, face and ears. After the session on the parade ground we would be dismissed for breakfast. Everything at camp seemed to be designed to make life difficult. The queues for the mess were long and it took ages to get to the line of huge pots with a variety of tasteless mush to choose from. The food was not going to win awards but nobody was going to complain. After eating you had to queue up to wash your 'varkpan' or 'pig pan' as were called the large stainless steel dishes onto which the food was slopped. If you were amongst the last to finish eating, the large tub in which you washed your pan was as thick as a good stew with the bits from the previous 1,000 pans!

The rest of the day would be filled with all kinds of exercises like doing leopard crawl backwards and forwards across a rough, rocky field on elbows and knees until bleeding. Eventually the skin on these strategic parts became thick and tough. Or we would take long hikes carrying a huge weight of equipment. We became like robots, which was the object of the whole deal. We learnt to do what we were told when we were told, quickly and efficiently. By the end of three weeks it all seemed like second nature which was quite scary. If anything vaguely resembling the communist enemy came over the hill at us we would have run at them like sheep.

I was fortunate to have been called into the Air Force as opposed to the army. Although we were doing the heavy basic training, including the use of our R1 automatic machine guns, it was unlikely any of us would do duty on the front line except in the case of running and maintaining aircraft and administration of temporary airstrips near the borders, under the protection of the army. The communist threat I jokingly refer to was at the time no joke. Young, fresh out of school conscripts and hardened permanent force soldiers were losing their lives on the borders on an almost daily basis and citizens were being killed in rare but effective bomb attacks in public places. At that time South Africa had Castro's Russian backed Cuban army in hostile Angola on our north west border training the Angolans in guerrilla warfare and leading incursions into South West Africa, (Namibia), which at that time was part of South Africa. To our north was Botswana, another hostile neighbour who insisted it was not harbouring any terrorists. However they were caught out a number of times when raids from South Africa's highly respected commando squads would destroy camps harbouring communist trained terrorists. To finish the bleak picture, Mozambique on the north east was a hotbed of Russian backed, trained and equipped guerrilla terrorists. Its borders were only about 400km from Pretoria, the military nerve centre of South Africa and Johannesburg the site of some of the world's richest goldfields and major financial centre of Southern Africa. There was more than one reason for these war games. Numero uno was that Russia viewed South Africa as a wonderful piece of real estate, not for holiday tours to beautiful beaches, but as a militarily strategic and wonderfully mineral rich country. If Russia could cause the downfall of the fiercely anti-Communist white minority controlled government and have a pro communist puppet government in power she would be in a great position to control both the strategic sea route around the southern tip of Africa and the vast mineral wealth of the sub-continent.

In the meantime back at Valhalla we gratefully came through basic training far tougher for the experience, but mostly not convinced about racing to our deaths for the Vaderland. We applied for placement in sections of the Air Force to undergo training in specific jobs. It could be in admin, as aircraft technicians, cooks, pilots, drivers, mechanics, do an officer's course or whatever. We filled in forms which asked us what we wanted to do and where we would like to do it. I naturally applied for a cushy desk job and for location at the Bluff AF base in Durban, nice and close to home. Instead I was placed in a telecommunications operators training course at the STO (Skool van Tekniese Opleiding) just down the road from Valhalla, a hell of a long way from my desired Durban!

The great escape

During basic training no one was allowed out of Valhalla for any reason except the death of a close family member or perhaps your own. Just after we had completed basic training, the oppression eased slightly. I had an important race coming up at Hesketh. I asked our Corporal, who turned out to be a nice guy and a race fan, whether or not sportsmen could get special leave for events. He said that the Sergeant Major was sympathetic and usually let sportsmen go on weekends if they could prove there was an important event. I arranged telegrams from the NMCC regarding the Natal championship races coming up to help convince the SM there was indeed an event. At my appointment with him I did not get a chance. He simply threw the telegram across his desk and stated in heavily accented English 'Motorbike racing is not a sport. Leave denied.' When I informed the Corporal of the SM's decision he came up trumps with an elaborate plan to enable me to orchestrate my own 'great escape'.

The race was on the coming Sunday. Maritzburg was 700km down the road and my desire to get there was great. The

Home-made chassis with trusty YF1 motor. In 1970 it was the fastest 50cc machine in South Africa

Corporal and I stood under a tree on the parade ground out of the way. He was on duty that weekend and would mark me as present at role-call on Friday and Saturday night, but that I should try to get back by role-call on Sunday so as not to push our luck. He figured the best thing for me to do would be to wear my formal Airforce trousers, big blue great coat and cap but carry civilian clothes to put on once out. The Military Police, always on the lookout for AWOL candidates, were less likely to question somebody in civvies. The best way to get through the main gate would be to climb aboard the truck taking the large contingent of Jewish conscripts to the synagogue on Friday evening. Although they had a head count going out it would be too bad if it did not tally coming back. We gambled that nobody would be able to pinpoint me as the missing party, so no one on the truck would get into trouble. Sounded good to me. Once out of camp I should get to the back of the truck to jump out at an appropriate set of traffic lights, then I was on my own. It was about 7pm when we started getting into the truck. I casually hung around looking invisible until I saw the driver take up his clipboard and come out of the office. I had my cap low on my face and coat collar up around my ears. I climbed over the high tailgate of the old Bedford and slipped quietly into a space on one of the benches that runs along each side of the back. The truck was full and nobody took any notice of me. The driver counted us half heartedly, fired up the motor and off we went, through the boom to freedom. It was such a good feeling. Phase one had gone perfectly. After about ten minutes we came to a stop at some lights. As quick as a flash I slithered over the tailgate and out into the night. With only a rough idea of the way to the main road I set off in that direction and started hitching. Eventually I was picked up and taken about 60km to Heidelburg. I stood there for a long time next to the deserted, thin black strip of tar, freezing despite the coat, until I got a ride with someone on their way to Durban. I had it made.

At about 3.00am the kind gent dropped me off at the Maritzburg City Hall. Half an hour later I knocked on the window at home. My parents were amazed to see me. They knew that I could not get a pass to leave camp. I enjoyed relating the escape to them. Johnno, whose nickname in his young days was Burglar, was impressed. He loved to sneer in the face of authority!

Next morning we were at the track for practice. The story of the great escape got around but mostly I had to take a lot of teasing from people regarding my stylish skinhead haircut.

Sunday's big event was a two hour race for proddies, with the richest purse to date in South Africa. I can't remember what was considered as rich in those days but it would have been no more than R200, enough to buy some racing fuel and a piston or two.

More important was the competition, to take up the challenge of two hours of hard and fast limit riding against the foe, the CB750 Hondas. I had pretty much got the measure of the other 500 Kawasakis like ours but the CB750s were more refined than the Kawasaki, with more power, front disc brake, better suspension and chassis. The race got under way and a guy by the name of Simon Fourie, an extraordinarily extroverted fellow, on a CB750, took the lead. I knew Simon seldom had control of his emotions if I was near. I knew that if I sat on his tail he would take care of himself for me. The bigger threat was Johan 'Bossie' Boshoff, the Grand Master, multiple SA Champ, tough gentleman of bike racing. Sure enough after a few laps Simon dumped it at Angel's Angle. I remember the look on his face as he hit the deck, looked back up at me with a surprised grimace, then bounced off into the dry, hard and dusty trackside with his untidy bike following him. In the next few laps Bossie came by. He was on a mission. I would have had to punish my fragile brakes to stay with him, so could not take up his blatant challenge. A few laps later he was out of the race having worn a hole in his left crankcase on the corners causing a terminal oil leak. This left me in the lead which I held to the flag. It was a newsworthy but comfortable win by one lap from Mike Grant.

My records show that I also won the 50cc race on the day. It was a very special win against another YF1 Yamaha from the Transvaal. It was a YF1 built and tuned on a dynamometer by a guy with a reputation as a great rider and tuner, Jannie Stander, and it was claimed to be South Africa's fastest 50cc. It was ridden by Freddie Van Niekerk, no slouch, and we beat them with a win as important as the one hour race, proving we had developed the fastest 50cc racer in the country. I imagine we cracked open a cold Lion Ale or two that afternoon, something that I had not had for over three weeks. After racing was over and we were loading up, Simon came over to our old Combi sporting a broken collarbone. He pulled out a gun and shot a hole through the roof of the Combi over the front seat, said 'Take that Ballington!' and walked off. We were dumbfounded.

I found someone at the track who was going straight back to Pretoria that night, so set off for the long haul back to camp. At about 10.30pm, in time for 11.00pm roll-call he dropped me right outside. I chose a quiet spot at the camp fence where I waited in the dark for a while, listening for the noise of a guard on the other side. When I thought all was clear, I climbed the fence, leapt to the ground on the other side and landed in the arms of a beaming guard. He was delighted to catch himself an AWOL conscript and marched me smartly off to the duty room with his loaded R1 in my back. I explained to the livid Sergeant that I had only jumped over the fence half an hour earlier to go to the shop to buy some food. As I was marked present on Friday and Saturday nights, he believed me and I was not severely punished. The common punishment for going home without a pass was seven or fourteen days detention barracks. I never made it there, but heard that it was soul-destroying and turned most men into mice. The days consisted of digging deep, perfectly square holes and filling them in again then re-digging them and other such monotonous morale-crushing tortures.

Soon afterwards we were all shifted to our various sections, mine being the STO located nearby to learn telecom operating. All we had to learn to do was touch type, operate telex machines, format messages and send and receive them. I learnt to touch type at about fifty words a minute, which has actually been useful in the processing of this story. Once qualified I requested to be sent to the signal department at the Bluff Airforce Base in Durban. When my posting came through, I was transferred closer to Durban. It was to the Airforce base at Waterkloof, down the road from the STO, about 5km closer to Durban! Here I spent the remaining seven months in relative comfort, sending and receiving signals in the nerve centre at the HQ of the formidable South African Air Force. During off duty hours I used to lie in a field alongside the main runway and watch the top gun aces putting the Mirage jets and older Buccaneers through their paces, trying to visualise what it was like controlling such awesome weapons. Around this time I was going home almost every weekend. Sometimes Dozy lent me his car to keep at camp, sometimes I would hitch and on one occasion one of the other guys in the bungalow who was also from Maritzburg, Pete Moolman, offered me and a couple of other guys a ride home with his father who was picking him up. Of course I jumped at a ride all the way home.

In an unbelievable turn of events I should have been killed that night. Moolman took over the wheel about half way home, late into the night. He and his dad were in the front and three of us were in the back of the Renault, sleeping. Sometime after he took over the wheel, I felt a lurch and woke up. When I looked out the side window I was looking straight down the road and the next second the world was upside down. Sparks were flying. Moolman must have fallen asleep and lost control. The car skidded along on its roof. The next thing I knew I was sitting in the middle of the road. I could hear swearing and groaning. I went to the edge of the road to find the car down the bank, on its roof with the headlights lighting up the veld. By some miracle no one was hurt. I had come out of the rear window while the car was sliding along on its roof and ended up in the middle of the road with one small scratch in the middle of my back. It is amazing that I was not killed or even injured.

During the latter half of 1970, although it became easier to get passes, I missed enough races to miss out on the Natal 50cc title but still won the Natal proddie bike championship for which I was awarded Natal Colours, one of the highest accolades a Natal sportsman can get.

Working on my Yamaha 50 with home-made frame. Note the military haircut!

Time out for a bit of hunting in Rhodesia after finishing military training. Bronnie poses with the Winchester.

Taking the H1R around Angels Angle.

1971 through to the 1972 national unlimited title

By the end of 1970, Club Motors, the Kawasaki importers in Pretoria, wanted to sell the H1R Kawasaki 500 race bike they had sponsored for a year in the hands of Errol Cowan in the National Unlimited Championship. Errol had little success with the bike because of poor handling and unreliability. It did not lack speed though, with over 75bhp it was a rocket. The Japanese factory produced it in limited numbers as a relatively inexpensive over the counter racer for Grand Prix and for the big money US National road race series. The bike had reasonable success in both the USA and in Europe where certain privateers challenged the superiority of the MV Agustas. In South Africa the hot shots were Gillie Cruse, Keith Zeeman and Les Van Breda from Johannesburg with the tried and trusted twin cylinder Suzuki TR500. They had pretty much dominated the unlimited national class for a couple of years.

Johnno, Dozy and my brother-in-law, Berry Bale clubbed together and purchased the well used 'state of the art' H1R500 Grand Prix type racer for R1000. Heady stuff! It was a beautiful looking bike and made the sweetest sound of all two stroke racers from the three unsilenced stingers, a kind of rippling, burbling howl. The handling was not the best, but we were not daunted. We had tamed worse beasts. Thus Team Ballington went into the 1971 racing season with an H1R for the Nationals, the H1 for Proddie and the YF1 for the 50 class. I had my first National Championship race on the H1R at Hesketh on my 20th birthday, 10th April and I could not have been given a better birthday present as I beat the reigning SA Champ, Les Van Breda into second with Zeeman third. By June I was finished with the defence force and back to work on the building site with Johnno. Now that we were contesting the nationals we would be travelling around South Africa to circuits we had not yet visited which was an expansion of horizons for us. Fortunately, being self employed builders we could load up in the middle of the week, send the labourers home and head for the next event. Johnno and I would sleep in the combi at the destination circuit and Dozy would drive to the event after work on Friday to help if the event was within reach. South Africa had excellent circuits in Johannesburg, (the original Kyalami Grand Prix circuit) Welkom, Bloemfontein, Cape Town, East London and there was a National leg at the circuit in far away Bulawayo in Rhodesia, and of course the best of the lot by a Swedish mile, Roy Hesketh!

Towards the end of the season we had mixed fortunes, experiencing some of the aforementioned unreliability with the H1R, but we also carried on our winning ways, notably, rubbing salt into the wounds of the Jo'burg Suzuki rivals by soundly beating Van Breda on his own track, Kyalami, in October. The Suzuki riders thought they were the big deals in the unlimited class, which they had dominated because of good backing and equipment, so it was a feather in my cap to break Transvaal dominance of the class and it was so sweet to beat them, especially at Kyalami, their home track. During the latter half of 1971 we made an amazing discovery. We had been using Dunlop triangular racing tyres as fitted since we acquired the bike. One day we got caught without a good set and ended up

KAWASAKI
KAWASAKI
Castrol GTX
72

Rear end of the TD2B 250cc Yamaha.

fitting the best road tyres we could get our hands on, a Dunlop TT100 rear and an Avon GP for the front, just to enable us to circulate to try out some motor mods. The result was uncanny. The normally skittish and wobbly bike was now as steady as the Voortrekker Monument. The bike turned better, stayed on line better, there was no tyre patter and I could detect no reduction of the grip capabilities of the road bike tyres compared to the racing tyres. At that stage we were admittedly being beaten by the rapid TR2B350 Yamahas but the newfound rideability of the bike made me instantly about 1.5 seconds a lap faster at Hesketh bringing me up to the times of the best on TR2Bs. At the next event, a provincial championship event at Hesketh, against TR2B Yams I set a personal best of 1min 18.8 secs. (Ago's record was 1min 18 secs. set in January) when I pulled through the field to finish second, half a wheel off beating Steve 'Granny' Thompson on a TR2B. This was significant progress.

Those who noticed were sceptical when we unloaded the H1R on race day with street tyres on. 'The Ballingtons have lost it. Street tyres will never do the job. He's going to hurt himself this time,' and so on but we caused yet another stir of disbelief. That tyre combo stayed on the bike until we bought the Seeley chassis. The H1R chassis design and construction was obviously not good enough to cope with the extra grip shape and construction of the racing tyres of the day. The road tyres had rounder profiles both front and rear which, I believe, eradicated the 'wobbles' I experienced on the racing tyres. Although the road tyres had less grip they made the bike easier to ride, enabling me to do faster laps. I think less grip was easier on the suspension and took away the 'tyre patter' I experienced with the racing tyres.

Around September we must have made a good profit on a house sale because Johnno splashed out and bought our first brand spanking and beautiful new racer, one Yamaha TD2B 250 (for R1480) destined to serve with distinction in Europe until 1975. However, things started badly. On its first try-out at Hesketh, the front tyre turned on the rim and ripped the tube valve, causing deflation which resulted in me dumping the brand new bike! I was never truly comfortable on the TD2B in South Africa and only achieved mediocre results on it, despite a lot of experimenting with different rear shocks and front fork settings. My first excellent ride came at Misano in 1973. Its rideability definitely improved after the frame got bent in my Nürburgring crash in early 1973. In the crash the steering head angle got knocked steeper by a degree or two and the bike simply became more rideable, so we left it thus.

So 1971 drew to a close with only one title, my second Natal production bike championship title, but we had prepared ourselves nicely for 1972 by setting up the H1R for a serious assault on Les Van Breda's South African unlimited title. Despite all the racing, about which we were all casually very serious, life went on in sleepy hollow with a lot of partying, almost on a daily basis and countless pranks. One evening Dozy, Berry, Mike Grant and myself were hanging out at Dozy's flat, no doubt consuming alcoholic beverages. Later on we decided we needed a swim. The nearest pool was in the middle of the nurses'

The H1R at the end of 1970 when we acquired it.

Flash transporter! The old VW bus.

complex at Grey's Hospital, Pietermaritzburg's main hospital. It was a secure area, no-one but the nurses and invited guests were allowed beyond the doors. We parked outside in Dozy's car and he agreed to stay behind the wheel and be ready for a quick getaway. The rest of us calmly walked up to the entrance and announced to the lady on duty that we had come for a swim and walked on into the forbidden territory, the home to dozens of young nurses. We stripped, and whooping and hollering, plunged into the pool. In no time nurses appeared at the windows and came out to watch, clapping and cheering, but the fun could only last about a minute or two. We knew from experience that the police, only about 3km away, would have been alerted by the Sister on duty and would be on the way. We jumped out and gathered up our shorts and shirts. With no time to dress we left, bidding a distraught Sister, 'Good evening and thank you very much!' To the sound of the approaching police siren we jumped into the getaway car, howling with mirth. But Dozy had reclined his seat and flat on

The Seeley H1R on the way to winning the 'Race of Champions', Hesketh, December 1972.

Fifty action at Roy Hesketh 1972. Alan North 14, Trevor Tilbury 2.

his back, had passed out. The siren was getting louder as we shook the bewildered getaway driver out of his slumber and urged him to get going. Dozy jerked upright taking a few seconds to grasp what was happening and without putting his seat up, started the engine and pulled off clinging to the wheel like a chimp. As we pulled off, the squad van came thundering around the corner at the end of the road and whizzed by, screeching to a stop outside the nurses' complex. That was the closest it had ever been. They ran into the building as we disappeared up the street, three soaked and naked idiots and one semi-conscious getaway driver!

We were all set for a focused onslaught in 1972 to try and claim the South African Unlimited Class Championship title. The racing season did not take a breather so we kicked off in early January with a win over the reigning open champ, Van Breda at the tough and bumpy Killarney circuit near Cape Town.

Two weeks later I was due to ride in my first International event. It was the third South African TT and I was entered in the big event. The overseas entries included 350cc and 500cc World Champion Giacomo Agostini with his three cylinder 500 MV. From Britain came, Ray Pickrell, three cylinder BSA750, Paul Smart, three cylinder Triumph 750, Barry Sheene, 250 Yamaha and 500 Suzuki, Derek Chatterton, 250/350 Yamaha and Yorkshireman Mick Grant, 250/350 Yamaha. I was inspired for this and in practice surprised the overseas guys, myself and my crew, by lapping faster than all of them, and 0.1sec under Ago's lap record at 1min 17.9 secs. Smart and Pickrell wandered over to take a look at our set-up. They nearly did backflips when they saw the road tyres and told us that our bike was as fast as any H1R they had competed against in England, 'and on bloody road tyres, mate!'

In the first race, for bikes up to 1000cc, an eighteen lapper, Ago, Smart, Pickrell and myself pulled away from the field which included Sheene. For seven laps I had no difficulty staying with them and in fact on each of the early laps rode around the outside of Smart and Pickrell on the difficult Sweep/Angel's section to lie second behind Ago as we passed the pits. Just before Henry's Knee the superior power of the factory three cylinder 750s would drive them past me. I tailed them until The Sweep/Angel's and then cruised around the outside again. The collective sounds of the three four strokes sporting a total of nine cylinders was so overpowering that I was battling to keep concentration. After seven laps the H1R lost a little power, as it usually did when the motor became thoroughly hot and they pulled away a bit each lap. By now I was safe in fourth, twelve seconds up on Sheene. On lap ten someone spilled oil at Quarry Curve and Smart and Pickrell went down. I saw them fall and automatically slowed, but still almost lost control as I rode through the spilled oil. Agostini must have missed the slick on the previous lap because one lap later on lap eleven, he fell victim to it, leaving me in the lead. Ago remounted quickly and continued to finish third. Unfortunately he would not come to the rostrum, otherwise I would have had a memorable photo of me standing on the sacred place above the multiple World Champion at my first International race. Les Van Breda finished second.

January 1972. My first international race at Roy Hesketh, I am number 72. 105 is Agostini (MV500), 101 is Paul Smart (750cc Triumph Trident), 104 is Ray Pickerell (750cc BSA Rocket 3) and 102 is Barry Sheene (500cc Suzuki).

Cranking the H1R later in 1972 with Rickman forks and a single disc brake.

January 1972 at Roy Hesketh. Not bad company at my first International event. Barry Sheene and Giacomo Agostini.

In the all-comers TT, a race over thirty-five laps, Ago tailed me for a couple of laps then opened the MV wide and scorched off to set a new and tough target of 1min 16 secs for us to spend the year trying to get close to. By lap seven my notes say the brakes were cooked and by lap seventeen that the motor was going off song. My lap times suffered accordingly by two seconds a lap and by lap twenty I was twenty seconds down on Ago. Eight laps from home Sheene started pulling me in, taking me on the last lap as my bike ran onto two cylinders. I was a bit disappointed to miss out on second, but very happy to make it to the finish and get on the rostrum with Barry and Ago. For the first time I well and truly beat the TR2Bs, the first of them being Granny Thompson in fourth, twenty seconds behind. In the post mortem column my notes read, 'Left piston broken in half and big end cage broken. Right piston cracked. Brake drum liner cracked and lifting.' The poor old bike was starting to feel the pace.

At Kyalami the following weekend, on the high speed GP track I got third behind Ago and Smart, earning the distinction of best South African performer of the series. The newspaper cutting says I won a battle royale for third with Barry Sheene, 500 Suzuki, Les Van Breda, 500 Suzuki and Johan Boshoff, 350 Yamaha, with less than 1.5 seconds covering us.

'The Teacher' , Roy Hesketh circuit. Diverse corners, steep ascents and descents and ample crash space created a superb learning facility.

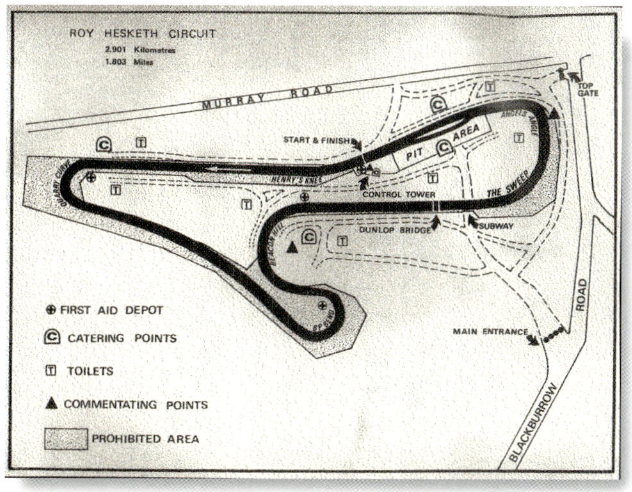

THREE 50 cc riders in the esses at the Westmead kart track during the meeting held there yesterday. Leading the trio is "Korkie" Ballington, provisionally the 50 cc champion of Natal and from whom greater things are expected by experts who have seen him ride.

In those two weeks I had my first taste of international competition and loved every dramatic second. So did Johnno, Dozy and the crew. The crowds at the circuits were huge, the biggest we had ever seen and they loved the show. The atmosphere was unbelievable and the sounds of the MV and the magnificent Triumph and BSA triples were awesome. In those days racing in South Africa was at an all-time peak, and talent development, of which Natal was streets ahead, was at an international level. Mike Grant, destined to leave to campaign in England after the series, and Jon Ekerold, beat Barry Sheene in the 250cc race at Hesketh. I realise Sheene might not have had his best bike there or might not have been sticking his neck out at the start of a season but the fact that Grant smashed 1970 250cc World Champion, Rod Gould's lap record at Hesketh and Kyalami, both set the previous year, was evidence of great talent. Other names like Ekerold and North would make their mark internationally. I can't over-emphasise how the 50cc school on the short go-kart tracks and on the full length of the Roy Hesketh circuit, played a big part in setting us up to become world class. Grant, North and myself were from that school. Ekerold was not, but where he did not have the short track grounding, he more than made up with piles of aggression and

1971. A cutting from a Durban newspaper. The caption says it all!

Autographed photo from Bazza, 1972.

At the SATT we found Kork Ballington and Barry Sheene with a Miss whose name (and phone number) we'd like to know. They are aboard the 750 Suzuki Three setting out for a lap of the circuit.

Doing a lap with Bazza in 1972.

grim determination. To complement the riding skill, we developed superb motor tuning skills through home tuning our bikes, experimenting and testing our ideas at the wonderful circuit. We also had some very clever people around like Dozy, Syd Stacey and one or two others to inject higher academic thought into the science of two stroke tuning. The support and encouragement of our parents, brothers and sisters also played an important role in our successes and then there was this intense inter-family, inter-team rivalry, especially in the fifty school, which sharpened our resolve and occasionally almost led to bouts of boxing between some dads!

Many have asked why the Natal Province produced the most successful of the motorcycle racing talent in South Africa. Bike racing is a most demanding and difficult sport because it demands absolute precision, skill and courage to do well. The penalty for making mistakes can be serious injury or even death. To develop the skill and precision to become the very best in any field one needs to go through a series of stages of development over a period of time, in the right environment. I believe I had this at my nursery school, the Circuit de la Casa around our old homestead then at the perfect primary school at Westmead go-kart track where Mike Hailwood recognised the merits of what we were doing. In Roy Hesketh circuit we had the high school and university to complete our training and we had free and unrestricted use of these very safe facilities. Safety is an important ingredient in the development stages of a dangerous pursuit. I don't think I could have developed to the same skill level had I lived in the Vaal and had to do my training on the old Kyalami circuit. It was simply too dangerous to allow the unrestricted mental and technical (from a riding point of view) development that Hesketh allowed. One could fall anywhere at Hesketh and not slide into anything hard, allowing us to test the limits of ourselves and our equipment with a relatively low threat of serious injury should we push it too far. If a rider fell at any point on Kyalami he would undoubtedly hit some obstacle, the catch fence poles, or unprotected steel barriers that were in place on the outside of every bend. Therefore there was a far higher risk of serious injury. This would have been at the back of my mind and slowed me a little which would have hindered the testing of limits, so important in the development process. I think this fact must have adversely affected the Transvaal riders' skill development to a degree. Another factor which helped a lot was the fact that the Natal authorities were very pro bike racing as demonstrated with the organization of the world class South African TT series and the steadfast refusal to erect steel barriers close to the circuit edge whereas their Johannesburg counterparts did whatever was necessary to please the car fraternity without concern for the bike racers. Roy Hesketh circuit was one of the finest circuits that I ever raced on with every type of bend to hone skills in a broad perspective. Kyalami was not in the ballpark. There was definitely an attitude of arrogance prevalent amongst some of the folk from the Johannesburg region towards the Natalians. This was probably brought about by the fact that it was an immensely rich area, indeed the financial centre of the country and they perhaps looked upon us as the poor relations from the coast. This sharpened our resolve to 'kick Vaalie butt' whenever we could.

After the highly successful SATT series, the international visitors went away, leaving me with a new pace goal in my mind to try and achieve. Mike Grant went overseas on his personally financed tour with his brother Arthur and his wife, Daphne, to seek fame and fortune, leaving us to get on with the job of trying to win the 1972 South African unlimited title.

Our racing program would encompass twelve Nationals in the

250cc and Unlimited Class, two Internationals already mentioned, seven Natal Championship races at Roy Hesketh in the 50cc, Production 500cc, 250cc and unlimited racing classes and eight Natal Championship 50cc events on go-kart tracks, plus the occasional hillclimb event. On one occasion, a Saturday in August, we raced in the Nationals at Killarney near Cape Town, with the H1R, and then drove the 1,600km through the night to get to Hesketh go-kart track for a Natal Champs 50cc event on the Sunday and won the championship race. Around this time there was a rumour of an extra race to take place some time in December at Roy Hesketh with talk of the winner being sponsored on an overseas riding campaign.

The 1972 season was a humdinger. All credit must go to our team and especially to Johnno for total commitment and focus. The time off we required to do the Nationals affected business and on top of that, the racing cost him a lot of money. As an opponent, reigning champ Les Van Breda was experienced and the 500 Suzukis were reliable. They were the Suzuki Importer team so had full backing and impressive equipment. Les also had the backup of a team mate, Errol James, also on a rapid TR500 Suzuki, to squeeze me out of points, whenever possible!

I kicked off with a win over Les at Killarney in the first round. The next race, at Hesketh, was a beauty. Les was determined that day. I led from the start but he hung on like grim death. Our lap times were almost a second a lap quicker on average than they had been at the SATT International in January which was a significant step forward. In the last few laps I managed to stretch the lead to four seconds at the flag. The significance of this race is that for the first time I was placed under intense pressure. It was an important race in an important season and I had no problem with it. The next good ride to back up my faith in myself was at Les's home track, Kyalami where I beat him to the

Aiming for Europe

DECEMBER 12 1972

IT'S ALL EYES on Europe at Hesketh on Sunday when 30 of South Africa's top riders aim at the "Mercury" Rider to Europe award. One of the hopefuls is Pietermaritzburg's Kork Ballington, national unlimited class champion, leading the pack in our picture taken at the Umhlanga Rocks Drive-In meeting

THE HEAT'S ON AT HESKETH!

By JOE MULRANEY

COUNTDOWN! Five days to go to December 17, the day on which Pietermaritzburg's Roy Hesketh circuit explodes into action with the "Mercury" Three-Hour and the "Mercury" Race of Champions.

One race for four-wheelers, the other for two – but both of them shaping up as the very best of both worlds.

Two races, the Three-Hour for sports, GT and production cars, the Race of Champions for racing solos, and between them they will decide two of the most important things in South African motor sport today.

The Three-Hour will be the final of the 1972 Castrol Springbok Series, most important TURN TO BACK PAGE

HEAT'S ON AT HESKETH!

FROM PAGE ONE

series of motor races in South Africa this side of the Grand Prix, while the Race of Champions will decide the two solo stars to be sent to Europe next year to challenge the world's best.

In the Three-Hour the world's top two-litre sports cars driven by the cream of Britain and Europe's sports car drivers will be vying with their local counterprarts – some of them driving the same top-notch cars.

Drivers like Britain's Gerry Birrell who streaked to a second position in the Nine-Hour behind the mighty Ferrari and then three straight victories in the three-hour races at Cape Town, Lourenco Marques and Welkom. The first three successes were with Jochen Mass, the young German who finished second to John Love in the series last year and who only missed the penultimate race at Welkom 10 days ago when he returned to Germany to be honoured for his European Touring Car title.

Drivers, too, like Peter Gethin who helped Birrell to his hat-trick at Welkom in Mass's absence and who stunned the racing world last year when he outwitted the top echelon of Formula One drivers in the last corner at Monza and won the Italian Grand Prix going away.

Drivers like South Africa's own Jody Scheckter whose meteoric rise has staggered racing men the world over and who will come to the Hesketh grid determined to shake off the ill-luck which has dropped his all new March BMW from the lead several times over in this series.

And what of the two-wheeler men? For them the stakes are high, higher than they have ever been in South African motorcycle racing.

For two of them, it will mean a chance to realise every racing man's dream – a chance to match skills with the world's best in the home of motor racing, on the tracks of Europe and Britain.

With a stake like this the pace will be torrid as it has never been before: "This race is going to be a killer, no quarter asked and definitely none given, a sort of a sudden-death, winner-take-all affair," gritted one of those invited to take part.

None but South Africa's best will be riding. Riders like double 250/350 champ Mike Fogg; unlimited title-holder Kork Ballington, people they beat for the laurels like Johan Boshoff, Les van Breda, Keith Zeeman, Alan North . . . to name a few.

It's difficult to imagine a formula for a meeting with more potential for excitement.

'Race of Champions' press blurb. Symbolic number 1 on the bike.

flag by 1.5 seconds. I loved beating Les at Kyalami. At Hesketh in July I dealt Les a crushing blow, setting a scorching pace to beat him by a whopping forty-three seconds. He was not slow on that day. Rather, Dozy had excelled himself because my bike went phenomenally well. The race was over eighteen laps, the same distance as the January International which I won when Ago crashed. My race time was now thirty-two seconds faster, with lap times just outside Ago's record!! This was some kind of progress, and still on road tyres.

At this stage I was leading the title chase. The second half of the season started out badly with a DNF at Kyalami with crank failure leaving Les to score maximum points. My ill fortune continued with a crash in the next round at Killarney, caused by a motor seizure, with Les again taking the win. In the next race in Bulawayo, Les beat me fair and square. At this stage we were about level, the championship could go either way. At the next round in Bloemfontein I oiled a plug on the line and by the time it chimed onto all three cylinders, Les, followed by Errol James was in the distance leaving me in third place. Having his team mate, James to take second place points tipped the scale towards Les and he was now leading the title chase. Things were getting tight with two rounds to go. The penultimate round was at Kyalami and I needed to win to keep our hopes alive so we would have our work cut out to beat the might of the Suzuki team on their own territory.

I am amazed at the timing of the good fortune that got us back on the winning track. During testing at Hesketh for the all important Kyalami race, we just could not get the bike to go properly. It was slow and although we checked everything thoroughly we could find nothing wrong. While out for a final few laps, one of the three tailpipes fell off. When I pitted we discovered what had caused the power loss which had been affecting my performances over the last few races.

Just before going tits up I was dicing with John Cooper on a 750 Norton

1973. Tits up at The Sweep, Hesketh. Just before leaving for England.

Carbon build-up at the rear section of the expansion chamber, at the narrowest point where the small diameter tailpipes are situated was chronic. It restricted the free flow of exhaust gasses from the motor, like cholesterol in arteries restricts the flow of blood. This had caused a substantial loss of power as the motor simply could not breath properly. We raced home and burnt all the carbon out of the expansion chambers and replaced the telltale tailpipe. That afternoon we were back at the track and the bike was a jet again. At Kyalami we got things back on track, beating Les by a mere two seconds, having led from start to finish. Again the pleasing thing about the race was that I was lapping some two seconds a lap faster than the last race at Kyalami and easily coping with the pressure. This meant we were progressing, I was becoming steadily better on the powerful 500. The championship was now down to the wire.

Whoever beat the other at Welkom would be the 1972 South African Unlimited Champion. For Welkom we fitted a rebuilt crank to ensure reliability from that quarter, otherwise we had no aces up our sleeve. Team Suzuki's ace was to draft former South African Champion, Keith Zeeman into their team on another 500 Suzuki to try and help Les. As it turned out, race day poured with rain, creating a dramatic final stage. At the end of the race the result was Zeeman first, me second and Les third. According to our scoring, I was a few points ahead of Les to win the title but before we had time to think about celebrating, Les came over and proudly proclaimed that he had won the championship again. They had him a couple of points ahead, but we calculated that we were the victors. Les firmly believed he had won and went off to celebrate. We decided to leave it until during the week to double check the scoring system with the Automobile Association, the controllers of motor sport in South Africa, before getting into any arguments. That night at the prize giving Les and the Suzuki crew displayed their lack of sportsmanship. As each recipient of a trophy for the days racing was being called up to be presented their prize the Suzuki crew were applauding, cheering wildly and stomping their feet on the floor, making a hell of a noise. The 500cc trophies came up and Zeeman was called to collect first prize to the wild applause and stomping of his crew. I was called up next for second place. There was a deathly silence from them. Next up was Les for third, again to deafening cheering and stomping from his table. As it turned out we had the last laugh. On checking with the AA about the scoring, they confirmed that we were using the correct system and were the winners over Van Breda by a few points. The scoring system had changed for 1972. Instead of all races counting, you could now drop your two worst results. Les and Team Suzuki had not read the new regulations and were using the old scoring system.

So, we had a tough, controversial but finally superbly

victorious season and proudly called ourselves the Unlimited South African Champions. My first love being 50cc racing, I just as proudly called myself Natal 50cc Champion (for the third time) as we clinched that title as well.

Around this time, Mike Grant, who was making his mark in Europe, had a bad crash at Tubbergen, one of the dangerous Dutch road circuits and received extensive serious injuries that would cause him to return home and prevent a great future in racing. Mike might have been on crutches with a badly broken leg when he got back to Maritzburg but he could still get up a turn of speed on them, as we discovered one evening. We were at Dozy's apartment doing the usual, listening to music, having a beverage or two and playing darts. As I recall there was Mike on crutches, Dozy, and myself plus our female friends. As night headed for morning and with the help of the brew, a game of strip darts developed. It was hilarious and cheered on by the 'ladies' who, despite our encouragement, would not participate. Once naked we decided to walk half a mile up the street to have a swim in the fountain outside the town hall, possibly before streaking was invented. At 2 am there was not much traffic in Sleepy Hollow so we got there without scaring anybody and had a raucous dip in the fountain. On the way back we werealmost at the apartment when a police patrol van pulled up at an intersection behind us. We were just fifty metres from home. We hoped they wouldn't notice us and we could get around the corner into Boom Street and nip into the apartment. We started running. I will never forget the sound of the patter of tiny feet, the childish giggling and above it all the sound of Mike on those crutches. Click click plop, click click plop as each crutch followed by the plop of his cast rattled out the beat on the sidewalk. Of course the cops noticed us and with a squeal of tyres pulled into Commercial Road in pursuit. By that time we were around the corner and into the dark apartment foyer. As the cops raced into Boom Street we crept into the apartment naked and wet and turned all the lights off, battling to suppress the laughter. Once we were sure that the cops were gone we cracked another bevvie and howled with mirth till sun-up. Pietermaritzburg's nickname of Sleepy Hollow had nothing to do with us.

Around this time the rumour of an important race at Hesketh was made official. There was to be a race on December 17th called 'The Mercury Race of Champions.' The winner of the race and next most deserving competitor would indeed be sent to Europe to have a go at the big time.

'Mercury Race of Champions' winner!

Part 2: In at the Deep End

Dozy cajoles a blown alternator back to life.

The big trip, UK here we come

By the end of January 1973, the bikes, tools and meagre, mostly used spares, had been despatched by sea and were half way across the Atlantic en route to Southampton. Dozy, then twenty-eight years old, had given up a good job as a technician at a cash register company to come on the trip. He was to prove to be the greatest asset a racing team could have. Dozy was never one to waste time on many words, however behind the sleepy exterior is a quiet genius. For as long as I can remember my older brother was always tinkering with and repairing stuff that most would deem well past it. I recall an occasion when his tinkering got us into trouble. When he was about fifteen years old, he tapped our phone which was located in our parents room and ran a wire through to our room where he set up a small speaker. We used to wait for my sister, just thirteen going on twenty-one, to call her friends. There was always a lot of whispering and giggling during these calls and now we were able to recline on our beds and discover their innermost secrets. My sister eventually discovered what was up and we were in trouble. When it came to tuning racing motorcycles Dozy was gifted and he was to play a major part in our success by making our equipment go faster than the manufacturers had intended. Bronwyn, then nineteen years old had given up her job as a pharmacist's assistant and pooled her savings to make the trip. We first met when she was fifteen years old. Nancy Egan, sister of two of my great friends, Mike and James in Pietermaritzburg, had decided we would make a good couple and engineered a meeting. Thirty very odd years later we are still together. We went steady for about five years, were engaged for three, then finally took the plunge on 15th January 1977.

The team of greenhorns Dozy, Bronwyn and I were feeling like lambs going to the slaughter house but nevertheless we were excited and eager to embark on the adventure. I had to keep convincing myself that we would at least learn something from the experience. We would see Europe, see real Grand Prix bike racing and the legendary men, machines and circuits that we only read about at the butt end of Africa. We would return at the end of 1973, financially poorer but theoretically far richer in experience. We could get on with what would most likely be a normal, average life, i.e. mundane job, babies, mortgage, etc! Every day I thank our lucky stars that we went on the big trip to Europe and stuck it out.

The night before we were due to fly out of Johannesburg for London we attended a presentation of awards ceremony for all 1972 SA champions from all motorsport categories, at the Wanderers Club in Johannesburg. At that time there was a World championship F1 car GP on at Kyalami. All of the top GP drivers were present. It was a momentous occasion. I recall after the ceremony Jackie Stewart came over to me and wished me the best of luck on the tour and that he would be looking out for the results. Many years later in about 1984 Jackie was present at a function in SA. I approached him to relate our encounter at the Wanderers Club in 1973 and let him know that I did all right. Before I could introduce myself he said, 'Hi Kork, congratulations on your fine achievements in GP. The amazing man had indeed noticed the results.

I looked through the window of the 747 as we descended over the suburbs near Heathrow. The sky was grey, the trees looked stark and dead. There was not a green leaf or blade of grass to be seen. There were row upon row of drab semi-detached houses huddled together as if trying to draw comfort from each other. The sight did little to relieve my apprehension.

We were to be met at the airport by Mike Grant's brother, Arthur, who was staying in London at the time. We had bought Mike's race transporter, a short wheelbase Ford Transit V4,

IT'S GOING TO BE TOUGH!

FORMER WORLD CHAMP WARNS NATAL'S 'RIDERS TO EUROPE'

THE START of the planning for the "Mercury" Riders to Europe racing tour. Jim Redman, former world champion (centre) Mike Fogg, Kork Ballington and Motoring Mercury pore over the calendar of the year's races in Britain and Europe.

Advice from Jim Redman before 'The Big Trip'.

which Arthur was looking after. Arthur also invited us to stay with him for a few days until we found accommodation. In the arrivals hall at Heathrow, Arthur was nowhere to be seen. On the other hand, Mike Fogg's chaperone, Bob Aldridge was there to meet the intensely focused Foggy who had been on the same flight. With Bob was Syd Stacey who was to be Foggy's help for the season. Bob was the eldest son of Doug Aldridge, a South African businessman. Doug had engineering shops in Pietermaritzburg and Beeston in Bedfordshire. Doug's clan of five sons all lived in Bedfordshire with their mother, Eileen. Doug spent time in both countries. The Aldridge family were staunch supporters of South African riders trying their luck in England. They had helped a number of riders in the past and were going to help Foggy set up his campaign. These good people were to be instrumental in our survival.

Bob insisted on taking us to Arthur's address in London. It turned out to be a tiny bedsit in Ladbroke Grove. Arthur's flat mate was not as happy to see us as Arthur was. The bedsit was one tiny room that quadrupled as bedroom, lounge, dining room and kitchen. Once we had brought our luggage in there was not enough room to swing the proverbial cat. That night after a pleasant trip to the pub, where we sampled warm flat beer for the first time, the three of us lined up on the floor of the bedsitter shoulder to shoulder for a bad night. We quickly realised that it was not practical for us to take advantage of Arthur's hospitality. We decided that the best move at this stage would be for us to check out of Arthur's place, into a B&B in Earl's Court with Dozy staying on at Arthur's. Although it would eat into the budget it was a better arrangement.

Earl's Court was a lot of fun. It was a Mecca for young Aussies, Kiwis and South Africans, mostly fresh out of school and looking to blow off some steam. During our short stay we spent a lot of time at a pub called The Tournament where every night we would cross paths with someone we knew from home. The vibe was excellent. What amazed me about the antipodean Earl's Court dwellers was the intensity with which they partied. Every day seemed like it was the last day of the existence of mankind. It had to be enjoyed to the max and we kept up with the best of them. It is amusing how the priorities stand when you are young and free. We would cut food to the bare minimum to ensure that we had a reasonable beer and cider budget. The cheapest alcohol at that time was cider and it was good value. It packed two punches though, one on the night of the party and another the next day.

During the day we continued our preparations for the season and had been accepted in four European races so far. The first was at Mettet in Belgium on the 15th April, the following weekend was at the French GP at Paul Ricard near Marseilles, Nürburgring was a week later and the fourth entry was at Misano in Italy on May 28th. What is more, we were going to be paid to go to these races. I can't remember the offer for the other events, but Mettet had offered 8,000 francs to start in the 500 race. Being paid to race was a new experience. 8,000 francs converted into about R140. My first job, as a motorcycle salesman for the Honda, BSA and Triumph dealer in Pietermaritzburg, paid R160 a month. This was heady stuff for a country boy from South Africa. Provided we did not break any motor parts or eat exotic food, we could make a profit. We might even score some prize money. Most of the preparations were formalities such as getting an Auto Cycle Union racing licence required to compete in International events. We also needed travel documents for the bikes and visas for us. All of these required getting around London and for some stupid reason, we insisted on doing this in our race transporter instead of by underground which would have been much easier. Dozy had nicknamed the van, Gossamer MK2. I can't remember why it got this strange name, Gossamer being a particular brand of condom. Perhaps it was because there were three pricks inside it! We got very lost quite often, had horrendous rows, battled to find parking, caused traffic jams and wasted a lot of time. I guess on the positive side we would accidentally ride by famous sights like Buckingham Palace, Big Ben, the Houses of Parliament and many others. Each time we would stop and stare but if an entry fee was involved we would satisfy ourselves with a photo and move on. One thing we did dig into the kitty for was a night at the movies. A porno movie called Trash, by Andy Warhol was on at a cinema in Piccadilly Circus. Coming from a country where pornography was totally and absolutely verboten we just had to experience the forbidden fruit. The movie was aptly named. We would have got far better value had we spent the money on a meal at the Bengal Curry House!

The bikes finally sailed into Southampton and we raced there in Gossamer to clear them through customs. Heading back to London

Dozy and Bronnie outside the luxury tent.

that afternoon with our little van loaded with the tools of our trade we started feeling like a complete team for the first time. Gossamer purred smoothly up and down the rolling Hampshire countryside without missing a beat and for a change it was not raining. Life was great. We went straight to the Tournament to celebrate. Before uprooting from Earl's Court we had to decide what we were going to use during the season for shelter, a place to call home and to work on the bikes. Hotels were out of the question. We could have stretched to a small caravan which would be expensive but the most convenient and practical way of touring the European circuits. The cheapest method would be some form of tent. For the difference of about £50 between a big three compartment luxury tent and a small but comfortable second-hand well-used caravan, we made a drastic mistake and chose the tent. A season of misery would follow this decision. Now the even more complete team with the luxury tent set off for a carefully chosen camp site in the Kent countryside near Brands Hatch. It would be our base for a week before we headed to Dover to cross The Channel. March in England is very cold. Most of the time the temperature can be around zero Celsius during the day and below at night. We should have known that living in tents in this kind of weather is only done by polar explorers. It was a crisp, sunny afternoon when we arrived at the deserted campsite and for the week we were alone. We unpacked our new tent and set about assembling it for the first time. It was very smart, in red and blue with two sleeping compartments and a small section for cooking and a larger section we were going to use for working on the bikes.

The first evening was terribly cold. We sat around our new camp table in our new tent with our new gas heater on full power under the table. To combat the cold we placed a blanket over the table and over our knees. The blanket trapped the heat under the table and warmed our legs. The risk of death by fire was not a consideration under the circumstances. At least we would have died warm! To combat the creeping freeze from attacking our upper bodies we donned almost all of the clothing we had with us. We sat like this playing cards for a little while, trying valiantly to be jovial before deciding we might as well go to bed. To crown it all, as we crept fully clothed into our sleeping bags we heard a rush of air followed by cursing from Dozy's compartment. He had somehow punctured his air mattress. Sleeping on the frozen ground was out of the question so we spent our first night camping in Kent in March huddled in a threesome on two air mattresses, in great discomfort. We soon developed a pattern. At the end of the day, as the temperature dropped, we would jump into Gossamer and race off to Farningham village a couple of miles away, to a wonderful old English pub with a huge fireplace. We would sit in great comfort in the warmth, share a coke and watch telly. Not surprisingly the landlord never seemed too happy to see us. We took up space, did not spend money and he would have to prise us out of our chairs long after last orders had been called. We would race back to camp, chip into the tent with an icepick and huddle together to stave off hypothermia!

The H1R Seeley.

Our primary objective while at the campsite was to manufacture the bottom half of a fairing for the Seeley. The original H1R fairing would not fit so we had fitted a small cowling with screen. By the end of our week at the campsite we had hand-built the required bottom half of the fairing out of beaten strips of aluminium sheet covered with fibreglass which we filled and sanded to a smooth finish. Once painted, it did not look too bad considering the primitive conditions in which it had been manufactured. It was improvisation at its best. One thing we were going to perfect and in fact elevate to new heights on this trip was the art of improvisation. South Africans, in those days were generally good at it. Being very much a developing country, many things weren't readily available, so one had to improvise until the part could be obtained. There is an old Afrikaans saying, ' 'n Boer maak 'n plan.' Translated into English it means ' A farmer makes a plan.' If you haven't the correct tools, you improvise to keep the show going regardless.

Boarding the Hovercraft at Dover.

Off to join 'The Circus'

We were now ready to load up, leave camp and head for Dover on the next leg of our journey to Mettet. We had pre-booked a trip across The Channel on one of the hovercraft that go back and forth between Dover and Bologne. We chose the hovercraft because it did not cost a lot more than the regular ferry. It was faster and anyway it sounded exciting to parochial Africans. Silly morons that we were, we could have taken a ferry from Dover direct to Belgium, landing at Ostende or Zeebrugge. Although the ferry trip was longer, it would have saved us a great deal of hardship by cutting out an entry and exit at consecutive French borders.

It would seem that to qualify as a passport control or customs officer, you must have the art of being as shitty and unfriendly as possible. In those days in Europe the borders had strict passport and customs formalities. Basically, crossing borders with racing equipment was a 'pain in the ass' experience. At French customs I lined up, with what I presumed were commercial truckers, to get our documents stamped in order to carry our racing equipment through France. It was slow going. What I did not know at that stage was that I had documents more appropriate to the import and export of commercial goods, instead of the RAC carnets which were specifically designed to streamline the movement of non-commercial equipment through Europe's borders. We were stuck with these infernal documents for the whole year. The fact that we were using commercial documents for private goods must have aroused suspicion with customs because the contents of our van were inspected thoroughly on a regular basis. Crossing borders was to become the single most unpleasant procedure I have ever endured. There was a long queue of lorries at every border crossing. Despite the most lavish promises and offers of reward I was unable to palm the job off onto either of the other two recalcitrant team members.

At Bologne I finally got to the glass window with the little hole in it and presented the paperwork to the bored, unfriendly man on the other side. He looked at the paperwork and fired a salvo of French at me. Of course I had not the faintest idea what he was trying to say. He had another try, slower and louder. By now I was starting to sweat. I suspected it might have something to do with our intended destination. I held my breath and croaked 'Belgium.' That seemed to do the trick. He scribbled something on the bottom of the page, stamped it with gusto and thrust the papers back through the gap at the bottom of the glass window, dismissing me with a string of unintelligible vernacular. I imagine the English translation might have been something like 'Now bugger off you silly imbecile.' I said, 'Yessir. Thank you sir!' and got out at speed. Driving on the right hand side of the road was a bit tricky to start with. I tried to go the wrong way around the first roundabout we came to which caused quite a stir. We learnt that French drivers love to hoot and flash their lights. Armed with a totally inadequate road map, we planned our route to go straight up the coast road to Belgium. A couple of hours later we arrived at the border where I joined the usual queue of truckers to get the paperwork stamped. Fortunately

Packing up to leave England for the first race at Mettet in April 1973.

the customs officer spoke a little English. Unfortunately he had some very bad news. 'Yew are et ze wrong bordair. Yew cannot pars ere. Yew must go to zees one.' Our friendly Inpector Clousseau prodded a spot on the map on his wall that appeared to be a very long way from where we were. The customs officer in Bologne had obviously been trying to find out at which border post we intended to enter Belgium! Then Inspector Clousseau did something unheard of. With a simple gesture he renewed my faith in the European Customs Service. He wrote the name of our allocated border crossing down on a piece of paper and handed it to me. He bade me farewell in his mother tongue with what I suspected was something like, 'Now on your bicycle you ignoramus.'

Fortunately our new destination was on our cheap map. Unfortunately it was a fair distance inland and there was no direct route. We had to backtrack to connect with a road that zigzagged across the French countryside. I cannot remember how these faux pas were affecting the friendship within the little blue Ford van but I imagine things were a little strained. No, things were very strained. There was probably some serious head biting going on as the weary threesome went the unnecessary extra miles as daylight began to fade. Just as well Bronwyn and I were not married. I think there were many occasions during this first European adventure when divorce proceedings might have been instigated. Just as well Dozy was my brother or we would have sacked each other a dozen times in those early, trying days. A trip from Kent to Mettet should have been a relatively simple procedure. Through lack of experience we had managed to turn it into a major expedition.

A big part of our problem was that we were basically very inhibited people. I had met a number of English riders who had come to race in South Africa. It would have saved a lot of trouble if we had contacted one of them for advice. Instead we chose to be as independent as possible so we had to pay the price by learning the hard way. In any case, at that stage there was nothing we could do about it. We were going racing in Europe. We were doing our own thing and damn, it was exciting to be where legendary riders diced it out on legendary circuits on exotic machinery, even though we were taking the scenic route!

Many hours later we entered Belgium and at about 2am arrived at Mettet. The Paddock was already crowded and in total darkness. We found a gap between some impressive looking equipment and parked. By the time we had rattled, clanged and sworn the tent up in darkness, I imagine our new neighbours and potential friends were asking themselves if these were not indeed the neighbours from Hell.

The next day was awesome. These were the thirty-fifth Grand Trophy races at Mettet on the Circuit Jules Tacheny, an annual and popular event on the international calendar which attracted some big names. The Italian legend and thirteen times world champion, superstar, Giacomo Agostini was the main attraction with the beautifully styled, blood red, Italian MV Agusta thoroughbred Grand Prix motorcycles. Ago would have been paid an extremely large sum of money to grace the event with his handsome presence. His popularity in Europe was of filmstar proportions and he was adored by his fans. He was hounded by journalists, photographers and strings of gorgeous chicks. Could I allow myself to dream? Nah, forget it, get back on the planet. The rest of the competitors were made up of well-known names from the 'privateer' contingent of the 'Continental Circus' as this spectacular show had come to be known, and a few rookies such as myself. On this, our first day in the big time, we roamed the paddock devouring the technology and atmosphere. This was heaven but I had not died. I was actually being paid to be there.

Mike Fogg also had an entry at Mettet so it was the first time we would see him since the day of our arrival in London. Foggy had set himself up nicely. He had a diesel-powered long wheelbase Ford Transit and hooked onto the back, bouncing along behind like a playful puppy, was a nice little caravan. Long wheelbase meant plenty of space, diesel meant cheaper running costs in Europe where petrol was wickedly expensive and caravan meant five star luxury. Trust Foggy to make all the right decisions.

Mettet circuit was awesome...unbelievable. The race track was 7.734km long and made up of country roads on the outskirts of the village. The start/finish line was at the end of a very long straight section. The riders would literally come howling (there were no sound regulations in 1973) along this section and cross the line in full flight and in top gear. After the start line the road peeled left into a huge, fast left-hand sweep that descended slightly towards the village. Being public roads and a part of the village, this section had kerbs, lamp posts and was lined with houses and although there were straw bales laid out I think a crash here was likely to leave the unfortunate rider seriously injured if not dead. I had never before seen or imagined anything like this. After the fast left hander was a short straight followed by a first gear right-hand bend which effectively set the course off out into the countryside again. The rest of the circuit consisted of long stretches of straight, narrow country roads connected by ninety degree right-hand second gear corners with the odd house along the way. The existing 500cc lap record average speed was just under 200kph. In the pre-chicane era Europe had many circuits, both on public roads and closed, which were biased towards high top speeds with very fast, and I mean very fast, corners of a nature I had never experienced. I was to be initiated into this culture at Mettet. I might as well start getting the hang of it.

Even though it rained for all of the allocated practice and we never got the 500 going nicely, I qualified for the race at an average speed of 163kph. This was a lot faster than I had ever lapped a circuit before, even in dry conditions. This new challenge... this new ultra high speed experience on road circuits was such an adrenaline rush. Mettet was an experience, but I still had to see some of the other fast road circuits dotted around Europe, both East and West, such as Chimay in Belgium, Imatra in Finland, Brno in Czechoslovakia, Opatija in Yugoslavia and of course the mother of them all, the most exciting circuit I ever rode, Spa-Francorchamps in the Ardennes region of Belgium. Five years later at the last event to be held on the original classic Spa-Francorchamps circuit I was to take pole position on the KR250 works Kawasaki at an average speed of 204.97kph This represented a lap of the 14.12km circuit in 4 mins 8 secs. That was in 1978 on a 250! That kind of lap required a special talent and a special precision that disappeared along with the circuit.

The weather at Mettet turned miserable. After Saturday practice a cold front blew over and sent the temperature back below zero which made a tough time tougher. During the night a blizzard set in but by morning it had subsided to a light sleet. Words such as blizzard, sleet and snow had until now been unnecessary in our vocabularies. I crept out of the warmth and security of my sleeping bag to take a look and it was not a pretty sight. Despite the foul, muddy, icy conditions, bikes were being started and people where milling around as if there were going to be races taking place. I didn't realise that humans could race under such conditions, I mean, there was ice coming out of the sky. The races, scheduled to start in the morning, would surely be delayed until the weather improved. So I crept back into the glorious warmth of my sleeping bag.

The 125cc race was first on the programme. A few minutes later I heard the collective howl of little two strokes firing up and accelerateing down the road for a warm-up, or closer to the truth, thaw out lap. The 500 race was after the 125 race and sure enough the public address system confirmed my worst suspicions, first in French (in which I was familiar with one word... merde) then in German which poor old Mrs Krull had tried to teach me and thirty other deadpans in eighth grade! 'Achtung Fahrerlager, alle Teilnehmer der 500-ccm-Klasse an den Start kommen, bitte! I jumped out of my sleeping bag. 'Come on guys, get up. I have to get to the pre-race paddock!' I cannot remember the expletives but the bottom line was that my crew had gone on strike. If I insisted on doing this, I was on my own. One thing I understood about the system was no start no pay. The rules clearly stated that if a competitor did not come to the start line, start his bike and ride off the line under power, he would not get paid. Not wanting to forfeit my first paycheque, I got my riding kit out. Everything was at the ambient temperature of the day, zero. The leathers were crisp from the cold. I was already in thermal underwear with a track suit over it, a sweater and two pairs of socks. I forced my way into the crisp, frozen leathers, squeezed into the boots, put a rainsuit over the leathers and an anorak over the rain suit. With a balaclava on under my helmet and gauntlets over my gloves, I must have looked like the Michelin man. I had great difficulty moving. With slick tyres not yet invented, the racing tyres of the day were for all conditions so fortunately there were no complicated tyre changes to make. With no help from the hibernating traitors, I wrestled the bike off the stand, got it started and wobbled off to the pre-race paddock. With all the apparel on I could not bend my legs to get my butt in the seat, so rode down to the pre-race paddock standing up, feeling like a real Charlie. There I readjusted the leathers and managed to force myself into a sprung sitting position with my bum hardly touching the seat. All the exertion had caused me to sweat like a pig which added to my discomfort.

Soon the track was given the all clear after the 125 race and we were sent out on a warm up lap but as soon as I closed my visor it misted up from my sweating body. I had to ride with the visor half open so the flow of air would prevent the mist forming on the inside, fine at low speed but as soon as we got going the sleet peppered my face and eyes. As well as intense pain, this caused my eyes to water profusely and my vision to become a blur of distorted objects. These were the most atrocious conditions I had ever encountered, yet the locals behaved as if it it was all perfectly normal! We got back to the line and cut the engines for the push start. With all riders in position the one minute board came up so I went through the last minute checks, fuel tap on, first gear engaged, clutch in, eyes riveted on the man with the flag. The last few seconds seemed like an eternity, there was a deathly silence and suddenly the flag came down and thirty riders lunged forward. The mixture of two and four strokes, single and multicylinder machines fired up almost simultaneously, emitting an interestingly diverse array of sounds from the open megaphones of the four strokes and unsilenced expansion chambers of the two strokes. Above it all I remember hearing the multi cylinder MV Agusta rip into life and howl off at high rpm. The second most prominent sound was the deep, sharp throb of the numerous low-revving single cylinder 500s. Beneath the four stroke symphony came the silky penetrating buzz of the two strokes.

I felt rather than heard my bike start, hopped on in a standing position and sped off down the track, slowly sinking into a more suitable, but less comfortable, sprung sitting position. By now Agostini had disappeared into the freezing mist as if it was a dry warm day, followed by the pack of hardened Europeans hard on his heels. The only riders that I was ahead of on the first lap were those whose bikes did not start at all and those whose bikes did start, but not on all cylinders! My main difficulty, as I had discovered on the warm up lap, was that I was unable to close my visor properly because it would simply mist up. Whenever my left hand was free from gearchanging I opened and closed the visor. This way I could see just enough to enable me to stay on the road. The spray thrown up by other competitors added to the general hardship, but the situation eased as everybody pulled away leaving me on my own wondering what the hell I was doing here. I stuck it out for a few laps until I could hear Ago's MV getting louder and louder behind me. At this stage I pulled into the pits and rode back to camp, parked the steaming, hissing bike against the side of Gossamer and dived into the tent. I ripped off the soaked outer layer of gear and crept into bed only to be criticized for having cold feet and hands.

This was our initiation into European racing. Eventually, we would get used to and cope with the conditions as well as anyone.The early months of the season in Europe were always dodgy, the weather tended to be foul and races in these conditions were typical. After Mettet I wondered why people had chosen to live in these parts in the first place.

The next morning in improved weather, everybody started packing their soaked equipment to move off to their next event. There was a great vibe and feeling of camaraderie amongst the competitors and their helpers. Most of us would be going to Paul Ricard Circuit in the south of France for the first round of the World Championship, the big time, the stuff that the dreams of a young roadracer are made of. Others might be off to smaller international events elsewhere. We met and chatted to a few people at Mettet and despite the debut debacle I felt a bit more relaxed about the whole trip. During the last week we had learnt a great deal about racing in Europe. The hardest part for rookies was getting properly organized, getting accepted by and communicating with the promoters at events, dealing with the weather and getting to the next race. The actual riding was, on most occasions, the easiest part of the whole deal. The world's best professional GP teams would be at Paul Ricard with their latest wares and the many different manufacturers would have been working feverishly and secretively off-season from September to April. The mission was to utilise the technological experience gained from the previous season and convert it into improved performance of their motorcycles for the following season, getting the edge on the opposition. Another area of immense interest was to see how those of the top GP competitors newly signed into factory teams from private participation and those who had changed camps were going to fare with their new teams.

Road to the sun

From Mettet, Paul Ricard was a distance of about 1,000km. We had been told that it would be best to use the Autoroute du Soleil to get there but that it would be expensive as it was a toll road all the way. The word soleil excited us because by now we were craving the sun, so we set out from Mettet in good spirits, believing things could only get better. Gossamer's heater worked well, so as long as we did not break down, we had the warmth generated by the motor to keep us alive. Although the weather was still grey and drab, the scenery was interesting. The little villages we passed through were quaint and everything was neat and tidy as if it had been just swept or scrubbed. We stopped along the way to buy food and got hooked on baguettes and the tasty cheese we would buy from the quaint shops in the charming little villages. This was the start of a decade of romance Bronnie and I would have with European culture. We came to love the diversity of the different countries which were packed into a relatively small area. The crossing of a border was sometimes a switch into a totally different time and culture, one side of the border like this, and the other like that. The people, the food, architecture, money and language could be very different. It was fascinating. We got to love European cuisine and in later years when we had money to spare we would stop at our favourite restaurants on the way to whatever Grand Prix we were going and dine in style. On most occasions, as I became a regular winner, we would be wined and dined by sponsors and promoters at the finest restaurants. Bronnie and I left South Africa as naive kids and ten years later we were confidently enjoying an incredible European experience together. I still get high thinking about those days. We were so fortunate to have had the opportunity, persevered and succeeded.

Once in France we picked up the Autoroute to Paris and started paying for the privilege. We had been wise enough to change some currency before getting on the toll road. With alarming regularity we would stop at the toll booths which reminded us of the starting gates at a horse race and feed more money into the basket or to the attendant. It did not take very long before we were getting close to the mighty city of Paris. Bronnie in particular was pretty excited. I guess Paris had associations of romantic things for a young girl, fashion design, perfumeries, designer this, designer that. The only merit of Paris for Dozy and me was the engineering feat of the Eiffel Tower and the controversial movie, Last Tango in Paris! It is a pity we weren't concentrating on the map. We missed the signs that said 'Peripherique', the ring road. We realised our mistake when we became the centre of a serious traffic jam. Paris drivers are fast and furious and giving way is against their principles, show one sign of weakness and you get trampled. London was fast and furious in comparison to Pietermaritzburg, where thirty cars constituted a traffic jam but tame in comparison to Paris. Later in the season we were to experience a drive eclipsing that of Paris, during a pleasure trip to Rome. One thing Parisian drivers are quick on is braking. We caused many emergency stops as we wobbled our way through the traffic until we gratefully recognised one of the Autoroute signs that led us back to the highway to the sun. Later on we would meet Pierre Soulas, a wonderful friend, and a resident of Paris under whose guidance, we would spend many fun days in this crazy, marvellous city.

Once back on the road south and with heart rates back to normal we decided to get off the toll road to save money. The little road. on the map next to the Autoroute wound its way merrily south through village after village. Yes, we saved on the toll fee, but at the end of the day it probably cost us more in petrol and wear and tear. We spent one night on the road, pulling up in a lay-by. The gross error of our decision not to buy a caravan became evident. As the day ended it would have been so nice to stop in a lay-by and put our feet up in a caravan with fridge for a cold beer and beds waiting for the weary bodies. Setting up the tent every time we pulled over was not feasible. We ended up with Bronnie and me sleeping in the back of the van where there was just enough space to crawl into our sleeping bags on the hard floor between the bikes. The two single front seats of Gossamer were about two feet apart and during the day, while travelling, Dozy would sit between them in a deck chair as if he was on the beach. At night we would put a tool box between the seats and he would have the front seats and tool box to call bed. Because it was raining we had to cook

Cooking between the front seats.

in the van so with the gas cooker on the tool box between the front seats Bronnie would heat up a can of stew, Vienna sausages or such delicacies for supper. Thereafter the kitchen would be packed away and the sleeping arrangements installed. This time of day, particularly when the weather was bad, which was most of the time, was a real pain. When the weather was good we could at least set up the cooker outside and boil Viennas al fresco.

The little road to Paul Ricard was painfully slow but the further south we travelled the better the weather became until it was blissfully warm and we could shed our sweaters for the first time in weeks. It took an extra day before we wound our way up the escarpment outside Marseille, on top of which was located the Circuit de Paul Ricard. We signed in at race control outside the circuit and received the necessary passes to enable us to enter the sacred domain of the GP competitors, where the privileged few had the right to enter. This GP was run by the eccentric Francois Chevalier. He was obliged by the rules of the governing body, the FIM (Federation Internationale Motocicliste) to pay each competitor a set, albeit rather small fee whether they qualified or not. This resulted in most GP organisers inviting as few riders as possible. But not Francois Chevalier! Francois had accepted about one hundred competitors per class. There were six GP and four national classes which meant that there were about 800 competitors present. This number was greatly multiplied by team members. There was a small city already in the vast paddocks, each team with colourful tent or caravan and transporter. It was spectacular. The tar paddocks nearer to the pits were full so we had to camp in one of the outer dirt paddocks with not a blade of grass to be seen. We found ourselves a nice spot next to some trees and set up camp full of enthusiasm and high expectation. The weather was good and we were actually at a GP. Regardless of how the weekend went I could have happily retired after it. The fact that I had got to Europe to try and qualify for a position on the grid for the 1973 French GP at Paul Ricard circuit was more than I had ever hoped to achieve.

The circuit infrastructure was impressive. There was a huge administration block, a four or five story building, running the full length of the substantial pit garages. An integral part of the admin block was a huge Press room, hospitality suites, restaurant and best of all, excellent shower and toilet facilities! Shower facilities were non-existent en route so we grabbed the soap and shampoo and got stuck in. Not only did the water come out with power, but it was hot. Alas, the luxury did not last. Day by day the toilet blocks became steadily dirtier, the water colder. By race day the queues were long, the showers dirty and the water cold.

We were awakened the next morning, the first day of official practice, by a howling gale which was hammering the tent and kicking up a lot of dust. We were told that this was the Mistral, which blew down from the north from time to time and usually lasted a few days.

250cc practice had been split into two sessions with about fifty bikes in each session. One hundred entrants were trying to qualify for about forty grid positions. I went out, eager to spend the first session learning the 5.81km circuit, but suffered a cylinder seizure on the first lap. We repaired it for the next practice, but it seized again. It turned out to be a faulty spark plug that caused the seizure which in turn cost us two practice sessions, not to mention expensive pistons rings and cylinders. The circuit was not too amazing. It had a long main straight, at least 2km long. It was modern for the era and designed with safety in mind, with plenty of run off area on the outside of the corners, and lots of twisty tricky parts, but no real character. The surface was impregnated with a very rough stone which gripped nicely but chewed your leathers and some of your backside if you slid off.

After practice we were in the tent stripping the 250 down in readiness for the following day. The irritating wind had been buffeting the tent all day and the dust from the bare ground was everywhere. Suddenly the wind picked up and the next second the tent took off, tearing the stakes out of the granite-like ground and spewing tent poles all around. We were left with the 250, a toolbox, kitchen table and the gas cooker on top. The tent was off to the blue yonder as were a lot of the other tents. Anything else light and capable of unpowered flight had gone. We retreated into a huddle in the back of the van and shut everything to keep the dust from invading more than it had already done. Fortunately it was just a passing gust which soon subsided to gale force at which time everybody came out of hiding to pick up the debris. We retrieved our tent and found no bad damage, but not wanting to risk a repeat, we stuffed it under the van. We would have to sleep the rest of the weekend in the back of the van in quiet discomfort and work on the bikes in the open, fully exposed to the dust and incessant bloody wind.

I didn't qualify for the 250 race. We had missed too much practice with the seizures, and although I managed to put in some reasonable lap times, in official timed practice the sheer numbers of fast riders in the class made it difficult to qualify. I did however qualify twenty-seventh in the less well-subscribed 500cc class on a rather sick machine. The 500 was never going to perform well again because it needed new crankcases and crankshaft. The cases were worn out and the crank had been rebuilt so many times that it had become a bit flexible and would not stay true. In the race the bike went badly, and according to my records I noticed excessive oil on my left boot so pulled in after ten laps. It was far more exciting to watch the rest of the race. Could the beautiful new factory four cylinder two stroke 500cc Yamaha match the spectacular three cylinder 500cc four stroke MV Agustas? A Finnish gentleman by the name of Jarno Saarinen, a man of phenomenal genius, riding the Yamaha, beat Phil Read on the MV into second. Ago crashed trying to keep up and Japanese ace Hideo Kanaya, Saarinen's team-mate was third. It was mind boggling stuff.

Another impressive rider at Ricard was an ace from New Zealand by the name of Kim Newcombe. Kim, Janeen and their three year old son Mark were the first folk we got to know well. Janeen, a very 'up front' person, came straight over and said 'How ya doing?' and created the opportunity for us to meet a lot of the other people in the race fraternity. Kim was more serious about things in general but certainly not afraid to have a good time. They were based in Berlin and Kim was racing for the Konig outboard motor factory. He impressed me not only because of his smooth racing style, but also because of his outstanding engineering genius. He adapted an outboard motor for use in bike racing. This is not easy because boat motors and bike motors have entirely different power characteristics and operate in totally different environments for different purposes. It is both an art and a science to extract power from two stroke engines so to adapt one for use in a different environment was no mean feat. The motor was a water-cooled flat four cylinder two stroke arrangement with one rotary valve on top feeding both banks of cylinders through one large downdraught Weber carburettor. Each bank of cylinders must have fired together as they shared a common expansion chamber.

Kim personally designed and built the unconventional chassis into which the motor fitted. It had a single large diameter round tube connecting the steering head to the swinging arm pivot point with the motor hanging under the tube or spine, rather than the traditional cradle-type frame in which the motor sits. It was beautifully engineered. As if all this was not enough, it handled well and Kim rode it brilliantly. Kim and his Konig were an irritation to the mighty factory teams of Yamaha and MV, constantly challenging their supremacy by setting lap times which kept them on their toes. He had a special talent, and was a brilliant rider and brilliant engineer.

Kim Newcombe with his amazing Konigs.

A section of the incredible 'Ring'.

The incredible 'Ring'

In two weeks in Europe we had already covered about 1,400km and participated in two race events, both in adverse weather conditions. In these two weeks we had been lost, wet, frozen, warm, blown away in a dust storm and blown off in the races! The trip from Paul Ricard to The Nürburgring, our next destination, was about 1000km north in the direction of the bad weather. Two days later we entered a cold wet Germany. It was our first trip to a country we had learnt so much about in history and it felt kind of weird being there. After clearing customs, the first road sign we came upon was the instruction for a 'Gute Fahrt'. Childishly it had us cracked up for miles. The Ring, as the Nurburgring was called, was built in 1927 and was Germany's first closed circuit. It was impressive to us with huge grandstands and an imposing control tower. There were lock-up garages available to competitors but they cost money or were allocated to the rich and famous so we set up tent with the damp campers in the damp grass paddock outside the garage area.

I knew The Ring was a long circuit, in fact 22.835km long. What I had no idea about was the complexity of this legendary circuit. It is located in the hilly, tree-covered Eiffel Mountains near the town of Nurburg and apparently has one hundred and seventy-two corners. I never counted them but what I did find out was that no two corners were the same and there was hardly a level section on the entire lap. Either you were going uphill or downhill, either a little or a lot! This was going to be a pig to learn. One section that I enjoyed a lot in later years after I became more acquainted with The Ring, was a section that descended straight down the side of a substantial hill. It was fast, as I recall, top gear type fast. At the bottom the track turned slightly left and at the same time headed straight up the opposite hill. You would hit the bottom at speed and lean over without tapping off to negotiate the slight bend. The middle of the bend was also the bottom of the valley, so as you hit this and began ascending, the suspension would bottom out and the G force would pin your head to the tank. You were stuck there for maybe two or three seconds before being released. It was crazy fun, like an extreme roller coaster ride at 250kph or whatever speed we were touching there. The green trees were very close to the circuit and at that speed it seemed that I was riding on a black strip through a tunnel of green. Straight ahead everything was in focus but as visibility spread out to your peripheral vision the picture became progressively more blurred as it flashed past. It was eerie and somewhat hypnotic. There was another interesting section further along where you became seriously airborne. It was very exciting, especially the first time. The section consisted of a fast left hand bend with a blind drop in the middle. On reaching the middle of the corner the track merely disappeared and you were launched into space. To make it worse the track veered slightly right at the bottom of the blind descent so if you were off line and flying in the wrong direction, as I was that first time, there was a lot of work to do when touching down. Once you learnt to get the approach to the blind rise perfect, the section was great. The better, or braver riders could get airborne and on landing keep the front wheel in the air for a long way. There were dozens of interesting sections on a lap of the mighty Nürburgring.

The Ring became one of my favourite circuits. Like Spa it was an ultimate challenge but for a different reason. It was the sheer length, character and technical complexity of it that appealed to me and I developed an intense desire to know every corner, every bump, every section intimately to enable me to ride the entire circuit on the limit and thus command the respect of, or dare I say conquer, this incredible circuit. Because of its length and difficult nature, it was extremely tough to learn. During the week the circuit was open to the public, and for a a small fee you could take a car or roadbike around on a lap. The rich and famous were buying laps during the week to familiarise themselves with the layout. A lot of us poor folk in the camping paddock sat and waited for the first of a limited number of practice sessions.

To make a tough time tougher, it rained persistently all weekend. In poor conditions the circuit was a beast, as slippery as a skid pan with mist on the higher sections. I had rides in both 250 and 500 classes so would hopefully carry what I learnt from one class practice to the next. In the rain the average lap would take a blind rookie about twelve minutes which meant that if your gearing, carburation or any other settings were not right you had to battle through the twelve minute lap before you could pit and adjust. This meant that in an hour's practice five laps were possible if no pit work was required. Five laps in the rain, cold and mist was not enough for me so it was not surprising that during one of the 250 practices I fell off and skated down the track next to the bike and crashed through a substantial hedge. I was not hurt, but the hedge had a huge hole in it, the fairing was ripped to pieces and the forks looked bent. I guess that was one section that I would remember, right down to the plant life! I was a long way from the pits so I would have to wait for practice to end for a pickup truck to collect the bits and return me to base. As I waited, a Flag Marshall came over with a little brown bottle which he offered to me. I gratefully accepted it thinking it would be brandy or some such desirable elixir as carried by St. Bernards. It turned out to be cough mixture, but what the heck. To the obvious surprise of the Marshall who was expecting some back for his own medicinal purposes, I drank it down hoping it would help ward off depression and the cold. It didn't.

Repairing the 250 was a challenge without the correct equipment. We eventually found a small workshop nearby

willing to let us use their press to straighten the forks. I dread to think what the 250 looked like after we glued the bits of fairing back together, but time was short so aesthetics would take a back seat until a better day. We later discovered that the 250's steering head had been bent straight back a degree or two from the crash. Ironically it handled better from that day so we never bothered to alter the geometry back to standard!

Both races took place in pouring rain so lap times were substantially slower than practice, which indicates how heavy the rain must have been. I finished twenty-sixth of fifty starters in the five lap 250 race and twenty-first of fifty-five starters in the 500 race. To us this was great progress; two qualifications, two finishes on a monster of a circuit in awful weather and DM700 for the effort. The money from each event was just enough to pay our way to the next. It would fill the tank with petrol a couple of times and buy basic foodstuff more akin to survival rations, the dreaded cigarettes and the odd bottle of plonk. At some stage we were going to have to dig into the savings to buy parts for the bikes. More specifically, we needed to buy the latest 398 compound super sticky Dunlops that everybody was using. We needed a Quaife six speed close ratio gear cluster for the 250 to replace the standard five speed one, and we needed to replace the points ignition on the 250 with the latest electronic Krober ignition system. These improvements would help me become more competitive and hopefully reach higher up the prize money scale. Our plan was to spend as little as possible on the 500 and use it as a 'start money special.' Two entries at an event usually paid a bit better than one and it was common practice among competitors to concentrate on their better machine for results, and use the other for additional pay.

Communications with organisers to get entries was the biggest hassle. It was difficult enough finding an international telephone, not all Post Offices had them. Calling the organisers direct was never much use. The person I needed was seldom available or did not particularly want to talk to me anyway, and language was always a stumbling block. The best method of communication while on the road was to write to the organiser using Arthur's address in London and wait for a reply. We would call Arthur once a week for news. However Arthur proved just as elusive as a GP organiser. It often took days to find him. Communications have come a long long way since then. We would have killed for a fax machine, cell phone or lap top computer with e-mail access. Communication or no communication, getting accepted at races, particularly Grands Prix, was to get harder as the season progressed. For the early Internationals and GPs, organisers were fairly accommodating to newcomers, giving a few a chance to qualify, but it became increasingly difficult to get entries except in the case of exceptional results or the 'old pals act', neither of which applied to us. During the Nürburgring event we learned from Arthur that I had been accepted in both classes at the Austrian GP at the Salzburgring but declined for the West German GP at Hockenheim and the Italian GP at Monza. Common practice for newcomers and some less successful old hands, was to travel to the next event and beg and plead for a chance to try and qualify, even for no money. As I was to find out, this was a harrowing experience for an introvert and particularly hard on the knees. It was another shitty job that I could not, by trickery or bribery, delegate to either of the other two team members.

I wrecked the 250 in practice at the Nürburgring.

Austrian GP, something to celebrate

After two standard, uncomfortable nights on the road, we crossed the border from Germany to Austria at Walserberg. The scenery through Bavaria and up to the Salzburgring was magnificent, like a big immaculate garden dotted with pretty chalets sporting ornate woodwork and flowers hanging from window boxes. The scenery instilled a peacefulness and even the cattle looked contented, chewing lazily in their lush green pastures. The sun was shining and it was warm which gave us a feeling of optimism. As we got higher up in the hilly country closer to the circuit the snow which was evident on the higher parts, became thicker on the ground, until there were drifts of up to a metre in places. Real snow was a new experience for us so like a bunch of kids we stopped and in warm sunshine had our first snowball fight and built our first snowman. The Salzburgring is one of the prettiest settings in Europe. It is situated about 20km outside of Salzburg nestling in a valley surrounded by stunning pine forests. The circuit was typically high speed with the pit straight running down one side of the valley and the back straight up the other side of the valley and into a natural arena. Here a series of very fast bends ultimately joined up with the pit straight and the plunge down the valley. The atmosphere on race day was incredible with many thousands of spectators sitting in the natural arena on the hillside watching the riders hurtling into the arena to the deafening roar of the spectators.

We found a spot, set up camp and rushed off to find the showers, standard procedure at each circuit after a few days on the road. The most disappointing thing at most of these so called world class venues was the lack of consideration for the comfort of the competitors. When it came to toilet and shower facilities nine times out of ten there were too few showers and toilets to cope with the number of competitors and team members, and most of the time there was no hot water. At some venues the toilets would be blocked and unusable by race day. The whole situation was ludicrous. Motorcycle racing's controlling body, the Federation Internationale Motocycliste (FIM) had set out fixed scales of pay and prize money which seemed, even to the newcomer, to be out of kilter with the huge spectator attendances. What's more, a lot of the members of the FIM happened to be GP organisers as well! These two issues, facilities and money, were two of many long-standing injustices that were to lead to dissent and the attempted formation of a breakaway series six years later at the end of 1979. There had been attempts in the past to force change by striking, but rider unity had never been strong enough for an effective walkout. The average GP hosted six classes of racing with a minimum of fifty riders per class accepted to qualify, totalling three hundred competitors. To get a small number, let alone a majority of three hundred riders to unite had so far proved impossible.

We fitted the last of our new cylinders and pistons to the 250, which made a big difference. The bike went great. Together with the improved handling caused by the 'new' geometry of the bent frame it helped me to turn some very encouraging lap times in early practice. To top it the weather was perfect. My notes say, '85 degrees, no wind.' By the end of two days of official practice we ended up an amazing twelfth on the grid of the Austrian 250cc Grand Prix. We were over the moon with this result as we had not yet upgraded the outdated TD2B Yamaha 250, or fitted new 398 Dunlops. At 1 min 31.3 secs., I was just two seconds slower than the pole position time of 1min 29.3 secs, set by Saarinen on the factory Yamaha. What a breakthrough! A factor in my success here and later at other events was my ability to learn new circuits quickly and my new found prowess (big balls) on ultra high speed corners. I loved the fast corners and the challenge they presented. The ability to cope with ultra fast corners was a useful weapon in the arsenal on the fast European circuits of the time. It was also after this performance that I realised, given the right equipment I could be up with the world's best.

Our mate Kim was also going great on the fast track and by the end of official practice had again split the factory riders. That night we sat with Kim and Jan and, high on the pre-race atmosphere, discussing our good lap times, how we might improve them and yarning about where we hoped to go and how we were going to get there.

Can you believe it, bloody race day dawned bloody raining. I had set my mind on trying to get tenth or better to earn championship points and I believed that I could. I knew that I could go faster after achieving twelfth with relative ease in practice but I also knew I would not be able to achieve tenth or better on a wet circuit. This was not pessimistic, simply realistic. We did not have the soft compound tyres that were crucial in wet conditions.

The 'Flying Finn' Jarno Saarinen lapped me at the end of the soaked twenty-seven lap race in which I finished twentieth. Despite the disappointment, we were optimistic about future events. The practice success at the Salzburgring had indicated that there was a dim light at the end of a very long tunnel. I had proved that I had the ability to compete at GP level. All we lacked was competitive, current equipment and the budget to keep it going properly. That night we had a hell of a bash with Kim, Janeen and many of the other competitors at the hotel where the Yamaha Team were staying. When it was time to return to camp, we could not find Dozy. He had chosen the time everybody had decided to leave to take a leak on the Yamaha transporter tyre, and was accidentally left behind! On his long trek back to the circuit he got lost and ended up trudging through deep snow-filled fields in search of home. The weather had turned very cold but luckily Dozy was well tanked on anti-freeze of the Stroh Rum variety. Eventually he roused a farmer at about 2am and in his best German asked 'Waars de fahrerlager?' Fortunately the farmer understood and pointed him in the right direction. The next morning we found him in his sleeping bag with his shoes on. One side was covered in frozen mud and the other side sported the contents of his stomach! Needless to say he woke up with a severe headache, but then so did most folk on a Monday after a GP.

Reluctant spectators at Hockenheim. Relieved spectators at Monza

We spent Monday recovering and cleaning and tidying up the bikes. We loaded up on Tuesday and got on the road to Hockenheim. Apart from border hassles and another uncomfortable night in the van, I felt that I could get to like the lifestyle. Imagine having good bikes and earning enough at each race to have a caravan at the race track and afford to stay in hotels with hot showers and real beds. Imagine stopping at quaint, classy restaurants when you felt hungry rather than parking in a lay-by with the truckers to boil Viennas on a gas stove between the front seats. At this stage I never seriously thought we would get close because we just did not have the cash or equipment. I was never one to build dreams and then relentlessly, fanatically pursue them. My attention was always on giving the very best account of myself. This never applied to school work though, only competitive sporting endeavours, especially bikes, where total comittment was essential. My goal in most races I entered was simply to go as fast as my equipment would allow for as long as necessary to secure the best possible position. There were races in different periods of my career that I knew I would win. Then this type of philosophy did not apply, the plan was to win by as comfortable a margin as possible. One of the biggest compliments I ever received, and I don't think Tom meant it as a compliment but as a comment, was in an interview after the 1977 Dutch TT 350 event, my second GP win, a race that I led from start to finish. Ulsterman Tom Herron, good friend and a great character, chased me for almost all of the race. He pushed me hard, but eventually fell back to finish fourth. When asked for his opinion of the race he said, 'The pace was too hard for too long and I could not keep it up.' Tragically Tom was killed some years later at the North West 200. There were a lot of riders killed in European GP and International racing until the safety revolution got going in '79/80. When Bronnie and I look through our photo albums from those days we are astounded at the number of pictures of friends subsequently killed at various tracks. On most occasions it was because circuit safety was too low on the list of too many promoters and circuit owner's priorities.

Back at Hockenheim I begged and scraped until my knees bled but failed to convince the dogmatic promoter to allow me the opportunity to try and qualify. We parked in the paddock and set about upgrading the 250 in anticipation of a crack at qualifying for the Italian 250 GP at Monza the following weekend or failing that, the International race the weekend after, at Misano at which I had confirmed entries in both classes. My notebook entry for Friday 11th May notes that I bought eight super sticky Dunlops for DM360 and the next day bought a second hand Krober ignition system for the 250 for DM300. I also noted that Kim and Janeen took us to dinner. What the notebook does not say is that it was a hell of a treat to have steak.

We spectated at Hockenheim on race day and saw a great 500 race. The most impressive thing, apart form the sound of Phil Read's MV Agusta, was the huge crowd that filled every inch of the vast grandstands which lined the track at the infield arena. I don't know how many spectators the infield arena seated, but it looked like 100,000. It was awesome. Each time Read and

Saarinen, who were having the mother of dices, came hurtling into the arena, the crowd would stand up and roar and wave. The gladiators would then head off through the forest section of the circuit for a good two minutes before re-entering the arena. It made the hair stand up on the back of my neck. Read was riding the race of his life and held Saarinen off to take the flag. That night we ambled over to the Circuit hotel for a drink. Jarno Saarinen was in the bar with his lovely wife, both in a very happy mood. Contracted rider for a factory such as Yamaha was certainly an enviable position and one that should have allowed him to reach for the stars. What impressed me about the man was that despite rising to a legendary status in a short period of time he had no airs and graces about him. He was very popular and highly regarded in the 'Circus' and still preferred to stay in the paddock in a small camper van among his friends rather than in hotels which was the norm for a person in his position. Alas I am sad to say that we never got to know him. He was to die an awful, and unnecessary death the following weekend at Monza.

I believe we are the master of our own destinies. If you choose to drink and drive or to climb Mount Everest, you might cause your own death. Every now and then, though, something happens to shatter this belief and I think all present at Monza on that fateful day were likely to be searching for answers. On arriving at the circuit, I went directly to the organisers and begged and scraped in an effort to get starts in the 250 and 500 races, without success. We were to be spectators again. As it turned out it was for the best. In what can only be described as a horrific tragedy caused by the unprofessional actions of the race directors, Grand Prix racing was to lose two great sons in one swift stroke. During the race which preceded the 250, one of the competitors had some kind of engine problem at the end of the race and spilled a lot of oil at the first bend, La Curva Grande, a very fast right hander. Despite the warnings and protestations of the riders, the organisers insisted on getting the 250 race under way without cleaning up the spill properly. Rider power was just not strong enough to take control of the situation and refuse to allow the race to start. At the time the oil spill was blamed for the multiple pile-up but there is an alternative theory supported by reasonable evidence that one of the leading rider's motor seized, causing the accident. Whether oil spill or motor seizure, the race began despite protestation and reluctance. It got as far as La Curva Grande where there was a big pile-up which culminated in the deaths of Renzo Pasolini, much loved Italian and the new superstar hero, Jarno Saarinen. Many other riders received serious injuries. As naive South Africans we were shocked and horrified by this unbelievable incident. We had not experienced the hard reality that riders do get killed. We had never had to go through this in South Africa and it was a serious wake-up call. That tragic incident spelt out a clear message. This could happen to me and I was going to have to be very careful in this dangerous pursuit of Grand Prix glory. The most frightening part was that if I had succeeded in getting an entry there was every possibility that I would have been involved in the fatal pile-up. In the final analysis I stick by my original belief that we are the masters of our own destinies. I do not believe that it was due to any divine intervention but it was simple good fortune that I had been refused a ride. I think it is true to say that people involved in a dangerous pastime mourn and regret the loss of a fallen comrade for a long time, if not for the rest of our lives. At the same time we pick ourselves up and hopefully wiser for the experience, go on to the next race where we again compete as hard as we can go.

We hit the jackpot at Misano and the bus in Rome!

The drive to Misano for the International event dedicated to the memory of Renzo Pasolini was a short drive south from Monza and we were there by Monday night. On Tuesday morning I parted with 3,000 Lire for a full morning's practice. The circuit was one of the future breed. It was new, relatively short at 3.488km, nicely designed and above all, the layout was safety oriented with ample run-off area at all corners. It was an interesting circuit with a variety of bends, fast and slow and an excellent circuit for testing. We would use it on a couple of occasions for exclusive pre-season testing of the prototype Kawasaki KR500 many years later.

The 250 was going very nicely. This was my first experience of the 398 Dunlops and they were fabulous. The extra grip gave so much confidence and enabled me to brake much later and harder, even while leaning over entering the bends. It was possible to get on the power earlier and harder when exiting the bends. The extra grip was causing the suspension to compress more than usual and was also allowing me to lean over further causing the fairing, pipes and foot pegs to scrape on the track. We had to stiffen the suspension up to alleviate the problem and I found that I was trying subtle technique changes to suit the slightly more aggressive riding style that the tyres were asking for. The bike felt crisper and stronger at peak revs with the newly-fitted second-hand Krober ignition system and after a very satisfying morning I was into competitive lap times so we parked the bike to save wearing it out. Something I found extremely useful in my bag of tricks was my ability to change my riding style to suit the circumstances. I believe my background gave me a very broad diversity of experience which enabled me to analyse and adapt to different circumstances fairly easily. At some events at Roy Hesketh in the early 70s, I would race in up to four classes on the same afternoon. I might step off our rapid little home-built 50cc Dozy-tuned Yamaha onto the H1R500 Kawaski for a big twenty-three second a lap change of pace. After that I would step aboard the TD2B 250 Yamaha then onto the hardest work of all, the H1 Mach III 500 production bike, which required a unique style of riding. These were usually short ten lap races so the transformation from one mode to the next had to be instant in order to be competitive from the drop of the flag. On a good day I might win all races entered. In one race I would be using a forgiving and non-fading Rickman disc brake that we had fitted to the H1R, then climb aboard the TD2B with its four leading shoe cable operated drum brake. The cable operated drum brake had far less feel in between off and locked up, so required a totally different touch to using the disc. In those days locking the front wheel while braking in a straight line was relatively easy, happened swiftly and often meant hitting the deck. The H1 had a tiny front drum not much bigger

The aged TD2B in action.

Big success at Misano, 28th May 1973.

Autodromo Santamonica, Misano Adriatico, 2·167-mile/3·488-km circuit

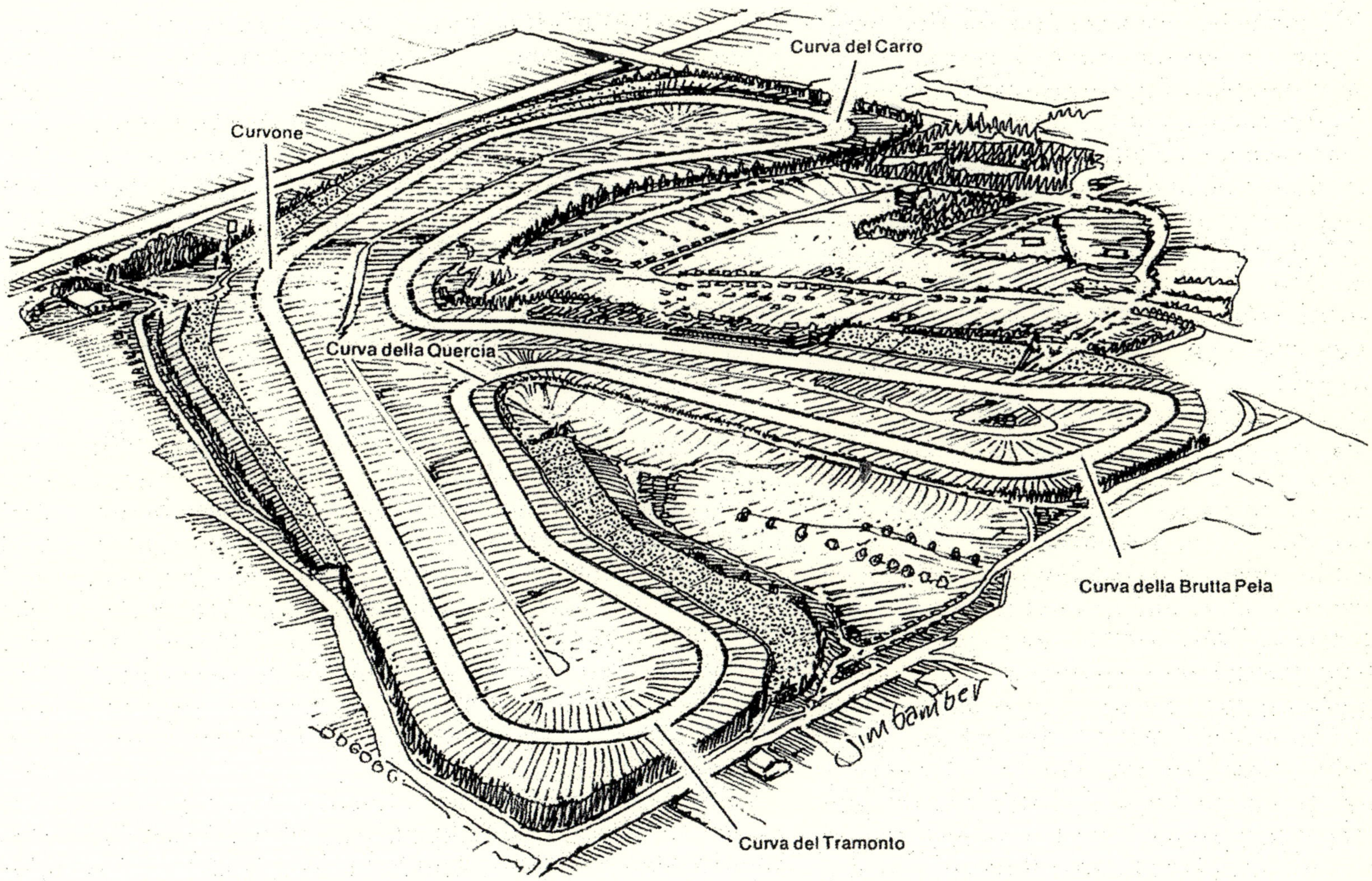

than my 50cc racer and it only worked okay once per race, and that was at the first corner! Thereafter it worked at varying degrees of inefficiency which was directly related to the time allowed for cooling between the corners. To top it all, the bike went like stink, had inadequate suspension, no ground clearance and was on street tyres. It was a wild ride to say the least. I won two provincial championships on that bike and on most occasions beat the mighty 750cc four cylinder Hondas. The 1969 H1 rocket which should never have passed beyond the factory gates, taught me a lot as a kid, particularly the art of survival. It is still in my possession, I ride it on the streets occasionally and it still tries to hurt me.

We were looking good at Misano and although still somewhat mellow after Monza we were optimistic about the weekend ahead. The track was super and we were told the weather was to remain perfect so having nothing more to do, we took time out to go and jump in the waveless Adriatic. When we got back to the paddock it was evening and Kim, Janeen and Mark had arrived and set up camp so we went to visit. We must have developed an insatiable weakness for European wine. Entries in my diary indicate that on Wednesday night 'We drank a bottle of Kim and Janeen's wine.' On Thursday night we 'Finished another bottle of wine, hic.' The entry does not specify whose bottle. On Friday night we 'Had big bottle wine with Newcombe'. All this wine. It was no surprise that by Friday night I had developed a writing impediment! That day's entry also stated 'N.B. Kawa seized on two pots.' Now it sounded like the bike was drinking as well! I must stress that Kim and Janeen never drank a lot of alcohol and I indulged in moderation on nights before practice sessions and races. I have never believed that you have to abstain from alcohol, sex or any of life's pleasures for days before an event to give your best performance, as some 'experts' claim. I found that alcohol in moderation did not impede my performance next day or that carbohydrate loading the night before the event helped any. Each individual is different and I found through trial, error and practical experience that whatever made me comfortable and got me into the right frame of mind was good. What I ate on the morning of the race was more important than the meal the previous day. On the sex front, well that's our secret!

Parties aside, Saturday was for official timed qualifying practice for all classes and we were truly ready for the first time during our brief European tour. The 250 race entry list had three names which will jog some memories. They became good compadres during the following decade; Roberto Gallina, Mario Lega and Dieter Braun. Gallina was a great rider in his own right but most will remember him for Team Gallina and his part in engineering Virginio Ferrari's brilliant but unsuccessful challenge for the 500 title in 1979 and back to back 500cc World Championship wins with Marco Lucchinelli in 1981 and Franco Uncini in 1982. Mario Lega was an up and coming young Italian star. We were to clash in 1978 when he was reigning 250 World Champion on a Morbidelli. Dieter Braun was on his way to becoming the 1973 250 World Champion. He was an older, experienced European campaigner on a very fast Yamaha, tuned by a noted German tuner, Sepp Schlogl, later to help my rival from Kawasaki Germany, Toni Mang in 1978, '79 and 80. At the end of practice Gallina was on pole and Lega was second. I was fifth and Braun was seventh. The lap times were all very close.

In the 500 class Kim was second to Guido Mandracci but was ahead of Read, Ago and Gallina. Astoundingly, Kim's mechanic, an excellent fellow and highly astute engineer, Rod Tingate from Melbourne, Australia, had his TR3 Yamaha in the back of his van. Rod had been accepted to start in the 350 race and was also going well and on the front row of the grid. Team Wine and Dine were hot that weekend!

My TD2B was the oldest bike in the race, but Dozy had it going superbly, our team was humming and I was ready to let it all hang out. I had not had a good old fashioned scratch for some time and felt the need. The race turned out to be a humdinger. Gradually Braun and I broke from Gallina and Lega and pulled away. Gallina's pole lap time was 1min 34.5sec. By halfway we were down to 34.4 and for the last ten laps were sub 34 with my best being 33.4. I was glued to Braun's back wheel. On the last lap my brakes could no longer take the punishment. Two corners from the end they gave and I found myself heading up the inside of Braun with the lever against the handlebar. I made an instant decision. Rather than take the future World Champ out and look like a dillbrain, I decided to dump it to avoid certain collision. I threw it right over onto its side. I can remember the sound of fibreglass grinding away on the ground as we skidded along on the fairing and my knee. I also saw Dieter lean safely into the corner out of immediate danger. I was all set to go bouncing down the road but instead, the bike having scrubbed off some speed going sideways, regained grip, slotted in right behind Dieter and we were away again. It was an unbelievable recovery. I crossed the flag right behind Dieter, with Mario Lega third to create a very interesting rostrum of future World Champions. The significance of the photo of the three of us on the rostrum would only be fully realised many years later as first, Dieter became World 250 Champion in 1973 then Mario's turn in 1977 and mine in 1978 and 1979.

This was a race that I will never forget. It was so good getting up on that rostrum, my first European rostrum finish. It was a great honour to receive the trophy with Renzo Pasolini's name engraved on it. What a weekend! Kim and Rod did very well, Kim getting third in the 500 and Rod third in the 350 race. This result reinforced the conclusion that I had arrived at in Austria. There was no doubt in my mind that with the right equipment our little team could reach for the stars. I was really lucky to have Dozy and Bronnie with me because it can't be done without the right kind of help. Mondays after a successful weekend were a mystical, pleasurable haze, a blend of total relaxation fulfilment and relief. We would sit around and dwell on the moment and lazily prepare to move on. They were a stark contrast to the intense pressure and hype of the build-up to race day and the final state of nervousness any top sportsperson suffers as the clock ticks steadily towards the moment of reckoning on the day of the challenge, when the starters gun fires or the flag drops.

Although we had bagged more start and prize money than usual, the kitty was low. Johnno approached his brother, Hardy, who owned a successful travel agency in Durban. Hardy was only too happy to help, and arranged to send funds in the form of traveller's cheques to Rome with his assistant. She would be in Rome for a few days on her way to London and we did not have a race the next weekend so we could meet her there. Rome was reputed to be a city overflowing with culture, some of which, with a bit of luck might rub off on us! At Misano we had met a really nice Italian guy by the name of Vincenzo Danielle who because he spoke perfect English was working as interpreter for the race organisers. Vincenzo, who lived in Rome, invited us to stay. We got to Vincenzo's small but comfortable apartment on Tuesday night and had the first taste of luxury since leaving home. His bath caused some mirth because it was so small that you could only fit in it with your knees jammed under your chin.

Our first trophy of the international tour at Misano.

The next day we were set loose on the city in Gossamer. The traffic was unbelievable with 90% of the cars being little Fiat Cinquecentos. No matter where you were the drivers were jostling for position, staring each other down in an attempt to intimidate the other as they raced for the same gap. At the last minute one would chicken out and give way, usually with a self conciliatory beep on the horn and wave of the fist as some sort of Roman salute. Amazingly these seemingly wild drivers were racing around with only millimetres to spare yet their bumpers and fenders showed little evidence of judgement errors. I am not sure who was responsible for this judgement error, but we had a coming together with a tourist bus, its door hinge ripped a nasty gash down the side of Gossamer ruining her previously perfect complexion. We engaged the driver in an animated exchange, but did not care to stop as we had no insurance! We met Jean at the appointed time to collect the funds and rushed back to Vincenzo's to park Goss and retire from Roman driving. Thereafter Vincenzo showed us the sights of Rome in his Cinquecento. It is without a doubt, the most amazing city in Europe. The ancient buildings, art, sculptures and the history of the place are truly incredible. That night we had our first taste of real Italian pizza which was nothing like the plump overloaded 'cheese pie' that seemed the norm outside Europe. My best memory of Rome is sitting on the pavement with Vincenzo, eating fabulous pizza, drinking fabulous wine to the fabulous sound of a million Fiat horns!

Sharing the rostrum at Misano with Dieter Braun and Mario Lega.

Retreat to the Island

Arthur informed us that we had not been accepted at the International race at Chimay in Belgium in two weeks but with nowhere else to go we set the compass for a long haul to Chimay to try and get a ride anyway. After two days and nights on the road we finally reached Belgium. We were pretty knackered and were ready to kill for a real bath with real hot water and a real bed with crisp white sheets to slip into. Driven by these visions and recent memories of Vincenzo's tiny tub, we unanimously decided to stretch the budget and check into a hotel in Phillipville. We were handed the keys and eagerly entered our room where we were in for a surprise. Our room which cost an arm, leg and foot, had no bath. The room had no shower. All it had was a basin in the corner and a strange looking thing which looked like a toilet except that it had a strange outlet not capable of passing large solid items! Dozy being the one with the enquiring mind, bent over the contraption and turned one of the levers on it and was immediately blasted in the face by a fountain of water. The look of surprise on his face was enough. Despite our despair we howled with mirth, the tears of disappointment turning to tears of laughter. The cost of the room with the shower was substantially more so we stuck with the economy room and did the best we could at bathing with the suave sounding 'bidet' butt washing contraption and the basin.

We arrived at Chimay track on the Sunday one week prior to the event, and after doing a lap of the circuit in Goss, decided that it exceeded certain parameters such as relative safety and enjoyment and would have to be treated with the utmost respect. The roads were narrow and the country sections comprised very high speed curves with no space for error. I tracked down the organiser, one Georges Annuzet who turned out to be a great guy with a good attitude and a smile. I suppose with such a lemon of a race track he needed to be thus. He was happy to give me a chance to start in the 250 race, but only for a small amount of money as his budget was spent. I had heard that one before.

The Paddock was locked so we found the local caravan park and set up home. Dozy got on with stripping the 250 which needed the crankshaft replacing. Bron and I jumped into Goss for a quick trip to Holland to deliver our spare crank to renowned Dutch tuning ace, Karl Zeegers for a rebuild. Karl had a great workshop with a dynamometer and all the toys and his tuning expertise was partly responsible for Holland's road racing hero, Wil Hartog's rise to stardom. Wil's bikes were rapid and reliable and he rode well, a winning combination. It was interesting that as time went by we were to meet many characters such as Karl who had a wealth of knowledge to offer and were always keen to help. Back at Chimay the paddock had been unlocked and Kim and team had arrived so we transplanted from the caravan park and pitched our camp next to them. By now I was feeling pretty sick. I had been drinking tap water at the caravan camp and was about to learn lesson number one in Europe the hardest and most painful way. Do not drink from any tap. I could not have picked a worse place to contract galloping gyppo guts because the paddock had one, I repeat, one toilet. As the paddock filled up with people for the weekend there developed a permanent line at the loo which increased in length as the population increased. My condition made no allowance for standing in queues as I needed instant access to a loo at alarmingly frequent intervals. I reckon this kind of situation is the worst a person can be caught in. The pain and anguish became so unbearable that I set upon digging a hole in the corner of the tent with my bare hands! Around the sacred hole I piled our suitcases on top of one another to form a wall behind which to

At the Aldridge's workshop in Beeston. Beds. Left to right: Roger Aldridge, me, Peter Aldridge, a friend and Dozy.

hide and let rip. My condition was so bad that I was to spend a lot of time in the corner or within quick access thereof. By Saturday practice I had improved slightly and with only a few laps under my belt qualified twelfth. I rode a conservative race finishing twelfth. On the fast sections my trusty old TD2B was outpaced by the current machinery even though it was going so well.

Whenever we moved from a location in Europe I was always left wondering if we would ever re-visit or would our trip end at the close of the season, after which we would go home never to return. The thought always left a sombre feeling in the pit of my stomach. During the three months that we had been on the road we had met some great and unique people who were fine examples of will and drive, negotiated a myriad of obstacles, made countless stupid mistakes, been through and raced in atrocious weather conditions, lived in great discomfort and had numerous tests of will and resolve. We had not cracked. We made it to the races, accepted the challenge and participated to the best of our ability. We had seen and experienced things that few get to see and do, experiences that money could not buy. We proved at the Salzburgring in practice and at Misano in the race that as a team, we were a force to be reckoned with. I had the vision of what was required and how getting to the top could be achieved. It would be a pity if we were unable to return to make use of our new found and priceless experience.

Chimay was to be our last contact with the Continent for a while. We had no more confirmed entries and decided it would be a futile waste of money to drive around hoping for starts in races in which we had little chance of doing well. Few of the circuits were like Misano where speed was not as important as ability. We would retreat to England where it was a lot cheaper to live, take stock of our situation and try some British style short circuit racing. The next day we hopped on board the ferry at Ostende bound for Dover. According to the diary entry for Monday 11th June, 'Great on ferry, cheap rum, and cigs only 8p a packet'! By Monday night we had reached Arthur's Ladbroke Grove flat. He had a pile of mail for us and it was nice to put our feet up, catch up with home via mail and catch up with the world via TV. We had been on the road for three months during which time we had been isolated from world events. The next day I called Bob Aldridge and we headed north up the A1 to meet him and the rest of the large family at their engineering works in Beeston, Bedfordshire. Peter and Roger Aldridge worked in the workshop doing crank grinds and rebores, Bob and mum, Eileen took care of the office, Michael was studying to become a chef and David was a student. They welcomed us and insisted that we use their racing bike workshop next to the engineering shop, to work on our bikes. We gratefully accepted, unloaded and set up in the pure luxury of a real workshop with benches and a vice. Next we found a farmer nearby willing to rent us the corner of his field to set up the tent. We would have to share the field with his donkey which seemed okay at the time.

This period was frustrating because our effort had stalled and we needed to formulate a plan to move ahead. We spent the days at the workshop working on the bikes and did a lot of thinking both at the workshop and in the wonderful old country pubs that we frequented on most evenings. Dozy and I started developing a taste for the warm flat and rather strong English beer. Bob, Roger and Peter had developed the taste long before. They were formidable drinking partners. Bob could drink all night without losing it. Peter would get progressively funnier and would laugh at any silly thing and Roger, with an insatiable thirst, became more vocal by the pint. We had many great times. On some nights the landlord at our local, the John 'O Gaunt in Sutton, would lock the front door after calling time and disappear to bed leaving his daughter, who would join in and serve us until the early hours of the morning.

A plan of action

The 'backyard' H2 Seeley scared the factory riders on occasions.

It was decided. I love it when a solid decision is made and the team rouses into positive action towards the goal. We would build a bike to participate in the remaining rounds of the Motorcycle News Superbike Championship for Formula 750 bikes, the most important series in England. We would locate a 750H2 Kawasaki motor and fit it into our Seeley chassis, a simple enough task as the 750 and 500 motors had the same mounting points. We would sell the H1R motor and parts and put that money towards race tuning the 750H2 which is a road bike motor. Bob located a 750cc motor from a write off for £300 and Dozy wrote up some specs for the cylinders, heads and pipes using his own ideas, and information from articles on race tuning the H2, by Kevin Cameron, a renowned American two stroke tuner. At the same time I had located a Quaife six speed close ratio gear cluster for the 250 to make it more competitive. Now that we had facilities, Dozy was starting to 'breath' on the 250 cylinders and heads to find more power. We were rocking and rolling again at last.

Bob arranged entries in 250 and 350 classes at a club event at Snetterton circuit in East Anglia. We were going to use this event to test the six speed box and Dozy's motor mods, and I won the 250 race by a long way. The bike was going great with Dozy's latest modifications and the gearbox was worth the money, the closer ratios improving acceleration all the way to sixth gear. Snetterton was not an inspiring circuit but with a long flat main straight was excellent for testing and being the closest circuit to base we often went there to try motor modifications. We went testing at Brands Hatch short circuit one day as a familiarisation outing, a very exciting prospect for me. I was impressed by the design and layout of the famous 1.94km circuit. There is hardly a straight or level section and the part called the main straight is in fact a slight curve. There are steep ascents and descents and the circuit is simply brimming with character. It rates in my top ten favourites, possibly as high as fifth. Ask anyone who follows bike racing about British short circuit scratching and I would put money on them saying 'Brands Hatch'. It is a very famous venue and synonymous with the traditional British short circuit brigade which was rumoured to be the toughest school of combat at close quarters in existence. One heard of the multi bike dices that took place where elbows and knees were banged together and fairing paint exchanged on every bend. This turned out to be the truth. In later international races at Brands and Mallory Park to name the two best, I was to be bumped, jostled, chopped up, run into, used as a burm and most of this attention was metered out by friends! I learned to give as good as I got. British short circuit racing was unique, requiring a totally different style and approach compared to continental racing. I really enjoyed it, was good at it and learned a lot from it. You had to be as sharp as a rotary valve and have eyes in the back of your head. You had to be constantly looking for the gap, reading body language, looking for a weakness to exploit ruthlessly. Later on, in September at the International Race of the Year at Mallory in the 250 class I got involved in a ten man dice for the lead. I finished sixth a few metres behind the winner and shared the fastest lap with three other riders. There was tyre rubber on the fairing as usual!

We took the 750 Seeley to a circuit for the first time to race at the International Hutchinson 100 at Brands Hatch short circuit. The 'Hutch' as the event was known, was a unique and famous event. Once a year this event takes place with the direction of travel of the lap reversed and the track turned out to be just as good in the reverse direction. The 'new' bike felt fantastic. It stopped well, turned well, accelerated phenomenally and by a long chalk, it was the fastest bike I had ridden. I was also entered for the International 250 race and after practice I was one second off pole on the 250 and two seconds off pole on the 750. Despite race day being very wet I had a very satisfying third in the 250 race at this, my first major British event. In the main race, the 'Hutchinson 100' for 750s I was in ninth place and going well when an exhaust header popped out of its flange, causing me to retire. It was luxury for Dozy and I to have extra hands at the races with Peter Aldridge helping with the bikes and Bob taking care of the paperwork and running errands. For the first time I was able to pose like a works rider. On the way back to Beeston we pulled up at the Taj Mahal in South East London and had a really good curry with pints of cold Harp Lager to cool things down. This was to become the traditional stop after Brands Hatch events, without fail.

Back at base we had little time to get the bikes clean and ready for the World F750 Championship race at Silverstone the following weekend. During the week Mike Fogg turned up at the workshop. He had damaged his leg in a crash at a French track a couple of weeks earlier. He said that another competitor had run into him and the disc had sliced his leg. He was throwing in the towel and going home. Like so many before him, he would have had a tantalising taste of the lifestyle and a glimpse of what could have been. It would likely remain on his mind as an 'if only' for the rest of his days.

A black week

Silverstone turned out to be one of the worst weekends of my life. We arrived at the circuit complex early on Friday, 10th August to set up for practice which started on the same day. Kim Newcombe had come over from Europe to compete and it was good to see them again. After practice Kim and Rod were too busy to go out so Bron and I went to dinner with Janeen and Mark. The next day Kim crashed at Stowe in the all-comers race and was rushed to hospital with severe head injuries. He never regained consciousness and was kept on life support until the Tuesday when it was switched off and he passed away. The next few days were very depressing. We spent a lot of time with Janeen and Mark and attended the funeral to bid farewell to a unique, kind and talented person we had only known for a short while. Kim's death was a point in my life when I was forced to recognise how very real death was in the crazy sport that I loved, that it would happen again to people close to us and perhaps for the first time I became aware that it really could happen to me. It was a very sobering experience. Although I was very shocked, I was slightly distanced from the Saarinen/Pasolini tragedy because I did not know them personally, but I had got close to Kim and his family. The experience hardened me to the realities of the sport in those pre-safety revolution days. Although deeply grieved at each of many future losses, Kim's demise was the first and last time I shed a tear for a fallen comrade.

The home straight

With about three months left before the season ended, Eileen Aldridge invited us to stay at their home. It was an inconvenience for them and we were grateful for their hospitality. Without their support we would most likely have ended up going home permanently. The guys were such a help with the racing. Peter was to become my right hand man the following year, wielding the spanners at the races when Dozy was forced to remain in South Africa to work. We checked out of the farmer's field and packed the camping equipment away, hopefully for good. I think the donkey would miss us. He used to come into the tent and chew on whatever he could find. One night we woke up to the sound of grunting noises inside the tent. On investigation we caught the donkey red hoofed chewing on a packet of our cigarettes!

Life at the Aldridge home, Kyalami or 'My Home' in Zulu, in the tiny Bedfordshire village of Sutton, was very pleasant. Michael was studying to be a chef and he used to practise on us whenever he was at home, which was quite often. His cooking was Cordon Bleu and quite fabulous. He did an outstanding Baked Alaska, which became our favourite desert. It was around this period we all developed weight problems for which Michael took the blame. He went on to become one of Europe's top chefs, receiving all kinds of awards and accolades.

September was a busy month because we had four International races in four weeks; Scarborough, Cadwell Park, Mallory Park and the West German round of the FIM F750 Championship at Hockenheim on the 30th. The final race of the season was at Brands Hatch at the end of October. Bronnie was booked to fly home after Scarborough and after Brands Hatch Dozy and I were to pack the bikes and equipment to ship home. At this stage we wanted to return to England in March 1974 but it was hard to say if it was going to be possible. We would leave Goss in England in case we needed her, but it made sense to send the bikes home. If we did not return to England we had the bikes with us and I could race them during Summer in South Africa.

Scarborough's Oliver's Mount road circuit must have been fun at some stage in its history, perhaps when the fastest bikes of the day produced 20 hp. Racing 120 hp Superbikes around there was not the wisest of ideas. The circuit was narrow, bumpy and very dangerous. Even the facilities were uncomfortable with the paddock, located at the lowest part of the circuit, in a narrow valley, being too small for the number of competitors and so steep that it was difficult to stand the bikes. We were sleeping in the tent and it was necessary to wedge against something to stop rolling downhill and out under the side of the tent.

A good start in the race was most important here. The first rider into the hairpin was likely to be the winner by virtue of the fact that it was so hard to find space to overtake. Thus the stampede from the start line to the first corner, a distance of some 100m, was frantic. It was better not to use your best leathers or fairing at Oliver's Mount as I discovered when I fell at the hairpin during the 250 race damaging both, but picked it up and continued to finish in fourteenth. The MCN Superbike race was much better. My Seeley was as well-mannered as Colin Seeley had designed it to be, which made riding on this rough, tough circuit a little bit easier. From a bad start, twentieth on the first lap, I squeezed by ten riders, usually while they were half on the grass, to finish a good tenth. The trouble that I saw other riders getting in and out of en route to my tenth place made me all the more impressed with my chassis. The MCN Superbike Championship was a spectacular series and was well supported by top British riders on factory-backed equipment. Suzuki had Sheene, Smart and Woods on the three cylinder water-cooled TR750s, and Kawasaki, only just establishing as importers in England, fielded Mick Grant on their three cylinder air cooled H2R750. Four strokes were still in the hunt with two Britiish factories evident. Dave Croxford and Peter Williams rode the amazing John Player Nortons and Percy Tait rode the melodious three cylinder Triumph. The same year(1973) the World F750 FIM Trophy was started which spurred the Japanese factories to produce even more powerful multi-cylinder rockets.120 bhp without suspension, chassis and tyres to match, set the stage for a very interesting period.

After Scarborough I took Bronwyn to Heathrow for her trip home then hustled back to base to help Dozy prepare the bikes for The International Race of the Year at Mallory Park, Derbyshire for my first ride at this popular circuit. I had heard a lot about the event but had no idea of the magnitude of the occasion. I am not sure what constituted a capacity crowd at Mallory, but I imagine there were at least 40,000 vociferous spectators squashed in around the tiny circuit that weekend. The atmosphere was more akin to a rock festival than a bike race. Attendances at the major British venues in those days were phenomenal. Later in the decade the top riders started demanding vast sums to appear. This prompted the promoters of Brands Hatch, Mallory Park and Oulton Park, a company called Motor Circuit Developments, to reduce the number of big names invited to an event. As a result, or perhaps it was coincidence, spectator attendances dropped dramatically, sending British bike racing into the doldrums.

The 250 race, true to British short circuit tradition, was fast and furious. As previously described, I remember being caught up in a train of desperados, fighting wheel to wheel, bar to bar, jostling for position all the way around the fun, fast and demanding circuit, where I finished sixth and shared the fastest lap with about three other riders! A lap of Mallory is worth description. From the start line on the main straight it was about

Scarborough, the dash for the hairpin.

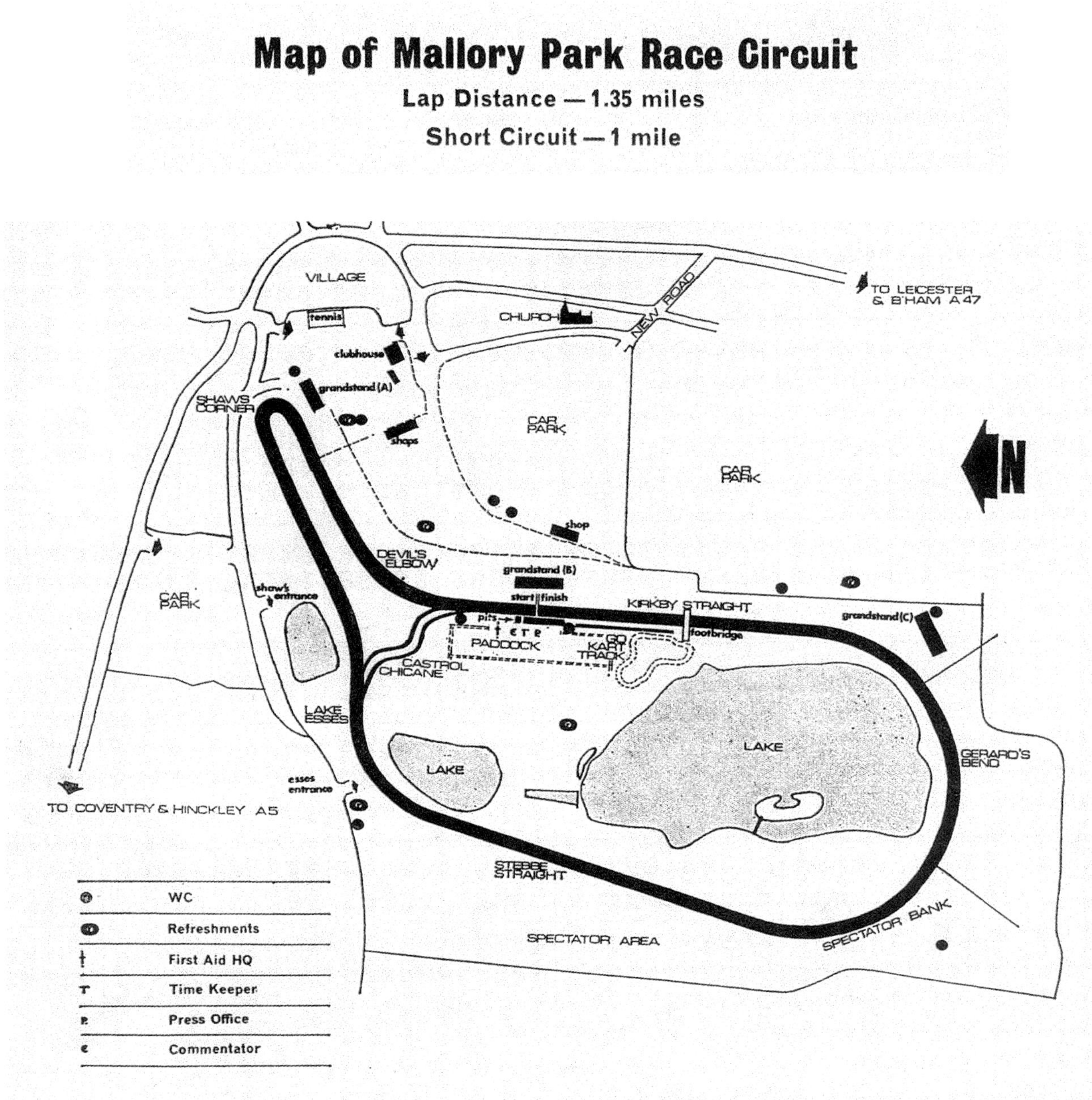

200m to the first bend, Gerard's, a right hander. Gerard's was basically a huge ultra-fast horseshoe shaped corner that turned 180 degrees to join the back straight, also of about 300metres. One of the world's special corners, the entrance to Gerard's required huge balls to do a good lap time. On either bike I approached it in top gear at peak rpm and simultaneously braked hard, changed down two gears and plunged in at about 160kph, riding over a big wallowy bump. Once over the bump it was necessary to get back onto the power to maintain momentum. From the middle of Gerard's, superb throttle control was required because the exit became progressively faster. Well before the exit the rev counter needle would climb to the red line and fifth gear (250) or fourth gear (500) would need to be selected, a tricky manoeuvre while scraping foot pegs at 180kph. By the exit the needle would again be at the red line and top gear selected at about 200kph. At the exit, the front end of every bike I ever rode there became frighteningly light causing the bike to twitch and wobble badly. I solved this the first time I rode there by pulling my body as far forward over the fuel tank as I could, with my backside right out of the seat! This enabled me to exit with far more stability and a little extra speed. It was also the only corner that I have ever ridden around where I had to get out of the seat and onto the tank to make the front end behave, even on the Seeley. At the end of the back straight the track peeled right into the first section of The Esses and immediately left for the short dash uphill to execute a harsh 'crash stop' at The Hairpin, a very tight, right-hand, first gear affair. It required skilful slipping the clutch to keep on the power for a quick exit. The front of the bike would lift off the ground with ease once the motor had been coaxed back onto the power band. From The Hairpin it was a fifty metre dash to the top of Devil's Elbow for the high speed dive down to the finish line. A fast lap at Mallory can only be described as exhilarating. On the 250 on that occasion the average speed was 147kph which, taking into account an almost dead stop hairpin, was fast motoring. It was and despite many changes, probably still is a unique but dangerous circuit. Many a rider has been seriously injured falling foul of Mallory's trickery.

The main race had a better line-up than the average GP. It was open to bikes up to 1000cc and the first prize was a whopping £1,000. The top 500cc GP riders, the top MCN Suberbike riders, the top FIM F750 riders and the best from the USA were there for a piece of the action. The promoters would have invested big bucks for the line-up in appearance money but would be amply rewarded by the spectator attendance. It was a dizzy thirty-five lap race and at the end of it I was a creditable eleventh in very good company on our amazing Seeley with a Dozy-tuned road bike motor. I rode my balls off as usual!

Again, after another hard and satisfying weekend of racing, it was back to base to service the bikes before heading for Cadwell Park, Lincolnshire for the next event, also an International. This circuit had a beautiful park-like setting with an interesting layout and was fairly long and difficult to learn. The paddock cafe made the best bacon butties on the planet. The bacon was fried expertly to the right crispness and set in between two thick slices of fresh white bread. The first image that came to mind when a race at Cadwell was coming up, was the sight, sound and smell of bacon butties being created in the paddock cafe. In the 250 race I got a good start and picked my way through to third until two laps from the end by which time I became more familiar with the circuit. I could see that I was gaining on the leader, Mick Grant and put in extra effort to move into second, closing rapidly on Mick. At the end of the main straight on the last lap I was right on his back wheel with my passing manoeuvre worked out. I pulled out of Grant's slipstream and slipped up the inside, braking for the tight right-hander. Mick saw my manoeuvre and was having none of that, so slammed the door in my face. My options were to force my way past him and possibly bang fairings or to concede, keep our paint intact and settle for second. At this stage in my British tour I decided discretion would be the better choice. As a newcomer on the British scene I would have taken some stick in the press and with the public if I had have knocked one of their favourite sons off his motorbike! It was at Cadwell that I started using the spectacles that I had acquired at the age of about seventeen but had only used to watch movies or for night driving. It was so gloomy at the circuit in that dark, overcast British way, that I was having difficulty seeing so decided that it was time to wear the vision aids. It was a revelation! The track edges and other features were brought into sharp focus. Wearing specs was to be a discomfort, particularly during races, that would stay with me until 1986 when I had a Radial Keratotomy performed on my eyes. The result of the amazing operation was the 20/20 vision that is still with me.

We were hard-pressed to prepare the 750 for the trip to Hockenheim for the FIM Championship round the following weekend. We were in a situation where we would probably lose money on the trip, but had to go to try and maintain exposure and learn what FIM F750 racing entails in case we got any opportunities the following year. We arrived at Hockenheim with time to spare for a wet Saturday practice but got in only eight troubled laps, not enough to learn the track or set the bike up. The Seeley was running on two of three cylinders, a problem which started at Cadwell. That night Dozy found a concealed wire in the Krober ignition system had broken and repaired it. At each event the F750 Championship races were held over two heat races of up to 160km each taking place on the same day, a truly gruelling test. Hockenheim was to be two heats of fifteen laps making each heat just over 100km in length. The problems experienced with the ignition had curtailed my practice. We would have to guess at the gearing and carburation requirements. I therefore treated the first leg as practice to come to grips with the track and brought my times down nicely to finish a credible fifteenth. In the second heat, after making adjustments to the bike based on what we learned in the first heat, I was able to give it some welly making a very good account of myself, finishing fifth with only factory bikes ahead of me. Considering the fast nature of the circuit and the 'home-made' state of our bike against current 'state of the art' equipment, the result was good. What is more, the returns from prize and travel expense money more than covered our costs, so the trip was worthwhile.

Back in England we had a month before the final event at Brands Hatch at the end of October. It was a frustrating time.

With Mick Grant in 1973 not suspecting we would be team mates in '78.

Not only did I want to return in 1974, but I wanted to return with better bikes and on a sound financial footing. That meant finding a sponsor before going home, a daunting task. I have always battled to talk my way into desirable situations, and had difficulty communicating generally, let alone approaching key people. Finding sponsors requires the gift of the gab as well as riding ability. I only had the riding ability! The few people who know and understand me well will know where I am at. Others may have interpreted my reticence as being aloof. I have always considered myself an introvert, a hurdle I would never fully overcome. I realised at an early age that I was short of communication and people skills. Later, when I started winning Grands Prix and world titles, it should have bolstered my confidence, but in many ways it had the reverse effect, like some kind of stage fright but it just did not hatch me from my shell! I learned to live with my shortcomings early on in my life, and was determined to succeed regardless. I had no problems when it came to the nitty-gritty of riding, with total faith in my ability to ride fast. Once I made it onto competitive machinery I knew that I would have the edge on my adversaries most of the time. I was also blessed with a temperament to suit the job. Out-psyching by opponents, and some tried, never had any effect on me. The pressure of riding for a factory, with millions invested in the cause, never worried me. I was very fortunate and grateful to be born with enough natural riding skills to be able to let the results do the talking.

We wrote dozens of letters in an effort to raise sponsorship but without success. My road to the top was destined to be the long route achieved purely by results on the track rather than by the elusive gift of the gab. There were a number of riders around who had sponsors and equipment I would kill for, who would never win a race. This is life! In the meantime while Bob Aldridge and I dwelt on the unsolvable sponsorship problem, Dozy was on a mission to try some ideas on the 250. He bored the carbs to 32mm, increased the volume of the inlet tract and port and raised the compression. On the 750 we fitted a wider WM4 rim to the rear wheel to fit a 3.50/18 KR83 Dunlop, a move that should increase traction by placing more rubber on the road, enabling me to use the power more effectively. The Race of the South at Brands Hatch, our last meeting of the trip, was an interesting weekend. On the Saturday certain events including the 250 race, were run on the short circuit. On Sunday, racing changed to the longer 4.24km GP circuit. The 250 was flying and in morning practice I lapped in comfort just outside the lap record. Strangely enough the winner of the 250 race was to be crowned British 250 Champion. There was no championship series for 250s that year, so the champion was to be decided from this race. In the race, I broke the old lap record on seven consecutive laps and was in the lead when the crankpin broke, slowing the bike and relegating me to sixth place. Dozy's tuning had worked. He had succeeded in making an outdated TD2B go fast enough to win a British Championship event! It was now producing a lot more power than it was designed for, so reliability was becoming a problem. On Sunday the first event for the 750 was the MCN Superbike final. I rode from thirty-first on lap one to twelfth at the flag. Judging by my lap times I was getting to grips with the new rim and tyre as well as the difficult GP circuit. In the actual 'Race of the South' International, open to GP bikes, F750 and MCN Superbikes, I chopped 2.5 seconds off my lap times and took an outstanding seventh. The weather was perfect and the crowd was huge. The large grandstands were full and the sunkissed hill opposite was covered with colour rather than the usual dark of Barbour suits. There must have been at least 50,000 people there. It had been a good weekend and a good end to our first season in the big time. The effervescent Bronnie was well missed both at the track and that night at the Taj Mahal where Dozy and I with the Aldridge boys drank copious quantities of Harp and feasted on a good hot Madras curry. British National and International racing was indeed in good shape in the early '70s. Because of the high spectator attendances the promoters could pay the drawcards reasonable appearance money. A guy like Barry Sheene would have been on substantial money at the major events. As a foreigner, and because I had made an impression in British events, my appearance money had increased slightly, making me more fortunate than most Brits who were not paid to ride. It is the old story, all the money going to a few, but that's how it goes.

One of the highest accolades for a South African sportsman is being awarded Springbok Colours.

Awards given to motor racers

IT WAS two wheels to the fore when Springbok motor sport colours were handed out in Natal last night. Grinning proudly are (from left): Horace Bergstrom, 1973 motocross champion; Alan North, 1973 350cc motorcycle champion; and Kork Ballington, awarded colours for "outstanding achievements" in motorcycle racing overseas.

Daily News Reporter

SOUTH AFRICAN and Natal colours were presented to Natal's top motor sport competitors last night at a function marked by optimism that motor sport would be allowed again soon.

"There are signs that the ban on motor sport may be relaxed — things are not as bad as they are made out to be," Mr Fred Sutcliffe, Automobile Association steward, told about 50 competitors and officials at the Polo Pony Hotel at Shongweni.

He was speaking after the presentation of colours to motorcycle and car racers and rallyists.

Three Springbok badges went to Natal motorcyclists for championship wins and other achievements during 1973. Horace Bergstrom (26) won the Motocross Championships; Alan North (20) won the South African 350cc Motorcylce Championship; and Kork Ballington (22) was given his South African colours for "outstanding achievements" in motorcycle racing overseas.

Natal colours were presented to Denys Currie, third-time winner of The Daily News Production Car Championships; Keith Berrington-Smith (sports and G.T. champion); Glen Martin (Formula Vee champion); Fred Franz (rally champion driver); Elton Prytz (rally champion navigator) and Eddie Izzard (karting champion).

Homeward bound. The oil crisis

Dozy and I delivered the bikes to Southampton for shipping home and picked up our air tickets in London. With the Aldridge boys we had a last blast at the John O'Gaunt and attempted to drink the cellar dry of Greene King bitter of which both Dozy and I had grown very fond. The next day, Thursday 1st November, Bob dropped us at Heathrow and we hopped on the South African Airways jumbo bound for Johannesburg. Twenty-four hours later we were back with family and friends in Durban.

I was eager to get back to work with my father in his home alterations and additions business, to earn money to return to Europe. I was also eager to get the bikes and go out to Hesketh to see if I could break the lap record. The 250 was, thanks to Dozy, much faster than when we left and I knew that my riding ability was a few notches higher, so I had a point to prove. Alas, while the bikes were on the water, the Arab oil-producing countries reduced their output which caused a shortage of oil that quadrupled prices overnight. South Africa was badly hit and the government imposed a number of emergency conservation measures. The speed limit was reduced to 80kph and vigorously enforced. Worst of all, motor sport was banned. In fact anything classed as recreational fuel use such as off road riding or water sports was banned. Petrol stations were closed at night and on weekends. In a nutshell it caused a lot of problems for a lot of people on a worldwide basis. If I remember correctly the crisis caused a severe world-wide recession. To crown the whole sorry situation, the 750 arrived at Durban Port as if it had been dragged through the bottom of the ocean. It was almost written off. The beautiful nickel plated frame was rusted and pitted in places. Everything aluminium, which was a large portion of the bike, was badly corroded, anything of unprotected steel was bright rusty orange. It must have been left on deck at the full mercy of the sea air. It was not insured and neither the freight agent nor the carrier would take responsibility. It would have to be stripped down to the last nuts, bolts and spokes and painstakingly restored at great expense.

Home from 'The Big Trip'.

The Natal Witness, Wednesday, November 7, 1973

● Pietrmaritzburg's "Kork" Ballington (left) with his fiance Bronwyn Randles and ~~her father~~ Dozy yesterday after "Kork's" phenomenal European motor-cycling racing eight-month tour.

BALLINGTON HOME FROM EUROPE

By Accelerate

"KORK" Ballington of Pietermaritzburg is home after a rather sensational European tour, and he's as poor as he left, but has a wealth of motor-cycling experience which money couldn't buy.

The pleasant "Kork" looks as young as that day he departed for Europe eight months ago (except that his hair has grown a few centimetres), but is brimful of confidence. And he hopes to return overseas next year.

World championship prospects? Not a chance, said Kork, with his delightful fiancée Bronwyn Randles celebrating the return in Kork's father's Pietermaritzburg flat.

"Although Kork's had a good Press overseas this year, it will take more than that to get factory recognition and the chance of a go at the title," explained Bronwyn.

But Kork's performance in his first overseas tour — the award for a great performance in a sponsored "Rider to Europe" event — has certainly improved his potential for a "works" offer.

So, at a preliminary cost of R8 000 (most of which was the Ballington family money) Kork has established himself overseas. Riding on virtually veteran machinery (an elderly Yamaha and a 750cc Kawasaki modified almost out of recognition), he had one win—at Snetterton — five seconds, and heavens knows how many placings.

Out of 31 rides, he was a non-finisher in only seven. He considers that his best two successes were a second at Brands Hatch in July, and also a second overall at Cadswell Park.

Part 3: Perseverance

1974, a factory ride at Thruxton

I made it back to England in time to get ready for the first race, a national event at Brands Hatch in murky March. I had worked hard with Johnno in Pietermaritzburg knocking in holes for doors and windows, adding rooms or doing whatever else came our way and had earned just enough for the air ticket and to restore the Seeley. Bronnie had to work a bit longer to save enough to return and Dozy would stay behind because he could not afford another year in Europe without pay. Our deal was that I would go back to get the show onto a firm financial footing then he would rejoin us if I could pay him at least a subsistence wage. We did not put a time frame on it because it was a tall order to start with.

I openly admit I was more apprehensive about 1974 in England than the first year. What lured me was the little tastes and titbits of success that I had experienced in 1973 which I hoped I could build on. Also the Aldridges had offered accommodation and workshop space. On paper we did not have 'a rats arse' of a chance of improving on 1973's results on the same bikes, mainly because during winter the manufacturers would introduce new upgraded models for the new season. They were always a bit faster, had better suspension, improved chassis or were lighter than the previous models so my task would be that much tougher. My plan was to concentrate on British international events, selected nationals and a couple of club events with better prize payouts than most of the nationals. The idea was to make contacts, get exposure, build up a good name, find sponsorship and hopefully make some bucks! It must be remembered that for a non-Brit to find sponsorship in Britain was and always will be a lot harder than for a local lad. If I had been an up-and-coming British lad doing what I was doing on old mokes, my path would have been paved with gold. The sponsorship that I desperately needed would lead to new, competitive machinery. It would lead to a reduction of the financial burden of paying all expenses and enable me to get Dozy back to what he was the best at...creating horsepower.

No Continental excursions were planned because they were very expensive and the circuits were generally more horsepower oriented than the British ones, therefore less suited to outdated bikes. 1974 was a depressing year, a year of marking time. I did all the preparation on the bikes, Peter helped me at the races and Bob did the entries, wrote letters and generally promoted me whenever possible in the hope of finding some backing. We did not hold out much hope of finding help during 1974 because sponsorship deals are arranged on an annual basis from the end of one season to the end of the next and usually negotiated well in advance.

Returning to Brands Hatch in the middle of March was a reminder of the start of 1973 when we first pitched our tent nearby. It was not as cold, but it was very wet. Most competitors in the pits had sparkling new 1974 bikes, some were the latest water-cooled TZ 250 or 350 Yamahas. They sound so good when they are new with a crisp zinging noise coming from new parts and clean expansion chambers. I had a painful crash in the 750 race when I lost traction at the rear tyre while accelerating through Clearways, the fast right hand curve coming onto the short main straight. The long wheelbase of the Seeley chassis and the narrow power band of our low budget home-tuned H2 made it a pig in wet conditions and I simply lost control and hit the ground hard. My body was cold so it hurt, the paint job was wrecked and the bike was badly damaged. I was so depressed by the incident and things in general that the following day I did not go to the workshop as usual but stayed at home. By Thursday I had not budged. I was doing some soul searching, trying to decide whether or not to carry on. On Friday Bob called from the workshop and asked me to come to the King's Arms for lunch. When I got to the workshop, parked outside was the Seeley. I was stunned to see that the guys had fully repaired it and put a great new paint job on it. What a surprise! I was overwhelmed by their kindness and support. It was just what I needed to motivate me back into action.

Bronnie arrived just before the next event at Brands in April which also lifted my spirits. It was good to see her smiling face again. She had managed to sneak some Biltong through customs which cheered me up a lot. Biltong is a dried, spiced meat, used by the early settlers of South Africa in lieu of fresh meat. It is something we South Africans can't live without. From birth most South Africans would have a stick of this dodgy smelling stuff stuck in their mouths. It kept the average baby quiet for hours and was especially effective for teething. Later when we had a home in Surrey, when I felt the need I would get into my Porsche and drive all the way to Kew Gardens to a butcher who sold Biltong and Boerewors (South African style sausage). I would drive home munching on a stick of 'tong' and we would have a 'lekker Boerie braai' (nice Boerewors barbecue) that evening! Small things make a difference.

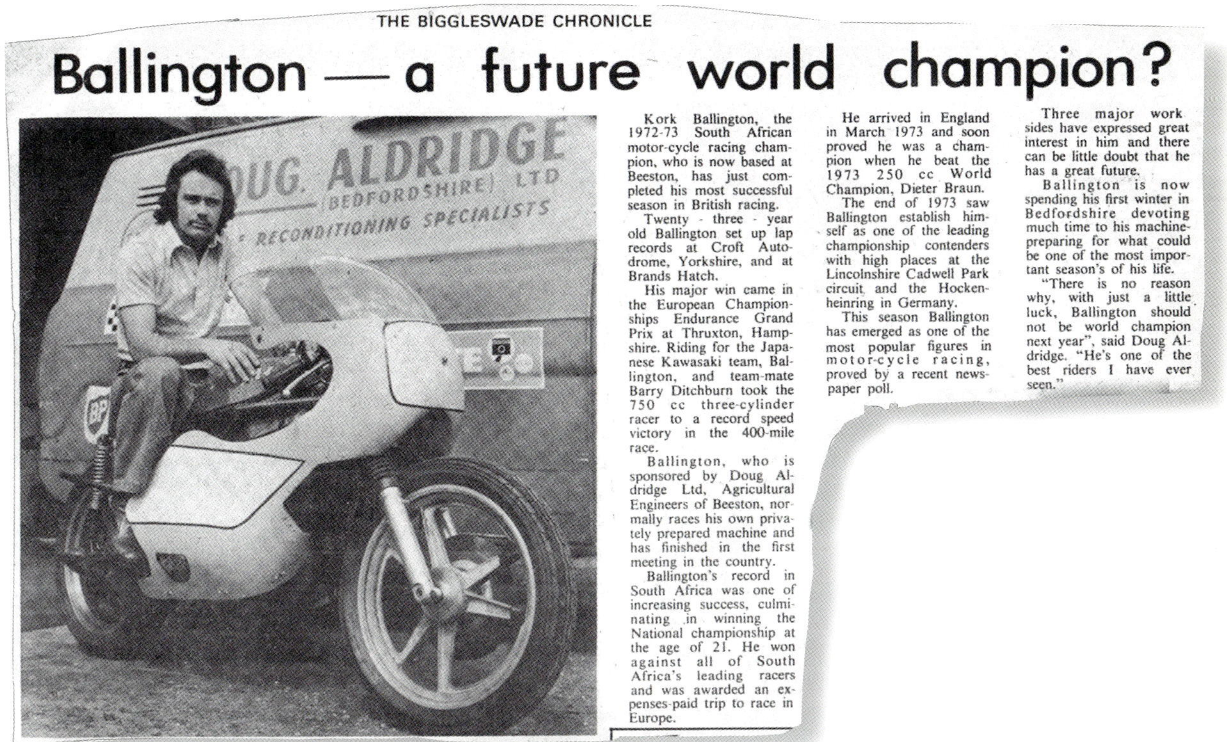

THE BIGGLESWADE CHRONICLE

Ballington — a future world champion?

Kork Ballington, the 1972-73 South African motor-cycle racing champion, who is now based at Beeston, has just completed his most successful season in British racing.

Twenty - three - year old Ballington set up lap records at Croft Autodrome, Yorkshire, and at Brands Hatch.

His major win came in the European Championships Endurance Grand Prix at Thruxton, Hampshire. Riding for the Japanese Kawasaki team, Ballington, and team-mate Barry Ditchburn took the 750 cc three-cylinder racer to a record speed victory in the 400-mile race.

Ballington, who is sponsored by Doug Aldridge Ltd, Agricultural Engineers of Beeston, normally races his own privately prepared machine and has finished in the first meeting in the country.

Ballington's record in South Africa was one of increasing success, culminating in winning the National championship at the age of 21. He won against all of South Africa's leading racers and was awarded an expenses-paid trip to race in Europe.

He arrived in England in March 1973 and soon proved he was a champion when he beat the 1973 250 cc World Champion, Dieter Braun.

The end of 1973 saw Ballington establish himself as one of the leading championship contenders with high places at the Lincolnshire Cadwell Park circuit and the Hockenheinring in Germany.

This season Ballington has emerged as one of the most popular figures in motor-cycle racing, proved by a recent newspaper poll.

Three major work sides have expressed great interest in him and there can be little doubt that he has a great future.

Ballington is now spending his first winter in Bedfordshire devoting much time to his machine-preparing for what could be one of the most important season's of his life.

"There is no reason why, with just a little luck, Ballington should not be world champion next year", said Doug Aldridge. "He's one of the best riders I have ever seen."

Roger Aldridge with the H2 Seeley after my Brands Hatch crash.

Easter weekend in the middle of April is worth a mention. It was a major weekend on the racing calendar in England. It was the traditional Anglo-American Match Races. A team of the best American riders would come over to race in a six race series at three different tracks on the same weekend. The first round was at Brands Hatch, the second two days later at Mallory, and the third the next day at Oulton Park in Cheshire. It was hectic but the Match Races were fantastic. The equipment was the latest 'state of the art' F750 Superbikes from the three big Japanese manufacturers and the last bastion of the British motorcycle industry, Norton. Under the friendly facade bitter rivalry lurked. Most of the American riders were more versatile than the Brits, being from a broad range of disciplines. Road racing was not the strong point of some of their team so they lacked road racing depth. The match races were therefore a bit out of kilter. A traditional British strength on British circuits was coping with British weather! If the British riders had had to compete in one of the American disciplines of mile or half mile dirt or a steeple

Waiting for the flag to drop at Mallory Park on the H2 Seeley.

chase, it would have been interesting. Each year the Americans were building depth and getting stronger as road racing improved in the States. It was just a matter of time before they would produce a string of talent, headed by a guy called Kenny Roberts, by my reckoning, the best of the Americans who ended up doing Grands Prix. My results at Brands Hatch were encouraging after the previous effort there a month earlier. I was leading the 250 race until the bike mysteriously cut out. In the unlimited race, I finished third on the Seeley and shared the fastest lap.

From Brands we all raced through the Dartford Tunnel onto the North Ring Road to the M1, and straight up to Mallory Park. We checked the 250 after it cut out at Brands, but could find nothing wrong, but after five laps it stopped again. I was lying third on the Seeley in the unlimited race until it became impossible to engage top gear, and I finished ninth.

The dash to Oulton Park is a race in its own right because getting there late meant battling for a piece of real estate big enough to pitch your tent. Oulton Park was quite an exciting

Navigating the Mallory Park Hairpin on the H2 Seeley.

track, being relatively fast with interesting turns and dips. This was my first visit to the picturesque garden track and I will always remember it for chaotic practice schedules. Practice was usually on race day so each class was given about five minutes during which you had to learn the track and get the gearing and jetting right! The queue at scrutineering was always long and slow. If you were not wide awake you could miss practice. Basically It was a shambles. I can't remember an occasion when it was not. It would have been better to give us less sessions and make them longer which was the format at most other popular events.

We could find nothing wrong with the 250 after the stoppages at Brands and Mallory. We replaced the Krober ignition with the original system as a guess at solving the problem. It was not the ignition, the bike stopped again at Oulton after four laps, one of those 'teasers' that turn out to be something simple that nobody thought to check. In the 750 race I was thundering along merrily in fourth place. On lap six of ten the bike started feeling harsh, as if something had gone wrong with the suspension. I slowed and finished seventh. On inspection we found both frame downtubes in the front had cracked through. That left the motor being held in by two skinny tubes at the back which would have been stressed to the max. It must have come within an inch of the rear frame tubes snapping and the motor falling out of the frame. Riding over the motor with the back wheel at any speed would have meant a horrific crash and serious injury! That was one of those occasions when you go white with fright.

The British beat the Americans in the Match Race series. It was the fourth occasion and the score to date, USA zero, Britain four. The depth of talent and local course knowledge gave the Brits the advantage. Americans hate being beaten. They had young emerging talent and would be back with a vengeance. The series probably pulled 120,000 spectators through the gates from all three circuits.

1974 had its moments; I fell off twice at Cadwell Park in one day, firstly the 250 then the 750 which was a clean knock out. I came round in the medical hut at the end of the day's racing with a deluxe hangover and a very worried team staring down at me. When I came off the 250 early in the race, I skidded down the track and wore a hole through the leathers on my shoulder. It also wore a hole in my best T shirt and my body. Before the 750 race I turned the T shirt round to shield the hole in my body from the hole in the leathers. Then I fell off the 750 and wore another hole in the T shirt at the same place, so it had neat matching holes on the front and back.

Throughout the year I had mediocre results, lots of middle of the road fifth and sixth places, some thirds and seconds and some moments of glory, such as winning the coveted Ken Redfern Trophy at Croft with lap record. At the last race of the year at Brands I finished second in the Bill Ivy 750 race and equalled the short circuit lap record held by Kenny Roberts, Yvonne DuHamel and Tony Nash.

At the end of August, after three years of unbelievable service, I decided to sell our TD2B. It was still good for top ten finishes in international events against TZ250A water-cooled Yamahas and top five placings in Nationals. I doubt if anyone else could boast such a long history of success at such a high level with the same old bike.

I was always good with racing bikes from the mechanical angle. I could strip and reassemble as well as anyone. In 1974 I got better. I also undertook some difficult modification work, the result of which I was very chuffed with. The 750 would never give nice clean plug readings and plugs would appear slightly oily and different from each other. I suspected that the autolube pump could be pumping uneven amounts of oil to each cylinder. I connected it to a lathe and spun it at a pre-determined speed for a while, measuring the amount of oil discharged from each outlet. The amounts were quite different and I couldn't be certain what the exact fuel-oil mix finally entering the combustion chambers was. I decided to remove the autolube pump and modify the crankshaft to run on a 20:1 fuel-oil mixture from the petrol tank. This involved stripping the crank to get to the conrods, cutting a slit at the bottom of each big end of the rods so the fuel-oil mix could lubricate the big end bearings. This was my first ever crankshaft strip and it was not a simple single cylinder crank but an in-line triple with six webs. Stripping it was tough enough. The real challenge was reassembly and getting the sucker straight. I stripped it, cut the slits and re-assembled the crank and got it within a thou. I confess, it took a couple of days but I did it. No one was more surprised and relieved than I was when the bike ran! It also ran cleaner and the plug readings were better. Another modification I made was to increase the size of the tailpipes by 2mm. I hoped this would ease a slight detonation problem, which it did. Judging by improved lap times, my mods had certainly not harmed the performance. Apart from this the motor remained the same from conception to sale at the end of 1975.

The crowning glory in 1974 was the partnership with Barry Ditchburn on a works H2R750 Kawasaki in the Thruxton 400 mile endurance race. I got to know Kawasaki U.K. Race Team boss, Stan Shenton and a director of Kawasaki UK, John Norman through purchasing parts from them and giving their rider, Mick Grant, a run for his money every now and then in MCN Superbike races. For some reason Mick was unable to ride at Thruxton so I was invited to fill his Yorkshire wellies and ride with Ditchburn. No two stroke had ever won the event and all the critics were saying the H2R750 would not do the distance and it would need too many fuel stops. For me it was a new high. A factory ride on no less than a legendary H2R750. What a blast. There were about six mechanics running around doing all the stuff and Stan was there calmly keeping the whole thing running smoothly, which meant that all I had to do was get there, put my kit on and ride. The first time I went out for practice was like going to heaven. The bike had power from low down and tugged with impressive strength all the way to the red line. It was smooth, it handled, it stopped. It did all the things a factory bike was supposed to do. There was only one problem. The rear brake lever and the gear lever were on the opposite sides to normal, as I knew it. The brake was on the left footpeg, and the gear lever was on the right side of the bike. British bikes,

Johnno sees Bronnie off from Durban Airport.

Our super H2 Seeley 750 poppin' a wheelie from Mallory Park hairpin, 1974.

from the beginning of time, were fitted with the levers thus, then the Japanese started building bikes and chose to place them on the other side.' Ditch was one of the old-school Brits who practised the traditional method. I don't think it was ever suggested that perhaps he should ride with the levers Japanese fashion, me being the visitor and all! It was extremely tough, but I managed to transfer my thought pattern across. The biggest danger with using these vital pedals on unfamiliar sides is to momentarily lose concentration and push the wrong lever the wrong way at the wrong time. This could cause engine damage or, if the bike spat you off serious physical injury. As it turned out, our race was flawless and we were the victors by a comfortable margin. The press coverage from the historic win was huge.

Stan Shenton remembers, 'When I agreed to run the Kawasaki Team for 1974 I insisted as part of the deal that we enter the Endurance Race, as I had been an entrant every year since 1966 and had been a winning entrant already with a 500 Triumph. Originally the idea was to get another rider to ride with Mick, and

One of the last bastions of British racers, the Norton, with ace rider and engineer, Peter Williams.

Barry was asked earlier in the year. In fact I think an entry had been sent in with their names. In the event, late in the year Kawasaki USA invited Mick to go to the States to ride a Kawasaki provided by a sponsor, I think the race was at Ontario, California. He agreed like a shot, so I had to find another rider for Thruxton. The rest is history as they say, with a convincing win, helped I am sure by the fact that I had put a rev counter on the bike which was reading several hundred rpm fast. This was based on past experience of this particular race, as I had found that two riders on one machine were as competitive with one another as they were with the opposition, and not too exact in complying with the maximum rev limit they were given. The win was very pleasing for me as it meant that the only time the race was won by a 500 and the only time it was won by a two stroke, I was the entrant. Kawasaki were so pleased with the result that they immediately sent me to America to see Mick race. He had a miserable time. The bike wasn't much good and he was thoroughly pissed off by the fact that Kork and Barry had given Kawasaki UK their first major win.'

At the time I thought my invitation to ride at Thruxton was for Kawasaki to consider Ditch or myself for the position of team mate to Mick Grant for 1975 to race in the MCN Superbike series and British Internationals. The position went to Ditch at the end of 1974. It is debatable as to whether it was good to get the contract to race Superbikes with Kawasaki UK in 1975, as they did not do all that well. Had I been chosen, would I have got better results for the team? Perhaps not. Had Kawasaki UK recruited me for 1975 it would have meant missing out on joining Sid Griffiths in 1975. Joining Sid led to my successes on his 250 and 350 Yamahas in England and on the continent in 1976 and 1977. This in turn led to Kawasaki offering the 1978 GP contract to me. It is funny how things turn out. Life takes some strange turns and there is no knowing what might or might not have been.

Stan Shenton told me later, 'Taking part in the Thruxton race was not an experiment to find a second rider. While I was in the race department of KMC in the States I was introduced to a rather shy young Japanese and told that he would be coming to England to be my Assistant Team Manager and Factory Liaison. His name was Ken Suzuki. At the same meeting I was informed that next year there would be new water-cooled KR750s. On my return to England I was called to a meeting with KMUK and told that as we were getting the new KR750s we would need a second rider and the discussion centred on yourself and Barry Ditchburn. Asked for my opinion I plumped for you. My reason was that I was impressed by your performance on a machine with the gearchange on the 'wrong side'. John Norman was adamant that as an English team we should have an English rider and pushed for Barry. Mick Uchida therefore had the casting vote and as usual demonstrated his commercial pragmatism, he said Ballington and Ditchburn are the opposition but Ballington is the friendly opposition as he is already riding a Kawasaki, it is more important to remove the opposition from a rival make, so we choose Ditchburn. I tried to sway him by saying that your Kawasaki was rather old and there

Joining Sid Griffiths in 1975 led to successes on his 250 and 350 Yamahas in England and on the continent in 1976 and 1977.

was no guarantee that you would stay on a Kawasaki but he would not be moved and said that we would supply you with our old bikes. The only improvement I could get was for the supply of spares as well'. Finally I was being noticed by the right people.

By the end of 1974 there was no way we could afford to return home, so Bronnie and I bought an old caravan which we parked in a trailer park near Biggleswade. We felt that we had abused dear Eileen's hospitality to the max and that it was time to move out of her home. Bronnie got a job at Boots The Chemist in Biggleswade and we remained in England for winter to work on the 1975 season. Winter in a caravan in England is not a pleasant experience. The site bathroom was in a small unheated room on the side of the park owner's bungalow. It was a mission to take a bath, you had to carry your kit there and back, often in atrocious weather. It was freezing at both ends of the procedure but at least the water was always hot. An English winter is a long, dark, damp, cold and depressing time. Apart from visiting pubs and the Aldridges, both of which we did fairly

The Mona Lisa Smile! Enjoying a ciggie in the back of Gossamer.

regularly, there was simply no outdoor life such as we were used to, so it was a tough and trying time.

The caravan park owners Wally and Reg were a queer old pair. One night they invited us into their home to show us 8 mm movies of their recent visit to the USA. During the movies, Wally who was sitting next to the projector, decided to put his hankie over the projector to stop the cooling fan from blowing in his ear. At this point we were looking at the Niagara Falls from the Canadian side. Next thing the falls started melting in front of our eyes as the film overheated. First the picture distorted and then took on the appearance of some alien molten landscape with craters and holes all over. By now the projector was smoking profusely. It took them some time to realise what was happening and to turn the projector off. It was so funny that we battled to keep straight faces and laughed ourselves to sleep that night!

Chasing Ago at Mallory Park Post TT, in 1974 on the remarkable Dozy tuned H2 Seeley.

BOYER KAWASAKI team chief Stan Shenton sips champagne in a toast to his riders Kork Ballington (left) and Barry Ditchburn after they won the Thruxton 400-miler on Sunday.

1975, the Sid Griffiths Racing Team is born

During the dark days of winter there was some news to cheer us up. Stan Shenton offered me the loan of two of the 1974 works H2Rs for the 1975 season with some parts to help keep them running. To me this was an important contact with Kawasaki and it provided lower running costs, even though it was designed to keep me as the 'friendly opposition'. Although these bikes were already obsolete due to the production of KR750 water-cooled triples for 1975, it was a step in the right direction. The H2R was more powerful than my Seeley H2 but revved at a higher rpm to produce the power, making it unreliable and particularly prone to crank failure. Fortunately Stan agreed to supply spares on a limited basis so if it broke I would not have to dig into the shallow cavity of my right pocket. My Seeley was remarkably reliable and had completed 1974 without parts failure on the same crankshaft. This was because its maximum rpm was lower than the H2R due to Dozy's cylinder and pipe specifications, so the only parts that needed periodic replacement were the pistons. Being roadbike pistons they were cast, therefore heavier and less resilient than the forged H2R pistons and prone to cracking. 1974 was cheap from a parts point of view. In February I took delivery of the works H2Rs, one with a standard frame and one with a British-made Reynolds frame. A couple of weeks later we took them to the frosty season opener at Mallory. The Reynold-framed bike turned out to be a delight in the wet. Its wheelbase was a lot shorter than my Seeley's and the motor had a wider spread of power with super torque at the bottom of the power band. These two traits make for happy wet motoring. The shorter wheelbase gives better grip at the rear and the good torque makes it much easier to ride. In wet conditions tractability at low rpm is far more useful than peak power at high rpm and vice versa on a dry road. I finished second in the main event, behind Percy Tait on one of the new, awesomely powerful TZ700 four cylinder Yamahas. The following weekend it was time for a trip to the land of the fabulous bacon butty.

Sid Griffiths.

Early March is far too soon for bike racing at Cadwell Park. My records tell me that it was wet wet wet and cold, oh so cold. In the 1000cc final, in atrocious conditions, I went from fifth on the first lap to second on the last lap, rapidly closing on the leader. Half a lap from the flag I swept past Peter McKinley, the reigning 'King of Cadwell' and stole the flag. The Reynolds framed H2R was indeed an ace in the wet. Sadly, Peter lost his life in a racing accident later in the year.

I was accepted for a start at Rouen in France the weekend after Cadwell. Need I say, the weather was miserable. It rained the entire weekend and to top it I had to go alone because Bronnie could not get time off work. As it turned out Bob and Pete turned up for the race. They left work on Saturday, caught the ferry to France and drove to the circuit to help! What can I say about these guys? I was very happy to see them. I had arrived at the circuit on the Friday afternoon and took a lap in Gossamer. Rouen was one of those typical country road circuits with plenty of character. It was fast, dangerous, long and had a unique cobblestone hairpin in the village that was slippery to walk on,

Last ride on the H2R 750 Kawasaki loaned by Kawasaki UK in 1975. Crashing at Barn Corner, Cadwell Park.

let alone ride over. That freezing night I bedded down in the back of Gossamer to the soft patter of gentle rain on the roof. In the morning the condensation on the bare metal roof inside the van had turned to icicles hanging above me. Being a hardened European private campaigner, I had experienced the worst Mother Nature could dish up. I had endured the consistently cold and wet British short circuits, I was not fazed by some little stalactites. I ignored them but was careful not to stab my head when I got up to get ready for practice.

The 750 event was made up of two forty minute races. In the first I never got to grips with things and finished tenth. but in the second race I let it flow like a ballerina and slipped past Chas Mortimer on the last lap to win by a wheel. It was very satisfying taking the race from such a seasoned 'circus' specialist. I could not put a foot wrong in the wet on this H2R. For the first time I started dancing for continual rain.

Back in England a dose of reality was ready to be dished up. The next race was an MCN Superbike round at Cadwell and for a surprising change the weather was fine and the track dry. The H2R, although going as well as it should, was outpaced by a rather large margin and I struggled to finish in the top ten. After Cadwell I was depressed. There was no way out this time. The opposition had progressed beyond us, the new works Suzukis and Kawasakis were rockets and the ultra fast TZ700 Yamahas, now prolific, were very much faster than the H2R which had reached the limit of its potential.

One afternoon at the workshop, soon after the Cadwell race, Eileen called me to say that Mick Woollet was on the phone. Mick is a renowned journalist and at the time was Editor of Motorcycle Weekly, one of the top publications. A call from someone of Mick's standing was something to get the heart of any struggling up-and-coming young racer beating at pace. What he had to tell me probably did not excite him too much. I am sure Mick had no idea where this telephone conversation would lead. He told me there was a gentleman in Birmingham who had a TZ250 Yamaha. He was looking for someone fast to try out on it. Mick had recommended me and I should call the gentleman as soon as possible if I was interested. His name was Sid Griffiths. No sooner had Mick rung off than I was on the buttons to Brum to talk to Sid!

Sid is from the Black Country and had that amiable drawl of the local dialect. He was quite a magnate, with a large Opel car dealership and very large transport company. He had style, our Sid. He had a new bike and he had enthusiasm. At that stage if he had said jump, I would have said 'How high would you like it Sid!' I had this feeling that things were going to happen from now on. I had a test ride on Sid's 1975 TZ250B at Cadwell Park at a national meeting on the 18th May 1975. In the race before the 250 event I had my last ride on Kawasakis for some time and ended the relationship with a neat crash at Barn Corner. Barn Corner was named after the large wooden barn on the outside. It looked fearfully close to the side of the track from the seat of a bike at speed and I often wondered whether you would hit the corner of the barn if you fell off at Barn Corner. I discovered the answer as I slid to a halt with a couple of metres to spare. The H2R, sensing it was about to get the flick, seized a big end and dumped me as if to say, 'Take that, you traitor!'

I got fourth in the 250 race. It was so nice to ride something younger than obsolete. Motor Cycle Weekly, 19th July 1975: 'I couldn't really shape up because my machinery was too old. But since I've been on good machinery, watch me go. Lots of the right things are happening at the right time, and it's like being liberated.' After Cadwell, Sid bought a brand new TZ350B and shortly after that a TZ700 to complete the line-up. It was just incredible! From being one of the poorest kids on the block I was transformed overnight to being the most spoilt brat north of Watford Gap. The new development meant returning the Kawasakis to Stan at Kawasaki race HQ, Boyers in Bromley. Stan was his usual sincere self and wished me well. I sold the Seeley, a truly sad moment which shut the door on a memorable chapter dedicated to succeeding against the odds.

The most exciting of the new bikes was the TZ700, the motor of which was basically two TZ350 motors with reed valve induction to tame them. The result was an immensely powerful smooth bike, an absolute joy to ride in a straight line. On the handling arena it required a distinctive style of riding to get the best out of it. It was schizophrenic. The moment I became aggressive and tried to make the bike do what I wanted, which was the way the

Posing with Sid at Croft.

Seeley liked to be ridden, the big, unforgiving TeeZee would turn into a pogo stick. The rear damping was way too weak so we tried every sort of back shock available and were able to cure the pogo effect, but without the original shocks, the bike lost its feel. It was very unusual and my best lap times came from the original rear shocks. The way to fast laps was smoothness and particularly a fine touch with the throttle when getting on the power. Rolling speed was the key as on small capacity bikes like a 125. If we had good rolling speed and delivered the power to the back wheel ever so softly it would behave acceptably but if you did not have optimum rolling speed from the apex onward, it was a task to get up to speed without the twitch and wobble. Basically the bike was just too powerful for the chassis, tyres and suspension.

My first outing in the new colours was at the Mallory Park Post TT International 350cc event. I felt like 'a pig in shit' out there on the lovely little brand spanking new water-cooled twin cylinder TZ350 Yamaha and won the race from a strong field, with the fastest lap as well. The bike was fast and light and a totally new experience for me. What a way to begin an association with your new team. For the first time in my life I was on a current and competitive bike and at last it showed everybody what I was capable of.

Second in this race was another South African, Alan North who started his European tour in 1975. Alan, also from the magic province of Natal, was my old adversary from the 50cc racing days on the go-kart tracks of Natal.

In sharp contrast to the elation of the 350 race, in the MCN Superbike race I was motoring merrily in fifth place with so much power on tap, keeping pace with the likes of Sheene and Grant when on the exit of Gerard's bend, a marshall ran across the circuit right into my path and I hit him. Dave Croxford on the works Norton, had crashed at Gerard's. Gerard's is a 160/170+kph bend under normal circumstances but with the yellow flags out I had reduced speed in accordance. The marshall was crossing the track from outside to inside and misjudged it and I could do nothing but close the throttle. At the last minute he leapt for his life which saved us both. I hit him a glancing blow off the right of the bike. How I stayed upright is a mystery but the poor marshall sustained a badly broken leg. I had to stop for two reasons. The handlebar was bent back into the side of the tank and I had to change my nappy! This was another occasion when one goes white with fright. Without a doubt, had I hit him full on at 150kph, we both would have been history.

In the 1000cc race I was back in action with fresh nappy and took a cautious and creditable sixth just behind Mick Grant on the works Kawasaki. Apart from hurting the marshall, Team Griffiths was quite joyful with the day. I was out of my tree. At long last, after years of struggle I had equipment that was on the pace, with which to do what I loved the most... race hard at the front.

Sid recalls: 'In the spring of 1975 the truck distributors to my Vauxhall dealership in Stourbridge rented a section of their showroom to Tony Rutter for the sale of motorcycles. Only knowing Tony by reputation, I wondered round for a 'natter'. I had an almost new Husquarvana 125 scrambler which my eldest

Another win for the new team.

son had learned the rudiments of racing on and which we had no further use for so I suggested to Tony that he could sell it on commision and a friendship that lasted for thirty years started.

On discussing his plans for the forthcoming TT he informed me that he only had one bike on which he had to change the pots and heads for each class, and if he had one of the latest Yamahas, he was sure he could win the 250 class. How to dangle a carrot to a donkey!

A new bike was ordered to which we fitted disc brakes and prepared it for its first TT win! I reserved accommodation at Castle Town Golf Club and let the excitement grow. Then just a few weeks before the race a very sheepish Tony came to my office to tell me that his sponsor was not amused and that he could no longer ride for me. Now what to do with the bike.

I telephoned Mick Woollet and he told me of a South African rider who he thought could be a world champion given the right machinery and he would get him to call me directly. When the phone rang, the strong accent told me I was speaking to Kork Ballington. He was entered for Cadwell Park the next week with his Kawasaki and was sure he could get a start in the 250 event.

My first impression of his ability as a professional racer was how well he could crash, he managed to do it just where I was watching. I had quite a long walk back to the paddock allowing me to think, it was a nice sunny day and there would be other opportunities. Arriving back at Kork's van, he was sitting at the back looking very sorry for himself. I said 'never mind there's always another day', to which he replied 'you are joking, I'm

In the beginning, left to right, Sid, me, Sid's son David and Fred Hadley.

going out on the 250'. He proceeded to tape up his leathers and went to the start line. It only took one lap to decide that this was a natural, professional rider. A new 350 and 700 were quickly obtained and painted in our new livery, the team was born!!

I went to the Isle of Man as arranged and on my return to the office, there on the desk was a large photo of Kork with a laurel wreath around his neck, the first outing of the team and a win!

Now was the time for a serious discussion. Kork felt he could compete in Europe. He could hone his abilities to win major races and even a Grand Prix. I think by now he had worked out how to tempt me and the decision was made.

My enthusiam was now running on all cylinders and I decided to expand the team to keep me occupied whilst waiting for Sunday nights to make sure Kork was safe.

The team which was created because of his tumble at Cadwell went on to prove it was still possible to win Grands Prix by enthusiasm and on a private budget, which now unfortunately are things of the past. Meeting Kork started a period of social and sporting pleasure allowing me to be a part of the highs and lows of the life of a privateer who reached the top'.

The deal with Sid to the end of 1975 was that he would supply a certain amount of spares for the bikes over and above the standard kit that new bikes came with. Thereafter I would be responsible for spares. I could keep all start and prize money but had to give Sid the trophies. I would transport the bikes to races in Gossamer and pay for the costs but as it turned out, Sid mostly picked up the tab. He was like that. One important fact

Mallory Park 1975. Mixing it with Grant and Sheene on a new TZ700.

was that Sid was eager to race on the continent, which was vital if I was to achieve success at GP level. Generally Sid was very laid back about things. We had our moments of strife, but they were insignificant. Whenever Bronnie and I were around the workshop near lunch Sid would whisk us off in his luxury Jensen V8 with leather trim, to his favourite haunt, The Pedmore House in Stourbridge. It was a place where huge deals were discussed, negotiated and concluded and perhaps where fortunes were made and lost in a moment. The car park was full of Rolls Royces, Bentleys and such, the food was outstanding and after lunch we would sip the finest Cognac and smoke opulently fat Romeo & Juliet cigars. After a trip to The Pedmore, which was often, I would be wrecked for the rest of the day.

Fred Hadley of Omega Engineering was vital to our maintenance of good results. His business, which specialised in the manufacture of racing pistons, was near to Sid Griffiths & Sons. He is a great engineer and renowned world-wide for manufacturing very special racing pistons for top manufacturers and race teams. Fred had the touch with two strokes. He modified the cylinders and heads on the 250 and 350 which gave them more horsepower. His tweaks were enough to give us the edge on most and keep us abreast of the faster bikes. He also did performance work for one of Britain's top short circuit runners and arch rival of mine, Tony Rutter.

After Mallory we entered the FIM World 750 event at Mettet in Belgium and in the first of two twenty-one lap legs I was going like a turbocharged Boeing. After seven laps I was fourth, behind Patrick Pons (TZ700), Barry Sheene (750 Suzuki) and Jack Findlay (TZ700). I was tailing the leaders fairly easily and was ahead of some very notable names. Then things went wrong. I think the 700 was jinxed, with the bizarre incident at Mallory and now another unusual problem in our second outing. On lap eight the temperature went into the red so I pulled in. A stone must have been thrown up by another rider's rear wheel and it had pierced my radiator, resulting in the loss of coolant. What a bummer. We plugged the hole with Araldite and in the second leg, which was wet, I had a race long dice for second with Potter, Newbold, Findlay and Pons. At the flag a blanket covered all five of us and I took fifth. The unfortunate thing about breaking down in the first leg, is that I would not feature in the overall results, missing out on a great result and some prize money. Sheene won and set a new lap record on the super fast circuit at 206kph, covering the 7.734km circuit in 2mins 16secs! I am not sure what the top speed of the F750 Superbikes were, but it must have been close to 300kph on Mettet's long main straight.

As I recall, 1975 was the first year slicks appeared. The power advance brought on by the F750 Superbikes forced tyre technology to step up a cog to keep pace. The slicks, at the time, were only available to certain riders and Sheene had them at Mettet. The tyre revolution was an interesting period. Slicks were developed to cope with increased power. They gave extra grip which caused chassis and suspension problems. Consequently, chassis and suspension were developed to cope with the extra grip. With extra grip and better

At the Aldridge home in Sutton. Left to right: Roger's fiance, Mandy Locke, Bob Aldridge, Roger Aldridge.

chassis/suspension, horsepower could be safely increased. It was a vicious cycle. What was lagging behind technological advances of the motorcycles was the safety development of most of the circuits. A place like Mettet was no joke on the 750 projectiles.

From Mettet it was a long trip to Croft in North Yorkshire. Races in England were social outings for Sid and his family and friends, which is part of what he wanted. It gave me pleasure to give him a day's racing worth talking about. In the 250 race, from an appalling start I worked through to third with a new lap record. In the 350 race I had a fine win and in the 1000cc race, a win with outright lap record. This was a good day. Despite the blemish of the 250 result, we would be assured of an obscenely opulent afternoon at The Pedmore on Monday!

The next outing was at Snetterton at a national event. In the British championship race on the 700 I finished second with fastest lap. In the Revetts unlimited race I finished second with new outright lap record. In the 1000cc race I took first with fastest lap and in the 350 race I was second to my good friend Steve Parrish and got the fastest lap. These kind of consistent results were more than I could hope for. Things were going well. After these weekends I would look forward to the next ride with extra enthusiasm. I was getting very good press coverage and managing to save some money which was a rather nice feeling.

The weather in early August at Brands Hatch for the Hutchinson 100 International was magnificent with sun all weekend and ninety degree temperatures. In the 250 race Tony Rutter and I had pistols drawn. We swapped positions throughout the race. I took the lead on the last lap but Tony outsmarted me at Paddock and took the flag by a gnat's knacker. I was sixth in the Superbike and fourth in the 1000cc event on the 700 and won the 350 race. Sid was accumulating silverware and I was accumulating prize money and job satisfaction. One thing that did not change was the fact that my mates the Aldridges were there to help, and still there when it was time for a 'shout' as we celebrated in the Brands pub afterwards and there when we pulled into the Taj Mahal for a fiery curry!

At this stage Bronnie and I were living in our flat in Wrestlingworth which we moved into in March. Wrestlingworth was and probably still is a tiny, quaint village with two pubs, nestled in the pretty Bedfordshire countryside. A certain measure of the size of an English village was the number of pubs located there. We usually drove the five miles to our favourite, The John O'Gaunt, Sutton's only pub, to socialise with Bob. We were still working on the bikes out of the Aldridge's workshop, a temporary arrangement until Sid completed plans for facilities to operate the team from Stourbridge. We were not in a hurry to move to Stourbridge so until Sid had workshop space ready we had the best of both worlds, being with our friends and having good bikes to work on.

We had made some good friends around England by this time. Steve Parrish and his girlfriend, Linda Davies were to become lifelong friends. Steve, a nutcase then and much worse now, was constantly playing pranks on anyone he could have a go at. His mother, poor woman, used to keep a few hard boiled eggs

At Bronnie's 21st party. Top left: Michael Aldridge, Lenny Locke, me, Pete Ort the Baker. Bottom left: Martin Brookman, Bob Aldridge, Peter Aldridge.

At Croft in 1975 with Sid Griffiths. We won the Ken Redfern Trophy on the amazing TZ700 Yamaha.

in the fridge. Steve would swap half of them for uncooked ones. Mrs Parrish thought she was going nuts when she would crack open what she expected to be a hard boiled egg and have it burst on her! The list of his pranks is endless, ranging from the sublime to the ridiculous; eggs in his mother's wellies, blowing up a brothel in Macau, there was no end to it. He was also a fine rider and rode 500 GP for Suzuki GB alongside Barry Sheene for a couple of years. Another good friend was Peter Ort from Leighton Buzzard, a master baker and racing enthusiast. They had a family bakery in Leighton Buzzard and the eccentric Pete used to arrive at the circuits in his British racing green Triumph TR4 with scarf and deerstalker, top down in the crappest of weather, with a box of Ort's Pizzas. These miniature pizzas, about four inches in diameter, ranked alongside Cadwell's bacon butties and Bronnie's scrambled eggs on toast, amongst the few things I could eat on a race day.

In the last six meetings of the season I continued to consolidate my good results. There was no doubt that I was missing Dozy and that we would have had better results with his full focus on motor development. Outside of the excellent mods Fred Hadley had already done, he did not have the time to take it further. Another thing that held us back was the decision to fit some magnesium rims to the 350. They messed the handling up and we spent too much time trying to get it to work by adjusting suspension settings instead of removing the wheels and putting the originals back in. At the same time I spent too much time trying to accommodate a project of Sid's. He wanted to turn the 350 into a special that he could name after himself. Unfortunately Sid saw a TZ350 with an aluminium monocoque chassis which was designed, built and ridden by a guy by the name of Richard Schultz and decided to go that route. I had a test ride on Richard's bike at Brands and was impressed by the handling although I did not take it to the limit which is where it counts. We spent a lot of time trying to sort out the Schultz bike without success because there were simply too many teething problems. Sid also gave him the green light on a monocoque for a TZ750 motor. Richard, essentially an eccentric nutty professor type, had some advanced ideas. His design for the 750 monocoque incorporated a twin spar layout for the basic strength of the chassis much like later Japanese works aluminium frames. For a variety of reasons he was never able to finish either project. In the meantime all the running around wasted a lot of my time and energy and had impacted negatively on results.

The highlight of the latter part of the season was the arrival of Johnno and Dozy for a three week visit. They arrived in time for a trip up to Croft for my defence of the Ken Redfern Trophy which I had won in 1974. It was Johnno's first trip out of Africa. He was amazed by the outside world. It was such a laugh showing him around. He had never seen so much traffic, so many people, such a big city, such bad weather and the list went on. Croft was a good location for him to see some racing. I retained the trophy with a convincing win and outright lap record, won the 250 race with fastest lap and got second in the 350 with new lap record. It was a busy season. In nine months I had competed in a total of forty eight 750 races and qualifying heats, eleven 350 races and nine 250 races. That kind of exposure to constant top class competition helped improve my ability bit by bit, so it was becoming easier to go faster.

Another end of season event which pleased me as it was proof of my value as an entertainer to the public was the Motorcycle News 'Star of '75' referendum, which included speedway, moto-cross, grass track, foot-up trials and road racing. I was voted seventh most popular competitor of these sections of motorcycle sport. This kind of competition, the results of which are from votes sent in by readers, is important for the promoters to take note of who the public want to see. This has some bearing on the amount of appearance money one can negotiate the next season. My goal, set at the beginning of the season, was almost fulfilled. It had been to make contacts, get exposure, build up a good name, find sponsorship and make a small profit. Unfortunately I could not yet afford to import Dozy.

Once the dust at the end of a totally exciting season had settled, Sid and I got together to discuss 1976. He was very happy with the results of our involvement and was positive. My 1976 priorities and requirements were logical and based on the fact that the key to advancing my career lay with the 250 and 350cc classes, getting Dozy back to Europe and success in continental internationals and Grands Prix. These two popular classes are usually the choice of privateers through necessity. Being twin cylinder they were far easier to maintain, cheaper to run and use the same chassis which can be useful for emergency parts swapping. Most important of all, factory participation, although strong from the Italian and Japanese manufacturers, was not as intense as in the 500 class. The 500cc GP and F750 classes were a waste of time without factory bikes or substantial financial backing. It would be handy to have a good F750 in the van for Internationals and certain FIM F750 races as an income earner. I was not worried about whether or not we had to do it all again, sleeping in the back of Gossamer, as long as we had some good equipment.

Sid had big plans. Big was the way he operated! Fortunately we were on a similar wavelength when it came to our projected race programme because had Sid wanted to race in England only, I would have been snookered. I would have no option but to spend another season hoping for an opportunity to reach continental races at some later date. This was a horrifying thought as I had outgrown British Racing and was not getting any younger. Time was no longer on my side. Sid's plan for 1976 was to order a new TZ250C monoshock, keep the TZ350B and upgrade to the forthcoming model C parts if there was a power improvement and we would return the chassis to standard specification. We could upgrade the TZ700 to 750 and if I wanted, get a monoshock chassis such as the Dutch one supplied by Nico Bakker. Sid would make space at the transport depot for me to work on the bikes when I returned to Stourbridge in February and Bronnie and I could stay with a friend of his nearby when we returned. Then he popped a cherry on top of the cake. It knocked me right out of my chair. He had arranged a Fiat OM55 transporter from Fiat UK for our use in 1976. This was a serious van, better than some transporters used by factory teams. There was more to come. Sid planned to have the area behind the driver's compartment fitted out with a kichenette with refrigerator and gas cooker. There would be storage for our clothes and supplies, and a dining area that converted into a double bed. In the back would be fitted a work bench and storage bins for spares and tools. An awning would be tailor made to fit on the back of the van and the bike ramp would double into a bench to stand a bike on for operations. We would be one of the best equipped private teams in Europe. I knew we would also be one of the most successful!

DURBAN, TUESDAY, DECEMBER 23, 1975.

Harold loses ground

PAGE 3

KORK COMES OUT TOPS IN BRITAIN

PAGE 15

An interesting headline.

1976, back to 'The Circus'

My goal for 1976 was to compete in as many Continental races as possible. I needed to see where we stood in relation to the private Continental Circus regulars in terms of organization, the performance of the bikes and skill level so we could take steps to improve the areas in which we were behind. It was accepted that European competitors were adept at producing faster motorcycles than their British counterparts. If this were true it would be because generally the Continental European circuits were more inclined towards top speed performance than the British short circuits where power characteristic requirements were at the other end of the spectrum for good acceleration. It was a 'rule of thumb' with racing motorcycles, both two and four strokes, that if you tuned the motor for top speed you sacrificed acceleration-producing performance. Likewise, tune for acceleration and top end performance is reduced. If you have a gifted tuner like Dozy and a handful of others that were with the more successful riders and you can find a little of both, you are in for a good time.

In March 1976 Sid Griffiths Racing Team assembled outside Sid's premises for a photo shoot. On display was the shining red Fiat transporter complete with large awning, three racing Yamahas in team colours, and the display of trophies won to date. It was impressive. I still could not believe that these 'tools of the trade' were for my use. Almost as soon as the shoot was over, Bronnie and I began loading in preparation for the trip to Rouen. It was exactly three years since we, as greenhorns had packed up at the caravan park in Kent to embark on our first trip to the Continent. This time we knew exactly where we were going. We had the correct documents and we had fabulous equipment. The only gap in the jigsaw was one Dozy Ballington, not present. The new 250 arrived days before we were due to leave for Rouen. All I had time to do was take it out of the crate, get the paint job done and strip the motor. I would have to leave it standard. There was no time to get the cylinder and head attended to by Fred. One little modification which I was going to try was a simple little tweak that I used as a schoolboy to get my Yamaha 50 to beat the bikes of my school mates. There was keen competition at school as to who had the fastest 50. I used to advance the exhaust port timing by filing 1mm off the front of the piston at the exhaust port. This was a mod that I had seen in one of Dozy's two-stroke tuning books. It used to give my otherwise standard Yamaha YF1 50 better top end performance but sacrificed low rpm pulling power. My mates would leave me from the school gates but by the time we had gone about 400 metres up the old main road towards Pinetown I would be hauling them in and would be ahead at the Cross-roads Tea Room which was the winning line. One day I fitted a new piston and instead of filing 1mm off the front I cut it in a curve exactly to the shape of the top of the exhaust port which I thought would give the same effect as a square top of the port but would not advance the port timing. My 50 now had acceleration and top end. My mates were gobsmacked when I led all the way from school to Cross-roads! Eight years later in Stourbridge, I had the cylinder off my new TZ250C and with the exhaust ports

Sid Griffiths set-up in 1976.

Pole position at Rouen on the TZ700 Yamaha.

crying out to be squared off, I decided to cut the pistons, as per my 1968 50cc road bike, as an experiment and because I did not have the time or equipment to cut the new cylinders. We picked up Peter Aldridge on the way to the ferry. He had very kindly taken time off work to come and help. A few hours later the three of us drove proudly into the Rouen paddock in the magnificent red Fiat loaded with good stuff. Hadn't we come a long way, and I do not mean in distance from Stourbridge.

Rouen was a fairytale. It was pure pleasure arriving in a van as good as a factory team's, setting up the awning, unloading new and almost new TZs from the van and then retiring to the comfort of the neat compartment in the middle for a cup of tea and a sandwich. We were all in a positive mood which seemed to help everything go so smoothly.

I was amazed in 250 practice because my bike with the cut pistons was a jet. At this time of the season most riders had new bikes which were probably not yet modified and there was not a machine except those of French and Japanese aces Patrick Fernandez and Takazumi Katayama, that I could not beat on the main straight. Katayama was a Yamaha factory rider so it is a certainty that his 250 and 750 were more than 'over the counter' bikes like ours. After simply adjusting the ride height and getting the jetting and gearing right, I qualified on the front row of the grid for the 250 race. The 750, at this stage still with standard chassis, was also going great guns. I was now on Michelin tyres and was getting on well with their big new rear slick which enabled me to use more of the TZ750's abundant power. Surprising myself and all others present, I qualified fastest on the 750 for pole position alongside Katayama and another French ace, Michelle Rougerie, former Harley Davidson works rider.

The 250cc race, a thirty minute plus one lap affair, was an 'absolute cracker, a beauty in every sense of the word' as described by Norrie Whyte of Motorcycle News. For the first ten laps Fernandez, Katayama and I swapped first place in a torrid dice. After ten laps Katayama broke away a little with a new lap record of 2min 13.5secs and held his slender lead. Then his Yamaha seized, forcing him out of the running. Fernandez and I went on into the last lap locked together, inches apart on the difficult and dangerous high speed circuit. On the last lap, at the final bend, I exploited a weakness of Fernandez by outbraking him and swept past to take the flag and reset the lap record at 2min 12.9secs! What an omen. On my first Continental outing with competitive bikes, the first stage of our planned assault on the Continent, we took the flag, set a new record, collected the silverware and pocketed substantial prize money.

The 750 race was no less spectacular. In the first of two legs of thirty minutes plus a lap, Rougerie, Katayama and I formed a high speed train as we scorched around the demanding road circuit. At the end of the race the on-form Frenchman, performing magnificently for his public, had an eight second advantage over me with Katayama four seconds aft. The second leg was no less hectic with Rougerie again winning, but this time by only two seconds from Katayama with me in third with cracked exhausts slowing the bike a bit. The overall result read Rougerie, Katayama,

With Peter and Sid at Rouen.

Ballington. It was to be some time before the elation of this days racing was to be eclipsed and it took my first GP win to do it.

At Rouen there was very good appearance money, very good grid position money and excellent prize money. I recall being paid out in those large colourful franc notes and it seemed like a huge bundle. In fact it was more money than I had earned during the entire1974 season in England. I knew Bronnie and I were going to enjoy 'The Circus' much more this time round. It began that night when, for the first time we went in search of a classy French restaurant to suit the occasion and indulged in a feast of fine cuisine. 'Park the Viennas missus, it's Chateaubriand from now on!'

After a heady Rouen experience, Sid Griffith's Racing Team headed south east towards Italy for the Imola 200, an international F750 event. Racing at or simply visiting Imola during a major race, whether it be cars or bikes, is an unforgettable experience. The grand old circuit is maybe 2km from the centre of town and surrounded by houses. Race week is a festival of excitement with the townsfolk a bunch of raving enthusiasts. On race day the locals would head down to the track carrying their picnic hampers, jugs of vino, chairs and whatever they needed for the day long vigil at the trackside. There would be three or four generations of Italians on the pilgrimage to the Autodromo Dino Ferrari of which they were immensely proud. I loved and admired the attitude of these people towards motorsport in their town. The noise did not matter because they all went to watch anyway, and the visitors must have brought huge revenues into the town.

I raced there many times and enjoyed the event for the nightlife, atmosphere and the racing. On each occasion, as soon as practice was over and changes to the bikes had been discussed and decided on, Bronnie and I would grab Croz and Brenda, Jeff and Zita Sayle or whoever was ready, if not all of them, and head down to our favourite restaurant to over-indulge on fabulous Italian food while moderately indulging in the old vino.

The 5.04km circuit was very demanding and interesting with ascents and descents, slow and fast corners to keep you sweating. It is a very physical track. The original was a classic high speed circuit but had recently undergone modifications to slow it down in certain areas. It was still very fast though and scary in places, particularly at the Tamburello, a left hand bend after the start line. It was fast, probably 240kph with no run-off area. In fact it has claimed a number of lives over the years. I qualified very well just outside the top ten in official practice but the jinx was still with us. In the first hundred mile race I was up to eighth at just over halfway when the water pump packed up and the bike overheated. There was a factory fault with TZ700s. There was not enough backlash on the small gears operating the water pump, and one gear stripped. The damage caused by the subsequent seizure was extensive and expensive and we did not make it to the line for the second heat. At Imola a gentleman from the AGV helmet factory gave me one of their latest helmets. It was my first free helmet and it meant that I was being noticed by the wealthy accessory industry, a small step towards entering the lucrative product endorsement area of professional motorcycle racing.

From Imola we had a lovely drive across to Genova on the Mediterranean coast then on to France along the incredible coastal route past Monaco, to Toulon to reach the Paul Ricard circuit for an International 200 mile F750 race at which we had entries. It was a single, mammoth fifty-five lap race with two fuel stops. There were no jinxes here, no wayward marshals, rocks in the radiator or faulty gears! I had an astounding practice with everything going just right. I finished third on the grid amongst the creme de le creme of F750 racing, the factory team supported riders from Europe and America. Things went smoothly in the race and I took a creditable sixth place. Everything was so different to our last visit to Paul Ricard. We now felt and behaved like we belonged to the European racing fraternity. The wind could no longer blow us away. Our roots were taking hold, cash was starting to flow and we were living a lifestyle that we had only dreamed about in 1973.

Thanks to Chas Mortimer I am signed up by Furygan.

Another South African in the race was Johan Boshoff, having his first Continental race on a new TZ700 Yamaha. Bossie was a lovely bloke and it was great to see him again. As a Springbok and multiple National Champion, he still is a legend in South Africa. Bossie qualified eighteenth for the race and despite severely injuring his knee during the race when it hit a kerb, finished fifteenth. Bossie died the following year after sustaining fatal injuries in a crash at Kyalami, another victim of the disregard of the powers that be with regards safety requirements for bikes. The mentality dictated that it was good enough for cars and therefore good enough. Bossie's death was a great loss to South African motorsport.

During the week before practice at Paul Ricard, Chas Mortimer, one of Europe's top riders, highly respected by all and a total professional, took me to see his racing suit sponsor, Furygan. They were located in Nimes, about two hours from Paul Ricard. Chas introduced me to the Seguras, a husband and wife team who produced beautiful leather clothing specifically for everyday motorcycling. The result of the visit was that they offered me a contract to wear their racing suit for the rest of the season. They took my measurements and we set up a small agreement that included free leathers as required and bonus money based on results in GP and International races. While we were at lunch in Nimes they cut and sewed my suit, which fitted like a glove.

They also gave us a range of their beautiful everyday leather goods and Bronnie and I walked out of there feeling like a million francs in our stylish leather jackets bearing the Furygan logo. It was really good of Chas to open that door to me. Not many riders would do that, especially not for an opponent.

My first attempt at GP racing since early 1973 was the following weekend at Le Mans for the French GP and it was abortive. At least I looked great in my new blue and white Furygan leathers. It was one of those times you want to rub out but can't. The 350 seized in the race before we had gone too far. A seizure occurs usually when the jets controlling the amount of fuel being metered to the combustion chamber are too small and not enough fuel is being passed. This causes overheating and the aluminium pistons expand quicker than the cylinder to the point where they jam in the cylinder. The best performance of a two stroke motor is in a narrow zone very close to lean. The trick was to get the jetting as close to the limit as possible. I ran it too lean and the 350 seized. Worse was to come. In the 250 race I was overeager to recover from a bad start and fought through from twenty-seventh to sixteenth. On lap five I overdid it and crashed, fortunately without injury. My lap times were good and I was riding well so we felt positive despite the lack of results.

My next confirmed ride was at Mugello for the Italian GP three weeks later. I was having problems getting accepted at most Grands Prix but was not going to drive to the events to beg for starts. There were enough high paying international races to keep us busy on those weekends and I was beginning to make a name for myself on the Continent so my appearance fee was creeping up nicely. This 'start money' was based on your results, your potential to draw a crowd and your ability as a negotiator. I was beginning to draw the crowds. No South Africans had been consistently successful on the Continent since Paddy Driver in the sixties so it was interesting for the promoters to have 'un pilote d' Afrique du Sud' on the line. The flag of the Republic of South Africa was flying around Europe again.

In the gap between the French and Italian GPs was the Austrian GP, where I had been refused a start and a Mettet International. I was now a regular Mettet visitor and negotiated a reasonable sum to ride the 250 and 750 there. It was a good day and we picked up second in the 250 and fourth in the second leg of the 750 races. Peter Aldridge had gone home after the Imola 750 race, so Bronnie and I were keeping the show on the road alone. It was very tough for both of us, driving the long distances to the races, unloading, doing the admin, preparing the bikes, riding them in practice, altering carburation, gearing and chassis settings, racing, sometimes one race right after the next without a break, fixing the occasional seizure and crash damage, packing again and then driving to the next event. Bronnie was flat out keeping house and helping me with the bikes. She would push the bikes through scrutineering and was the prettiest fuel mixer in the paddock, an excellent timekeeper and giver of pit signals. It was tough but when you are getting good results and can sense a breakthrough, adrenaline and enthusiasm keeps you driven. I often drove through the night to get to an event on time during the first half of 1976, but nothing was too much trouble to get there and get the job done as efficiently and effectively as possible.

Mugello GP circuit was south of Florence near the quaint old town of Mugello. Part of the fun of going to a venue for the first time was the discovery of a new location and the exploration thereof to see how other folk do it. We were getting a far deeper experience than tourists could ever hope for. On arrival we would explore the local town to find the lavanderia, macelleria, panetteria, supermercato and the best restaurant. Once familiar with the territory and stocked with local delicacies we would set up shop at the circuit. Things went smoothly in practice and at the end of the officially timed session I was eighth on the grid in the 250 and seventeenth in the 350. The classes were very competitive and the qualifying times extremely close. In the 350 I was within one second of fifth on the grid and in the 250, within one second of third. I was excited because I knew I could go faster on both bikes. I had spent practice setting the bikes up as best as was possible in the allotted time and learning the ins and outs of the difficult 5.245km circuit, rather than focus on doing my best lap time. The circuit was a relatively safe 'modern' layout so I would be inclined to have a full go in the races, let it all hang out so to speak. I did just that in the 350 race and by lap three had chopped one second off my best practice time to go into fifth. At the end of the race six seconds covered second to seventh with me in sixth, ahead of World Champion, Walter Villa on the factory Harley Davidson. This was an excellent result on last years outdated twin shock TZ350B against the current monoshock TZ350Cs! Sadly, at the end of the racing, we learned that Paolo Tordi, fifth on the grid, had crashed and been hit by his bike sustaining serious injuries from which he died. Bike racing is dangerous, always was and always will be, even on a relatively safe layout like Mugello.

I fancied myself to have a go in the 250 race after the great 350 ride and I did. I chopped 1.5 seconds off my practice time and went into third on lap eight, pulling away from Katayama. I was now catching Finnish ace, Pentti Korhonen in second. Unfortunatly over-exuberance got the upper hand and I crashed in a big heap on a big corner, aptly named Curva Arrabiata. Early 'pioneer' slicks were nothing like today's radial ply slicks. On those early suckers there was no warning when you stepped over the limit of their adhesion. They let go so quickly that the best you could do was hold on and hope. My first experience with radial slicks was on a MacLean Racing NSR 500 Honda ten years later in 1986 at Laguna Seca. I could not believe how much easier they made limit riding. When you got to the limit the tyre would send a loud, clear message saying, 'Hey man I am about to slide but don't worry about it. Feather the throttle a little if you want me to come back in line, otherwise just keep the gas on and either way you will be okay.' Back at Mugello, I was so close to holding the huge slide on the Curva Arrabiata, but as quickly as those slicks let go they might grip again. Mine did and I got flicked off. In the process my boot got caught in the chassis and the bike dragged me down the road behind it. When we hit the slightly ramped curb on the outside we started tumbling. With my leg stuck in the frame I was being beaten on the ground every time the bike somersaulted until finally we parted company and came to halt in a dusty heap on the side of the track. Remarkably, nothing felt broken but when I stood up I had this excruciating pain in my crotch. I had banged the old goolies a good one and the pain made me double up in agony. I think the crowd thought that I was a showman bowing to them because they cheered vehemently every time I bent over. When the pain subsided a little I noticed a neat round hole in the ankle section on the outside of each boot. Holes in the protective gear usually meant there was some kind of hole in your body and on this occasion my ankles were stinging. The interesting part was finding out how bad the injury would be. If you crunch your hand it is always a relief to find your fingers remain attached to your hand when you remove the glove. I waited until I got back to the paddock before removing the boots so I could share it with Bronnie. She would almost faint whenever I brought in gruesome injuries and sure enough, on this occasion, there was a matching pair of deep holes, almost to the bone on each ankle. To this day I have these neat matching scars to remind me of the moment I took my bow at the Curva Arrabiata.

During 1976, the Dozy-tuned TZ350 was a jet.

After Mugello the 250 had to go back to England for the Isle of Man TT races. Sid was obsessed with the TT races and wanted the 1976 monoshock there for Geoff Barry to ride. The 1975 250 twin shock was delivered to us at Mugello and the Monoshock was taken back to England. This meant we would not have the monoshock chassis for Osterreichring, Nogaro and Chimay. We would get it back at the Post TT races at Mallory after Chimay. The '75 twin shock Yamaha did not handle anywhere as well as the monoshock so this made things much harder for me and would impact negatively on results.

The following day I woke up feeling very sore. The family jewels were okay but my ankles were swollen and painful and one leg was stiff and sore. It was a problem walking but it was not a worry as I had raced well. A bit of pain was a part of the job. We had to get to the Osterreichring for an International meeting taking place in ten days, where I was being very well paid to race in the 250 and 750 classes. Before Mugello I had promised Bronnie we would go to Venice on the way to Austria so we loaded up and headed off. Venice is an amazing place but because of all the walking it is not the place to go if you have two bad ankles and a wrecked leg.

With time to kill we took a slow scenic drive north through the Dolomites to enter Austria at Villach. En-route we stopped wherever took our fancy simply to admire the view or walk through a quaint village, sit at a pavement cafe and take in the 'old Europe' atmosphere that was still so strong in the smaller towns. We arrived days early at the Osterreichring. It was the

Winning at Nogaro in 1976. Me, patrick Pons and Gerrard Choukron get a good angle of lean.

On the rostrum with Phil at the Osterreichring.

middle of spring so the weather was European perfect with warm balmy days stretching late into the evening. We set up at the circuit and popped a cold bottle of chateau 'not-so-cheap-as-last-year' out of our little fridge and sat outside watching another good day fade into darkness.

We had a pretty relaxed time at this event. There was a fairly small entry and so the pits were not too crowded. There was not a great deal of practice so we would not wear out too many parts. Phil Read was the main attraction and Steve Parrish and myself possibly the next highest paid. I got pole position for the 250 race and second on the grid for the 750. In the 750 race Phil, multiple World Champion and legend in his lifetime, led from start to finish while Steve and I had a good dice for second which I took by metres. In the 250 I came second to Austrian tuning ace Harald Bartol on a Yamaha. I missed the well-behaved monoshock chassis on which I could possibly have won. The twin shocker did not have as good manners as the mono, which illustrates technological progress at work. The Monoshock, or cantilever Yamaha frame allowed the rear wheel far more movement. With more grip from slicks more workload was put onto the rear suspension. This meant either running harder suspension to prevent bottoming or designing a suspension system with more travel. Enter the Yamaha Monoshock system in 1976.

Four days later we were set up at Nogaro in the south west of France, near Spain for the French round of the FIM F750 Championship. The thing that I remember most about this event, apart from a blistering win in the International 250 race against hot opposition, was that the strain of doing all the work was starting to tell. In the first 250 practice I blew a crankshaft which requires a major motor strip to replace the part. I had to leave the bike until after 750 practice before I could repair it, thus missing the next practice session for the 250. That night I worked until 2 am to finish the 250 crank replacement and also did a strip, check and rebuild on the 750, which being a big four cylinder was not a simple job. I remember putting the 250 motor back into the frame and it slipped and squashed my fingers. Sombody's famous saying was that cowboys don't cry. Well this cowboy was close to tears. As I crawled into bed in the early hours, exhausted from a rather busy day at the office I made a firm resolution to make that phone call to Pietermaritzburg, South Africa, first thing Monday, to tell Dozy that it was time to pack his port grinders and get his butt back to Europe!

The next and final day of practice went well. After only eighteen laps on the short but tough and bumpy circuit, I made third on the grid for the 250 race behind Fernandez and Bouzanne. I would have had a far easier time if I had the monoshock chassis at this venue. The line up was classy. Factory teams stayed away from most of the 250cc Internationals which left the GP privateers to battle it out to see who was the top gun. On the 750 I qualified fourteenth just behind the factory bikes. There was strong factory support for the F750 and the entry list was basically the 'Who's who' of F750 racing. In the first 160km leg I finished a very good eighth. In the second, the bike developed a misfire after three laps, so I retired.

Directly after the first fifty lap 750 race with no time for a shit, shave or shampoo, we lined up for the twenty lap 250 race. This turned out to be one of the more exciting races of the year. I beat the French aces on their own territory. After twenty laps of the closest racing one could wish to see, I took the flag from Bouzanne by a whisker, with Fernandez third by another whisker. This was my second international win in 1976 with three second places and an outstanding Grand Prix performance in the Italian at Mugello. These results were pretty good for a 'Circus Rookie', it was what we were hoping for and the season was still young. The 750 was proving unreliable otherwise I would have had all top ten results in the Championship events. On Monday I made the phone call. Dozy must have been bored, he did not hesitate, he would be with us in England for the Mallory Park Post TT International in a month.

On that cheerful note we left the gorgeous location of Nogaro with superb and unique south country style cuisine and the laid back French rural way of life. Apart from regular trophies, I received four large bottles of prunes soaking in Armagnac brandy from the region. These prunes were fabulous eaten as they were, or when warmed and served with ice cream. The only problem was the after effects which were socially unacceptable!

We journeyed north, with the windows open, to Chimay in Belgium, the scene of our last Continental ride in 1973 before we had retreated, broke, to England. I recall pondering at that moment whether we would get the opportunity to re-visit as we left Chimay in 1973. Well, here we were, stronger than ever, ripping around Europe as if it was our playground. Chimay had the makings of another good 250 result. I was second fastest in practice and was lying second behind Australian ace and seasoned GP veteran, John Dodds, after seven laps when the bike stopped with engine failure. We packed and headed back to England to pick up the monoshock and get ready for the Post TT races at Mallory, a premiere British event.

It made a change to be somewhere we could understand the language. We had become proficient enough in French and Italian to be able to ask for food and wine. An area of language I excelled in was counting because when negotiating with the promoters you had to be 100% sure you were asking for the right amount, and understand what amount the promoter was talking about. I also learnt to cross my sevens. A European one and an uncrossed seven look the same. The first time I wrote to a promoter asking for 7,000 Francs without crossing the seven I got a reply saying that of course I would be welcome to 1,000 Francs!

The 350 race at Mallory was a good one. Katayama took first from Mortimer with me right behind. It was fun to be at Mallory again and I was surprised that the regular British short circuit aces were not in the running. The pace set by the Grand Prix set was hot with Katayama and Frenchman Bernard Fau sharing a new lap record at 51.2 seconds. Sid was happy to see us, collect a swag of trophies, a bottle of volcanic prunes and to see his team, now an established force in International racing, in action at Mallory. He had been unable to visit us on the Continent as he originally planned to do, due to pressures of business. He was understandably not totally happy about us disappearing again, but fortunately he did not prevent us from getting back to the serious stuff across The Channel, and I was grateful.

The return of Dozy

Mid 1976 was busy. We picked Dozy up at Heathrow before Mallory Park. He had shipped his Maximat V10 lathe across weeks before so we had to pick it up at Southampton and fit it in the van. As far as I know we were the first team in Europe, including factory teams, to have machining facilities in the transporter. We mysteriously became more popular amongst the circus dwellers around the same time and that old V10 did a lot of work. After Mallory we bade Sid farewell and headed back to the Continent to resume our mission, to seek and win races preferably of the Grand Prix variety. We headed to Germany for an unusual race event that was to take place at a street circuit called the Norisring in the infamous town of Nurnburg. The circuit just happened to race around the big concrete structure atop of which was Hitler's podium from where he delivered his speeches to the fanatical multitudes. I finished second to Patrick Fernandez in the 350 race. We got paid and moved on from that eerie place. With no race the following weekend, we went to Assen to watch the Dutch TT. It was notoriously difficult to get entries at this event and I had tried every angle to persuade the promoters, but without success.

We picked a good venue to be spectators. The weather was hot all week but on race day the temperature soared to thirty-five degrees Centigrade. The humidity must have been up there close to 100%, and some competitors collapsed from heat exhaustion. The winner of the sidecar race, Hermann Schmid collapsed after the race and had to be given emergency treatment to get his heart beating again. To compound the problem Assen was a physical circuit without many straight sections where one could relax briefly. In such harsh conditions it was interesting to observe the riders' physical conditions immediately after their race. From this it was possible to analyse a rider's physical state of fitness and state of tension at the controls. The negative effects of fatigue are compounded by tension. A lot of riders who had to be helped or carried away after the race, if simply not fit enough for the conditions, were probably over-tense during racing thus putting more physical effort than necessary into riding and suffering the consequences. Riders with the right level of relaxation while racing in adverse conditions would step off their bikes without assistance. Most of the top riders fell into this category. It could be down to superb fitness. However I, for one, although very fit, did no special training and I don't believe any of the top stars spent hours in the gym. Barry Sheene is a good example of a relaxed rider. He won the 500 race in this heatwave by forty-five seconds and got off the bike looking almost as fresh as when he started. The Venezuelan GP in 1977 at San Carlos was probably hotter than Assen in 1976. Simply walking fifty metres to the toilet was an energy sapping experience. Barry won under pressure from Steve Baker by three seconds and looked like he could go the distance again. Giacomo Agostini was another example of a relaxed rider. He would step off his bike and onto the rostrum looking as if he had not done a single lap. He won the 350 race at Assen in the heatwave by twenty-four seconds yet his MV Agusta had been outpaced by the faster Yamahas in practice at Assen and at all other GPs that year. Part of the skill of racing fast hinged on the state of your body and mind while out there. Aside from increasing fatigue, which also affects concentration, a tense body cannot get accurate feedback from the tyres, chassis and suspension, through the seat, foot pegs and handlebars. If your arms and hands are tense you cannot analyse the slightest signals through the handlebars. For example, if your front tyre is starting to break away, you need to sense it immediately. If you are tense, particularly in your arms and wrists, the small movement of the tyre across the track surface will increase in size before you can detect it, by which time it might be too late to do anything about it. Your whole body has to be in the correct state of relaxation in order to go fast smoothly. Smoothness is another area of riding that is vital to performance. It goes with being at the right level of relaxation because you cannot achieve smoothness without it. I have often been told that it looked as if I was not trying. I loved to hear this, especially after a win or a new lap record. I first learned about the effect of smooth driving when I was about eight years old, with my wooden soapbox racer. Near our house in Pinetown in Natal, there were beautiful smooth surfaced hard packed dirt roads. The terrain was very hilly so there were some lovely downhill sections complete with a variety of bends. I used to spend hours after school and on weekends riding down and then pushing that old cart right back to the top of my favourite hill. Luckily traffic was very sparse but occasionally I would surprise a housewife in her car and have to execute emergency avoidance procedures, which I guess was a part of the thrill. My favourite section was probably three or four hundred metres long and would proceed up the next hill after bottoming out over a small stream. One of my games was to see how far I could get up the other side before rolling to a stop. From a fixed starting point, my soapbox and I could only get to a certain point if I drifted too much on the bends on the way down. I learnt that the softest of touches, the gentlest of movements on the steering wheel and keeping my body as still as possible would help to create the smoothness that would enable me to take the bends without drifting and thus reach the bottom of the hill with more speed to reach a higher point on the uphill. Drifting was a lot of fun though and it was also fun seeing how far I could get the tail of the cart out without losing control and spinning out. The all-steel wheelbarrow wheels on the rear were ideal for sliding and my super-low cart was very difficult to turn over, so spinning out was not a problem.

A truly smooth riding style also makes for easier limit riding. When on the limit of tyre adhesion, at the point where the tyres want to start sliding across the track surface, any sudden or jerky moves get transmitted through the handlebars, seat or footpegs via the chassis and suspension to the point of contact with the track, and can advance the breaking of adhesion at the point of contact. This can cause a situation that requires negative throttle action to rectify and thus a slower lap time or worse, loss of control. On occasions riders have fallen off when seemingly going around a bend at the same pace as another rider, despite being on similar bikes with similar tyres. I reckon it has something to do with lack of the finesse that I have been mentioning.

Analysing riders during the Assen heatwave or at any other opportunity, gave me a valuable insight into potential strengths or weaknesses of certain key riders. This information could be useful if I was racing against them. There were many areas of opportunity to collect vital information about the opposition both on and off the track, which might be useful in combat at some time or other. It is very useful to have an idea of how an opponent might react in the last lap when you are right behind him, or what you can expect him to try on the last lap if he is on your tail. It could help you to beat him or save some skin and a repair bill.

With nine races left, we were pleased with the first half of 1976, and looked forward to the remaining races. Now Dozy was back I knew we would be in a position to improve. The simple fact that I would not have the extra pressure of working on the bikes to silly hours of the morning would make a big difference. Dozy had some ideas to create power, which if successful would get me one or two positions closer to the front. While at Assen I spoke to the organisers of the Swedish GP for entries and was rejected. I will never live this down..... Bronnie spoke to the Finnish GP organiser on my behalf and I was given entries in both classes. I guess I just did not have the legs of a dancer! The Scandinavian trip to do these two events is very expensive so unless you get accepted in both classes at both meetings, it does not make sense to go at all, so we gave them a miss. We were turned down for the Czechoslovakian GP which left the West German at the Nürburgring and the Spanish at Montjuich Park, Barcelona as the remaining GPs for the season. I was accepted for the West German but the Spanish promoters turned me down. I would keep sending them letters to try and change their minds.

After Assen we were entered to race at Zandvoort in Holland in 250 and 350 races. It would be an opportunity to try some ideas of Dozy's. He modified a set of 1975 cylinders and exhaust pipes for the 250 and bored the carburettors to a larger size and modified the inlet ports on the 350. During this period sound restrictions were introduced by the FIM. Bikes were to have mufflers fitted to reduce the readings to around one hundred and fifteen decibels. The Zandvoort organisers were adhering to the new regulation so a lot of people were running around trying to 'maak 'n plan' to quieten their bikes. The new regulations were a good move. Unsilenced two strokes make a big noise at a high frequency. Apart from damaging our hearing inevitably they would annoy residents near circuits. In some cases, circuits were under fire from local resident groups on the noise issue. The factories would supply bikes in 1977 with factory fitted mufflers but during 1976 we had to find a way to reduce noise levels ourselves. Our saving grace turned out to be the tailpipes from the VW beetle. They had a perforated pipe of our required bore size inside the chrome outer pipe, with fibreglass matt between the outer and inner pipes. We cut off the existing tailpipes of our exhaust and welded on the VW tailpipes. This reduced sound emissions enough to pass at some of the circuits. Where the sound checks were more stringent we had special plates to slip inside the tailpipe for the sound check! The sound regulations took something away from GP racing by muffling the magnificent sounds made by unsilenced high powered racing engines, but by the same token were necessary to ensure the survival of racing on circuits close to populated areas.

At Zandvoort we had a lot of practice to experiment with motor modifications and mufflers. I ended up third in the 350 behind Alan North and Tom Herron. I was third again in the 250 race behind Patrick Fernandez and Pentti Korhonen. Dozy analysed everything, usually uttering his favourite saying, 'Oink!' while scratching his beard and burying his head deep in his books to make calculations that only he understood. After Zandvoort we went back across the water for the Hutchinson 100 'reverse direction' race at Brands Hatch then to Silverstone for the British round of the F750 series. At Brands I had a solid 350 ride recording the fastest lap but got beaten to the line by Alan North. Alan was having a good year. He was travelling with his girlfriend and did all his own mechanical work. His bikes were fast and he knew how to ride them.

Silverstone was a rare day when the 750 did not give trouble. After two gruelling one hundred mile heats I was an excellent fifth overall in the F750 results. I was fifth again in the 1000cc race followed by fourth in the 250 race, and third in the 350. I reckon the riders of that era, such as myself, riding three classes in five major races, some extraordinarily long, must have been pretty damn fit to do so many races on the same day.

Silverstone was so different from most circuits. It had big, wide, fast sweeping bends and required a certain rhythm to get the best out of a lap. You had to flow with the circuit. It was very hard to find the optimum braking and peeling points because of the speed at which you approached the bends and the width of the track. I always felt that I had not yet got it right. I could go in faster and roll through to the apex faster. It was a challenging circuit and I enjoyed racing on it. Although it did not have long straight sections the average speeds were high. At the time the F750s lapped at 182kph average, the 350s at 174 kph and the 250s at 168 kph! Races at Silverstone were Sid's best event. He always hired a double decker bus with catering facilities, parked it at a good vantage point and entertained his clients and guests in style.

Our first Grand Prix rostrum at 'The Ring'

The Nürburgring was the ultimate challenge. In 1973 I learned about a third of the incredible 22.835km circuit and hoped to get to grips with the rest during this trip for the West German Grand Prix. I could now afford to buy laps to facilitate learning the way around but did not have a car or road bike at my disposal, so again my learning was confined to official practice, made difficult by intermittent showers. After two days and only ninteen laps on the 250 and 350, I started in the 350 race with a lot still to learn. From fifteenth on the first lap with a time of nine minutes thirty-six seconds I reduced my lap time to 9mins 8secs. on the last lap, finishing twelfth. The guys who knew their way around had an advantage. The fastest lap and new record went to Johnny Ceccotto on a factory Yamaha at 8mins 57secs.

I started the 250 race feeling more confident knowing a little more about the track after the 350 race. At the end of lap one I was seventh and steadily picked up places. One and a half laps from the end, I overtook Bruno Kneubühler, Dieter Braun and Jon Ekerold in one go, to take second. We had a hell of a dice for the last 22km, never more than a few wheels apart. I held them off to the line with fellow Natalian, Jon Ekerold taking third from Braun and Swiss star Kneubühler fifth. Only 2.5secs covered us. Villa, officially the 1976 250 and 350 double World Champion on his rapid factory Harley Davidson, was in a class of his own. He beat us by just over a minute with a lap record of 9mins 3.2secs. My best lap was 9mins 17.4secs. I was ecstatic with the result, Bronnie and Dozy were happy too. They were jumping up and down.

This was our first rostrum position in Grand Prix racing. It's hard to believe that three chumps who had got lost on their way to Mettet back in 1973 were on the rostrum next to a multiple World Champion at the West German Grand Prix, one of the most demanding circuits in history. As far as I was concerned, Bronnie and Dozy were standing with me, as were my mom and dad, smiling for the dozens of photographers who clicked furiously as reporters scribbled notes and raced to wire the news to the world. 'Kork Ballington, the quiet guy from Natal who only ever dreamed about racing bikes as he gazed at magazine cuttings of his Grand Prix heroes, was standing on the rostrum at a Grand Prix, laurel wreath around his neck and silver trophy in his hand.' This was more than I could have ever wished for. I was high on that magic moment for days. Not only had I stepped onto the rostrum but I had come closer to fulfilling my desire to know every inch of that incredible circuit. In 1978 I achieved that dream when I won the 250 West German Grand Prix on the factory KR250 Kawasaki with a new race record and a lap record of 8mins 49.5secs.

From the Nürburgring we floated at 30,000 feet in the red Fiat OM55 on our way to Assen for the Dutch round of the FIM F750 series. Practice was plagued by rain as was the first hundred mile heat of two. It was a case of stay upright during an incident wracked race. Basically I hung in and stayed out of trouble with the result that by the first fuel stop I was eleventh, and at the end of one hundred miles I was ninth. By the second hundred mile heat, the circuit was dry but the sky did not look promising.

My first Grand Prix rostrum finishing position at the incredible 'Ring'. Walter Villa won with Jon Ekerold third.

MOTORRÄDER
AUTOSONIK
frigikit
air conditioning
Harley- David
Klassen-

I opted for an intermediate tyre, expecting rain at some time during the race. Well I got that wrong. Without rain an intermediate tyre, which is a slick with a pattern cut on it, overheats and requires tender care to last one hundred miles. I got a great start and lay second at the end of the lap. I dropped to fourth by lap six as I was riding to conserve the tyre. A few laps later the three riders in front of me were not pulling away. My tyre was feeling good so I stepped up my pace by two seconds a lap, and went back into second place. On about lap thirteen Agostini pulled in for fuel and I went into the lead. Agostini, on a slick, was fast and went back into the lead and kept it to the end. It was frustrating because the bike was going so well and I was wasting about three or four seconds a lap conserving the tyre. Once I realised John Newbold, in third could not catch me I eased two seconds a lap and cruised home second. My ninth and second placings gave me fifth overall, well into the big prize money. The good results on the TZ700 were a confidence booster and proved that I was just as capable on the big gun as on the lightweight 250 and 350.

We had a busy run up to Mallory Park's Race of the Year the following weekend. At Nico Bakker's chassis factory in Holland we picked up one of his monoshock style chrome molybdenum tube frames, which Sid had bought to replace the standard TZ700 Yamaha frame. We raced back to Stourbridge to set it up for Mallory. Something new like this usually takes a lot of test sessions to get used to it and make adjustments to set it up to one's liking. We left it standard for Mallory and it felt pretty good considering. In practice I beat my previous best time on the stock TZ700 consistently lap by lap. In the main event, The Race of the Year, one of the premiere events in England, I was challenging the big guns on their factory bikes. I was mixing it with Sheene, Hennen, Agostini and Ditchburn for second place but tried to put down too much power coming out of the hairpin and spun out. My lap times were good though, with my personal best at 50.2secs whereas Steve Baker, the winner, set a fastest lap of 49.8secs. A contributing factor to the crash was probably the setting on the rear shock unit. It felt too harsh, possibly too much rebound or compression damping. The rear shock unit had adjustable damping functions, a new experience for me, so I would have to learn to set it up.

I got back into winning ways and won the 350 race in fine style from Frenchman, Christian Sarron. Sarron gave me a run for my money and led on two of the laps. He claimed a new lap record for his efforts at 50.8secs. The race was cut short by one lap when Bill Henderson had a bad crash at the entrance to the high speed Gerard's. Unfortunately Bill died later in hospital. It was scary how we had become hardened to the death of fellow riders. It was astounding how many had been killed since we arrived in Europe, mostly due to primitive safety standards. We all mourned a fallen comrade but we knew it was dangerous from the start and always would be. After Kim's death I accepted it could happen to me. You had to work at reducing the risk as much as possible yet still give your best.

Kim's death intensified my awareness of the dangers of the sport. It was a big advantage to have some extra riding ability. This is not an idle boast but a simple fact, otherwise I would not be consistently taking the first few places in races. This ability combined with bikes that could go a bit faster than standard, gave me an advantage. My 100% effort was good enough for me to be at or near the front. Riders with an ability level, say, outside the top five would have to perform over 100% to keep up with the front runners, thus putting themselves in the danger zone. The more you overextend your limit, the higher the risk of an accident.

The two main areas for risk reduction were circuit layout and equipment condition. When we arrived at a circuit I would jog around it, studying the corners, condition of the track and particularly what was on the outside of the bends. If you crash, this is where you were headed. If there was plenty of runoff and no chance of hitting the straw bales I would value the corner as good for limit riding and over. If there was limited space I would calculate the risk based on the speed of the corner, the amount of space and the number of straw bales, if any. If there were catch fences I checked to see if the poles were sawn almost through the base as dictated by regulations, so they would snap easily on impact, and whether each pole had a straw bale against it. I would set a standard for each corner and try not to ride outside the prescribed standard on that corner, unless there was a championship at stake. Key corners are at the back end of a lap leading back to the flag. In a last lap, duelling riders are likely to throw caution to the wind. Better to overtake on the safer corner and hold the line on the last couple of bends and let the others do the desperate work to pass you. There is a good chance that I would qualify as the least injured multiple World Champion in the history of the sport, implying my approach to safety management was right on the button.

I insisted on the highest preparation standards possible, whether it was when I was doing it alone or with Dozy then later with the Kawasaki technicians and I was prepared to get in and help if necessary. I could prepare a bike as well as anybody and could feel a problem with a motor, therefore, rather than thrash it around the track taking a risk of being thrown off by a seizure or whatever, would pull in and find the problem. Even when I became a factory rider I watched preparation like a hawk. On the odd occasions I would pick up something that had been overlooked which might have caused a problem. I was fortunate to have Dozy and later the highly skilled Kawasaki technicians because there is no substitute for a fast and reliable bike to reduce risk. There were many occasions when riders experienced problems caused by poor preparation, alias 'bad luck' which caused them occasionally to break down or even crash, sometimes with serious injuries.

I adhered to my safety management plan as closely as possible. It was difficult from 1973 to 1978 to balance safety with the need to have a go. I desperately needed results to further my career. Occasionally I would slip up and ride over the top, as at Mugello in the 250 race of 1976. My injury record speaks for itself. In my racing years between 1967 and 1988 I only broke three bones, my left collar bone in 1968, my left scaphoid in 1977 when I was knocked off by another rider and my right scaphoid in 1988. I had my share of crashes in the early days, but as I became better the crashes were few and far between. I also attribute my lack of injuries in part to the fact that I had trained myself to fall properly, as I believe most professional riders do. I was able to remain focused while sliding down the track on my butt and would avoid tumbling at all cost as it is a bone breaker and causes disorientation. I preferred to slide along the ground controlling body position for impact against bales or whatever. It was imperative to go in feet first, using the legs as buffers or slide in sideways spreading the impact along your body. I would rather break a couple of legs than go in head first and break my neck. Avoiding a crash was of course the best way to avoid injury. I fell off my 350 Sid Griffiths Yamaha at Zandvoort on 10th July 1977, did not crash for the rest of that year, joined Kawasaki and rode through 1978 until Imatra on 29th July 1979 before taking my next tumble. During that two year period I rode in thirty-eight GPs, winning twenty-one and I clinched three World Championship Titles. I also rode in about twenty-three International races, winning fifteen of them. That has to be some kind of record. Some say I was lucky. Some say the bikes were so fast that I did not have to ride hard, forgetting that I won four Grands Prix on private Yamahas against the factories. The truth of the matter is that we had a system of our own making in place that was hard to beat. We had the most astute tuner in GP racing in Dozy. With Kawasaki we had some of motorcycle racing's finest engineers and dedicated team of expert technicians and management that did not try to obstruct or dictate the path along which we were travelling. We had superb equipment and on occasions we had the fastest bike in the race, because we planned and worked to get it that way. Also, we had me. I was better than most. On a good day with this great team and those great motorcycles I was unbeatable. We had all the ingredients of a winning team, we used them properly and we won. That is why Kawasaki hired us.

Whenever I was doing one of my private circuit inspections, I would contemplate how ridiculous it was that most circuit owners and race promoters had so little concern for the safety of riders. When Kim was killed at Silverstone, the circuit owners or the race promoters, whoever was responsible for the lack of adequate safety, should have been in serious trouble. The argument that no one was forcing us to race if we were unhappy with the safety standards has no bearing on the subject. The circuits were built to race on and we were racers. Most of the circuit owners did not finish the job properly by not protecting competitors from unnecessary risk. To cite economics as an excuse is ludicrous, especially at circuits like Silverstone where huge crowds were paying a lot to see badly paid performers putting on a great show. Surely there was enough profit in it to put a little back into moving a wall of sleepers, or even getting more straw bales. There seemed to be a mentality that dictated that the circuit was good enough for cars, therefore good enough. Kim hit unprotected sleepers. His death was unnecessary as were most others over the years who fell victim to inadequate safety standards. Straw bales were later placed against the sleepers where Kim crashed. Afterwards another rider, Stan Woods, fell off there and slid into the bales rather than the sleepers and was not injured. Why were there not enough bales in the first place? As a rider I take a part of the blame. We were partly to blame for not standing up and demanding extra bales be put in place. European riders had been dictated to for too long, told to like it or lump it by many promoters. Numerous attempts at forming riders associations or boycotting events had failed because there was no unity amongst the riders. When Kenny Roberts arrived in Europe in 1978, his fresh and forthright views on the poor state of safety, paddock facilities and pay at Grand Prix venues were welcomed by most riders. Views do not change anything unless there is energy and vision to create action. Kenny seemed tailor-made for the job. He was a great motivator and almost effortlessly stirred the key riders into action with his no bullshit attitude. Kenny was genuinely interested in improving the sport as a whole, not only for his own interests. As if he did not have enough on his plate in the tough 500cc World Championship!

Place of dreams

After Mallory we decided to go to Spain for the last GP of the year. Despite constantly contacting the race promoters I had not secured entries. Barcelona was a long, expensive drive, about 1,200km so it was a big gamble to undertake the trip to more than likely end up spectators. The race was the weekend after Mallory so we had to get a move on to see the promoters, beg for an entry and hopefully practice on Friday, the first session. We arrived on Wednesday and I went straight to the promoters. There was no chance of a ride, the classes were full and there were no cancellations. Cancellations! This might be the way to get in. We went to the circuit, set up shop and began asking who had entries here but might be injured, sick or unable to participate. Alex George had 250 and 350 starts but had accepted a lucrative ride with Honda at the Bol D'Or 24 hour race at Le Mans the same weekend. Ironically he and Jean Claude Chemarin won the event. Armed with this information I raced back to the office to try and take over Alex's entries. Since Alex had not withdrawn his entries, they weren't available to give to me. If Alex sent a telegram saying he was not coming they would re-consider.

To cut a long story short, I sent Alex a barrage of telegrams via the Le Mans organisers. He must have eventually got the message and sent a telegram to Barcelona race office withdrawing his entries, asking the promoters to give them to me. By the time the director agreed to my entries it was Saturday morning. I had missed Friday's practice making it that much harder to learn the circuit and set the bikes up. My perseverance had paid off, although on a couple of occasions I was tempted to say 'stuff it' and give up. On Saturday I got two sessions on the 350 and one on the 250 with a tenth placing on the grid for both events, a fine effort on a difficult circuit I had never seen before.

1976 Spanish GP at Barcelona. Leading Walter Villa to my first GP victory.

The circuit was unique. It was set out in Montjuich Park in Barcelona City and relatively short at 3.791km. Being a street course it was dangerous with walls, poles, trees, road signs and other such hazards that are an integral part of a typical street course. Learning the circuit was not a problem as I had by then become experienced enough to suss out a new venue very quickly. Setting the bike up to find the optimum gearing, jetting and chassis settings was the tricky bit. My 350 lap time was 3.4 seconds slower than pole position set by Walter Villa. My 250 lap times were in a similar situation. With so little practice it was impossible to set the bikes up properly. I would have to estimate the final gearing and guess at suspension settings by trying to anticipate any handling problems at the faster pace which I knew I would be doing in the races. I fancied my chances on the 350 with the monoshock chassis as it was easier to go fast on and the motor had gone very well at Mallory Park. The 250 in its 1975 chassis, was the less competitive of the bikes.

15 Bruno Kneubühler, 7 me,10 Alan North, 1 Johnny Cecotto, 8 Victor Palomo, 39 Boet Van Dulmen and 9 Walter Villa, 1976 Spanish GP, my first win.

On top of everything we had technical problems to deal with. Dozy remembers, 'After 350 practice we found one cylinder had detonated through to the 'O' ring seal between the cylinder and head. The 350 was a jet but we had no more practice to run in new parts nor did we have suitable used parts in stock to correct the problem. To solve the problem step one was to hand modify the combustion chamber, using a hand file, to reduce the compression ratio which would ease the detonation problem. Step two was to nip a piece of alloy off another part of the cylinder block and gently hammer it into the damaged area of the squish band, leaving it slightly proud. These 'farmer's repairs' were more than adequate to secure an amazing GP win!'

The 250 race of thirty laps was first. I used it to become more familiar with the track and progressed steadily until around lap twenty-three when I was two seconds a lap quicker than in practice. I took eighth place at the end, not exactly a mind blowing result. Had it been worth the arduous drive and horrific hassle to get on the start line? Maybe. The 350 race was definitely worth it. I was in an acutely determined mood and from the drop of the flag was in the hunt. I went into second on lap four of the thirty lap race and sat comfortably on the tail of Spaniard, Victor Palomo, the local hero, until Bronnie's signals told me Cecotto was gaining on us. Apparently the partisan crowd was shocked into silence when I overtook Victor on the eleventh lap. I went into the lead, cutting a second a lap off my lap times. After fifteen laps I was five seconds ahead of Palomo, Cecotto, Villa and Kneubühler with Franco Uncini making a charge and catching these four. After twenty laps I had eight seconds on Palomo. Disaster almost struck on lap twenty-three, coming onto the start finish straight I got into the biggest slide imaginable. This section was very fast and dangerous, taken in fifth gear and almost flat out. There was no run off area so if I lost it here, the consequences would be serious. I hung on. The rear wheel was by now about two feet out and laying a thick black stripe. It gripped as suddenly as it let go which sent the front wheel into a slide and simultaneously threw me into the air right out of the saddle. It felt like I was doing a 160kph handstand on this wildly bucking bronco. All logical analysis of the situation said I had no chance of saving myself from disaster. I saw the headlines across the front pages of the papers. Instead of saying how I won the Spanish GP they were describing how I made a messy splash on the stone wall next to the track! No one was more surprised than I when my bum came down, right back into the saddle. I still had both hands on the handlebars and the bonus was that I was pointing the right way up the track. By this time I had lost a lot of speed and had to slip back a couple of gears to get the motor back onto the power curve. The whole episode cost me about four seconds so Palomo and Uncini, who had broken from Villa and Kneubühler, closed in by that margin.

The slide and near crash was caused by a combination of factors and triggered by rider error. There was a subtle bump on the racing line in the middle of the fast curve leading onto the main straight. There was no choice but to ride straight over it. During the limited practice I never got down to very fast lap times, so the bump was not a major problem. I started noticing its potential as a problem in the 250 race when my lap times got faster. We had time between the races to adjust the 350's suspension but I was reluctant to do this without being able to try it out. During the 350 race I was nailing this curve way faster than in practice and it was evident that I would have benefited from softer rear suspension settings, making it easier to ride over it with the power on hard. The hard rear suspension would make riding this section a bit more difficult than if the settings were correct and I would have to ride accordingly. This entailed rolling the throttle off a little just as the bump was about to be hit, riding through the bump, letting the bike settle, then immediately, smoothly getting the throttle back open again. This procedure took a split second and hardly affected lap times but required extra effort and precise timing. Rolling the throttle off that little bit would reduce the power at the rear wheel. This was necessary because as the rear wheel hit the bump the hard suspension would force the weight of the bike upwards instead of just absorbing the bump. The momentum of the bike's weight moving up to the top of the rebound stroke in turn caused the rear tyre to become lighter on the road for a millisecond. This was enough to cause traction to be broken if the power at the wheel was not reduced by closing the throttle a little. On lap twenty-three, I miss-timed the procedure and hit the bump before closing the throttle. The wheel broke traction, a rare mistake that could have cost me my life! After regaining control I rode the next few corners cautiously until I was satisfied that the slide was rider error and not oil or water leaking onto the back tyre. Once satisfied, I got back on the gas, back down to 1min. 43 secs a lap to take the chequered flag from Palomo by 1.71 secs with Uncini 0.82 seconds behind Palomo.

I could not quite comprehend the magnitude of the occasion. I pulled off the race track after the start finish line in a daze and handed the bike to a beaming Dozy. We had the award ceremony to get through straight after the race. The officials in their dark jackets with identification armbands were ushering me through the crowd towards the rostrum. They each placed a hand on my arm as if I was a dangerous criminal heading for the gallows. There was so much back slapping and handshaking going on. There was Bronnie, a long relieved hug. I think she was crying. There was Chas Mortimer with his posh accent, 'Bloody hell, Ballingthrop. That was a f....ing huge slide. We thought you were history!' There was a sea of faces, all smiling, smiling at the winner. It's funny how things turn out. I was within a gnat's knacker of being either dead or seriously maimed, the non-winner in the hospital bed or on the morgue slab, tears of sorrow instead of joy. By a slim margin I regained control of the bike to be the hero privateer giant-killer at the Spanish Grand Prix in Montjuich Park on the 19th September 1976. I won my first Grand Prix, the first South African in history to win a World Championship Motorcycle Grand Prix. I cast aside all thoughts of my close shave, as I stood on the rostrum in front of the huge crowd holding the silver and blue glass trophy aloft in a victory salute.

The following morning, despite the dull thud in my head, I felt an intense serenity, a light-bodied comfortable feeling of total fulfilment. I lay in the bed of our compartment in Sid's van next to Bronnie, and listened to the sounds of people dismantling and packing their equipment. The slamming of doors, the clank of awning poles being pulled apart and stowed, the throb of a diesel transporter bursting to life, ready to move on. The sound of voices, a myriad of different languages drifted into my consciouness people with dreams and goals, plans to move on and try again, optimistic that the next will be better than this one. Most would never achieve whatever it was they were seeking. I thought, you can kill me now, I have achieved things which as a little boy I dared to dream about as I lay on my bed gazing at my posters, as I raced my soapbox down the dirt road in the bush, as I rode my bicycle with drop handle bars as fast as I could on the footpath to school, imagining I was on some racetrack in another world. To have visited my place of dreams was just awesome.

I came back to earth, rejoined the planet and left Barcelona. I left Barcelona physically but Montjuich Park would conjure up an exciting memory for the rest of my life. We took a leisurely drive through the French countryside to Bordeaux and north about 100km to reach the quaint and famous town of Cognac where we had been invited to race. The first thing we did was pull up outside the Martell factory for a guided tour which included some tasting of the different classes of Cognacs. By the time we walked out of there we were a bit pickled from tasting and the general alcoholic haze which permeated the factory. In fact there was a strong aroma enveloping the entire village. The townsfolk probably spent most of their lives slightly tiddled from pollution of a different kind emanating from the distilleries. Fortunately the circuit was far enough out of town to escape the addictive smell otherwise there could have been a lot of weaving on the main straight!

The venue was a disused airfield in very bad condition, with the layout of the circuit demarcated by straw bales. I was entered in the 250 class only so we took the motor out of the 350 and replaced it with the 250 to have the benefit of the better suspension system. The usual French aces were there, much the same as at the Nogaro international. In the race, I led from start to finish and set the fastest lap, with Fernandez second and North third. The race was very amusing. On every lap someone would bump the straw bales somewhere and modify the shape of the track so each lap was a bit different to the previous one. At the end of the day when it was time for payout the promoters said they were broke and could not pay anyone. Their race office was a small caravan parked in the middle of the paddock. When they announced this bad news the French riders got very agitated, so the promoters locked themselves in the caravan and battened down the hatch. The French riders started rocking the caravan with the officials locked inside, threatening to overturn it if they did not come out and pay up. By now we were cracking up at the sight of the little caravan with each wheel coming off the ground as it was rocked from side to side by the irate riders. Eventually the officials capitulated and came out with their moneybag open and paid up!

We had one more race that year, The Race of the South at Brands Hatch, but were reluctant to return to England as I had a problem with British passport control. With the constant travelling backwards and forwards during the year I must have said something wrong on one occasion and was given permission to enter for only thirty days instead of the normal six months. Once this happens you never get permission for a longer as the officers are suspicious about why you were only granted thirty days. It does not matter where you are, once on the wrong side of bureaucracy you have a problem. We were about two months away from flying to South Africa for the end of season break and it would have made life difficult if I could not stay that long. If I got a nasty passport officer, who knows, he might refuse me entry. By a stroke of fortune Johnno was born in Cornwall, so I was entitled to a British Passport. It looked as if I would have to begin application for one soon. Certain governments were also getting sticky about South African passport holders entering their countries and visa requirements were becoming stricter all over Europe. It was just a matter of

Good buddies, Patrick Fernandez and Vic Soussan.

The Sid Griffiths Team at the end of 1976.

time before they started shutting the door. The old green South African passport of which I was immensely proud was becoming a hindrance. We re-entered England and I suffered the usual suspicious interrogation about the thirty day visa but was granted another thirty days. We were going to be in the country longer than that so I decided that all I could do was become illegal and hope it was not noticed when we left. When we got back to South Africa I would get a new passport so I could start afresh in 1977 and begin an application for a British passport.

We had nearly four weeks to kill before Brands Hatch so we caught up with the Aldridges for a few days, pub crawling before moving on up to Sid's to sort out the equipment and discuss plans for 1977. It was always a pleasure to see the Aldridges and sad that we had moved on. Pete Aldridge recalls, 'During my association with Kork we shared lots of ups and downs but we had plenty of fun. One of my best moments and there were plenty of them, was in 1976 when we set off for a three race tour which was at Rouen, Imola and Paul Ricard and in the first event Kork came in first in the 250 and third behind Rougerie and Katayama in the 750 race. I felt very proud that Kork was competing at world class level and that he could ride with anybody and beat them on an equal bike, a definite world champ and I had helped him in getting this far. Really, the worst and saddest part for me was that I would not be involved in the following years of Kork's career when all the hard work gave him the success which we all had wished and hoped for. On a lighter note, I recall an incident at a Silverstone event when Kork, Bronwyn and I were sleeping in the back of the van. Kork was in the middle and sometime during the night I woke up startled with someone rubbing noses with me. It turned out to be Kork who must have been facing the wrong way and thought that I was Bronwyn! We had a good laugh about that one.'

Understandably Sid was unhappy about never seeing his team race. Our appearances in British races were rare, however I think the success we were having was as exciting for him as it was for us, so he agreed to another continental bash in 1977. By entering so few races in England things worked out well from a financial aspect. I had become a rarity and with the good results abroad I was able to negotiate a more substantial appearance fee at the English races. My income from racing at the time was far more than a very good job. Competitors were paid in cash after an event, so between events on the Continent, it was handy to detour into Switzerland to do the banking. We could not have looked too impressive pulling up outside the SKA in Seefeldstrasse, Zurich in a large red van with a graveyard of bugs squashed on the front, we were probably in need of a shave and wash, as we scurried into the bank clutching the tin box! I eventually got to know the investments manager at my bank in Zurich, Ludwig Takacs, himself a racing enthusiast. We would on occasion go around the corner to a restaurant and discuss where the hot investments were. Although at that time I knew little about global investing it felt kind of audacious to be sitting on the pavement in Zurich with the chief investment officer from the SKA enjoying fine European cuisine.

Brands Hatch came and went, I got a good fifth in the Gauloises Powerbike main event on the 750 behind the factory boys and we had a good end of season celebration at the circuit pub, followed by the traditional team trip to the Taj Mahal. For my spirited 1976 effort I was voted fifth in the 'Star of 1976' poll in Motorcycle News, finished twelfth in the 350 and thirteenth in the 250 World Championships and was ranked seventeenth in the world's top twenty riders by Motocourse which predicted, 'Kork could well prove to be the really hot property of the 1977 season.'

The 1977 roller coaster starts in hell... San Carlos

The first Grand Prix of 1977. The bikes arrive at the dusty hell hole San Carlos, Venezuela. The gringo with the sexy legs is Alan North.

The 1977 Venezuelan GP at San Carlos was, as far as I know, the first ever motorcycle world championship Grand Prix to take place in South America. It was an incredible journey. Words fail to conjure up the whole affair, except that it was a load of bollocks. The circuit turned out to be hundreds of miles from nowhere, and the hot and dusty hell-hole of a town, San Carlos looked as if the one horse had left a while back. I will never forget arriving there. We were on an organized tour from Holland so hotels were pre-arranged and we had journeyed from Caracus to San Carlos in an air-conditioned bus, which was to be our last taste of luxury for a while. We passed by the one decent-looking hotel in town, but the bus did not stop there. Not surprisingly, as we learned later, it was reserved for the FIM officials and their friends, which included one or two of the top riders. Our hotel was a cockroach-ridden dump and the room was tiny with three or four beds crammed in. The air-conditioning unit produced a lot of water and noise but no cool air, which was a bit of a set-back, considering the ambient temperature was forty degrees or more, day and night. There was no better accommodation in town.

The event was arranged by Venezuela's FIM official, who also happened to be the Venezuelan Yamaha importer. It was strange that some bikes, (non-Yamaha) had trouble clearing customs so got to the track after first practice. I remember the treatment we received from officials was more shoddy than usual. Frenchman, Ollie Chevalier tried to argue a point with an official and was severely threatened by a very mean-looking policeman brandishing a very large dangerous-looking sword. We had journeyed long and hard to be there to put on a show for these guys, putting up with sub-standard accommodation and inferior facilities in town and at the track, so to be shown such contempt was incredulous. I am actually embarrassed that such talented, seemingly intelligent humans as we GP competitors agreed to go there in the first place. Then, not learning a thing from the experience, we went back the following year. Okay, we were riding on some awful tracks in Europe but at least their locations were civilised and easy to get to.

When I was about fifteen, during a camping trip, my father took me mullet fishing one night in a lagoon on the Transkei's beautiful and remote Wild Coast on the east coast of South Africa. We rowed out into the middle of the lagoon and lit a powerful gas lamp. It did not take long before these fair sized mullet started jumping into the boat. It was unbelievable how stupid they were. Soon we had to turn the light off before the boat sank. We struggled to catch the little bastards during the day with fishing rods when we were offering them something to eat. Yet here they were jumping into the boat for nothing. When I think back to Venezuela and other unacceptable venues that we travelled miles to, only to put up with untold hardship, I think of those mullet jumping at the light, desperate to get there only to be eaten as reward for their effort.

We practised and raced in the most atrocious hot weather imaginable. At least the featureless circuit was safe enough, but I don't think it would have been a good idea to get injured. I did not dare to find out about the medical facilities, or how far it was to the nearest hospital. I figured it would be better not to know, to ride with extreme caution, get done and go home.

At San Carlos I was trying contact lenses for the first time, to try and replace my spectacles which were a hassle to race with. Sometimes the spectacles would slide down my nose during a race until I could not see through them anymore. The contact lenses turned out to be a real pain because they had to be cleaned and stored properly which was a lot of work. They were large in diameter and extremely difficult to place in my eyes. I had to get them in at the first attempt before my eyes started watering profusely or it could take forever. Once in they were very uncomfortable and it felt like there was sand in my eyes. In the 350 race I fell off on a corner on the outside of which was a rather large puddle, the remnants of a huge rainstorm which had occurred during the week prior to the event. As I slid into this huge puddle a stream of dirty brown water came under my helmet and washed the contact lens out of my right eye. As I did not have a spare, I rode in the 250 race with only one lens which made it difficult to judge braking for the corners. Perhaps I would have been better off taking the other lens out and have evenly blurred vision. Then I would not have been able to read my pit board, which I was managing to read with my lensless eye closed! In that kind of heat one had to set an easy pace and ride for a finish. After twenty-eight gruelling laps I finished a useful fifth for six points in the 250cc World Championship.

At least the bus back to Caracus had air conditioning that worked. We made it through the vehicular hell of chaotic Caracus, and out past the massive tomato box and cardboard communities which were clinging to the hillside on the way out of the city, to get to our hotel on the coast near Maiquetia Airport. The hotel was fabulous compared with San Carlos, and the mood amongst the thirty odd riders in the group was lively. I think the relief of escaping San Carlos and the fact that in two days we would be out of here created the festive mood which led to trouble!

The hotel had a relaxing pool area and the cerveza was very palatable. We were horsing around in the pool, throwing each other in, making quite a noise and consuming quantities of the amber beverage. Tom Herron, the likeable Ulsterman and vociferous prankster, must have reached the stage where the demon inside takes over. A pair of giggling, sallow-skinned, dark-haired waitresses in their neat uniforms went for an involuntary dip with a bit of help from Tom. That was okay. Management smiled the artificial smiles of nervous and irritated people who hoped that was the end of it. The loco gringos had had their fun, got a laugh out of the prank and would now settle down and behave. Wrong! Tom, encouraged by the fact that he did not get into trouble and by our amused guffaws did a flying tackle that would have made the captain of the Irish rugby team proud. The victim was an immaculately dressed waiter with shiny black shoes, neatly pressed black trousers, virgin white jacket and dress shirt with bow tie. He came striding past Tom's table with his tray up high, white cloth over his arm, with a round of drinks and sandwiches for a destination that he would not reach. Tom caught him around the waist and the two of them splashed into the pool a tangle of arms and legs. The tray and contents went flying into the pool, the sandwiches bobbing up and down on the waves as the metal tray sank to the bottom. Tom came up with that big mischievous smile of his, eyes twinkling with satisfaction and emerged to the sound of the cheers of his audience. The look on the waiter's face was scary. He jumped out the pool, all of his finery a soggy mess, the sandwiches slowly disintegrating into mushy bits on the surface of the pool. He strode over to Tom who by now was seated, acting as if nothing had happened. The cheers subsided as Pedro confronted a poker-faced Tom. It would have been good to understand what he said as he strode up and down in front of Tom shouting at the top of his voice prodding his finger almost up Tom's nose at each pass, ranting at the top of his voice, a staccato of Spanish curses! Tom remained poker-faced and stared into the distance. By now the management were running around and Pedro was taken away, suddenly a deflated person, with his Latin ego in tatters, shamed in front of his peers.

Add a caravan to the equation for total luxury.

The rest of us, a mixed bag of European and colonial gringos realised that things had gone a little too far. Within minutes the cops arrived and were directed to Tom's table by the manager. Tom and the two other innocent suckers at his table were physically lifted out of their chairs and frog-marched out, bundled into the back of the cop car and raced off.

We had difficulty getting any co-operation when trying to find out where they had been taken, but eventually learnt where the police station was. Myself and a couple of others were dispatched as a delegation to locate and retrieve our compadres. Venezuela was a police state so we were concerned that the Boeing could take off the next day with three empty seats.

I think they were very lucky. The station commander spoke English and seemed a reasonable type. He explained that the offence was grave and that normally he would keep them in jail for a few days, but under the circumstances, us being the Grand Prix gringos, he would let them cool off and release them that afternoon. We were allowed to see them to give them the good news. They were three very worried-looking guys in this dirty cell together with what looked like murderers and rapists. First we told them they were being held for a week, just to piss them off, then told them the good news and left them with a few cigarettes to puff on. One of the innocents was a mechanic in one of the teams, a character called Long Bob or Brothel Bob as he was also known for reasons that I will not get into!

The following day at the airport, on the way through passport control, there was an official from Inland Revenue with a list of riders and what they had been paid by the promoter. He was pulling the riders aside and his assistant was collecting the tax on what they had earned at the event. The FIM's minimum/ maximum payment and the prize money at Grand Prix was not a lot, so to have tax removed would be more an inconvenience than a financial disaster. I got to the official and he looked down the B's to find Ballington Kork. My passport says Hugh Ballington so he was a bit confused 'Senor do you know where eez Korka Ballinton?' 'Sorry, never heard of him!' and on I went. Tom, behind me had heard the chat. As I walked away I could hear the broad Irish 'I don't know Tom Herron. My name is Thomas Herron to be sure.' He was at it again. I did not stick around!

Back in Europe, Dozy and Bronwyn were waiting at Amsterdam's Schipol Airport. They had driven from Stourbridge to collect me and the bikes so we could get to Tilburg in Holland where we were to race in an International event that weekend. Our 1977 team improvements included a new TZ350D and a well appointed caravan in tow behind the van. This would make life a lot easier as Dozy could have the comfort of the compartment instead of the back of the van and Bronnie and I would have the luxury of the caravan. We kept the TZ250C which was new at the beginning of 1976 and the Nico Bakker TZ750, also one season old. Contracts negotiated and signed in January started with a marriage contract with Bronwyn. It was a lifetime contract, although not financially lucrative. It was conducted on the 15th January at a small church in Durban. I renewed the existing contract with Furygan leathers and with

Bronnie's dad, Peter Randles, Johnno, myself and my best man, Mike Grant, all looking cultured for a change.

It's a life sentence.

With Dozy and the TZ250 Yamaha in 1977.

the help of Pierre Soulas, my Parisian buddy, clinched a lucrative deal with GPA helmets in Paris, to use their lightweight Kevlar helmets for the year. Another contract which would last until I quit Europe, was with Antonio Ronzoni of Ray Boots. It involved no payments but Antonio would treat us to fine dining at gourmet restaurants around Europe, something money could not buy. Wherever we were racing he would take over the best restaurant in the area and treat his riders and crew to the finest food and wine we would ever experience. There were contracts with Regina Chains and Castrol Oil which involved product and result bonuses. The choice to use these products were fairly simple decisions. The oil, chain, helmet and boots were not going to make a difference to lap times. The tyres, however might make a significant difference and if you decide to go with a manufacturer and they do not come up with the goods, you will have a tough year. Dunlop were keen to break Michelin's dominance in the 250 and 350 classes and they talked me into leaving Michelin and joining them. Peter Ingley, Chief Tyre

The 1977 Austrian 350 GP at the Saltzburgring. Christian Sarron took me out on the first corner on the first lap.

Technician, Dunlop Racing explains, 'One of the most difficult facts of racing at the top level for privateers to understand is quite simply that you have to be fast to get the good equipment, i.e. factory bikes and factory tyres. This special equipment in the right hands increases the potential to go faster. Many riders have found this to be unfair, needless to say they were all too slow to be considered. The same equipment in the wrong hands will certainly cause a lot of grief. We had a situation the following year when a reasonably talented private rider nagged us to try one of Kork's specification slicks. We gave in and let him try one but he could not get it up to working temperature!'

One of the biggest benefits of becoming an emerging star on the GP circuit is that the tyre companies start to give you special attention. I was happy to move from Michelin. Their product was very good and was dominating the 250 and 350 classes. What worried me was their partisan attitude towards French riders and the communication problem. I was afraid that if a situation arose where there was a shortage of the desired compound, which occasionally occurred, certain riders of lesser ability would be ahead of me in the queue and I might end up having to race on tyres with compounds not suited to the conditions. I had a much better rapport with the Birmingham based Dunlop dudes and unlike with Michelin, understood where they wanted to go. Peter Ingley, Dunlop's chief tyre technician was wide awake and Dunlop was on a mission to develop their new slicks. I gambled that I had a better chance of getting their 'special' tyres than would be the case with Michelin. The drawback of being in the front line of tyre development was that you would constantly have untried new designs to evaluate. For privateers with limited resources it could be tricky and time consuming. It was the price you paid for reaching the top and it was also a bloody interesting preoccupation to give the boffin from Dunlop your opinion on what they needed to do to the compound and construction to improve their tyre!

We got rolling at Tilburg where the weather was very bad and the track rather grim. I hardly recall much about the place except that I was off the pace and not committed to trying in such conditions without more experience of the track. To risk injury in tricky conditions so soon in the season was not wise. We had a long hard season ahead with many important races such as the annual big bucks Imola 200 mile F750, and 100 mile 250 races the following weekend.

At Imola our 250 was flying and I ended up fifth in practice in what would have made a spectacular GP grid. All the regular GP contenders, including the factory teams, were present. Added to the star-studded line up were the legendary USA number one, Kenny Roberts, another USA road racing ace, Steve Baker and Australia's number one racer, Gregg Hansford. Roberts and Baker were on factory Yamahas and Gregg Hansford was on one of the new in-line twin cylinder, rotary valve 250 Kawasakis. Kenny Roberts won pole position with the rapid factory 250 Yamaha from Kneubühler, Uncini, Ditchburn, Ballington, Baker, Villa, Herron, Mortimer and Hansford. The outcome of this 100 mile 250 race probably caused more press interest and public

I cop a big pay day at the controversial 100 Miglia at Imola.

debate in Italy than any other race in history. Roberts stopped with a broken gear lever on lap eleven while in the lead. This gave Steve Baker the lead from Barry Ditchburn, also on a new lime green Kawasaki, with Villa third, Uncini fourth and me fifth. Uncini dropped out with engine problems leaving me fourth. I overtook Ditchburn on lap twenty-five to go into third. Baker ran low on fuel on lap twenty-eight and had to pit to top up, rejoining the race in third promoting me into second. I was now less than one second behind Villa, the new leader. Here is where the controversy arose. The Harley Davidson pit crew never noticed me quietly circulating, never more than nine seconds behind Villa and they never warned him that I was sneaking up on him. My crew had kept me informed and I judged the race perfectly. When I overtook Villa with three laps left his crew still did not realise that I was in the lead. I was piling the coals on with my last lap being my fastest, one second faster than Villa's best lap of the race. His crew believed Baker to be in second spot and thought I was a slower rider unlapping himself, a fatal mistake to make with a hungry South African on your tail! At the flag it was me from Villa by one second, after 100 miles. Third was Baker, fourth Ditchburn and fifth Hansford. After the race the rostrum ceremony was delayed, while Villa's team argued frantically with the race officials, believing that they had won and that I was a lap behind. They had stuffed up, I was over the moon to collect the laurels and the richest ever prize fund for a 250 race in Europe. It was a huge pile of lire notes for the tin box that took a very long time for the paymaster to count out!

The next clash of the 250s would be at Paul Ricard, two weeks after Imola. I had another great ride. Hansford and I duked it out for the 100km with him taking second, ahead of me by less than half a second. Roberts streaked off to win by thirteen seconds. I felt pretty important on the rostrum with these two great riders. My win at Imola and third at Paul Ricard gave me overall victory in the two series Bayer Makrolon 250cc championship series.

The next major event was the Austrian GP at Salzburgring and it turned out to be a lemon. After practice I was looking good in the 350 class, qualifying sixth on the grid. My race, however, only lasted two laps, eight laps for some and seventeen laps for the survivors. On the second lap at the bottom of the hill, Frenchman, Christian Sarron got out of control under braking and centre punched me, taking us both into the catch fence. Although we weren't badly hurt, the medics insisted on taking us to hospital for a check up. On the way out of the paddock I was watching life go by through the ambulance window when I witnessed a horrific pile up on the fast right-hand bend above the paddock. Bikes and bodies were flying all over the place. To cut a long story short the accident unmasked a lot of gross inefficiencies in the system. The race should have been stopped immediately to allow the medics to tend to the injured on the trackside in safety. Instead it continued for nine laps before being stopped. Because the race was not stopped, the ambulances took too long to get to the scene. The crash resulted in the death of Hans Stadelmann from Switzerland who died on the way to hospital. Other seriously injured riders were Cecotto, Braun and Fernandez. Uncini crashed first and the fuel spill from his tank caused other riders to go down. He was unhurt. I had cursed Sarron for taking me out on lap two, but later was more inclined to thank him. When I think about how close we came to being involved in that deadly crash, I shudder.

Barry Sheene and Phillipe Coulon tried to persuade the officials to stop the race then tried to stop it themselves, but were forcibly removed from the start line. After the display of inefficiency and lack of decisive action, a group of the top 500 class riders, having lost confidence in the ability of the officials, called for a boycott. Half the riders stood together and did not go to the start line for the 500 race, but some did, so the race took place. Lack of unity among the competitors in such situations always was the main stumbling block for negotiating for improved standards of professionalism by the race promoters and the FIM officials. Jack Findlay, winner of the depleted 500 race said the riders should have said the track was dangerous before practice started. That is all very well, we all knew the circuit was dangerous, as were most GP circuits but no one knew that the officials had their heads up their backsides and would not do the right thing by stopping the race immediately to allow the medics and marshals to do their job quickly and in safety. Supporting the call by the officials to ride in the race merely sends the message that they can get away with being slow and inefficient again and again. A better supported boycott would have given them a much needed wake up call.

Grand Prix racing was a 'Catch 22' situation. The World Championship was the ultimate series. In order to make a name, attract sponsors and the cherry on top, a factory ride, we had to bust our arses to get results. The promoters and FIM, often in the same bed, had us by the balls and exploited this fact by setting a level of pay that barely filled the fuel tank. Worse still, they did not care to raise their level of professionalism because they knew the mullets would jump into the boat to try and reach the light!

Ludicrously, I was still having problems getting starts at Grands Prix. According to FIM rules, the promoters need only accept the first ten in each class in the previous year's championship standings and I was twelfth and thirteenth in the1976 350 and 250 results. I was initially turned down for the Austrian GP but went to the Salzburgring and successfully begged a start. My begging technique must have been improving after years of

MOTO
Radio Mont
RMC
CAMEL
BATES

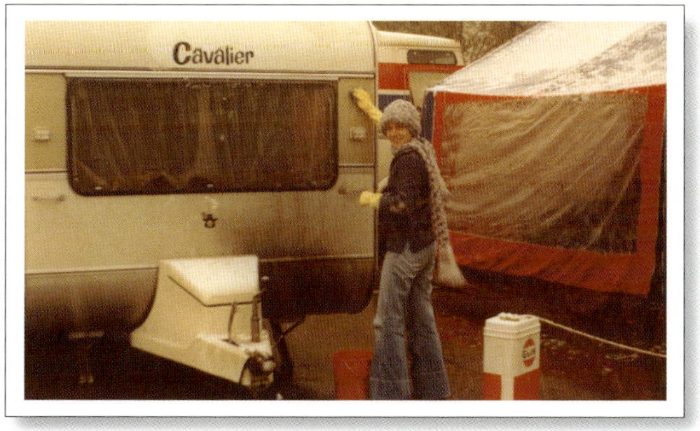

The caravan gets a wash after a long haul despite the snow!

practice. At Hockenheim for the West German GP, I again begged and succeeded to get a start in the 250 class but failed to convince them that I was any good on a 350!

At the end of the 250 race I was at the receiving end of the stick when Venicio Salmi and Pekka Nurmi got ahead down the long back straight and beat me into seventh by inches. The race was won by Christian Sarron by one tenth of a second from Kawasaki factory test rider by the name of Akihiro Kiyohara on one of those unusual, rapid little Kawasakis. Something was brewing at that factory. They had never before seriously contended the Grand Prix series as a full factory effort, yet to date we had seen Hansford, Ditchburn and now the Japanese development test rider himself in Europe.

The following weekend was the Italian GP at Imola where six weeks earlier I had run off with the gold from the 250 race. Dozy, Bronnie and I were in the full swing of things and still enjoying the travelling, although it was far more hectic than the early days when starts were thin on the ground. The caravan made life much easier, and pulling up for the evening en route was luxury. We would always pick a good spot next to a lake or nestled in the trees to set up the deck chairs and ponder life over a glass of wine, cold from the fridge. The caravan had a bathroom and toilet so a hot shower at the end of a hard day on the road was no longer a dream.

Whenever we entered Italy via Como where Antonio Ronzoni's leather factory, producing fine quality motorcycle street and racing boots, was located, Antonio would whisk us off to his favourite 'pesce ristorante' on the shores of beautiful Lake Como. It was more a private home than a restaurant, one of those very old Italian style houses with the uneven half pipe terracotta type roof tiles, wooden beams and grape vines climbing haphazardly up the wall onto the pergola. There was no sign outside and the small dining room overlooking the lake only had about three tables. Dozy, Bronnie, myself, Antonio and his wife Armella, would eat divine food, drink divine wine and solve all the world's problems using pidgin English, pidgin Italian and pictures drawn on bits of paper!

Things were looking good and bad at Imola. The 350 was going like stink and I qualified third fastest behind Alan North and Mario Lega with 0.25 of a second covering the three of us. The 250 had a terminal illness and kept stopping out on the circuit. I ended up borrowing Sarron's spare 250 just to qualify. In the race my 250 mysteriously conked out again on lap two. The 350 race turned out to be a humdinger. From the start we circulated like a train with Alan holding the lead from the first lap. On lap two, I scrapped my way out of the traffic into second. Lega followed and went past me. I clung to him like a dag to a sheep's butt. We swapped second and third a number of times and started to gain on North with me breaking the lap record on four consecutive laps in the process. Half way round the last lap we were right on North's tail when my bike started spluttering, cut out and coasted to a stop with an empty fuel tank. North went on to win with Lega right behind. I could not believe it. I was comfortable behind Lega and North in the last few laps. All the pressure was on them, I had no one to worry about behind me and I thought I had a chance at least to beat Lega if not Alan as well. Running out of fuel is unforgivable if the tank had room for more at the start. Dozy was being helped by Syd Stacey, who had been spannering for Ekerold until walking out on the temperamental Ekerold at a previous race. The pair of them got smart and calculated the fuel to one lap over the total to avoid filling up, thus saving a few ounces. They disappeared like scalded rabbits when they discovered the tank had run dry, before I could save them weight by cutting off their balls! At about two in the morning Dozy was delivered back to the caravan. He had been drowning his sorrows and was a little under the weather. By then I was over the grumps so we tucked him into bed to let him sleep it off. At the end of 1977 those lost ten points added to my total would have elevated me to second in the world championship behind Katayama. Unfortunately ifs, buts and maybes mean nothing. What a roller coaster ride the season had been so far. We packed and headed off on the long haul to Madrid blissfully ignorant that things were to get a lot worse before they would get better.

On the rostrum with the top guns at Paul Ricard. Centre, Kenny Roberts and right is Gregg Hansford.

The wheels come off at Jarama

I liked Spain. Driving through the remote areas reminded me of those old Clint Eastwood movies with the dusty villages of quaint whitewashed adobe haciendas. The villages were very quiet but there were always a couple of guys in the saloon bar drinking cold cervezas as if waiting for Clint to come and shoot the place up. Once in the outback and regardless of time of day, I would pull up at a cantina, with the stark furnishings and high ceilings, for one of my Spanish favourites, chorizo soup, a delicious, garlic laden soup with bits of chorizo sausage. Dozy used to be the most adventurous, often ordering stuff with an unrecognisable name. Sometimes it looked good but sometimes it was better not to ask what it was. Anyway, he always ate it with an 'oink'! On one occasion the meal looked suspiciously like little eyeballs.

The circuit of Jarama, on the outskirts of Madrid was a fairly modern 3.404km layout and looked as safe as they get. It was not a difficult circuit, shortish in length so practice times were always very close. The fastest twenty in the 350 class were covered by 2.8 seconds and in the 250 class by 2.9 seconds. Alan North, the tall slim South African was setting the GP circuits alight. He had pole position in Austria, Germany and Italy where he claimed his first GP win. Now in Spain, he had pole position in the 350 class again. Alan was quiet and efficient and went about his business without fuss, He had picked up a Dutch sponsor, Hennie Ten Dam, and was certainly justifying Hennie's belief in him.

Takazumi Katayama. 1977 350cc World Champion.

Racing in Spain always takes place early in the mornings, probably so that it can be all over by siesta! The 250 race got under way in the cool of the early morning and by the tenth lap, Ditchburn was ten seconds clear in the lead on the magic little Kawasaki, until he fell. Those bikes were clearly something special. I was with a group in seventh until halfway through the race when my throttle slides started sticking causing me to slow. I ended up a disappointing eleventh with no points scored. The race was won by Takazumi Katayama.

In the 350 race I was in fifth place after seventeen of thirty-eight laps, dicing with Pons, Kneubühler and Chevallier. On the eihteenth lap it was a case of being in the wrong place at the wrong time. I was lapping a slower rider, Peter Balaz from Czechoslovakia and happened to catch him at the very fast kink between Virage Fangio and Virage du Mans. It should have been no problem as he was going much slower than us. I lined up to take him on the outside. As we went around the kink I got next to him, then he fell off. I can only imagine his bike must have seized at that inopportune moment, causing him to fling it down the road, taking me with him. Apparently he was in and out of the pits messing with things on his bike and was lapping so much slower than the rest of us that he should have been black flagged as a hazard, a procedure the start line officials could implement. Typical of the officials, to be sleeping on the job again instead of noticing such things. The result was a broken left scaphoid for me and a broken leg for Balaz. The medics loaded us into the ambulance and as we sat nursing our wounds. Balaz piped up with, 'Vot happened to you?' The man did not even know we were coming up to overtake him or that he had taken me out! I felt like punching him but instead said, 'Well... you knocked me off.' He was amazed! I don't think he believed me. Anyway, after a roller coaster of a season the wheels had well and truly come off.

A broken scaphoid is a tricky injury. It is a bean shaped bone in the wrist and a very commonly broken bone amongst racers. The problem is that the blood supply enters the bone from one end only. Once broken, the supply to the other end is stopped so the far side could die in some cases and never graft together. From what I gather the injury must be put into an effective cast or better still be pinned or screwed immediately for the best chance of joining. If it does graft it might take a very long time. The Spanish doctors put my forearm and wrist into a plaster cast. It was my first cast so I did not know any better when they applied it directly onto my skin without padding which caused me great discomfort in the following days. The next step for me was to find a doctor to take a look at the injury. We were advised by the French contingent at the circuit to go to see Professor d'Autry at a hospital in Paris. He apparently had a reputation for finding solutions to such problems as inconveniently broken bones. I called Pierre Soulas in Paris and asked him to make me an appointment with d'Autry. Halfway on the marathon 1,500km trip to Paris my fingers swelled up like pork sausages and ached unbearably. The only way I could get relief was to hold my hand straight up in the air so the blood would drain away. I ended up hanging the cast from the ceiling of the van because my arm became too tired to hold it up. Sleep was impossible.

Two days later Professor d'Autry's assistant cut the cast off. The relief was amazing when the blood circulation to the fingers returned to normal and the incessant pain subsided. D'Autry, an elderly but kindly fellow said that in the case of such an injury I had a couple of options. I could have an operation and have it in plaster for the rest of the season, or, as a racing motorcyclist, I could continue to race with the wrist tightly bound and try an operation at the end of the racing season, though the chances of it joining would be slim. The latter was good enough for me. D'Autry suggested I should start exercising the wrist in warm water immediately to prepare it for use. I thanked him, paid and we moved off to book into the caravan park in the Bois du Boulogne in central Paris where we would stop for a few days to rehabilitate the wrist and contemplate our next move. I must be honest, I had my doubts. My wrist was totally useless. I could not squeeze anything. I could not hold anything. I could do nothing with it and every movement hurt but I was determined to overcome this minor obstacle. The Boer was going to maak 'n plan!

'n Boer Maak 'n plan

We had entries at a Dutch circuit, Raalte in Holland on 12th June where I wanted to try and ride. We had about six days before practice started, so I needed to get onto a bike before then to see what I could do with the broken wrist. We left Paris and drove to Nivelles, in Belgium, a good circuit where we could rent the track for a few hours and do some laps. At Nivelles we set up shop in the pits to begin analysing the situation. The first problem was that I could not pull in the clutch. Dozy modified the leverage to make it soft enough for me to operate. The second problem was that the left wrist could not support the weight of my body in the racing position on the bike. We had not even got the bike off the stand at this stage and I was already having major problems! I rode one lap but it was hopeless. I was having to sit awkwardly and lean on the tank to keep the weight off the left wrist but I persevered and did a lot of laps. Gradually I became accustomed to the new scenario. Basically I was riding with one hand, the throttle hand. All my left hand could do was to work the modified clutch, which was only required to pull off and for smooth down shifting. The trick was to keep the weight off the left arm as much as possible which was almost impossible as the arms take enormous strain, especially under braking. That afternoon as I sat considering the situation the brainwave struck me... build some kind of knee-peg onto the left side of the bike that I could set my left knee against. If I was right this would take all the load off my left wrist. We found a plank and built a padded knee-rest and bolted the contraption onto the frame on the left side of the bike. It worked perfectly. My lap times came down dramatically to what we were told were competitive times. At the same time we found an interesting added benefit from the new idea. The front forks were not getting as close to bottoming out under heavy braking as was normal on the TZs. Everybody countered this by fitting air valves and pressurizing the forks slightly. It was now not necessary to put air in the forks. Air in the front forks had a similar effect to hardening the front springs, which might not be an ideal set-up for other aspects of riding so in fact was a compromise. Under braking, the left knee pad actually took most of the weight off both arms. Most of the upper weight of my body was now transferred to the suspension at a much lower point on the motorcycle, which in turn meant the angle of force on the front springs was now coming from behind them rather than above, thus placing less kgs downforce on the springs. This gave a similar effect as the hydraulic anti-dive front suspension systems which became fashionable years later, except that there was no interference with the compression rating of the fork under braking, as was the case with the hydraulic anti-dive. It also meant that I could use a bit more back brake because there was less weight transfer to the front of the bike under braking, so I could brake a little later.

I was now confident we could go to Raalte and race. When I think back to the dogged determination with which I was trying to get myself killed, it makes me chuckle!

Although I was now capable of doing good lap times, what if something happened that required strength to control, like a huge slide or tankslapper? I would not be able to handle such a situation with one arm and could basically get myself up shit creek without a paddle if I was not careful. Careful is what I programmed myself to be, to avoid situations, at all costs, that would put me in a dangerous position. Strangely enough, when under such pressure I found my concentration would step up a cog or two and I became ultra smooth and focussed. Determination usually heightens under this kind of pressure and faced by this level of adversity.

Raalte was a smooth but dangerous track made up of narrow farm roads with trees and fences. Not the ideal venue for a one armed bandit to make his one armed debut! It turned out to be a dream and I rode faultlessly to finish second in the 350, less than two seconds behind Jon Ekerold, and I claimed the fastest lap. I could have beaten him and would have tried with two good arms but I engaged my brain and settled for second. In the 250 race I got third, close behind Ekerold and winner, North. The result was astounding under the circumstances and showed what can be done against all odds with a bit of perseverance and determination. I just couldn't sit back and say, 'Oh dear, there is nothing I can do about this,' and give up.

Opatija, home of the Yugoslavian GP, was, and might still be, a romantic seaside town on the Yugoslavian Adriatic coast not far from Trieste on the Italian border. This was my first visit behind the Iron Curtain, so I looked upon it with apprehension, having read books on how terrible conditions were. Yugo was therefore an anti-climax. It appeared to us visitors to be just another capitalist society with some luxury German cars and a few affluent-looking people running around. The race circuit, if it can be called one, was horrendous. I had been warned by the other mullets, but I needed to go and see it for myself. It was a narrow strip of road which ran along the ocean front with a rock cliff on the one side and low stone wall on the other. At a very tight hairpin the track switched back on itself and ascended the cliffside very steeply. Now the rock cliff was on the left and a low stone wall with a sheer drop on the right. The track went straight up the top of the cliff where it levelled off and started a long fast and twisty descent down the cliffside and back to the section running along the seafront. It is hard to describe how dangerous this little number was. The lap record was about 160 kph so it was not just a dangerous track but also a fast one, a deadly combination. As it turned out two riders were killed that weekend. I never had my heart in the event and with the bad wrist, did not really try, something which was against my competitive nature. I basically started in the race to qualify for travel and expense money, rode a few laps, pulled in, loaded up and hit the trail for Assen for the next round of the World Championship. After that event, the circuit of Opatija was closed and the Yugoslavs set about building a new circuit at the nearby town of Rijeka. It is a pity that it took loss of life to finally prompt the decision to discontinue using the circuit. It is interesting that pre-race medical checks were such that people such as myself, with broken bones, and nowhere near 100% fit could pass the medical examination to compete. Another case in point was Takazumi Katayama. He broke his collarbone in a race in Belgium the previous Sunday, had it screwed together on the Monday, started practice at Opatija on Friday and won the 350 GP on Sunday with a record lap of 161 kph!

We cap it at 'The Dutch'

Assen turned out to be the reward for dogged perseverance and our refusal to lie down when it seemed all was lost. The visit to the Professor in Paris produced a fork in life's journey at which point I had to make a choice to go one way or the other. Had I capitulated and taken the easy route and been out of racing for the rest of the season, I would not have become the hottest property in Grand Prix racing at the end of 1977, under consideration by factory teams. For me the choice was easy and logical. I was not going to win races and earn prestige sitting at home with a cast on my arm.

At Assen my knee crutch caused huge interest and sniggers, 'He's bloody daft isn't he. Trying to kill himself,' which of course was warranted. The race got under way and from the second row of the grid I blasted into the lead on lap two, a lead I held unchallenged until the flag. This was my second GP win and no less emotional than the first. The difference was that I did not put a foot wrong. Mentally my first GP win at Montjuich Park had prepared me for the next, and it was very much easier. I remained focused and relaxed for the whole race and avoided making mistakes. It was the 350 race and I got a good start which encouraged me to employ my chosen tactic in this situation, of going at it 100% for the first few laps to suss the opposition out. This was the opposite of Barcelona where I followed the leading riders in order to evaluate what was going on, picked up the pace and then set it. At Assen I took Herron on the second lap to lead and set about lapping as consistently fast as I could. It worked and I built up a small lead by halfway. Towards the end I eased slightly and won by 1.2 seconds from Rougerie and Fernandez, with Tom fourth. After the race Herron said, 'The pace was too hard for too long,' which chuffed me no end because it was my aim to set a hard pace. Assen always had a huge spectator attendance and I won in front of about 150,000 people. It gave me cold shivers standing on the rostrum in front of the cheering grandstand while the South African flag was raised and 'Die Stem', my national anthem was played. The whole race was captured by a film crew who were doing a

1977 Dutch TT, 350cc. 4 Tom Herron, 11 me, 16 Patrick Fermandez, 30 Mario Lega, at the rear is Jon Ekerold. On the way to my second Grand Prix win.

documentary for Castrol on Castrol-sponsored struggling top privateers, myself and Tom Heron. I just love getting the old silver screen and projector out occasionally and showing the kids. The cold shivers at the end are no less severe than they had been on the day.

So after the astounding Assen win, we were back on track and not too soon. We were entering the latter part of the season, coming down the final furlong so to speak, so it was vital to close the season with good consistent results, hopefully to impress someone out there who might be talent-scouting. We followed up with sixth in the 250 at the Belgian GP at Spa where there was no 350 race. After Spa we raced at Zandvoort where I had a minor slip off in the 350 race, my last crash for a long period until July 1979.

At the Swedish GP I came within an inch of my third GP win in the 350 race. Leading into the last corner after a hectic race-long dice with Katayama, he literally 'moved me out of the way,' in a manner of speaking, almost knocking me off on the last corner, to claim a desperate win. I managed to stay upright to take second. Johnny Cecotto was also chopped up in a dangerous move sometime in the race by Katayama and contemplated protesting. Takazumi was on a works TZ yet I set a new lap record and would have beaten him but for his last corner 'do or die' effort. The true genius of brother Dozy had developed our 'out of the crate' twin to a state in which it challenged the might of Yamaha.

The interesting thing about this race was that I was using one of Takazumi's spare rear Michelin SW4 tyres, which might be why he got a bit narked on the last bend. He helped me out after practice and I thanked him by nearly beating him! I had been struggling to get the right grip at the rear with our Dunlop slicks. We tried every available rear tyre in Dunlop's arsenal without success. Andersdorp's abrasive surface was being particularly hard on the rear slick, and perhaps my new broken wrist riding style was placing more emphasis on the rear because the other Dunlop riders were not having as much trouble. Checking on the opposition's tyres, Michelin's harder compound rear slick, the SW4, appeared ideal for the conditions. By the end of practice Pete Ingley had run out of options. Being under contract to Dunlop meant that I should use their rear tyre in the race. Peter and Dunlop Race Manager, Roger Saunders agreed that it would be better to use a Michelin to give me the best chance of a good result. The problem was finding an SW4 rear good enough to use. Michelin would have laughed me out of town had I asked them for one to go with my Dunlop front! We found out that Takazumi, a Michelin-contracted rider, had a good SW4 in the back of his van. With a happy smile and, 'No ploblem Kork san, I herrip you!' he handed it over. Such was the decency of the guy. Dunlop fitted the Michelin to my rear wheel and off we went with the warm up lap as first trial. It turned out to be the best combination of tyres that I used all year and I nearly won the race. I had all the grip that I needed from the rear, and the front Dunlop was a better tyre than Michelin's PZ2 front tyre. The Michelin rear and Dunlop front worked perfectly together at Andersdorp.

Peter Ingley, 'At Andersdorp we had an unfortunate set of circumstances that could have upset an important relationship. There is no gain for a technical sponsor to harm a competitors's potential for success. We did not have a rear tyre that would last more than half race distance and if we had insisted that Kork run our best rear, it might have led to a split. The race result kept our rider happy and evolved a new clause in our contracts stipulating that if our product was considered to be uncompetitive, by mutual agreement, then the team was allowed to run with another manufacturer's product for that event. The object of an agreement of this type is to avoid having a sponsored rider sliding all over the track with the potential to crash and risk injury.'

After Sweden was the Finnish GP at Imatra. It was my first trip to the venue and I looked forward to seeing the road circuit about which I had heard so much and visiting this 'out of the way' country. It was a dangerous circuit situated on farm roads in the countryside next to the small town of Imatra, very near the Russian border. It was nowhere in the league of Opatija as a dangerous venue, but nevertheless not a place to go making mistakes. Despite the fact that this circuit would eventually be shut down, and I was in full agreement that it had to happen, I enjoyed riding it and certain other 'pure' road courses, on the smaller 250cc and 350cc bikes. These circuits were exciting and demanded precision. There was little room for error.

I finished out of points on the 350. After lying sixth on the second last lap, the bike conked out and I coasted in thirteenth. I made amends in the 250 race, claiming third on lap nine and keeping it until the flag on lap twenty to bank a useful ten points. Second in this race, standing on the rostrum next to me was my old adversary on the British short circuits, Mick Grant. Kawasaki now had him drafted onto the green machine with Ditchburn. It was obvious even to the blind, that they would set up a Grand Prix team for 1978. Above both of us on the sacred part of the rostrum, was reigning world champ, Walter Villa.

Katayama clinched the World 350 title at Imatra with a win in the 350 race. Courage and grim determination are apt in the description of his successful assault on the 350 World Title. What a tough competitor and great guy. He earned his title by hard work and dedication and he deserved it.

This was our first Scandinavian foray. The racing was successful and the trip was an experience. The ferry boat that the entire 'circus' travelled on from Stockholm to Helsinki was a huge luxury liner. With a few hundred mad Grand Prix fanatics on board it turned into a party of note. The trip was overnight and the boat had discos, bars, superb restaurants, a casino, games rooms, sauna, swimming pool and every conceivable luxury. The special cocktail on board was a 'Thor's Hammer' and quite a number of us got hit on the head by it!

After such splendid luxury we faced the border post between Austria and Czechoslovakia with trepidation. We were on our way to Brno for the Czechoslovakian GP and the scene which faced us was unnerving. After the long, tough haul from Imatra, we were in a queue on the Austrian side of the border, waiting to be beckoned past a huge steel barrier which was raised and lowered slowly by guards. Two cars at a time were allowed into a holding area in what appeared to be no man's land. Off to the left and right, a set of impenetrable fences ran perfectly parallel, about ten metres apart, off into the distance. Between the fences guards with powerful looking German Shepherds pulling them along, patrolled the gap. There were guards manning machine guns on either side of the border post waiting for a chance to drill you full of holes. On the Austrian side a healthy looking crop was growing in neat square fields. The farmhouses and barns looked recently painted and everything was clean and tidy. On the other side it was a stark contrast. Our turn came to pass from the holding pen to the immigration shed where we were barked at by mean-looking officials. A team of inspectors walked around the van tapping the walls. They went into the caravan and van to check every square inch for contraband of some sort. We were made to change a minimum amount of currency into their Crowns and curtly waved on. It was a nerve-wracking experience and a relief to get beyond the final steel barrier with the machine gun following you out, down the now very rough road. Along the way we noted the fields hardly had anything growing in them and the houses were ramshackle. Every now and then we would pass a farm implement that must have broken down at some stage in the past and was left at the side of the road, now a deep rusty orange with flat tyres and weeds growing up through it. We passed through a small community. The people were poorly dressed, the kids dirty and the thin dogs looked as pissed off with heavy socialism as the folk did.

We drove into the paddock at the circuit and chose a spot. Within seconds the cops were there to check our passports and look us over suspiciously. High on poles throughout the paddock were surveillance cameras keeping an around the clock vigil. The whole scenario was just unbelievable. You felt as if by some innocent action like giving a local an old motor part or T shirt,

Putting our private Yamaha on the front row next to the big guns at the 1977 Czech Grand Prix. Far side on pole is Franco Uncini, works Harley, 2nd is Walter Villa, works Harley and 3rd is Mario Lega, works Morbidelli. The finishing position was the same order. A total of ten World Titles was achieved by this front row.

My second Grand Prix win in front of over 100,000 spectators. On the rostrum with the first Dutch rider, Jack Middelburg. Assen circuit's smooth and ultra grippy surface made it a pleasure to race on.

you could get arrested and taken to break rocks in Siberia never to be seen again. Friends who had been here before warned us not to sell or give anything to anyone in the open, better not to sell or give anything to anyone, full stop.

The circuit was made up of dangerous country roads with a very poor surface. It was our mission to race, stay out of trouble, and leave asap. The circuit was long at 10.92km and fast with the 500 lap record at 187.477kph. The worst section of the track was at the end of the start finish straight where it wound through a small village. It was a high speed section and the houses were so close to the track that if you lost control you could end up in some folks front room. I scored points in both events with seventh on the 350 and fourth on the 250 and we got the hell out of Czecho, not without having a mirror pushed under the van at the border to see if we had any stowaways clinging to the suspension! The guards looked disappointed that we did not give them a reason to shoot us as we moved through to the free west as fast as we could.

Pure magic at Silverstone

Sid had not seen his multi thousand pound race team since the beginning of the year. The British GP at Silverstone was going to be his chance to party. It was also the first time in history that the Grand Prix was being held on the mainland. The previous events were always on the Isle of Man TT circuit, which had been stripped of World Championship status after last year's event. By now Dozy had both bikes going superbly. Average results in Imatra and Czecho were more down to conservative riding on those types of circuit than poor machine performance. By the end of practice I had amazingly, in the face of factory supported opposition, claimed pole position for the 350 race, but was only seventeenth on the grid for the 250. We had trouble setting the 250 up the way I wanted it, but had it sorted out by the end of practice so I was not concerned about my grid position. My wrist, although gaining strength little by little, still needed the support of the crutch.

As at Montjuich Park, the 350 was going like a jet but examination after final practice revealed severe detonation on one cylinder. Dozy, 'After careful examination and measurement I discovered that one connecting rod of a new crankshaft we had fitted for Silverstone was 0.3 mm longer than the other. As

1977 British 250 Grand Prix at Silverstone. Me 20, Franco Uncini 13, Tom Herron 5, Aldo Nannini 47, Jon Ekerold number obscured, Vic Soussan 21, and Patrick Fernandez 11.

at Montjuich there was no more practice to run in new parts, and no time to do any extensive work. I removed the piston and simply machined 0.3 mm off the top of it, cleaned it up and re-fitted it. These type of improvised modifications go to show how much abuse a two-stroke can take and still, in the hands of an ace, go like hell.'

Race day was a fairytale. Sid hired a double decker bus for his clients, friends and family and it was parked in a good spot after Copse Corner. Team Sid was about to put on the show of the decade. In what was described as the most exciting race of the day, the 250 race was action-packed all the way through, with a variety of riders challenging and taking the lead throughout the race. By lap eleven of twenty-six, there were ten riders within two seconds of each other with me in the lead. According to my lap chart I increased the pace at this stage by just under one second a lap and pulled away from the mob with Venezuelan Aldo Nannini and talented young French rider, Eric Saul, coming with me, right on my tail. I was very comfortable with the pace, with extra in reserve. So rather than play cat and mouse, I held the pace as it was right to the flag, beating Nannini by two seconds and Saul by four. Saul set a new lap record but it was not enough to challenge my cool consistency. That was a hot race. I never put a foot wrong, despite being under intense pressure. I had been tested to the limit by the opposition and was not found lacking. I managed to stay calm and relaxed throughout. I believe at this moment, my first 250 and third in total GP win, I had matured into a complete Grand Prix winner.

Feeling pumped up and high as a kite, I took the 350 to the line to park on pole position with a nervous Dozy alongside clutching his rag and spanners. The klaxon sounded to clear the grid of personnel, followed by the green light to proceed on the warm-up lap. What a great feeling to have just won the 250 race and go right back out to pole position for the 350 race. I had no thoughts of repeating the 250 performance. That would be too presumptuous. At the start of any race, just before the warm up lap got under way, I would switch focus totally to the race at hand, do a mental lap to remind myself of the different brake markers and lines used on the more powerful 350, and concentrate on getting a slick start, the result of which together with the early performance of the other players, would dictate early race tactics.

The race turned out to be less of a problem than the 250. I took the lead easily on lap nine of the twenty-eight lap race, where I stayed to the flag. I won by sixteen seconds, with a new lap record at 167.5kph. A privately sponsored rider does not win two Grands Prix on the same day. It is just not feasible. I would not be surprised if I was the first and possibly only privateer in the history of Grand Prix racing to do it. It was an achievement normally only within the realms of possibility for factory supported riders. We, the quiet team had done it, Bronnie, Dozy and me, a combination of skills, from our first win at Snetterton to the strategic win at Rouen, the phenomenal first Grand Prix win at Barcelona, the Dutch TT comeback win with a broken wrist and now the fantastic, unbelievable, double win at Silverstone in front of about 60,000 spectators. Where would this end? I asked myself that night as the celebrations raged on to the early hours of the morning. Can this get any better? I was at this stage inclined to do the unthinkable... to let myself dream a little that maybe, just maybe, given the right opportunity, I could one day wear the ultimate crown of the World Champion. The recent successes and continued personal development as a rider nurtured a belief in myself that anything was now possible. I could succeed even beyond my dreams.

Heading for another win over Ekerold on private Yamahas at Schwannenstadt in September 1977.

The call

It happened before the weekend of the Race Of The Year at Mallory Park on 9th October, officially my last ride of the year. Stan Shenton called me and invited me to his end of season party at his home in Kent. The obvious implications made my heart race. Stan suggested that in the meantime I should not sign any agreements with teams or sponsors until after the party, but he would not elaborate.

Wow! So this is what it was like to enter the twilight zone between maybe and maybe not. It was hard not to get my hopes up and hard not to consider the disappointment if nothing came of it. We had travelled such a long hard road to get to this place. I wasn't sure I could survive the disappointment if this was not an invitation to join Kawasaki. I tried to put all thoughts and hopes on the backburner, won my last ride of the season, the 350 at Mallory Park Race of the Year International and went to Belgium to have my wrist operated on as d'Autry had suggested. Amongst riders, Doctor Derweduwen in Mol had a reputation as an expert. He was the one that screwed Takazumi together days before the Yugoslavian GP. A number of other riders had been boldly repaired by him in an effort to get them back on the track quickly. I did not know it at the time, but it was futile. I have yet to meet someone whose scaphoid has mended after months of abuse, with any kind of operation. Derweduwen grafted a piece of bone from my hip into the wrist and I sat with a plaster cast on until February 1978 when X-rays revealed the bone was still in two pieces.

Giving thought to something.

Many years later Stan explained what was going on at Kawasaki at the time. 'Towards the end of the 1977 season I was again called to a race meeting at KMUK, I don't remember who all the personnel were but there were a number of visiting Japanese management types as well as Mick Uchida and John Norman. They were so pleased with the promise shown by the 250 in 1977 that they said a 350 would also be available in 1978. They said that they felt that with the right rider it should be possible to win a World Championship. The senior man asked me who I could guarantee could win the championship for them. I needed to divert focus from British riders, bearing in mind John Norman's preference for a British rider, which he had voiced several times over the intervening years, so I said Kenny Roberts. There was utter silence for a few moments until one of the Japanese asked eagerly if he would sign for us. I quickly said no, because they didn't have a 500 machine. But if they were open to a non-British rider I would suggest Kork Ballington and I gave a brief outline of Kork's recent 250 and 350 successes. I heard no more for a few days until I had a phone call from John who asked if I could arrange an informal meeting with Kork to sound him out. The Japanese didn't want to make a formal approach in case they were rebuffed and it was reported by the press. I was already planning an end of season party at my house and John agreed that this would be the best way to speak to Kork informally. The rest is history.'

As the end of the year drew near and it was time to set up plans for 1978, I had to make a choice and gambled on getting the Kawasaki ride. I felt that their presence in 1977 was too serious and successful to have been a whim. I was clearly one of the better options for Kawasaki. I had done phenomenally well during the year, made a bit of history and was by far the best privateer of the season. I had past ties with Kawasaki with the Thruxton event, and my British 750 exploits on the Seeley Kawasaki were well known to Stan and John. I was a resident in the UK which was convenient for co-ordinating a season's racing within a team set up. This gamble meant that I had to end my relationship with Sid Griffiths after two and a half fruitful seasons. Unfortunately the impending parting got into the press before I had time to tell him so he was upset to read about it. Nevertheless we parted best of friends. To this day I am grateful to have met him and had his support during those two critically important years in my career, 1976 and 1977. I thought I was good after Rouen in early 1976. By the end of 1977 I was better but I knew I still had a lot to learn as I prepared to step into the most challenging and telling time of my life, as a factory rider for a top Japanese team.

Two key things happened in December that were vital to the continuation of my unstoppable climb up the ladder of success. The first was the granting of a British passport at the Consulate in Durban. The second was an official cable from Kawasaki UK Managing Director, John Norman on Tuesday 13th December, officially confirming that they wanted me to race for them in the 1978 World Championship in the 250 and 350 classes. We had secretly negotiated the terms of a contract around October. The contract, on their part, was subject to my getting a British passport and to my wrist healing. The former was vital. South African passports were becoming unusable in certain countries and understandably Kawasaki could not back me with millions of pounds worth of equipment, personnel and research and development to have me turned away from certain countries where we needed to race. The wrist did not heal but I seem to remember telling them it was just fine! I insisted that Dozy be an integral part of the team, in charge of my bikes which was something Kawasaki wanted to happen in any case. Through our success Dozy had made a name for himself and could have stepped into big bucks with any of the factory teams. Financially, my contract was rich in bonuses based on results and short in retainer but I was completely happy with the deal. The money was not important at that stage. I needed the ride to win races. The money would then take care of itself.

Life was great. I had been racing for such a long a time and we had achieved so much, yet it felt like we were at the beginning of a great new adventure.

Time out at the end of 1977 in Bulawayo with Mom, Lynn, Dozy and nephews Lan and Wade.

Part 4: Kawasaki Years

Stan efficiently managed the team to two titles in 1978.

1978, a new lifestyle

1978 dawned with the promise of a new lifestyle, a new and exciting elevation to the status of factory rider, every racer's dream. Above all with some serious effort on my part, it promised the opportunity of winning the World Championship.

To win in the first year was an outside possibility in most people's eyes. The bikes had shown excellent speed and reliability in the 1977 Grands Prix they had contested. The components were in place to enable us to do it. We had 'state of the art' equipment and the might of Kawasaki behind us. We also had superb technical expertise and dedication in Dozy and boundless enthusiasm of the young and eager-to-learn Stuart Shenton as technicians, and an astute team manager in Stan Shenton. By now I knew enough about Grand Prix racing to realise that it was possible to win a championship that year, but adopted my standard 'I will give it my very best shot and see what happens' approach which had always worked for me. This mindset eliminated a lot of pressure that I would have attracted had I made bold predictions about winning a series that had not even started, on bikes I had not yet ridden. The 250 class in particular was going to be one of the most hotly contested for many a year with the entry of Kenny Roberts and Gregg Hansford into the already highly competitive 250 arena, and the supply of KR250s to a number of European Kawasaki importers to contest the Grands Prix. Another thing that was going to work in my favour was the fact that, being a quiet person, I would avoid a lot of the added pressure that the media tend to put on the flamboyant riders by simply hounding them. Sure, my face would never be seen on billboards around the countryside and I might not attain the earning level of one or two of the showmen but I knew that I was about to earn more money than I ever dreamed possible, and that was enough for me.

A new ball-game would be having a team mate, Mick Grant, contesting the same championship. In terms of seniority within Kawasaki, although we were never, as far as I can remember allocated status by Kawasaki, Mick would be the number one rider. Certainly in the eyes of the British press and public he was understandably the favourite choice. My 'don't shake the bee-hive' policy towards racing in foreign countries paid off because, I provided no reason for the media, particularly in Britain, to give me negative press. In fact my long and positive association with Britain, now entering its sixth year, created only good press reports about me. In the annual Motorcycle News rider popularity 'Star of '77' poll, I was voted fifth most popular overseas rider by the readers. Barry Ditchburn, a true blue and popular Brit had been dropped from Kawasaki when I was drafted into the team, yet I never heard or read a word against me or Kawasaki U.K. for their decision.

On having a British team-mate in a British team, I could not foresee a problem. If Mick could beat me I would be the first to congratulate him and I knew he would do the same. Mick was a tough competitor and a good bloke. Yes, we would be competing against each other and if, at the end of the day he were leading in the championship I would not hesitate to ride to orders if asked by Stan Shenton. I was simply too happy to have

The new 'Factory' look for 1979.

End of 1978 in Durban with my sister Lynn and Johnno.

Team launch in Italy.

got this far in the sport to become jealous or possessive over team positions. I was quietly confident that Dozy and I would come up trumps. One thing I love about racing is that you do not always need words to make statements or answer critics. The results can do all the talking!

A part of the reward for attaining the level of factory rider was the quantum leap in lifestyle. Financially it was unbelievable. I would receive a retainer, all expenses would be paid and bonuses based on results were extremely generous. I would keep all appearance and prize money from each event as well as the money from any personal endorsements that I could negotiate that did not clash with Kawasaki's sponsors. As a factory rider for an elite team I could negotiate very large sums to appear at the international events where Kawasaki agreed to let me compete. The lifestyle became a glamorous one, the factory rider and entourage in stylish team uniform, constantly sought by the press from dozens of countries for comments, words of wisdom, predictions of who was going to do what, all hoping for some inside titbit they could call a scoop. Spectators were constantly on the lookout for their heroes for an autograph and souvenir photos. Arrival in the paddock would no longer be at the wheel of a big diesel truck but at leisure, or in time for practice, but not days earlier to set up the workshop and do all the preparation. Most of the time at the circuits we would be whisked off by sponsors for lunch or dinner, sometimes both, at the most superb restaurants. Bronnie and I could now choose to drive or fly to the circuits. For 1978 we chose to drive to some, fly to some and stay at hotels at all of them. What a luxurious step up from a tent, van and caravan. Freedom of choice is a wonderful thing. Basically, our new lifestyle was plain bloody marvellous and Europe became our playground.

To kick the season off on a high note, we were treated to the most luxurious of ski trips in the Italian Dolomites by Team Kawasaki's main sponsors, the Italian-based helmet manufacturer, Life Helmets. It was their official press launch of the team and Italians love a party so it was a big extravagant event. Over five days we skied and ate and drank plenty of delectable Italian food and wine. It was our first attempt at snow skiing so there was much hilarity and spills aplenty.

I was introduced to the new bikes at Snetterton on a cold wet day in early March. It was one of the most memorable days of my life as the unpainted, 'state of the art' factory thoroughbreds were unloaded and started up. Four of these sophisticated little beauties were for me, two 250s and two 350s, especially put together at Kawasaki Racing Division at the Akashi factory in Japan for my exclusive use. Mick and I did as many laps as possible to run them in and familiarise ourselves with them. They were then raced back to base in Bromley for painting and crating for the first GP of the season, the Venezuelan at San Carlos on March 19th. The timing felt good with regards to tyres and tyre development. I had built a very good relationship with the Dunlop guys, particularly Peter Ingley, during 1977. We had grown together in the 250 and 350cc classes, the product was constantly improving and they were committed to breaking Michelin's

Looking flash in new team colours.

Dozy and me at a wet Snetterton for the first outing.

domination of the classes. Pete and I had a common bond, we both wanted to win, now had the opportunity and were focussed on making the best of it. Because I had signed with a top factory team with substantial resources we would be in a position to give more time to tyre testing and development, which would be critical to the degree of success the team would achieve.

Peter Ingley, 'The late 70s arrival of this amazing talent Kork Ballington and his genius brother 'Dozy' coincided with the serious beginnings of my GP career and the Dunlop transition from treaded tyres to slicks, front and rear. To be able to develop any racing product on a regular basis against serious competition requires certain ingredients. Firstly, a factory needed to be serious about the business of winning and not just being involved. The workload can be phenomenal and the requests on the production facility extremely unreasonable most of the time. Winning GPs and World Championships is not a nine-to-five job starting Monday and finishing Friday. It is almost twenty-four hours a day 365 days a year. Secondly, you need a rider fast enough to push the product up to and beyond the limit on a regular basis. During a test day the rider will be called upon to lap at close to lap record pace for up to six or seven hours, running many different specifications for five lap runs at a time, sorting good lines of development, both front and rear, from not so good lines. As a test progresses, the number of variants is quickly reduced and the length of the runs is increased. This will lead to a smaller number of variants to be tested during the limited GP practice sessions and if good enough, one to actually race on. Thirdly, you need a team with sufficient budget and infrastructure to run exotic, fragile, expensive race winning machines day after day without breaking down or wearing out, because some tyre engineer keeps wanting to do 'one last run!'

We had all of this, and the timing was just about perfect. Motorcycle racing, unlike car racing depends more on the human contribution than the machinery. Winning requires confidence and self belief. It also requires a lot of support from the team and technical engineers. The relationship between tyre engineer and racer is very special when intensive development is taking place because of the mutual requirements, ultimate trust and faith, very important. It hurts when you fall off a motorcycle. One of the most important ingredients in the Ballington/Ingley winning recipe was that we both had incredible self belief and at the same time absolute trust in each other. That is not something that had to be worked on, it just happened because of the intensity and importance of the situation and oh boy, was the rest of the world in deep trouble! We worked very hard, we played very hard and all of the time we worked at refining the two areas. The work rate never diminished or reduced, quite simply because everyone involved thoroughly enjoyed the whole process. As a group of people we were inseparable after the work. We ate together, drank together and plotted late into the night on how to make things better, faster, easier and on Sunday nights we partied, perhaps to release the tension. Then on Monday we travelled off home or on to the next race, usually with a fair headache.

Nothing had changed at San Carlos. It was the same hell hole

A nice close-up of the lengendary KR250.

Opposite: close-ups of the 1978 KR250, a 'state of the art' masterpiece.

At San Carlos for the first Grand Prix of the season. Neville Doyle and Gregg Hansford in the background.

except that this time we were in a luxury hotel, not in San Carlos but about fifty miles away in the nearest substantial town, Valencia. The drive every day was a small penalty to pay for the comfort. The same disorganisation and corruption prevailed as in 1977, illustrated by Stan's experience while trying to clear our equipment through customs.

Stan relates, 'We arrived at Caracas Airport in the late afternoon and I went to customs to clear through our machines and spares. The officer in charge told me that they would not be available until the next morning as they were closing for the night. Next morning I went to customs at opening time to be told they had already been collected. I asked how this could be when only I had all the documents. They just shrugged and went away. I just didn't know what to do and as I was walking away I bumped into Vince French, (a mechanic for Team Yamaha). I must have looked very bemused because he asked me what was wrong. I told him the story and he immediately said, 'I know where they are, I bet Ipolito has them.' Señor Ipolito was the Venezuelan Yamaha importer. Vince had worked for him the previous year and knew what he was like. He said, 'Go and hire some trucks and I'll take you to his compound.' I duly hired two trucks complete with Venezuelan drivers and we drove up into the poor area of Caracas where people were living in packing cases. A high wall surrounded the compound but through the metal gates I could see our bikes and spares still on the palettes on the bare earth. We gave the gates a push and they opened, almost immediately a large swarthy ruffian named Angelo who was mechanic/minder for Ipolito appeared and asked what we were wanting. I said we had come for our bikes whereupon he pulled out a very large knife. Before I could get terrified one of the Venezuelan drivers pulled out a very large revolver and Angelo changed his mind. Venezuela is not like anywhere else in the world. Some days later Ipolito came up to me at the circuit and said he was only looking after them for me!'

The 250 Kawasaki was a treat to ride. It was smooth, had a good spread of power and handled very nicely although very different from the monoshock Yamahas which I had ridden intimately for over two seasons. The 350 was a different story, basically an overbored 250, it went like stink, had a narrow power spread and was a handful. It was a very exciting ride! Both bikes had identical frames with Kawasaki's own Unitrak rear suspension system, which incorporated a rising rate of spring compression, which gave the suspension at the rear a very firm feel once the first few centimetres of travel was used up. It was designed to cope with the new forces being placed on rear suspension by the new breed of super sticky slicks. It would take some getting used to. Another area that would take us a while to get the hang of was in the carburettor settings department. Hansford and his manager/technician, Neville Doyle had a couple of years experience with the KR250 and were using the previous year's 250, so had it running sweetly. Even with Gregg's extra weight, it had the edge in a straight line therefore was making more horsepower than ours. In practice I noticed

Hansford, on Michelin slicks front and rear, was phenomenally fast into the corners. I noted this as a problem to which we would have to find an answer. Mick and I were clad with Dunlop tyres and still using their patterned front tyre, waiting for them to produce an improved front slick which they were working on. Like the previous year, the mission at Venezuela would be to stay out of trouble, get a result and get back to Europe in one piece for the real racing. I got a fourth in the 350 and fifth in the 250. Tom Herron stayed out of jail this time, as far as I know!

Back in Europe we headed south for two International races which we were going to use as extra track time to help set the bikes up before the Spanish GP. The first was at Imola where we made little progress. I achieved a poor sixth in the 200 Miglia 250 International event and the second was at Paul Ricard for another hundred mile 250 race. I cannot remember the results but I do remember the fire which almost burnt our hotel to the ground.

A large contingent of the teams, including Team Kawasaki, traditionally stayed at an hotel in Bandol on the Mediterranean Coast called Pieds Dans l'Eau, right on the beach. Two paces and your feet were literally in the water. It was during the night before the first day's official practice that all hell broke loose. The first person to realise there was a fire was Bonny, wife of USA Formula 750 rider, Steve Baker. At about 2am we were awakened to the sounds of her shouting and we could smell that something was burning. I jumped out of bed and went to the door to investigate and found the passage full of thick smoke. Bronnie and I scrambled into some clothes and went out onto the balcony to try and work out what to do next. By now most of the guests had stirred and there was a great deal of commotion. We were on the first floor directly above the kitchen which was burning furiously. The fire had spread along the entire ground floor and from the balcony we could feel intense heat coming off the large plate glass windows below us. We also noticed that the floor was becoming steadily warmer. There was no way out down the passage so our escape was going to have to be over the balcony and it was going to have to be soon, because if the plate glass windows gave in the fire would become a raging inferno that could prevent us from going over the balcony, and possibly spread throughout the entire hotel. Steve and Bonny had knotted their sheets together and had already climbed to the ground. We followed suit and secured the sheets to the balcony railing. Bronnie went over first with Steve down below to help her out. I grabbed my briefcase with the important bits in, hurled it over the balcony and climbed down the sheets to safety.

The situation was very scary and very serious. The folk on the upper floors were in big trouble and some were coming down from their balcony to the one below and so on, the risk of slipping off the knotted sheets or having the sheet tear meant a long fall to certain serious injury or death. British journalist, Chris Carter was on the second floor and because of his large size there was no way he was going to be able to descend via the sheets. We found a long, robust plank and set it up against his balcony rail and somehow manipulated him down to safety. Most people on the upper floors had no alternative but to stay

We found time to unwind on a fabulous beach in Venezuela.

'State of the art' KR250 motor.

on their balconies and hope for a good outcome. Chris was later heard to say, 'All of me was terrified.'

At some stage the Fire Department arrived and brought the fire under control. Fortunately the glass had not given in and the fire doors were all functioning, so the fire was contained to the ground floor. Miraculously no one was hurt and a couple of hours later we were allowed back into our rooms to retrieve our goods. Everything was sooty and stank of smoke but otherwise no damage. Dawn was starting to break and most people were packing to leave. To cap it all, the hotel manager was running around with our bills, demanding payment for the night's accommodation!

At Jarama in Spain for the second round of the World Championship there was no 350 race, which gave us the chance to concentrate totally on setting up the 250. I was pleasantly surprised when Barry Sheene, whose team was parked next to us, hearing the 250 was not running cleanly, came over to help. By just listening to it Barry, known for his carburation wizardry, was able to make suggestions and in fact supplied needles and needle jets from his collection. This cleaned up the carburation from throttle closed to about half throttle which helped performance off the line at the start and while accelerating out of the corners. We were to use these settings often during the rest of the season. I was still not to grips with the chassis and still had no front slick. Although better, our straight line performance was still not up to that of Roberts and Hansford. Gregg won by ten seconds from Roberts on a Yamaha with Uncini also on Yamaha third and I came in fourth, a whopping fifty seconds behind Gregg. Mick was also having trouble getting to grips with the ride and was thirty-two seconds behind me. At this stage I was not in the least worried because I knew where the seconds were going to come from. Stan Shenton, 'I believe Kork was under a psychological disadvantage at the beginning of the season because he was so new to the bikes, whereas Gregg had been riding them in Australia for between three and four years and knew exactly how to set them up.'

It is amusing how most of the reporters tend to ignore you in such circumstances. Gregg was a tall, good looking charismatic guy with blonde hair. They loved him. Roberts was Roberts, an amazing character and commanded the attention of the press without trying. These two guys were setting the pace on the circuit in the 250 class and rightfully getting the attention. It did not worry me and I knew that when we made the breakthrough, the results would do the talking!

At the 100 Miglia 250cc International at Imola two weeks before Spain, I had a dismal ride into sixth, a long way behind Kenny and Gregg. An Italian journalist, Giancarlo Galavotti bitingly asked me why I was being blown off now I had the Kawasaki ride. I did not bother to try and explain our problems, but instead asked him not to count us out. After we made the breakthrough a few races later, he was the first to congratulate me on the cool methodical way we had sorted things out without panic, slowly closing the gap on the pace-setters and then setting the pace. The sign of a great team.

Dozy and Barry chat at Jarama. Alberto Pagani looks on.

Off on a victory lap with Takazumi and Franco at the Salzburgring.

The next round, the Austrian GP at Salzburgring did not cater for the 250 class so it gave us the opportunity to concentrate on the 350 which, being a hastily created machine, still needed a lot of development to get into good enough shape to win races. I believe the Japanese back in Akashi expected the first year of the 350's life would be mostly a development year and did not expect to win any titles. We had other ideas and intended to optimise this opportunity by doing whatever was necessary to overcome any problems. One such problem was with the swinging arm. Dozy relates, ' Dunlop came up with a rather larger, new generation rear slick. Our designers had not foreseen the inevitable probability of slicks growing in size so this new monster tyre would not fit the swinging arm. To remedy this in a hurry we had to revert to 'bush mechanic tactics' by heating and crushing each arm in a large vice until the desired clearance was obtained. These methods were unorthodox but were dictated by the needs of the moment. Practice was imminent and GPs wait for no man! Another example of niggling problems we had to cope with was that we had received lightweight fibreglass tanks from Japan but when we tried to use them we discovered they were dissolving gel from within so we quickly reverted to the alloy tanks. All of these little problems took up valuable time to fix and during official practice at GPs time was limited.'

Some drastic setting changes to the rear suspension and an effective front slick together with the improved rear slick started giving me the rideability I was looking for, so things started to happen around the corners, particularly entering them. In Venezuela I had seen Gregg braking far later and entering corners faster than I could on the 'old' patterned Dunlop triangular design front tyre. We focussed on improving this area, which relied mainly on Dunlop coming up with a good front slick. During practice, apart from major technical problems with crankshaft bearings, the motor was proving very difficult to tune. Dozy; 'Feedback from the rider indicated that the 350 would not rev out to maximum rpm in sixth gear and when inspecting the spark plugs the readings were incomprehensible. We fitted larger float needles... no improvement. We checked the fuel tank breather....all ok. However the fuel flow rate from the fuel tap looked a little slow as we let it drain into a container. On measuring we found that the fuel tap bore was the same as the 250 at 4mm so we enlarged the bores to 5mm and 'Voila!', the 350 was transformed. The next plug reading was way too lean and after a few sizes up in the main jets, Kork had a rocket!'

First 350cc GP win for Kawasaki at Salzburgring in 1978. Left to right: Jim Fitzgerald, Nobby Inoue, me, Dozy, Stuart Shenton.

Another win for the new works team in 1978.

The difference was amazing, the bike began responding to jet changes and ran much sweeter. This fault had not become evident on the relatively slow San Carlos circuit (350 record lap at 154kph) but on the ultra high speed Salzburgring (350 record lap at 177kph) fuel consumption was greater which highlighted the problem. Stuart calculated after practice that it was going to be touch and go as to whether one tank of fuel was going to make the race comfortably. Therefore, he topped the tank right up on the start line after the warm up lap.

From pole position, I blasted to victory by fourteen seconds from Franco Uncini, giving Kawasaki their first 350 Grand Prix win in the bike's second GP outing and in the process set a new lap record. I can't describe what it felt like to achieve this for my new team. It justified to them and to me their choice of rider and faith in me. It was a relief to tee off on the title trail in Europe with a long drive down the centre of the fairway.

I would say that the win in Austria and the 350 Championship that year belongs to Dozy. What the record books don't reflect

KR 350 inspection.

because problems such as these were kept under wraps, is the serious trouble we were having with crankshaft main bearings. They were cracking across the outer race causing it to disintegrate. There were cracks evident after Venezuela and in practice at the Salzburgring yet another failure! The Japanese technicians now travelling with us had no answer to the problem except to refer it to Japan. There was a chance Kawasaki would be forced to withdraw from the 350 GPs until they could remedy the bearing failure. Enter Dozy. He had been quietly analysing the problem. With one day's practice left, he came to a conclusion and volunteered the solution. Dozy noticed there were faint scrape marks on the crankcase walls. This meant that the crankshafts were flexing or bending enough to touch the case. This was putting a load on one of the main bearings which was prevented from moving in the crankcase by a tight-fitting steel dowel pin. The force on the bearing was causing the pin to try to bend in the outer bearing race, the leverage causing the crack. Dozy's solution was to grind the dowel pin down in size on the half that located in the crankcases so that the bearing was allowed some free movement. This, he theorised, as he tugged his scraggy beard, would prevent the bearing from cracking, but would be hard on the cases. His theory was correct and this ended the bearing failures .... and enabled us to win races. Dozy; 'The damage to the bearing was being caused by flexing crankshafts and the dowel pin prevented the main bearing from a little free movement to absorb the flexing. I reduced the locating peg diameter to allow it to move freely in the bearing locating hole. The bearings had grooves in them, so I made a fly-cutter from bits and pieces and cut a matching groove in the one crankcase half. This enabled me to make a retaining ring which held the bearing in place yet allowed some movement. I also ground the case away where the crank was touching to allow the crank to flex happily!'

It is interesting to speculate on how much money Dozy's simple solution saved Kawasaki. Because the Japanese are so thorough and concerned about safety, the correct protocol would have been to send reams of notes on the subject to Akashi where a team of technicians would analyse it and start the process of redesigning the bearing, the case or both. This process would take a long time because of red tape, meetings and the manufacture and testing of the new bits before releasing them to us. One thing is certain. We would not have won the 350 World Championship without Dozy's simple solution. Whenever Dozy improved something or as with the bearing failures, solved a serious problem, our good work was shared with the other Kawasaki teams present at the GPs so they would benefit as well but as I remember it, it was basically a one-way information stream.

One week later at the French GP at Nogaro, a circuit I knew and had won at, but did not particularly like, Gregg, who was slowed by injuries in Austria, beat me in the 350 race by eight seconds. In the 250 race Gregg stormed off and beat Roberts by two seconds. The suspension settings and new front slick that we had tried in Austria on the 350 helped the 250 and I took third, twenty-five seconds behind Gregg. We had reduced the deficit since Jarama by twenty-five seconds.

The KR350 was an interesting machine, being simply an overbored 250. As I said earlier it was hastily created and relatively undeveloped . The crankshaft, except for balance and volume details, was the same as the 250 which meant that it was overworked. Dozy; 'Kawasaki were surprised that we started winning so soon. This caught the factory wrong-footed. The 350 ate cranks for breakfast with an average life a lowly 400km which caused a shortage. Subsequently a large crate of 250 cranks arrived post haste for our delectation. We removed the tungsten stuffers and converted the majority to 'throw away parts' for the 350. This was to save our bacon and kept us in the winners circle during the rest of the year. This meant that most of the 350 GPs were started on brand new cranks. The only run in they got was the warm up lap, which was not ideal! However, we never had a problem with the new cranks or our pre-race rebuilds...a tribute to the Kawasaki quality and our teamwork.'

The breakthrough

Pete Ingley, Dozy and Stuart waiting for action.

Things came together at Mugello the following weekend in both classes. The important result happened in the 250 class. Dozy started coming to grips with the motor, Dunlop came up with a new construction and compound, pure magic rear tyre which proved to be as good as if not better than the Michelins of our opponents, and I finally learnt how the KR250 wanted to be ridden. It wanted to be ridden hard, almost aggressively. It loved to be pushed to its absolute limits. Its roadholding was so forgiving and with the new rear tyre I felt I could do anything. An area which I had worked hard on with both 250 and 350 was late braking and going into corners faster with more front brake on. Front slicks were allowing a much higher entry speed into corners and hard braking was now possible while leaning right over. Gregg had the jump on me in this area, not only because he was so good at it, but because Michelin were ahead in slicks development. I started the '78 season on a patterned front, with Dunlop working feverishly to get their front slick up to scratch. At Mugello I started equalling Gregg at braking and entering, stealing precious time at each corner! Dunlop were putting in a huge effort and it was starting to pay off.

Pete walked into our pit early on the first day's practice at Mugello carrying a new rear slick and told me in his Brum drawl that he had the tyre of my dreams. It was hot out of the R&D department in Birmingham and had just arrived at the circuit. Would I please try it but be careful to allow it two or three laps to get up to working temperature before giving it a work out. Peter said the 726 compound would suit me and that it would grip the entire race without going off, as was wont to happen once the rear tyre got too hot... and that my last lap will be my fastest. As usual I said, 'Ja, ja, tell me another one, I'll trash it for you in five laps!' The tyres felt great in practice and I opted to use them in the race on both bikes.

Peter Ingley, 'It is not very often that you know something with such certainty that you would bet your life on it. I was a trained and qualified mechanical engineer but relatively new to tyre engineering and development. I fought long and hard for this particular development, simply because I knew it would work! I also knew that my secret weapon in the right hands would be a sure fire winner. There was only one man for the job, Ballingthrop, fast and rarely fell, a tyre engineer's dream. One of Kork's strong points was his ability to pay attention, listen carefully to a briefing and after his own evaluation take 110% advantage of the tyre.'

At Mugello I was feeling ever so good about how the cards were falling into place for us now that I had, cautiously, over the space of three GPs come to grips with riding the lovely little KR250. I would unhesitatingly state that my ride in the 250 Grand Prix at Mugello that year was one of my very best. It was possibly the hardest race I ever rode, but possibly the most rewarding, influential and strategic win of my career. As usual I did not have much to say afterwards, the victory spoke volumes!

The result of the win over Hansford was the breakthrough we had been working towards and it gave me the edge over him from there on. The most impressive thing about this race was how Gregg and I, locked in combat, riding on and often over the absolute limit, with our bikes skitting and sliding on every corner, pulled away from Roberts at lap times that were over a second a lap faster than Kenny's pole position setting time. As Peter Ingley predicted, my last lap was my fastest, and I squeaked in inches ahead of Gregg with a new lap record 3.3 seconds, better than the previous record held by Walter Villa. Our race times were actually identical but I was judged the victor by half a tyre.

Peter Ingley; 'That 250 race at Mugello was one of the all time greats. It was absolutely awesome and to be able to race Gregg Hansford that hard for that long was incredible. The start and finish straight at Mugello is quite long and you can see the last part of the last corner from the pits. They came into view for the last time and Hansford was heading for the chequered flag after this titanic battle. Neville Doyle and team were going beserk with excitement, screaming and yelling after so much tension. Then WHAMMO! just like an electric light switch Neville and team were silenced with disbelief and the Ballington pit erupted. This was better than a dream. They don't make movies like this. Kork used the secret weapon when it most counted, when the opposition and the whole world were convinced he was beaten into second place. Taking a wide line and getting the power on

Vital win in the 250 at Mugello in 1978.

Leading two greats in the 1978 title battle, Hansford 4 and Roberts 7.

harder, earlier and totally abusing the rear tyre, Kork got a better run into the final sprint to the flag and inch by inch gained on Hansford to win by the smallest margin. This was an unbelievable victory, the whole team, the whole package had come together with perfect timing and our man had put a new manoeuvre into the Mugello book of impossible passes, on the last corner, on the last lap with perfect rear traction, throttle nailed to the stop to beat the world!

'Elated is how we felt that day. This rear tyre, T17 726 was the exact specification number, was to become a legend. I would be very happy to get back to the office on Monday, with a hangover, to present the weekend report! Not only had we won two Grands Prix on a first test for a prototype tyre, but I had battled for months with my boss to build this particular specification for 250/350cc machines. Basically it should never have worked on these smaller, lighter machines. The compound had originally been developed for endurance racing... intended to run for eight hours on heavy 1000cc four stroke machines and needed a long slow warm up but gave low wear rates and very stable performance. The construction was similar to that used on the 500cc GP bikes. My thinking was crystal clear, if Kork could get it to work within five laps, then it was going to be dynamite! My main goal with this tyre was to solve performance drop off during a race, a problem we were having with the current designs. The downside was that it would be very difficult in the first few laps, because of the construction and hard compound, to get the tyre up to working temperature (no tyre warmers in those days) and stay with the front runners. We were never outside of the first three, and Kork's last lap was a new lap record, say no more! We never counted them up but that specification rear tyre was fitted to many, many GP winning machines in the following years.'

The 350 race was simply a dream. To beat someone of the calibre of Gregg twice on one day was a great thrill for me and a tribute to the team effort. I had to crank it to stay ahead of him, winning by only 0.4sec. This time it was Gregg who took the lap record, taking exactly three seconds off the old record held by Johnny Cecotto. These two race performances from Gregg and myself were phenomenal. GP lap records are seldom broken by such significant amounts, about a half a second a year being more the norm. Cecotto and Villa's records that we smashed had been set two years previously. The next 250 GP to take place at Mugello on an unchanged track, was four years later, when the fastest lap set by Carlos Lavado was 0.11 secs. outside of my record. It took six years before my record was beaten when Martin Wimmer shaved 1.9 secs off during the San Marino GP. The fact that it took so long to crack my 250cc lap record is an indication of the pace and intensity at which Gregg and I were going at each other at Mugello in 1978 in our battle for psychological supremacy!

At Mugello a set of experimental pipes had arrived from Japan for the 250. Ken Suzuki, overall Team Manager of all Kawasaki teams in Europe decided I would be the one to try them. 'Kork was the top rider in all of our teams so as team manager giving Kork the pipes was a natural decision for me.' In the days, months and years

During 1978 from left to right Stan, Stuart, Jim, Bud, Dozy and Ken.

after, there was debate as to whether I would have beaten Gregg without them. They were a slight improvement and probably raised the 250's straight line performance to equal Gregg's bike which was faster than ours from the first race, having had the benefit of two or three seasons of Neville Doyle's tuning expertise. Gregg and Neville would have received a set as soon as more were produced so they were not our exclusive property for the rest of the season.

Pipes or no pipes, the result at the end of the season would have been no different and there were no special parts on our 350 at Mugello. Ken Suzuki; 'I think beating Gregg Hansford at Mugello was the beginning of Kork's four times World Championship. I think that race was very important for his riding career.' That night at the restaurant next to the Motel Barberino we sat and feasted on good food and better tales, with my ecstatic crew and Team Dunlop who were jumping up and down at finally breaking the Michelin dominance in the 250 and 350 classes, not once, but twice. I might have become a factory rider, but one thing that would never change... Monday morning, the day of the big headache!

Peter Ingley again; 'Just off the Florence autostrade at the Barberino turn off is the Motel Barberino. Next door is a truck stop which is famous in Italy for the magnificent food and wines served there. We stayed at the motel because it was convenient and ate at the truck stop because the food was better than the motel! Anyway we had a lot to celebrate and copious amounts of vino rosso were consumed with our victory feast. In fact we drank the place dry! After much protestation I was despatched to the cellar to see what I could find. I surfaced from the gloom clutching a dusty old bottle, the last remaining bottle of alcohol in the place, an excellent vintage port. Such was my excitement at discovering more grog that I failed to notice one of the household dogs sleeping peacefully at the top of the stairs. I

1978. The KR250 sporting number 6 which was my finishing position in the 1977 250cc World Championship on private Yamahas. Here Stan and I discuss how to change the plate to number 1!

tripped over the dog, waking him in the process, so he leapt in the air and bit me on the thigh! Nothing too serious but a further contribution to the inebriated hilarity of the night!'

At the next round, the Dutch, I won a wet 350 race from Bonera and Ekerold. Gregg could only manage eighth in the conditions. In the half wet 250 race I was second to Roberts with Gregg third, some thirty seconds behind. I had a huge thirty point lead in the World Championship over Katayama in the 350, and lay third in the 250 title chase behind Roberts and Hansford.

A highlight of the season was qualifying on pole position for the next event, the 250 Belgian GP at the 14.12km Spa-Francorchamp high speed road circuit. A lap in 4min 8sec at an average speed of 205 kph is an unforgettable experience. Gregg could not get his lap times down on the unique high speed circuit. After practice, in his lovely dry way, he asked me to show him where the shortcut was! Unfortunately it rained for the race and I went into survival mode, accepting fifth place. The winner was Pileri followed by Uncini, Villa and Fernandez. That was to be the last GP on the classic long circuit and one I would have sorely liked to try and win, given good weather. After Belgium I went into the lead for the World Championship, three points ahead of Roberts who was two points ahead of Hansford.

Classic Spa was hated by most but I found it unique and intriguing, a circuit I actually enjoyed riding, a challenge, like the Nürburgring yet totally different in character. A fast lap at The Ring was mostly a memory feat. A fast lap at Spa was an art. I don't think I would have enjoyed it as much on a 500 though as Johnny Cecotto's pole lap at Spa on a YZR500 Yamaha, that year, was at an average of 222 kph! It must have been a bit hairy at that speed. The circuit was dangerous on any size of bike and it was irrefutable that its days were numbered, yet I felt very comfortable there on the 250. A high speed lap such as my pole position setting one was an unsurpassable exercise in precision. My favourite section and the most important to get right, was the run up from the Virage de Stavelot to the La Source hairpin, near the start/finish line. It was about the last 5km of a lap and consisted of a series of ultra high speed fifth and sixth gear corners taken at around 200 to 220 kph, perhaps faster! It was quite a steep run up all the way to the hairpin, so to perfect this section made a big difference on the stopwatch. If you made the slightest mistake and had to roll the throttle off a little or lift your head out from under the screen it would be like putting the brakes on, the needle on the rev counter would drop down the scale a couple of hundred rpm which translated into lost speed for which you paid the penalty in terms of a slower lap time. A fast, clean lap of Spa was an immensely satisfying experience.

There were continued technical challenges. Dozy; 'During practice at Spa, Mick Grant's 250 broke its piston ring on one of the transfer ports. We had been sent a new batch of cylinders and examination showed that one of the transfer ports on each cylinder was misaligned. This caused the end of the ring to protrude into the port and break after a few laps. I remedied the situation by banging the piston ring locating pin deeper into the piston and drilling and fitting a new pin at a safe spot on the piston. It required precision machining but we were equipped with my trusty Maximat V10 lathe/milling machine in the race transporter. Thus we customised each piston to each cylinder until a new batch of good cylinders arrived.' For this kind of swift efficient problem solving, Dozy had no peer, and it set us apart from most other teams. It was directly responsible for our great reliability record without which we could not have won the Grands Prix which brought us the titles.

By the Swedish TT at Karlskoga I was battling to find reasons why I could not win both World Titles with some careful planning.

1978 British Grand Prix. Setting the scene for our first World Title.

The only thing that would prevent it, would be mechanical breakdowns and crashes. The former was a slight consideration but the possibility of a crash is what led me to choose to finish second in Sweden. One look at the track, a short twisty, tricky little number more like a go-kart track than a GP track, told me that to beat Gregg here we would end up in a risky dogfight.

Gregg excelled on small, tight circuits so there was a 50/50 chance I would finish second anyway. I decided that it would be prudent to go hard, keep in touch and exploit any opportunities which might arise, yet avoid confrontation on the crappy circuit. I implemented my plan and finished seven seconds aft in the 350 and six seconds aft in the 250, both times behind Gregg. I maintained my lead in both classes, although Gregg was now only two points behind me in the 250.

Gregg and I had a good relationship. We had a common ideal. The racing was dead serious, but never serious enough that rivals could not let their hair down and party together. Many a time Gregg, girlfriend Julie, Bronnie and I would talk long into the night, always with a bottle of good wine on ice, and occasionally a few flaming Zambucas at the end of the evening for good measure!

At Imatra the following weekend I knew that I should be in a position to try and win. The circuit would favour me over Gregg on the 250 because it was fast. He would suffer a little on top speed because of his bulk. He was fairly tall and broad at the shoulder which made it difficult for him to get down out of the airstream behind the perspex screen. The 350 race would be closer because the extra power of the larger motor negates a lot of the losses caused by inefficient aerodynamics. Katayama supplied the surprise in the 350 race. As reigning champ, he was making a big effort to stay in the hunt. His three cylinder special Yamaha was flying and he was riding it with the heart and

A winning combination. The Dream Team!

determination that made him the champion he was. Had he not suffered from a very poor start and have his work cut out to scythe his way through the field to within three seconds of me with four laps to go, we would have had a classic battle, the victor anybody's guess. I saw him coming from my pit signals from early in the race, but he was many seconds behind. I was nursing a slight flat spot in the carburation and fearing that the settings were too lean, kept peak revs down. This left me circulating around 2min 16 secs, which I hoped would be enough. In the last three laps Takazumi went for it, setting the fastest lap of the race at 2min 13.8 secs to close right up on me. My bike had not got any worse during the race. So with one eye on the temperature gauge, I decided to go for it. I wound her up and responded to his attack, turning just over 2min 14 secs for my last three laps to hold him off by three seconds.

After missing out Karlskoga, Roberts came back into the 250 fray at Imatra, but went out of the race with problems. Lega on the rapid Morbidelli had the potential to challenge us, but his team was disrupted by politics within. Also in the race were the Factory Kawasakis of Mang, Balde and Mick Grant. I had an impeccable ride to win by 29 secs from Gregg with Lega third. Of the top seven bikes five were Kawasakis!

The KR250 Kawasaki was the best bike I ever rode. It handled fantastically, had a wide power range, was as smooth as silk and was extremely reliable. Now that I was as one with it, it felt like it was an extension of my arms, legs and mind. I felt invincible. With the smooth running team of pros expertly taking care of everything, solving problems before they could effect results, we were a perfect example of what is required, as a team, to win titles...a dream team.

Lap of honour with Mick third and Tom second, after clinching my first title on the KR350 at Silverstone in 1978.

CHEERS!

One down, one to go

At Silverstone a week later I won the 350 British Grand Prix to become the 350cc Champion of the World. Both Gregg and Takazumi, the only riders who could have prevented this, retired with mechanical problems. Although it appeared that I won the title easily and it was said that the Kawasaki was so fast that I did not have to ride hard, take myself and Dozy out of the equation and reassess the situation. I am not saying Stuart and Stan had nothing to do with the winning, they played very important roles, but when it got down to the nitty gritty, Dozy's technical prowess was second to none. All other Kawasaki teams had identical bikes to ours and were supported with technical feedback from our team and Akashi through Ken Suzuki, the overall manager, as improvements were made, yet they could not get close to us. It is one thing having the info and another thing to get it working. After Silverstone, Mick Grant was still not in the top ten in the standings and ended the year fourteenth. Had Ditchburn been contracted instead of me, would he have been doing much better than Grant or Hansford? Doubtful. After Silverstone, Gregg was in third, eight points behind Katayama and he ended the season third, two points behind Katayama. Removing all my results from the log and elevating Hansford and Katayama a position at each event, the final tally would have been Katayama by five points and Katayama never went to the final round in Yugo.

This is hypothetical but food for thought. It is possible that Kawasaki would have lost the 350 title to Yamaha if not for the polished 'old team'. One example was the irreparable bearing failure and fuel flow problems in Austria. Dozy solved them, keeping our championship hopes alive. I believe Stan Shenton astutely recognised our determination, drive and exceptional ability to 'maak 'n plan' when he suggested to John Norman that Kawasaki should give us the call.

Becoming the World Champion is indescribable. It was a mixture of emotions, tears of joy for us, the team, the guys back in Japan at Kawasaki whose dedication and ingenuity played a leading role in our victories, intense feelings of gratitude for those who had helped along the journey, Mom, Dad, Lynn and Berry, Dozy and Bronnie, the Aldridge family, Sid Griffiths, Fred Hadley and many others. Above all it was the final arrival after an enthralling journey, the culmination of a long hard road from the 'Circuit del la Casa' in Pinetown to the sacred place on the rostrum at Silverstone Grand Prix circuit in England as the new World Champion.

At Silverstone we had our first mechanical breakdown of the season. It was the trusty 250 which succumbed. On lap nine, while having a mother of a dice for the lead with a flying Tom Herron we had a rare big end failure and I rattled to a stop. At the end it was Anton Mang on Kawasaki Germany's KR250 who just beat Tom by 1.9 seconds. Anton was learning to use his KR250, starting to show good form and would need to be watched! Things were not going well for Gregg and he crashed out after a bad start. He failed to get vital points at Silverstone, which could have won him the 250 title. What would ultimately win me the title would be our machine

Victory lap with Tom Herron and Gregg Hansford.

reliability and lack of crashes. I had one DNF and no crashes as opposed to Gregg's two DNF and one crash. We each won four of the 250 GPs and I beat Gregg by only six points, so the championship was a close affair.

For the first time I went to the Nürburgring for the West German GP feeling that I could race knowing every inch of the circuit. On our last visit in 1976, I came to grips with about 80% of the track and achieved my first GP rostrum position, second in the 250 race. Now as a factory rider, my practice laps were paid for by Kawasaki and I had the use of a road bike, courtesy of Kawasaki Germany, for the exercise. It was ironic that now I did not really need extra practice at The Ring, everything was available. When I had desperately needed the tools in 1973 and 1976, they were out of reach! We had a laugh during one of my sponsored unofficial practice sessions on the loan bike when Dozy got into my spare leathers and we did a few laps with him on the pillion. We looked like a set of identical twins and it had the press rushing for their cameras.

The American Kenny Roberts, who was leading the 250 world ratings, crashed in Sweden leaving Kork's team-mate, the brilliant Aussie Greg Hansford, to head the list.

But Kork neatly served it up for himself by chalking up a 250 - 350 double in Finland to lead both classes in the world ratings.

Yet another win in the British GP gave him the world's 350 cc championship for 1978, a brilliant achievement.

On the famous (or infamous?) Nurburgring circuit in Germany, the most tortuous and dangerous circuit in the world, he won the 250 class and was runner-up in the 350.

There only remained the 250 title chase with the last race in the championship to count — the Yugoslav GP. Here he needed a place in the first six to clinch the rare double for 1978.

This he did last Sunday when he took third place, leading the race until hit by mechanical trouble.

He became the first South African motorcycle rider to win a world championship when he clinched the 250 title and made it a triumphant double.

He's a korker

DAILY NEWS 18/9/78

Chasing one of ny heroes, 1977 World 250 Champion, Mario Lega on the 250 Morbidelli.

The 350 at Brno with Gregg and Michel Rougerie.

The first race was the 250 and I led from start to finish, winning by forty seconds. I had a wonderful time out there alone, racing against the circuit and the stopwatch. I accomplished the goal I had set at that first experience of the Ring back in '73, to know every inch of this unbelievable circuit. I set a satisfying lap record over thirteen seconds up on Villa's 1976 time at a speed of 155 kph and a record lap of 8min 49.5 secs. The race was a Kawasaki benefit with four Kawasakis in the first five. Tom Herron on his Yamaha, proving to be the best privateer of the year, took third, splitting the green onslaught.

I was very pleased that Takazumi and his team did not get their act together sooner in the season, or the 350 title might have gone down to the wire. I had to chase him for the entire 350 race and at the flag we were like Siamese twins with Takazumi winning by 0.002 secs! Takazumi's new record of 8min 39.7secs at 158 kph was very fast. I gave the challenge everything I had, but could not pull it off. It was actually good for the knockers, and the 'Ballington's bike is so much faster than everything else' merchants, to see that other teams with other makes of bike were capable of matching and beating us when they pulled their fingers out!

In Czecho, my least favourite destination, for the penultimate round of the championship we did a smash and grab raid, winning both classes, the 250 comfortably and the 350 after a great dogfight with Gregg. It is really hard to get enthusiastic about scratching on a circuit like that. It had a slippery, dusty surface with horrendous bumps in certain sections and no run off area at all. Gregg and I were trying to be conservatively aggressive, if that makes any sense, and were getting into some good slides on the twisty bits. Eventually Gregg got a mother of a slide and I managed to pull a small gap on him because of it and took the flag. It had been a long hard season and I was glad it was coming to an end. The 250 title was up for grabs and would keep us on our toes, going all the way to the final round at Yugosavia before the championship would be decided.

Between the Czecho and Yugo GPs, Bronnie and I were flown first class to Johannesburg, courtesy of the Sports Car Club to receive

The 250 at Brno with Gregg and Mario Lega

Team shot. From left: Stan, Stuart, Nobby, Dozy, Doug, Me, Jim, Peter, Ken and Bud Satoh, designer of the KR250 motor.

The Daytona Beach Sheraton.

the Ken Lee Memorial Trophy, an award for the person who has made the greatest contribution to South African motorsport during a given year. It was a great honour and very emotional for me. Another award bestowed on me in South Africa that year was the State President's Award for outstanding achievement. It is the highest accolade a South African sportsman can receive, coming from the leader of the country, no less. I was to receive another State President's Award at the end of 1979. It would have been great if these recognitions came with a title of some sort. The British do it right, I mean, Barry Sheene MBE, now that sounds groovy!

I remember the Yugoslavian GP at Rijeka clearly. It was the first time that we were caught out for an ideal front tyre compound. In the all important 250 race, if Gregg won I would only need five points from sixth place to win the title. That should have been easy. As it turned out the circuit was working the front tyre very hard, and our hardest front compound was a shade too soft. Hansford and Mang were on Michelins, which appeared to have a suitable compound. In the race, there was nothing I could do to hold Hansford once he came past. Next came a train headed by Mang, with Ekerold, Herron and Pileri in tow. I knew that any faster into the bends would overheat the front tyre causing a big problem. I had to change tactics by going into the corners slower then getting on the gas earlier and harder to place more emphasis on the trusty T17, 726 rear tyre. This would conserve the front tyre and hopefully keep me in the hunt. I had to keep cool. Losing the front end could mean that I end up in a dusty heap on the edge of the track which would lose me the 250 title. At the end of the race Gregg took the flag, with Mang four seconds behind him. I managed to clear Ekerold, Herron and Pileri and hang onto Mang, crossing the line third, glued to his rear wheel.

No one can say it was not an exciting end to the 250 Championship, my second title in my first season as a factory rider. Double 250/350 titles are almost unique, only ever being achieved by a select few: 1962 and 1963, Jim Redman; 1966 and 1967 Mike Hailwood; 1976, Walter Villa and in 1978, and 1979 yours truly. In 1978 I won six of eleven 350 GPs and four of twelve 250 GPs, to bring my tally up to fourteen career GP wins, fourteen more than I ever hoped to win when we first arrived at Mettet back in 1973! Other wins during the season were at lucrative International races. We entered about ten Internationals at various circuits, winning seven of them.

Congratulations from Franco Uncini after I won a 250cc International at Misano.

An interesting angle on the KR250.

Back in South Africa and cocktails with Minister of Sport, Piet Koornhof.

1979, the reunion

1979 started in the nicest possible way. The Natal Motorsport Union, an amalgamation of the old clubs from Durban and Maritzburg, organized the fifth SATT and I was billed as the star attraction. It was to be a great moment to take my World Championship winning KR250 to my old stomping grounds, and it was heaven riding around Roy Hesketh again. The circuit was under threat from home developers and a motorsport-hostile mayoress, who was determined to cut off a major source of revenue for the city, and it was certain to close in a year or two. It would be a crushing blow to Natal motorsport, from which it would never recover. I was over the moon to be able to race there one last time before the circuit closed. The whole event was fraught with nostalgia for the exciting times as a rag-ass kid, riding my guts out on homebuilt fifties and ill-handling production bikes, breaking out of army barracks to win the one hour race, seeing and hearing Mike Hailwood on the Honda six and riding around Pickerell and Smart on my H1R with road tyres. Now I was back after a six year expedition to the pinnacle of Everest, but this time as the 250 and 350 World Champion factory rider. Oh, the sweet memories of my youth spent at the sacred citadel and the memories of the long, heady journey from the Race of Champions right back to the spot where the journey started. It was sheer bliss that day. There was nobody else in the race, it was me and the circuit, alone together in an intimate secret sharing ritual. I loved that circuit, it was a part of me and I a part of it.

Hot 250 action 1979.

Pretty pit crew.

The double double

At the end of 1978 things changed at Kawasaki UK. Seth Nagatomo took over as Managing Director, and in the racing division, Ken Suzuki, who was overall manager in Europe also became Team Manager for Kawasaki UK, replacing Stan Shenton.

Fortunately, we were left much to our own devices as in 1978 when Dozy, Stuart and I could operate relatively unhindered. Ken Suzuki, an accomplished engine designer and fluent in English and Italian, was very experienced in European ways, having worked for Piaggio in Italy from 1970 until joining Kawasaki in 1974 when Team Kawasaki was formed at Boyer of Bromley. Ken understood how we worked and was not in a hurry to mess with a winning formula. He let us be and concentrated on the smooth administration of day to day team business, which he did with great efficiency. Ken was a reasonable man and a pleasure to work with. If we had have been placed under an inexperienced company man from Akashi there is no knowing what kind of rules and restrictions might have been applied to stifle the team's creative genius and make the job of winning harder. Mick Grant moved to Honda to help with their new 500 four stroke GP project bike as well as Suzuki to do the MCN Superbike Championship. Barry Ditchburn was hired by Kawasaki to contest the British 250cc Motorcycle Racing/Vladivar Vodka championship on a KR250. Mick was not replaced in our team so we hit 1979 as a slimline, one rider, entity. I preferred it that way, but think it was a bit of a gamble on Kawasaki UK's part. If I were to get a long-term injury it would cause them headaches, although the other Kawasaki teams from Europe or Australia might keep the flag flying.

The most effective weapon that I ever rode, the KR250, total harmony.

On the way to Venezuela for the first round of the 1979 World Championship at San Carlos on 18th March, we scheduled a ride at Daytona in the hundred mile 250 race as a shakedown. A lot of Americans did not consider the bike World Championship as such, because most of the races took place in Europe. I seem to recall an American national baseball series called the World Series of Baseball! I was introduced as the European 250 Champion by the commentators, probably the same guys who would be calling Kenny Roberts the World Champion. I was determined to let the results do the talking and after cruising into third in my heat, felt that if that was the pace, I would cream it in the race. It was not to be. On the line for the main race the bike started overheating and by the time we got to Turn Two the kettle was boiling. The thermostat had packed in and failed to open, causing the motor to overheat and the water in the radiator to boil. It was very frustrating that I would not get the opportunity to silence the commentators.

On we went to Venezuela. In survival mode with the race-ready 1978 bikes. We got fourth in the 350 race and second in the 250 race. Once again there was drama with Venezuelan 'hospitality'. Ken-San learnt a valuable lesson about Venezuelan authorities and how to get them motivated. Somehow our bikes got lost at customs again as in 1978 when Stan went to collect them. It seemed traditional that most non-Yamahas never got through smoothly, perhaps because the Yamaha importer sponsored the event and was connected with the FIM. Also, there were two very good Venezuelan riders, on Yamahas, Johnny Cecotto in the 500 class and Carlos Lavado in the 250 class! Anyhow, our bikes were lost in customs and practice was getting nearer. Eventually Ken pulled out a wad of cash which did the trick and the crates containing our bikes were immediately located by the customs officers.

Thankfully there were to be no more GPs in Venezuela after that year. Before we left for the last time, Tom Herron succeeded in throwing substantial journalist, Chris Carter, fully clothed into the pool at our hotel which caused quite a splash! At least he wouldn't go to jail for this offence.

Driving or flying to circuits and staying in hotels had been an interesting experience but such a hassle with packing and unpacking and driving from hotel to circuit with big traffic jams commonplace on race day. Once in the pits, there was nowhere to sit in comfort. We were at the mercy of circuit toilet facilities which, at most circuits were still a disgrace. In fact it had been far better when we had the caravan at circuits. We had our clothes hanging or packed in drawers, toilet and shower facilities, a fridge, in fact all the relative comforts of an apartment. Kenny Roberts had brought a big American-built motorhome to Europe at the beginning of 1978. It was a magnificent beast with more built-in luxuries than the average house. For 1979, Bronnie and I decided we would go that route and imported a superb Chevrolet-based luxury apartment on wheels. Gregg did the same, as did Suzuki factory rider from New Zealand, Graeme Crosby. We fitted CB radios and kept in touch between races, often meeting at favourite restaurants or beach locations en

A left side view of the neat and well mannered KR250.

Outside our cottage in Everdon, Northants in 1978.

route. For the next four years Bronnie and I, later with our son Craig, the cute little guy who joined us on 7th May 1980, travelled Europe in luxury with friends, having a marvellous time.

At the beginning of 1979 we bought our first home, a little 150 year old cottage in a tiny one pub village in Northamptonshire called Everdon. The cottage was quaint, with original oak beams and wall studs, all exposed. The village was nicely isolated and surrounded by farms with sheep and cattle. There were also a lot of horses around as the area was noted for equine events. We would spend the time we were not in the motorhome at races, in our gorgeous cottage in this peaceful and quiet village, off the beaten track. Nearby was a fabulous golf course which I would frequent when the weather allowed and there were Green Lanes for public use all over the area. I used to go for long jogs along them and the deserted country lanes in absolute peace and tranquility.

We loaded up our Chevy motorhome in a cold and wet mid April for the long haul to Salzburg for the first Grand Prix to hook up with the rest of the team who had made the trip from Slough in Surrey, where Kawasaki race HQ had been relocated. Miserable weather at the Salzburgring made the time-consuming task of setting up our new 350 impossible, so I opted to use the '78 race bike which we had in the van for such an emergency. Conditions being what they were, I never managed

Warming up the 'weapon'.

Toni Mang and Sepp Schlogl could not keep up so decided we must be cheating!

to get in a good practice time and was way down the grid, somewhere in the middle. I got a great start, clearing most of the traffic and systematically chipped away at the competitors one by one until I caught and passed the leader, Jon Ekerold, to win with a new lap record.

Here we ran into the first protest action against our result since the old days at Hesketh when my bikes were frequently stripped and then cleared by officials, after protests by beaten competitors. It was like being back 'ome, as it was fellow South African Jon Ekerold who filed the protest, claiming that I was using some kind of illegal fuel. Normally after any GP race the first three bikes were impounded by officials and sent to the parc fermé immediately after the race ended. In the parc fermé the bike would have been kept for the regulation time period for protests, if any, to be filed. Unfortunately the officials slipped up on this occasion and did not impound our bike. Apparently one of Ekerold's crew saw the bike being wheeled directly back to our awning and alerted him. The fact that the bike was not in the parc fermé meant someone could protest about almost anything and it would arouse suspicion. Ekerold chose the fuel as the target of his complaint. As it turned out the amount of fuel left in the tank would not have done another hundred metres and even though we emptied the carburettor bowls into the vessel containing what fuel was left in the tank, unfortunately there was not the minimum amount required to do the test, so the protest was sent to the bin. It is a pity because it would have been very satisfying to silence him there and then.

I bear no grudge. It is the right of every competitor to file a protest if they so wish. Ekerold states that he was put up to the protest by Anton Mang and Sepp Schlogl, our own Kawasaki Germany counterparts. It seems that they were having a hard time keeping up with us on the track so decided we must be cheating! I believe they probably did put Ekerold up to it but I don't think he needed too much encouragement to do it.

I find it hard to believe that he could be so naive to think that the Kawasaki Factory Team would jeopardise their reputation or that I personallly would risk losing everything that I had worked so hard to accomplish by doing anything illegal whatsoever. We were achieving success through hard work and ingenuity as a committed team and we would never have compromised that.

I believe Ekerold's actions were a reflection of how resentful he had become towards me, because contrary to what he has said we had enjoyed a good relationship as struggling privateers in 1976, until I won my first GP in Barcelona at the end of that year after which he never spoke to me again. It appears he, too, was having difficulty handling my success. In any case, after Ekerold's protest we went faster and faster as the season progressed with records aplenty, yet he never protested again.

Leading Ekerold at the Salzburgring in the 350GP. My win prompted him to file a protest, accusing us of cheating.

Mang looks for clues as we wait in the pre-race paddock.

NOLAN
Kawasaki
GAMA
AKAI
Shell
1 T
AKAI
CHAMPION
DUNLOP
AKAI
TONI M

Stan doing the 'Statue of Liberty' to the amusement of Nobby.

Ironically, three weeks later, at the Spanish Grand Prix at Jarama, Ekerold, unable to qualify for the event, engaged another rider to participate in official qualifying practice on his behalf, wearing Ekerold's leathers and on Ekerold's bike in order to secure a grid position to claim start money. This was a flagrant contravention of the FIM rules and strange behaviour for one who had so sanctimoniously lodged a protest against a fellow rider just a few weeks prior.

After the race, Steve Parrish, Linda Davies, Bronwyn and myself went to a local hotel where some of the teams were staying, for a thrash with our buddies. It is hard to describe how a bunch of people who have come through a weekend of the toughest sport on the planet get down and party. The tension release is amazing after three or four days of intense focus and graft which constitutes the average Grand Prix. Everyone usually let their hair down! We were right into it and I remember there was a very droll 'oompah' band competing unsuccessfully with the general din and revelry. At some stage Bronnie's demon took over and suddenly she was up on the long wooden table at which we were seated, followed by Linda, where the two of them proceeded to goose step up and down in perfect timing to the band, left finger under the nose, right arm out in a Nazi salute, John Cleese fashion. It was so spontaneous and silly that it had us rolling on the floor. Nothing beat a post GP party.

At the next GP at Hockenheim we suffered another practice calamity and qualified way down the list in both classes. Early in the 350 race I was third until I suffered what felt like a mild seizure. I pulled the clutch in and free-wheeled for a bit then decided to try and start up and continue. It fired up and ran perfectly but I had lost about sixteen seconds. I got my head back under the screen and pulled through from ninth to fourth at the end. Ekerold on a Yamaha won from Mang after a close dice. The 250 went great and I won with a new lap record. Second was whizkid, 19 year old American Randy Mamola, on a Yamaha, in his first GP season. He was going well, beating Mang by one second.

We had a good laugh one day in the town of Hockenheim. After practice was over, a group of us decided to go to the health spa to have a sauna and relax in the hot tub. At the main entrance we said goodbye to our girlfriends and wives and went through the respective male/female entrances. What we had not bargained for was that the day we went was unisex day so it was boys and girls together. When we came out of the men's changing room stark naked we came face to face with our partners who were in a similar state of undress. There was a lot of laughing and shrieking going on as we tried to maintain our dignity. The girls went off to the sauna and Steve Parrish and I ended up in the hot tub with some lovely German frauleins. Stavros, who will do anything for a laugh, kept dipping his head below the surface of the water with eyes wide open obviously hoping to catch a glimpse of something interesting. The fact that the water was extremely hot and probably scalding his eyeballs did not deter him!

At Imola for the Italian GP, big end failure on the last lap put paid to a win on the 350. On the first lap Ekerold out-braked himself and me at Curva Tosa, but ran wide past my front wheel almost taking me out, totally out of control. On the next lap I was not surprised to see him tangled in the catch fence at Rivazza. I think he used to see red when he saw the green bike because, by his own admission, he lost his cool and crashed. He would regret not exercising self control, because he could have picked up second or third place points to stretch his lead in the Championship over me by at least eleven points. I set the fastest lap but it was small consolation. Hansford, who was just three seconds behind me when I stopped, took the flag for his first win of the season. On the classy KR250, a bike with which I was so much in harmony, I ripped to a clear win from Mamola who was performing very impressively on a private Yamaha. Barry Ditchburn, also on a KR250 and having a rare GP outing, took third just ahead of Villa and a huge fifty-seven seconds behind me. I was now twelve points clear of Mamola and very surprised that there was no challenge coming from the other factory teams including our Kawasaki counterparts.

In Spain at Jarama for the next round, the chorizo soup must have turbocharged me. Maybe Gregg had tried some as well because I won both races with Gregg second. He was at last starting to get his act together after a lack-lustre start to the season. Ever since I beat him twice at Mugello in 1978, he seemed to lose a bit of fire. Michel Frutschi, the likeable Swiss rider, showed his face on the rostrum for the second time in two weeks. third in the 250 was Graziano Rossi on the Morbidelli. Rossi would spring some surprises as the year went on.

Winning races still gave me the biggest thrill ever. One of the most enjoyable things at the time was the complete unity of the team. Every success welded us more firmly together and automatically sharpened everybody's senses and resolve. There was never an occasion for harsh words between any of the personnel. It was never necessary to motivate them... the results were our leader. The best part of winning, such as at Jarama, was to have dinner with the team afterwards and relive the moments and plan the next. We were not a flamboyant team so did not attract a lot of the media. Often there were times when it appeared that some of the media were offering explanations for our wins. The bikes are faster, or so and so got a bad start, instead of accepting that such a quiet bunch of non-showmen can do great things. Most, but not all of the press, understandably prefer showmen and sharp talkers because it is easier to write about them and they create more public interest. In many ways I knew that we would achieve more and do it easier without the pressure and distraction of too much attention. The fact that none of us were extroverts helped set the game plan, action rather than attraction. I believe for the two years, 1978 and 1979 Dozy, Stuart, Kawasaki and I were by a long chalk the most organized and effective combination of all and without any fuss whatsoever. Had we got our mittens on a competitive, race-ready 500 we would have made an excellent account of ourselves, giving the same level of performance in the awning and on the track as Dozy and I gave with our outdated TD2B and the Seeley H1, the Griffiths Yamahas and the KR250 and 350 Kawasakis. How it would have panned out in terms of finishing positions? I immodestly state that I know it would have been very good.

Alas, on the weekend after we raced and celebrated the double victory at Jarama, we were devastated by the news of Tom Herron's death after a high speed crash at the North West 200 in Ireland. All who knew him went into deep mourning for the loss of one of our favourites. Tom had picked up a ride for 1979 with Suzuki GB to do 500 GPs. He turned in excellent, impressive results in the first four GPs, including two thirds and a fourth, consistently ahead of team mates, Sheene and Parrish. Tom, a product of Irish road racing was racing at home, in front of his own people when he lost his life to the sport he loved.

At the Austrian GP the team recognised and solved another problem which would have caused a retirement from the race, which I won. Dozy; 'The new 'pork chop' style crankshafts for the 350 were more robust than the 250 ones. However, to save money the young designer was ordered to use lead-based metal to balance the cranks. This was not a good idea. At Yugoslavia the matter came to a head with the motors running with '100% leaded' petrol. We found during practice that under the heat, vibration and centrifugal forces, the lead in the crankshafts was undergoing plastic deformation and looked as if it was going to spread itself about. We decided that we would revert to the 250 cranks and built some press tools required to remove the aluminium 'stuffers' from the 250 cranks and fitted them to the 350. Gregg's team opted for the leaded jobs and paid the penalty. The lead came out during the race forcing Gregg to retire. His engine ended up with a perfect lead moulding of the combustion chamber!'

At last another 250 team got going and in the next three 250 rounds Graziano Rossi, on the Morbidelli, gave us a hiding. He won at Yugoslavia, he won at the Dutch and he won in Sweden. The man had become so quick off the line and into the first bends, it seemed like he was starting on hot tyres, yet warmers were not yet invented. We had some problems but not enough to take anything away from Rossi. The question on everybody's lips was... how long could he keep it up? I won the 350 at Yugo but went out at the Dutch with an engine seizure on the first lap. There was no 350 race in Sweden.

Kenny's winning crew: Kel Carruthers, Nobby Clark and Trevor Tilbury at Finland in 1979 with their TZ500.

Strike strife in Belgium

Traditionally the Belgian GP is the weekend after the Dutch and nothing about the date had changed. What had been changed, however, was the circuit. In accordance with plans agreed at the FIM congress at the end of 1977, Spa, Imatra and Brno had to be substantially modified by their respective 1979 GPs to improve safety if they were to retain World Championship status.

Over a year before the 1979 race, work at Spa began on a link between two sections of the old circuit, reducing it from 14.1km to 6.95km. The new section had good run off area and the average speed of a lap would be brought down from 222 kph to about 150 kph for 500s. This was good news. The bad news was that the surfacing took place only days before the GP, the result being that the surface had not cured and was unusable. We tried to practise on it but there was no grip regardless of what tyres we tried. Oil is an ingredient of asphalt and with newly laid asphalt of the type laid at Spa, a film of oil sits on the surface and causes poor grip until the asphalt has effectively 'weathered'. The Belgian GP is well supported by spectators

The new and old Spa circuit. It was reduced from 14.12km to 6.947km reducing the average lap speed for 500s from over 220kph to 152kph.

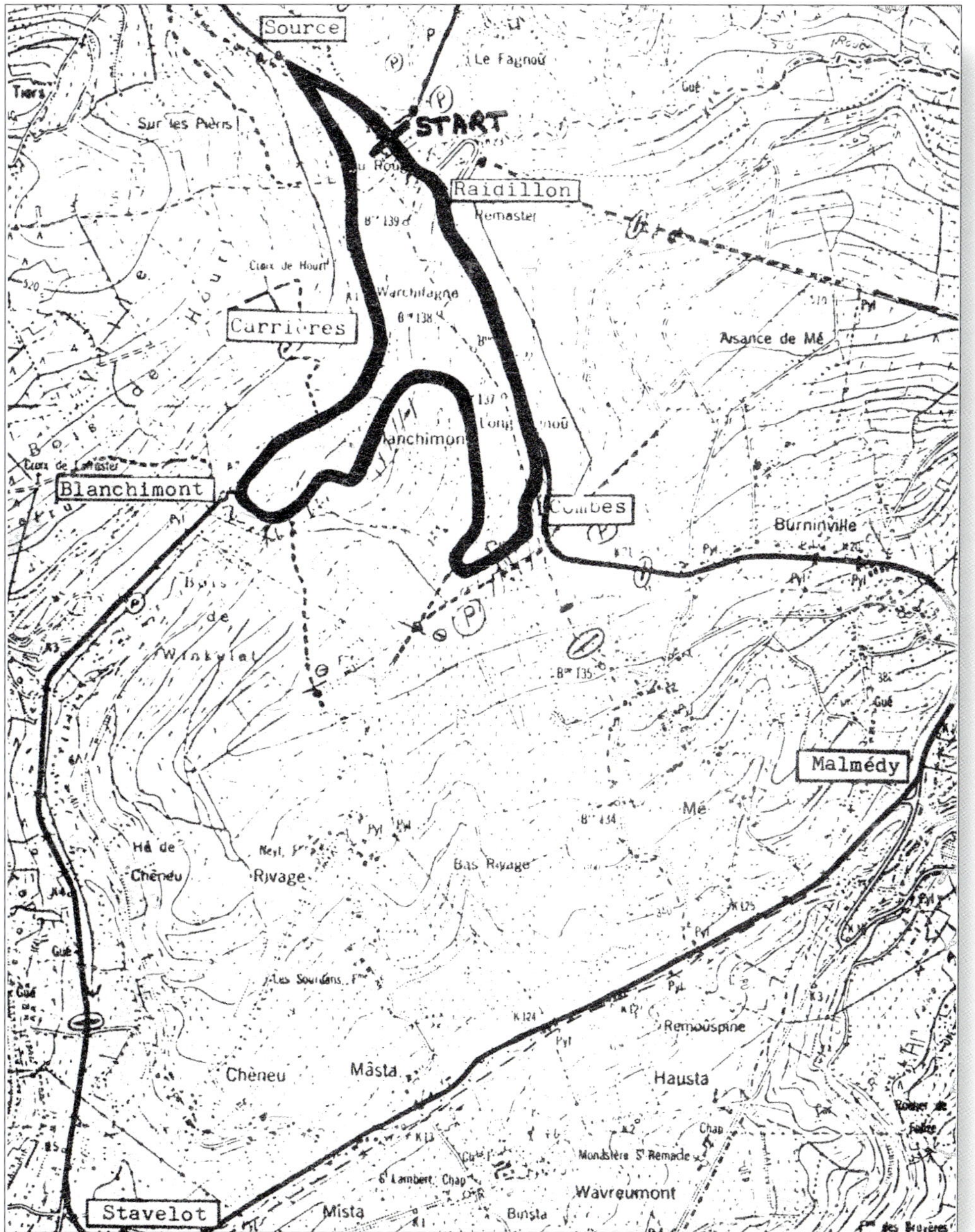

Media interest in 1979.

with about 60,000 people from all over Europe. The promoters, not wanting to miss out on the huge revenue from the spectators, wanted their race to go ahead whether the surface was safe to use or not. As in the Monza tragedy of 1973 the organisers were determined to continue regardless of the potential to kill. To cut a long and involved story short, the majority of riders from all classes including the top Championship contenders, having no alternative and after countless heated discussions, packed up the afternoon before the race and left the track.

I believe Kenny Roberts was mostly responsible for the inspiration that created the unity. He brought together the top riders and other key people from the media and other areas who were interested in a better, more professional future for GP racing as a whole. Had this episode happened two or three years earlier it is almost certain that the races would have taken place with no one determined and passionate enough to lead the competitors on the correct path.

Gregg took it this time.

Racing did take place but only with riders who would normally have battled to qualify further forward than the last few rows of the grid. The spectators arrived, the vast majority of them expecting the usual spectacle. They were not warned at the gate that there had been a walk-out by the top contenders. Many demanded a refund but the promoters refused. Altogether the affair brought out the worst in the promoters and the FIM, exposing their total and blind self-interest.

Walking out of a Grand Prix is a very complicated matter and a decision not lightly taken. Everybody would lose money from it. Sponsors would not get the mileage they were paying for and that had been written into legal binding contracts. The factories would have spent a fortune preparing for the race and getting personnel and equipment to the venue. Associated trade such as the tyre companies would have incurred heavy expenses to be there. The competitors, many not of excessive means, would have spent to be there and not get paid the FIM pittance for it. Media personnel would have travelled from all over the world, although the sensational turn of events would probably sell more copy than the usual Grand Prix! Spectators would have travelled from far and wide only to be charged unfairly full price to see a non-event. The list of casualties from such a walk out is endless. Ken Suzuki, on behalf of Kawasaki, without hesitation backed my decision to take whatever action that was deemed necessary by the united riders.

Desperately wanting vengeance, the FIM imposed fines and licence suspensions, firstly on Kenny Roberts and Virginio Ferrari, who they considered the ringleaders. Eventually they levied fines on all participants of the walkout. As far as I remember no-one ever paid the fines. There were never any hearings or charges along with the fines so I imagine they would never have stood up should the affair have been taken to a court of law. The FIM realised they could no longer be judge, jury and executioner as they had so often got away with in the past.

There was to be a lot of positive kickback from the walkout. The most positive outcome was that competitors had united and this sent a signal to all promoters that the tide had turned. More than a safety or money dispute, the rider's dignity was at stake and some of us took a bold step to restore some of it.

Back to racing. After 250 practice at Karlskoga in Sweden, Gregg was 0.036 sec faster than me with Rossi one second behind me. The three of us set a tough pace with the next rider, Mamola, over one second behind. The stage was set for a potential showdown as both Gregg and I wanted to challenge Rossi's audacious onslaught. A part of successful Grand Prix racing in that era when riders had to push-start their bikes, was the art of fast starting. A polished and practised starting procedure increases the potential for a swift getaway which could set a good platform from which to analyse the situation and plan race tactics. Losing time at the start simply made it tougher to challenge the opposition. From a poor start you had to make up time and negotiate traffic and with races often being won by fractions of a second, losing a few seconds at the start could mean the difference between winning and losing.

Gregg Hansford had made life hard for himself in 1978 by starting badly too often. He was much better in 1979 and Rossi had been outstanding in the last few races. Unfortunately on race day a shower just before the 250 race wet the track taking the edge off what could have been a good dice. On an extremely rare occasion, I was left on the line with a loaded up motor. By the time it fired up I was last, but at the end of lap one, was up to twenty-sixth. Rossi took the lead from Gregg on lap four and took the flag by just under four seconds. I climbed steadily through to fifth at the flag. So Rossi zapped us again but they had left their charge in the 250cc championship a bit late, so at that stage I had a comfortable lead of twenty-four points over Gregg while Rossi closed to two points behind Gregg.

We were entertained to the most amazing display by an aircraft from the Swedish Airforce on the day before practice started. One minute we were going about our business in the paddock and the next minute all hell broke loose as a Saab Viggen ripped past, barely clearing the flagpoles. For the next half hour we were treated to some awesome manoeuvres by that beautiful delta wing aircraft with the extra little wings on the front. It buzzed the paddock, did rolls, steep turns, climbs, dives and plenty more. It passed so low and close that you could almost feel the heat from the jet nozzle as it went by. Bronnie and I loved staying in the paddock in our motorhome while on the GP trail. It was a fun and interesting place to be. All of the privateers with whom we had spent so many good times stayed in the paddock and on most evenings someone would have a barbecue going. We would get on over, hurl a steak on the grill and have a beer or glass of wine. If there was nothing going on in the paddock, we would go to the nearest town and dine or find a cosy bar or just sit in someone's motorhome and chat. To this day most of our best friends are from those Grand Prix years. There was an incredible bond between most of us, brought about by sharing this incredible lifestyle and adventure.

One particular night a lovely character by the name of Victor Soussan, one of the leading privateers with whom I had crossed swords on the track on occasions, turned up at our motorhome with a lamp and baseball bat and invited me to go hunting with him. Vic, an Australian citizen, was born in Morocco of Jewish parents who moved to Australia when he was a teenager. He had spent a lot of time in France, was fluent in French and spoke English with a French Australian accent. Vic was a fiery and temperamental person. We loved him and his Australian wife Jenny, great characters of the sport. I asked him what in hell we would hunt with a baseball bat and lamp. Of course it was his secret and I would have to go with him to find out. We went deep into the bush near the circuit before he gave simple instructions, I was to walk along slowly in the bush shining the light until we found a rabbit. It would be mesmerised by the lamp and he would attack it with the baseball bat. Voila! mate, next day's meal. We trudged around for ages in the forest getting bitten by mosquitoes, stepping in mud and tripping over logs, but never so much as even saw a rabbit. This ruined Vic's evening but I was rather pleased. I was not keen to be an accessory to bunny bashing!

Gregg and I at it again - somewhere.

Cat and mouse again.

The Finnish GP the following weekend was another controversial event. At the 1977 FIM Congress it was agreed that Imatra was one of the circuits which had to be modified to conform to certain safety standards. In response, the circuit was shortened from 6.030km to 4.95km cutting out a section with some dangerous curves which resulted in reducing the 500 lap speed from 168kph in 1978 to 152kph in 1979. The alterations however, did not come near to upgrading the circuit to acceptable standards. The rest of the tree-lined circuit had not been altered and was still very dangerous. Emotions were still running high after the Belgian debacle. New thinking and professionalism in motorcycle Grand Prix racing had outgrown that style of circuit. The newly formed Association of Professional Motorcyclists tabled a number of demands regarding Imatra, to be set out at the next FIM congress, and reluctantly agreed to compete. To make matters worse for the disgruntled riders it started raining just before the 350 race. It was wet when we went to the start line but minutes before the start, the tap opened wide and it began bucketing down. The race was delayed long enough for riders to fit full wet tyres before re-assembling for the warm-up lap. We, that is all of about thirty riders on the grid, possibly should have decided to park our bikes indefinitely until conditions improved. On the grid, minutes before the start when everyone is on edge is the most difficult time to get a consensus, particularly from such a diversity of personalities, a lot of whom did not want to be influenced or united, each with their individual beliefs, suspicions and responsibilities. Everyone was focussed on the race and eager to get going, so after a short delay off we went.

In the race, Hansford led from Patrick Fernandez. I was in third, merely circulating at a safe pace....until after a few laps, the deepening puddles at the end of the main straight caught me out. I estimate that I was doing about 240 kph, some 20 kph down on the normal top speed which the 350 would probably attain at the end of the long main straight. In these dangerous and difficult conditions, rain smeared the screen and visor, blurring and distorting vision. I sat up a touch early from a half-crouch to find my braking point, found it and gently applied the brakes as in the previous laps. The front wheel locked, aquaplaned and dumped me unceremoniously onto the track. Falling on a wet track is okay, it hurts less than a dry one because the friction of the leather suit rubbing on the surface is far less. The downside is that you slide further, which is okay if there is nothing to slide into. There I was, skating down Imatra Straight, on my back at over 200 kph, watching my 350 skidding along in front of me. Just when I thought that this was going to be okay, I started drifting towards the left edge of the track. The camber of the surface was slightly inclined towards that side and was redirecting my direction of travel. The big problem was that about two metres off the edge, trees lined the length of the straight. It was not going to be too long before I would leave the track and make painful contact with the trees. I was still going fast enough to get seriously hurt, even though the straw bale tied to each tree would soften the impact. I set myself up on my

Imatra 1979.

Big get-off at Imatra in the 350 GP, my first crash in over two years.

right side facing forwards, and by kind of paddling my right arm and left leg, controlled my direction and managed to remain on the track, eventually coming to a stop about 40 metres past the corner on the slip road. I picked the bike up and was surprised to see that the screen was not even broken. After a quick check to see if the handlebars, footpegs and front brake lever were usable, I restarted and jumped on to rejoin the race in ninth place. I climbed back to seventh place but the crash had worn through the outer clutch plate so the clutch was slipping badly. I slowed down to prevent cooking the plates and limped home in ninth to score two points. I recall sliding down the track very clearly. In life-threatening situations such as this, my focus was razor sharp. There was so much water on the surface of the track that my body never came into contact with the surface until it broke through the cushion for the last ten metres. Until then it was an almost enjoyable, silky smooth, ultra high speed slide a few millimetres off the tar. I did not have a scratch and my leathers were not damaged at all. In a way I was relieved to have got the crash out of the way. It broke an amazing crash-free period of just over two years, which had become a bit of a distraction! I made no mistakes in the 250 race which took place after the big crash. In treacherous conditions of a track that was beginning to dry in places, I won, beating Gregg by a miniscule 0.3 secs. Rossi broke his good run with a DNF and the likeable Fernandez was third. He was having an impressive season.

One day Vic and Jenny invited Patrick to their caravan for breakfast. Being a good Aussie, Jennie always had a jar of Vegemite on the table. Patrick took a piece of toast and laid it thick with the dark salty tasting substance and took a huge bite. Once his fussy French tastebuds got the message that it was not chocolate spread he got the fright of his life and rushed outside to spit it out. We never let him live that one down!

After Finland Fernandez took over the lead in the 350 championship two points ahead of me, with Gregg six points behind me. In the 250 championship I had a comfortable twenty-seven point lead over Gregg. Rossi failed to score in

Pole position for the start of the 1979 250cc British Grand Prix. I exercised my option to start from the right of the grid rather than the traditional left to have the safer inside line during the scramble for Copse Corner, a right hander.

Finland so lost some ground, still third on the log. With three rounds to go in Britain, Czecho and France, I was feeling confident of doing the double double. Superb preparation by our mechanics gave us an enviable 100% reliability record that ensured that we scored points in every race started. In a fine, flawless end of season display, I clinched my third World Title, the 250, at Silverstone with a win and went on to win the remaining two rounds in Czechoslovakia and France, for good measure.

The 250 race at Silverstone was memorable. Rossi was back on form and raced off at the start, opening quite a gap. I gradually hauled him in, setting a lap record of 178 kph in the process, to close within three seconds on the last lap. I knew I could not catch and overtake him unless he made a mistake, but kept the pressure on. I knew he would be getting the message from his pit crew and there was no knowing how he would react. Approaching Club Corner, the third corner from home I was about two seconds behind. I could clearly distinguish his classic 'knees in' riding style and see his long hair trailing from under his helmet in the breeze behind him. He tipped it into the corner, and to my surprise, lost it and went bouncing off into the catch fence. I felt a twinge of disappointment for him at having slipped up after such a good ride as I took the flag for my fourth British Grand Prix win and third World Championship.

My fifth British GP win came on the same day, about two hours later, when I took a close 350 race from Gregg by 1.5 seconds to go back into the lead in the title chase.

At Silverstone, Dozy got the chance to test some theories he had been working on. For a couple of weeks before he had had his head buried in an old set of 250 cylinders and heads, cutting, machining and grinding until he had what he wanted. He cut two small extra ports through each side of the exhaust to increase the port area, machined the bottom of the cylinder to lower the port timings by about 2mm then raised the top of the transfer ports about 2mm to get them back to where they were. He modified the cylinder head to make space for the piston that was now protruding at the top of the stroke. Finally he changed the angle of the expansion chamber header. If I remember correctly he steepened the angle of the first cone by about a degree. I took a few laps on his creation and found that it would not pull to as high rpm as a standard motor by about 500rpm, but seemed to pull a bit better at the bottom of the range. It did not feel all that impressive but when I pulled in I was astounded to see my lap times. At the end of the day when we had set up both bikes, a standard one and the Dozy-tuned one, the latter was one second faster than the standard one I had ridden all year. I took pole position for the race on the Dozy-tuned bike. His capabilities never failed to amaze. All his working out was done on paper and in his head and he never, throughout our association, had access to a dynamometer. He simply created more power from the KR250 at reduced rpm, a phenomenal feat. We reverted back to standard components for the race because we would have been in trouble if the modified bike had broken down.

1979, British Grand Prix, high speed at Woodcote, number 5 is Anton Mang and 39 is Roland Freymond.

At Brno in Czechoslovakia the following weekend I got the measure of Rossi, only this time we were joined by his team mate Paolo Pileri who was going like a rocket and who had set the fastest lap in practice to claim pole position. The Morbidelli team was really getting their act together, fortunately for me a bit late in the season. Brno is a fast, dangerous track made up of country roads, similar in character to the Belgian road circuits, with little or no run-off space on the outside of the bends. When someone falls the bike and rider have no option but to thump into the straw bales lining the circuit and get bounced back into the track, making it rather hazardous for those following. For this reason I did not want to hang around behind the furiously duelling Morbidelli teamsters for too long lest they tangle. I decided to make a break and try and pull away a little so I would have the clear road. I put my chin on the tank and opened a five second comfort zone, in so doing set the fastest lap of the race at 167kph, over two seconds better than Pileri's pole-setting time. At the flag I was 5 seconds up on Rossi who squeezed past

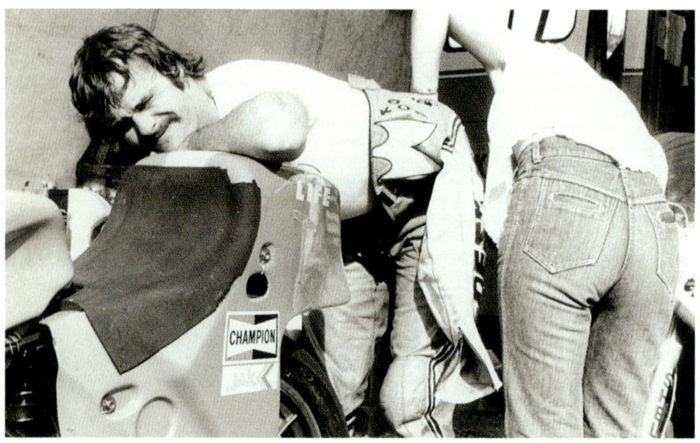

Bottoms inspection time!

On the left is Graziano Rossi and on the right Paolo Pileri, 250cc race, Brno.

Going through the Village at Brno 1979.

Pileri on the last corner to beat him by 0.01 of a second!

The only impressive thing about Brno was the size of the crowd. Brno got about 200,000 or more people at the event every year, mostly from race-starved East Germany. The huge hill overlooking the paddock and a section of the track was covered with about half of the total. You could tell the leading riders were coming into the hillside section because of the sight and sound of 100,000 people cheering and waving. It made the hair stand up on the back of my neck every time it happened. The East Germans once enjoyed their own Grand Prix at a circuit called Sachsenring. The story goes that during the 1971 race at the Sachsenring, Dieter Braun caused the 300,000 strong East German crowd to stand and sing the West German national anthem. Dieter Braun remembers it clearly; 'When I was catching Rod Gould I had to pass a backmarker. For that reason I had to leave the normal line and ride into the dirt a bit, which created a big cloud of dust. The political agent who supervised the GP for the government told the Clerk of the Course, Zacharias to black flag me for leaving the circuit, It had nothing to do with safety, he just did not want a West German to win. But I had not taken a short cut so Zacharias was brave and did not listen, which made him a hero in town. But the following year he was no longer Clerk of the Course.

'The East German politicians had completely underestimated the wish for freedom amongst the DDR public. The emotions were unbelieveable after I won. Because of the FIM rule, they had to play the anthem at the start and finish area. But around 300,000 fans around the circuit could not hear anything, as the promoters had switched off the speakers. So they started singing the anthem. Ten thousand fans climbed the fences and started a riot because they wanted to hear the West German anthem for the first time in so many years. The East German anthem never aroused such emotions. Because they had been denied TV and newspapers from the west, a fantasy West Germany had developed. They thought it was total paradise with everybody driving big Mercedes Benzes instead of Trabants. Anyway, I was scared that the riot would get bigger and was relieved when the police put me in a small Wartbug bus and drove me away.' `The 350 race was more important because I was only nine points up on Gregg as we went to the line. Nine points is not a big margin with two races left, so the Championship could boil down to overall consistency, reliability and lack of crashes such as had helped us win a comfortable 250 title. From start to finish the race was an exciting four-way dice between Gregg, Toni Mang, Patrick Fernandez and myself. We exchanged positions constantly, almost by corner. A dogfight at close quarters on Brno was the last thing I needed at that stage in the title chase. It was an occasion when I had no option but to fight for my space regardless of the consequences. Simple arithmetic dictated that if Gregg won and I was fourth he would catch me by seven points, so we would go to Le Mans with me only two points in the lead. It would be a 'winner takes all' shoot-out.

On the rostrum with Mang and Fernandez.

On about lap nine of the dogfight, a superbly on form Fernandez with his privately entered Yamaha was teaching us factory Kawasaki riders a lesson. He broke away to secure the lead by a couple of bike lengths. As we came up to lap a slower rider on the fast downhill section, the guy mysteriously crashed and hit the bales, which caused bike, rider and bales to bounce right into Patrick's path. There seemed to be no way through the debris, I thought Patrick was a goner. We had just enough warning to slow down and take evasive action, picking our way through the carnage. Patrick somehow made it through safely but had lost his momentum. Once past the mayhem, we all sped by, relegating him to fourth. We immediately got back up to race pace and duked it out to the end with me taking the flag by 0.5 second from Mang, followed by Fernandez who made a remarkable recovery, in third with Hansford on his tail in fourth. Brno was not the style of circuit to go mixing it like that. Nevertheless, I had not enjoyed a race so much for a long time. It was a real shit or bust for all of us, caught up in the moment when man and machine pushed themselves to the absolute limit, challenging for supremacy regardless of the danger. It was a fitting way to clinch my fourth title. I scored seven points more than Gregg which gave me an unassailable lead of sixteen points. My rare gamble had paid off.

Peter Ingley and I left the circuit shortly after the race to drive to Vienna to celebrate with Team Dunlop, who were spending

Looking relaxed at Brno.

350 action at Jarama 1979.

the night there before flying back to England. We went on the town to let off steam until the early hours of the morning, eventually getting back to the hotel as the sun was coming up. We showered and checked out without having turned back the bedspread, sporting the biggest of Monday headaches in living memory, a fitting tribute to the celebration of an incredible fourth World Championship title in two years. Unfortunately my soul mate, Bronnie, on a South African passport had not been able to get a visa to go to Czechoslovakia. She had stayed put in Everdon, missing out on another good weekend.

The French GP was a formality and I can't remember why we went, having tied up both titles before the event. Le Mans short circuit was not inspiring to ride and the team and I, having had a tough season would have happily left out the last Grand Prix. It was most probably some commercially based reason or obligation by Kawasaki to generate publicity in France that dictated that we compete there.

The 250 race was run on a dry track and my rivals seemed to lack inspiration so I had an easy time winning it. The 350 on the other hand, started in drizzle which turned into heavy rain. The track was extremely slippery in wet conditions, probably due to excessive car use and I could not get switched on. In contrast to Brno, I had an uncomfortable, lacklustre ride and finished a poor unsatisfying fourth. That evening the whole paddock erupted into party mode as everybody celebrated the end of another Grand Prix season. The 1980 season opener was not until the Italian Grand Prix on May 11th so the 'circus' would disband for the traditional Winter break. We had competed in thirteen rounds crammed into twenty-four hectic weeks between March and September. Everybody was determined to let their hair down so we did just that!

Winning at Donington again in 1979!

Other notable occurrences of 1979

For a long time the united riders had been talking about forming a breakaway series, the World Series, to be run in direct opposition to the FIM World Championship. This was a huge undertaking and I supported it wholeheartedly but never believed it would be made to work in such a short time in such a complicated sport. It was to be a professional package consisting of only the 250cc and 500cc classes with twenty-five of the very top riders guaranteed entries and a further ten getting the opportunity to qualify at each event. The package would be professionally marketed and offered to circuits passing certain safety and other standards, at a fixed price. The prize fund would be very big with all riders getting a good share of the pie instead of the top few, as with the FIM system.

The hurdles were numerous and high though, and at best I thought the threat of a new series might motivate the FIM into improving their performance. One thing that was clear to me at the outset was that without the blessing and support of the factories, it would be a dead duck. I am not sure about the Italian factories, but the Japanese are very conservative and would be very wary of such proposals. To get the collective decision to support a new, unproven idea would take more time than was available so I suspect that they would have stuck with the FIM series. Most of the riders would have been forced to split from World Series to preserve their rides rather than go through the immense problem of finding sponsorship for a new series. The only dilemma I would face in agreeing to support the World Series was when negotiating my 1980 contract with Kawasaki. If they refused to follow me to the new series I would most likely find myself prematurely retired. Maybe Roberts and a few others had earned enough to retire, but I had only just begun to run the printing press. I decided to agree a contract with Kawasaki first and then argue about where to race later if there was a choice. Kawasaki were non-committal about the new series but I knew from experience that they would not have supported it. They would have stuck with the FIM until the World Series was up and successful before thinking about getting involved. They did not have the resources to run two teams, I don't think the other factories did either and I don't think any of them could have come up with extra sponsorship in such a short time to fund extra teams. As it turned out the World Series never came to fruition in 1980 but at least we, the competitors and entertainers were becoming better organized on all issues. I don't claim any credit for the improvements, I merely lent moral support to the idea. The main efforts of Kenny with journalist Barry Coleman and a small band of active supporters resulted in improvements across the board. Prize money was substantially increased but was still poor in relation to the effort. As the attitude towards the riders improved with more respect being shown now that we were prepared to walk away from races rather than just talk about doing it.

With the great artist, Jock Leyden at Roy Hesketh circuit in 1979.

Ultimately, after many years of political warfare, the FIM would be defeated by the year 2000 by the ultra professional world championship series run by IRTA (International Race Teams Association) which came into power embracing most of the basic ideas of the original World Series breakaway movement of 1979.

Team Kawasaki UK's international races were curtailed somewhat with just four outings, Roy Hesketh, Donington Park, Oulton Park and Raalte for seven races. I collected six wins and a third from these outings. The reason for less exposure at Internationals was directly as a result of Pat Hennen's crash at the Isle of Man TT races in the middle of 1978. Pat was a sensational young American who, after some good rides in 1977 on private Suzukis was drafted into the Heron/Suzuki GB team as Sheene's team mate. Pat was going great and by the end of the Italian GP was second to Roberts in the World Championship. There was a chance he could shut out the determined Yamaha man, Roberts and carry Suzuki to another title. From the 1978 Italian Grand Prix, Pat went to the Isle of

Jean Francois and I teamed up for the Bol d' Or 24 hour torture session!

Man to race in the Senior TT 500cc race, not a part of the World GP series. In an awful crash he received head injuries from which he would never fully recover. Roberts went on to win the World Title for Yamaha and Suzuki were left pondering the wisdom of their decision to allow Pat to race at The Island in the middle of a Grand Prix season. Thus and understandably, Kawasaki were very reluctant to let me ride at as many international races in 1979 as I had during 1978, lest unforeseen injuries interfere with our multi million dollar Grand Prix effort.

Once the Grands Prix were over, I agreed to ride at the Bol d'Or, the most famous twenty-four hour race, at Paul Ricard circuit in France. The invitation came from Kawasaki France chief, Xavier Maugendre to team up with my mate Jean-Francois Balde on a modified 1000cc Kawasaki. I admired endurance riders but was never interested in getting involved in long distance racing. Like long distance running, I think the tedium would kill the fun. My agreement to ride had a little to do with my 'try anything once' attitude and a lot to do with the money offered. It was to be a once only experience. Twenty-four hours is a hell of a long time for two riders to share, so at the end of it I would be cured of long endurance events and the big pay seemed like small change for the unbelievable hardship suffered. Anyone who has not experienced a twenty-four hour race with two riders per bike will not realise how strenuous it is. In 1983 the number of riders was increased to three per bike which would make it a hell of a lot easier.

The huge four cylinder Kawasaki 1000cc with the monster tank could run for forty minutes before needing refuelling, at which time we would change riders. This meant we would refuel and change thirty-five times. By half way I had raw palms and bum, my left toe was bleeding from changing gears and my body ached all over. The forty minutes break at first seemed plenty of time to freshen up but after twelve hours it was forty minutes too short. We had a masseur and a chef to take care of us. On completing a stint it would be straight to the masseur, then to the chef who would prepare whatever you wanted. By eighteen hours I was staggering straight to the masseur and spending thirt-five minutes with him and the remaining five bandaging up my palms and toe before getting back on the bike. This was self-inflicted misery beyond belief. All I wanted was a cold beer! Towards the end everybody was circulating like robots. I remember the last lap. I was following someone and they appeared to slump onto the petrol tank and crash. Jean-Francois and I had done remarkably well on the badly handling not so fast 1000 Kawasaki, bringing it in seventh. After the race I crawled into the motorhome and slept through to the next day. When I did get to that cold beer it was the best ever. Team mate for the twenty-four hour race, Jean-Francois Balde also rode in the Grands Prix for Kawasaki France on KR250 and KR350s. He is a charming, good looking Frenchman who fancies his prowess with the ladies. His claim to fame was meeting a gorgeous woman who turned out to be a lesbian. He proudly stated with his sexy French accent, 'After one night with Jean-Francois she was a lesbian no more!'

By the end of the season Bronnie had stopped throwing up in the mornings but was sporting a rather large belly! Our first child was due to enter the world in May 1980. The other end of season big news was that Kawasaki had secretly developed a 500cc bike, the KR500, to compete in the 1980 500cc Championship. Kawasaki UK would drop out of the 350cc class and would contest the 250 and 500 races. They offered me the contract to undertake the daunting task of racing an untried prototype alongside the KR250. At about the same time Suzuki GB with whom Sheene had fallen out, approached and offered me an opportunity to race for them in the 500 World Championship. It was a pretty easy decision to reject the Suzuki bid. Despite the fact that it would be a chance to race a bike capable of winning the World Championship, their proposed retainer was so poor that it made me doubt what their level of commitment to us would be. They seemed to be in the habit of supplying two or three riders with bikes but not supporting them properly. In any case I was very happy with Kawasaki and figured it would be prudent to go the distance with them, rather than change to an unknown quantity.

The end of each Grand Prix season when riders begin negotiating with new sponsors or teams to try and set up for the following season is known as the 'Silly Season' because of all the confusion and bullshit that goes on. After finalising the 1980 contract with Kawasaki and renewing my personal endorsement contracts around Europe, Bronnie and I headed for Durban to spend three months in our apartment on the Golden Mile on Durban's then world class beachfront. Our apartment overlooked North Beach and if I sat up in bed I could see the surf. If it was good I would jump up and go surfing, if not I would simply roll over and go back to sleep, or pester Bronnie and her big round twitching belly!

Escorted victory parade through the streets of Pietermaritzburg at the end of 1979.

The view of North Beach from our apartment in Durban.

First trip to Japan to meet the top brass, World Trade Centre, Tokyo, Kawasaki headquarters.

Japan

A highlight of 1979 was my first trip to Japan. I was to be honoured for all the titles and would have a token two hours of testing the new KR500 at Yatabe and three hours at Fuji circuit. I arrived at Narita Airport on December 13th and was met by a gentleman who would become one of my best buddies, Shigeki 'Scott' Iwasaki. Scott, a great, lively, fun-loving character, was to be my chaperone for the trip and he sure took good care of me. Our first port of call in Tokyo was to his favourite form of eatery, a sushi bar. Thus began the Japanese gourmet experience with Scott, which would last throughout our association. 'Do you want gaijin food today, Kork-San?' 'Nai, Scott-San, Nihon tabeta oh kudasai.' My philosophy on eating in any country is when in Rome, do as the Romans do, so I sat in a sushi bar in Tokyo, for the first time, looking at the raw fillets of fish neatly lined up behind the glass counter. Along one side was a fish tank with live fish inside. Scott asked me if I liked the fish in the tank and I said that it looked okay. He had a word with the chef who instantly netted one out of the tank. Before we could drink a 'campai', the fish was gutted and filleted and on a plate in front of me, the head and tail still twitching on the chopping board. Talk about fresh! The stuff was still alive! I admit to not wanting to eat it but I did not want to display any rudeness or weakness to Scott. I tweezered it with chopsticks, dipped it in soy sauce, added a little wasabe as directed by my mentor and ate it. Scott thought I was not bad for a 'gaijin' so kept on ordering different delicacies, which I devoured with seeming gusto and washed it down with copious quantities of that lovely Kirin beer. After two or three visits to Japan I acquired the taste for sushi, some of which is excellent, and I became an enthusiastic regular at the sushi counter. Years later I was fishing off Glenmore on the Natal coast with my old mate, Mike Grant. That afternoon we were gutting and filleting our catch. I was eating raw fillets as we worked which had Mike in horrified hysterics. No amount of persuasion would get him to try it. It is funny how the concept of eating raw fish was unacceptable to a lot of people in those days.

Another fresh food occasion was Tempura, a great Japanese dish. As Scott and I were sitting at the counter of a Tempura restaurant, the chef came in with a large bowl of live wriggling prawns. When he set the bowl down one of the prawns saw his chance, jumped out the bowl and came scurrying along the counter towards us. The chef quickly reached over before it could get away and grabbed him, ripped his head, legs and shell off, rolled the tail in Tempura batter and fried the little fella. There was never a dull moment in Japanese restaurants and the food was always outstanding.

Scott, even more than the average Japanese, loved and had an insatiable appetite for beer. On my first night in Japan we ended up in a German style beer kellar drinking pints. I engaged in a private dice to see if I could keep up with Scott, who must have been very thirsty. The Japanese have a wonderful custom during social drinking. You never pour or top up your own drink, it must be done by another in your party or your waitress, and the glass must be lifted off the table before the liquid can be poured

Mr Tsukamoto, Managing Director and Senior General Manager Engine and Motorcycle Group.

Top brass at Akashi 1979, T. Takahashi General Manager Motorcycle Division, on my left. Scott Iwaski in the middle and Mick Uchida on Scott's right in 1980.

in. The vessel holding the liquid would never be allowed to run dry unless you fell over or declared that you had stopped drinking. We were topping each other up with alarming regularity and Scott was a couple of jugs ahead when he said it was time to go. I thought it was the best idea I had heard all day because I was knackered and beaten at beer swilling. Scott, however, did not mean we were going to the Shiba Park Hotel where I was staying but to a Karaoke bar to drink some whisky! So we walked to a narrow side street and into a building, entered a tiny lift and stepped out a couple of floors up into a small lounge bar. There was a Japanese guy at a microphone on a tiny stage sort of yodelling out a sad lament and a couple of cute looking geisha girls mincing around in Kimonos serving drinks and snacks. Scott knew the owner of the bar and kept a personal bottle of Scotch there, in which we made a serious dent. I can't remember what time my head hit the pillow, but I do remember that when the phone started buzzing I thought I had only just fallen asleep. The schedule was strenuous and mapped minute by minute. Despite my exhaustion, it was quite a kick to meet the World Marketing Director, Mr.Takahashi at Kawasaki Heavy Industries headquarters in the World Trade Centre and engage the Japanese Press at a press conference there. What I was really looking forward to was meeting the engineers from the race department and testing the 500 the following day.

Precisely at the scheduled time, not a second sooner, or later, the Shinkansen or Bullet Train pulled up on the platform at Tokyo Station, the door lined up perfectly with the yellow lines where we stood in an orderly queue. It whisked us off at 200kph to the town of Yatabe, near the JARI (Japanese Automobile Research Institute) test circuit. It turned out to be a narrow, bumpy, banked oval of 5.5km length, certainly an interesting place to introduce me to the new 120bhp KR500. A lot of the testing since the inception of the KR500 had been done there. Professional test rider for Kawasaki, Akihiko Kiyohara cautioned me before I went out, that the front wheel of my bike, the one with Dunlop on, was prone to 'shimmy' or twitch, at high speed. He was far happier on his bike with Michelin tyres. The Michelin front tyre he was using had a more flexible sidewall construction so would have a less harsh feel. After a few laps I built up to a frightening full speed in sixth gear and the bike was clocked at around 276 kph! The circuit became about the width of a cycle track at that speed and although the front was a bit twitchy, causing concern for the test riders, I found no cause for concern with the high speed stability under the circumstances.

What I was to learn after a couple of Grands Prix once we had analysed the overall performance of the prototype and done some comparisons was that the wheelbase of the bike was three to four inches longer than that of the Yamaha and Suzuki. A long wheelbase bike is very stable but does not lay the foundation for a good, raceable, responsive Grand Prix bike. I would place bets that the test riders, testing a lot on the fast bumpy JARI oval circuit evolved the horrendously long wheelbase to increase the stability at full speed on the scary oval, a design fault that would cause the most problems for us on the tighter

My introduction to Japanese cuisine by Scott in 1979.

Ken Suzuki and I tour the production line at Akashi in 1979.

Introduced to karaoke by Scott.

race tracks of Europe. A lot of Kawaski's large street superbikes also had very long wheelbases and I know they used JARI for testing. A lot of disadvantages are caused by a long wheelbase which I will explain later. The next test, at Fuji circuit, with the majestic, snow capped Mount Fuji towering above in the distance, turned out to be a waste of time. The temperature was below zero in the morning and the circuit was covered in ice. By the scheduled test at 1pm, the ice had thawed and there were some patches of dry track so I took a token ride but learnt nothing. The lack of pre-season testing was to be a big drawback each year, and would result in us using the early GPs to do the stuff that should have been done in the off-season.

At JARI and Fuji I spent many hours with the engineers and tried to learn what they were up to with the 500. It was overweight, a whopping 20kg heavier than a factory 500 Suzuki, but they were addressing the problem. It was also a little short of torque at the bottom of the power band and they were working on that. They claimed peak power was about the same as the opposition.

It was a pleasure to meet the guys who had designed the magnificent KR250 and KR350. The KR500 motor, simply two sets of KR250 cylinders in a square configuration, was to prove to be the strong point of the prototype, having benefited from years of KR250 development and the excellent engineering standards of Kawasaki. What was to be the biggest problem with the project would be the weight, chassis dimensions, and the suspension shock absorber units. The chassis, designed by Cowboy Hiramatsu, was an ambitious departure from conventional frames used by other teams, and a first attempt by Kawasaki at an aluminium, monocoque style construction. The shock absorber units, manufactured and supplied by Kayaba, were simply not up to the job in their standard form at the outset of the project.

Before leaving Japan I spent a day at the factory in Akashi to meet almost everybody throughout the works. I went cold and sweated at the unexpected respect the personnel showed me for bringing their factory so much Grand Prix glory. Even the little secretaries screamed, covered their mouths and gazed in admiration when I was introduced by Scott, who was loving every minute of showing me around. That night we went to Kawasaki's own restaurant in the hills with the top brass and I was introduced to the speciality, Sukiyaki, which became one of my absolute world favourites. After the meal we did the normal thing and went to a Karaoke bar in Kobe, where the party really got going. By now I was ticking like a bomb having consumed dozens of tiny cups of powerful hot sake. Before long Scott was

The R&D team during our first outing on the prototype KR500 at Fuji Raceway, early December 1979. We had to wait for the ice on the circuit to thaw before we could do some laps!

KR500 launch in London.

up on the stage and elected to sing 'It's a long way to Tipperary' which he did with the aplomb of one who frequents karaoke bars! I knew my time would come and I was dreading it. The only song I could find in the book that I recognized was Tom Jones, 'Green Green Grass of Home'. It started out fine and I thought I was sounding good when I got the words out of synchronisation with the music. Shit, what could I do? The Kawasaki brass were looking at me expectantly, perhaps not yet knowing that I was making a cock-up. I broke into whistling to the music and managed to get it to sound pretty good, then I picked up the words and music again towards the end and closed it out with a beautiful crescendo. My buddies from Kawasaki erupted in applause, Scott the loudest of all. They had struggled to get me onto the stage at first, but by the end of the evening were battling to get the mike out of my hands. It was great fun.

By the time I got on the plane out of Osaka I was exhausted by the whole fantastic experience. Sitting with my eyes closed as we taxied for takeoff, I wondered whether there would be another visit to the Land of the Rising Sun. I certainly hoped so.

Group pic at Kiyo's shop in Kobe.

1980, 250 title goes due to illness

I had my first race on the KR500 at Donington Park on April 13th in the Shell 500 race. The seventh place result was good, with my best lap time within a second of the fastest lap. I could tell from then that we would have to work on getting the heavy bike to change direction quicker. In Donington's low speed chicane it was a mission to heel it over from right to left and maintain a good rolling speed. I would lose valuable time in this section and any sections where a quick change of direction was required such as the Craner Curves and the approach to Maclean's. Adjustments can be made to the attitude of a bike to steepen the front fork angle or shorten the trail by changing the top and bottom yolks holding the fork legs, both of which make the bike turn quicker. We already had these settings at the point where it would be unwise to steepen the fork angle or shorten the trail any more. A long heavy bike with a steep fork angle and short trail loses a certain feel that a well-balanced bike has. They are a contradiction in terms of what is ideal. If the bike were lighter and shorter we could use middle of the road fork angle and trail setting as a starting point. We would then have a racer.

In 1980 Martin Carney took care of the 250.

Craig, a handsome dark-haired little fellow, was born on May 7th at Barratt Maternity Hospital, Northampton. Regretfully, I kissed mum and son goodbye and jumped on a flight to Milano for the first World Championship round at Misano. We had a mediocre 500cc GP debut, qualifying twelfth and then dropped out of the race with ignition problems.

By the second round of the Grand Prix series at Jarama we were beginning to pinpoint the main areas needing attention with the KR500. Jarama is a demanding circuit. It works the suspension and tyres of any bike very hard. Warm weather and an overweight bike compounded our problems. The rear shock was simply not in the ballpark and on the firmest settings would become sloppy after a few laps. The tyres which had evolved around feedback from the lightweight Suzukis and Yamahas, were being overworked causing them to overheat and lose grip within two or three laps. The motor was short on torque at low rpm so would lose ground out of the slower corners as it battled to pull the weight. If I geared it for higher revs out of the corners for more power on tap, it would spin the wheel and compound the tyre heating problem. Once going, the straight line speed, although understandably slower than the factory Yamahas and Suzukis, was not too far off. On the whole the bike's engine performance was very similar to the average over the counter Grand Prix Suzuki RG500 and Yamaha TZ500 as available to privateers. There were about twelve full factory riders on Yamahas and Suzukis at the Grands Prix and about five very good private entries. In the races that I finished it read, Spain thirteenth, France eighth, Finland fifth, Britain seventh and Germany eleventh, which were pretty good results considering.

Craig joined the team in 1980.

At this stage, after Jarama, I would say we had a stalemate situation on our hands. The weight situation could not be solved during the season because the chassis would need to be redesigned. Having our own made by one of many chassis experts in Europe or England simply was not an option the factory would have even considered. Likewise, the length of the wheelbase could not be shortened without major chassis re-design. The tyre problem could not be solved because there was no way Dunlop could set about the enormously expensive task of designing tyres to suit one heavy bike. We would spend the season doing the best we could. The suspension problem could be addressed and towards the end of the season we had upgraded units which were more efficient than the earlier ones.

The 250 championship, which was going to be dominated by Kawasaki, started badly for me. In the first round at Misano, Mang and I were pulling away from the field in what was building into a battle royal when we came upon a pair of fallen riders on the corner at the end of the main straight. There was a patch of oil or water spilled on the corner, and no warning flags were being shown by the marshals. I hit it and joined Lavado and Marchetti on the side of the track. Mang made it through and went on to win and chalk up fifteen points to my nil. I got the fastest lap of the race but it was small consolation.

Gregg Hansford was conspicuous by his absence and would only appear in Europe for Kawasaki for the last round of the championship at Nürburgring. He was possibly a victim of his own indecision regarding whether or not to accept an offer to join Yamaha to race 500s in the FIM races. Because of his support of the attempted World Series breakaway movement it was difficult for him to decide. Morbidelli were fielding a one

Kawasaki's monocoque, technically interesting and beautifully engineered.

man team with Swiss rider, Roland Freymond on the rapid 250. They would not however, feature as prominently as the previous season with the dynamic pair of Pileri and Rossi at the bars. Jean-Francois Balde was again on the French KR250 and would have a consistent season claiming third in the championship. The rider to pick up his performance compared with 1979 was Anton Mang. Not only had his riding improved steadily during the previous season but with the help of German tuner of much repute, Sepp Schlogl, he had the KR250 running very well. Dynamometer facilities found extra power and the use of a wind tunnel developed the original fairing into a more aerodynamic tool. Mang's bike would pull away slightly in certain situations, but we would have to make do with the 250 the way it was which was basically, out of the crate. Dozy was now totally consumed by the KR500 so there would be no horsepower development work on the 250. Our new man to take care of the KR250, Martin Carney, former British 250 Champion was one of the best guys I ever worked with on setting up carburation and suspension. Being a successful racer himself, we would get the settings as close to optimum as possible in the shortest possible time.

I won rounds two and three in Spain and France by slim margins from Mang to pull up to nine points behind him. I felt confident that I could steadily chip away at his lead and retain the 250 world title. The French GP at Paul Ricard was an excellent, technically interesting race. The circuit had a very long main straight which was a good place to compare the speed of Mang's and my bike back to back. The difference was that Anton could pull out of my slipstream and get ahead of me by the end of the straight, but I could not do the same to him. Whether it was his 'aerodynamic' fairing or maybe a little extra power is hard to say. I would hazard an educated guess that, by the sound of his motor they had tuned the cylinders for more top end power, and in so doing sacrificed power at the bottom of the power curve. If correct, this would make choosing internal gear ratios difficult for Toni at Paul Ricard with its diverse collection of corners. Early in the race it became evident to me

Close-up of the square four stripped for inspection.

Close up of the 1980 KR500.

1980 KR500.

Cranking the 1980 KR500.

that Toni had not chosen a workable ratio for the exit of the fast right hand corner at the end of the main straight, Courbe de Signes, because I could hear the flat sound of a motor not on the torque band, coming from his bike. I could see that he was not getting powerful drive out of that particular bend. I had chosen internal ratios very carefully and with that particular bend being in the first of a series of seven crucial corners in the final kilometre I made sure I had optimum drive from it and those following. In the race I found that provided I was right on Toni's back wheel in Courbe de Signes, the fact that I was well up the power curve near peak engine revs at the exit gave me enough extra speed to overtake him in the short straight leading to the next bend. I was planning to save this manoeuvre for the final lap and make it as hard as possible for Toni to overtake me between there and the flag. Toni must have made a mistake somewhere on the last lap because I led him onto the main straight by a few bike lengths. If he was planning some kind of manoeuvre in the last few bends, he would have made sure he was an inch from my back wheel coming onto the main straight. I was still ahead at the end of the straight, was not put under pressure, negotiated the last seven bends as planned and won by just under two seconds. I remember that race vividly because I spent many a lap planning exactly how I was going to take those last seven bends and leave no opportunity for Mang to come back at me. It had been a long time since I had to think so hard. I was a bit disappointed not to get the chance to test my plan.

The setting up of a racing bike for each circuit was an area of the profession that I enjoyed very much. I was very good with chassis geometry, gearbox, motor performance analysis and okay with carburation but don't think I was particularly good at setting the suspension. My background of racing on older and unsophisticated machinery had taught me to get it as close as possible and then change style to make the most of the set-up. Each circuit required different setting across the board and at each venue, if we had raced there before, we started with the settings we had last used. If we had not raced there before, we estimated what we would require and started with that. Practice was taken up sorting out the various aspects of the bike to get as close to the best of everything as possible for race day. This meant sorting out the complex carburation system to ensure the best motor performance throughout the power range while constantly analysing the performance of the motor. Analysing and deciding on front and rear suspension adjustments to both spring rate and compression and rebound damping, analysing tyre performance and perhaps testing new compound and construction tyres, hot off the drawing board. Making adjustments to the chassis regarding ride height and fork angle for the best cornering performance and perhaps re-adjusting some of the above if a different tyre design made the bike behave differently in the corners. The best overall gear ratio was adjusted by changing the front and rear sprockets and at the same time we had to decide on and try different internal gear ratios. Choosing internal ratios was crucial to good lap times at any circuit. If the ratio was too high on a certain bend, the bike would

Good shot of Dozy playing with the magnificent KR250.
Barry Ditchburn looks very thoughtful.

Ready to pop champers with Shell's Keith Collow after a race win.

1980 KR500 and li'l bro' KR250. It was very interesting racing both classes with the bike's totally different personalities and the 60 odd bhp power difference.

not accelerate powerfully from that bend. If the ratio was too low the motor would be revving too high in the bend but hindering acceleration and the smooth exiting of the corner. The KR250 had a six speed gearbox and we had a choice of about five different gears for each of the six speeds, giving a wide combination to choose from. As motor performance changed by tuning the carburation or trying different motor parts, or both, so the internal ratios might again need changing. As we improved the suspension settings or tyre performance so too might the internal ratios need adjusting. Setting up the bike was a highly complex task. I enjoyed it immensely and with our excellent team, we excelled. In such a situation there is no such thing as overall perfection of all adjustments but the team that can get it close has the advantage. The team whose rider has the capabilities of changing style to make the best out of the imperfections was a step ahead of most of the opposition.

The French GP was to be my last ride until the Finnish GP two months later. In early April Bronnie, Craig and I were visiting

The paddock was always a fun place. Patrick Fernandez feeds me.

Team chat.

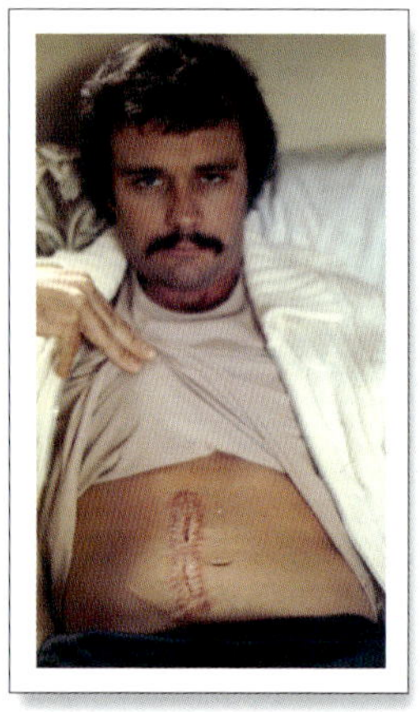

Nice scar.

friends near Derby when I started getting unbearable pains in my stomach. That night I ended up in the Derby Royal Infirmary. The doctors had no clue as to what was wrong and gave me indigestion tablets. During the night the pain was so intense that I was unable to lie still or keep quiet. I recall the doctor reprimanding me for the commotion but to my great relief, he injected me with morphine. The relief was short-lived as the drug wore off so they continued to administer doses of morphine through the night. Meanwhile no-one seemed to be making any decisions about my condition or attempting to determine the problem. Bronwyn arrived early the following morning and seeing the state I was in started making plans to have me moved to a private hospital. The hospital staff said she would have to be responsible for removing me from their care, that I could only leave in an ambulance and that they would not supply one. As luck would have it John Newbold, a fellow rider and good friend, lived nearby so Bronwyn phoned him for help. John suggested we go to the Private Patients Unit at the Mansfield Hospital and called Donington Park Circuit to ask for the loan of an ambulance. They were happy to help out so with John behind the wheel of the ambulance I discharged myself from the Derby Royal Infirmary and we rushed to Mansfield PPU. Mr Greatrex, a specialist surgeon, immediately diagnosed a blocked intestine and performed an operation to have a look. He found a section of the small intestine to be gangrenous and promptly removed it. He said it was a matter of a few hours before I was a goner. Subsequent tests showed that the most likely cause was a blood clot in the intestine. It was not related to bike racing in any way or even eating too much curry!

Recovering from the operation meant that I would miss the Yugoslavian, Dutch and Belgian Grands Prix, a situation which would eliminate me from the championship. By my next ride,

On the 250 at Brno in 1980.

the Finnish GP, I was third in the championship with Mang an unassailable forty-nine points ahead. In Finland I got back into the winning ways, beating Mang comfortably with fastest lap. Mang was now World Champion and although handed to him on a plate, he was a very worthy champion. He and his team had worked hard over a period of years to achieve their successes. Had I not taken ill I believe I could have won the title but it would not have been easy.

We followed up Finland with my sixth British GP win at Silverstone. At Czecho I accepted second to Toni without a fight on the dangerous Brno, and closed the season with a fine win at my old adversary, the Nürburgring, my third German GP win and thirty-first Grand Prix win in total. This would be my last 250 GP ride and Grand Prix win. As it turned out I finished runner-up in the championship.

Kawasaki wanted us to concentrate totally on developing the prototype KR500 during 1981 and leave the 250 GPs to the other European Kawasaki teams. At the end of the season, before all the Japanese technicians returned to Japan with their reams of notes on the season's progress, we had a meeting to discuss the season, our main problems and what we needed for 1981. Of course we emphasised that we would never be in the ballpark with the massive weight deficit and the chassis geometry which might suit JARI test track but not modern GP racing. As the safety revolution gathered momentum, the circuits were moving away from long straights and high speed corners and turning to the use of irritating and characterless chicanes to slow the pace down in certain sections of a lot of the older circuits. Given this new style of circuit, the new generation of bikes would have to be light and nimble to flick through the chicanes with more emphasis on bottom-end power for smooth acceleration from them.

1981, slow progress

Although our express requests for what we needed to get to the front in GPs were noted in miles of paper with nods of understanding, they must have been cast aside by the technicians, test riders and administrators back in Japan at the collective think tank as not what they thought we needed. The KR500 was completely redesigned but emerged negligibly lighter and with the same 'cruiser' chassis geometry. Kenny Roberts joked at the time that it was impossible to get past the Kawasaki in a chicane because it was so long it blocked the entrance and exit at the same time! Clearly we had come up against the stonewall illogical side of the Japanese. We knew what we needed to win races, but they would not listen to us. Despite all the evidence in our favour, they spent zillions of Yen building something we had proved would not do the job. Sticking to the use of an overweight chassis was the first bad decision. It was obvious that they were having great difficulty reducing the weight of the monocoque. There seemed no way Kawasaki would change from their chosen path and replace it with an infinitely cheaper and simpler conventional chassis. Whatever

The 1981 team at Donington in pre Grand Prix testing. Ken Suzuki, Dozy, Stuart and Stuart. The front mudguard was ruled illegal at technical inspection for the first Grand Prix at Salzburgring and had to be modified by cutting holes in the sides to meet regulations.

In practice at Paul Ricard on the way to claiming a front row grid position with fourth fastest practice time.

Dicing Croz at Paul Riccard.

the reason we were stuck with the 'log' for another season.

From the outset I embarked on a campaign at least to get a shorter swinging arm manufactured to try. Every time I spoke to Ken Suzuki or the Japanese technicians, who were now prolific in the pits, I harped on about needing a shorter swinging arm. 'Ken san, we need a shorter swinging arm oh kudasai. Please tell Japan.' 'Ah so, Kork san, dai mondai, it is not possible. Japan will not do it.' The bike was proving hard to ride and tried to hurt me a number of times. Eddie Lawson was racing one in America and he crashed it with injury at Laguna Seca and in Europe my old pal Gregg Hansford was back to compete in the Grands Prix, also on the lastest KR500. Unfortunately he crashed at the Imola international in April during his first ride on it and sustained injuries that would keep him out of the saddle until the Belgian GP in July.

Ideally, what I wanted for the KR500, apart from a 20kg weight reduction, was for the wheelbase to be shortened at least 80mm and the motor to be moved forward about 40mm to maintain the balance and keep the front stable. Moving the motor forward was a major task but shortening the swinging arm and adjusting the suspension linkages was possible. Shortening the swinging arm without moving the motor forward would cause the bike to become too light and twitchy at the front but would improve the lap times through improved traction at the rear wheel, better manoeuvrability amongst other benefits and prove to the Japanese that we were right.

By the Belgian GP in June, Gregg had recovered enough from his injuries to get back in the saddle which was good news for me as his input, particularly about the chassis would be very welcome and might help convince the Japanese. In practice Gregg was going very carefully but his feedback concurred with mine about the less than ideal handling characteristics of the KR500 and how it could be remedied. Unfortunately for the whole team, Gregg was to suffer another accident which would effectively end a brilliant career. During the race it started raining and Gregg, who had started on slicks, was having problems so pulled into the pits to fit more suitable rain tyres to the front and rear. When removing and refitting the front wheel it is necessary to remove both of the front brake callipers. To facilitate doing this, the brake pads need to be pushed apart and when replaced it is necessary to pump the front and rear brake lever a number of times to get the pads back to the brake discs. Nobody did this and Gregg was sent on his way with front brakes that were not going to work the first time he was to apply them. It is a pity that he had a clear run onto the circuit from the pits for if there was traffic coming down past the pits the Pit Marshall would have flagged him down and he would have discovered while going slowly that he had no brakes. The run up from the pits to the new section of circuit is very fast and Gregg would have been doing at least 240 kph or more when he would need to be slowing down for the second gear right hand bend, which was the start of the new section of circuit. Fortunately for Gregg the old circuit ran straight on at this section so there was a fair amount of space for him to lose as much speed as possible. Had there not been a fair amount of run-off Gregg would have suffered horrific injuries as

1981, KR500 at Paul Ricard.

KR500 crossing the rail at Imatra.

he would have collided with whatever kind of barrier that might have been in place, at a very high speed. Once Gregg realised that he had no brakes his first reaction would have been to pump like crazy to push the pads back to the discs. At the speed that he was travelling he was unable to stop in the given space. Eventually he collided with an official's car parked up the run-off area, at about 60kph. He suffered serious injuries including a broken femur. Gregg's demise left me once again as a lone campaigner. Sadly Gregg Hansford lost his life in an accident at Phillip Island circuit near Melbourne while competing in a Super Touring Car race in 1995. With his death motorsport lost a great personality and a truly gifted sportsman.

Despite the shortcomings of the KR, my qualifying and finishing positions were up on 1980. The big improvement over the 1980 KR500 was far better front forks and rear suspension. I qualified mostly in the top ten with impressive front row positions; Monza sixth, Paul Ricard fourth and Finland fourth, so we were starting to raise eyebrows. We suffered five minor breakdowns but finished the other six Grands Prix well in the top ten with two magnificent rostrum positions with a pair of fine thirds at the Dutch and Finnish GPs. The other four GP results were; Austria sixth, France seventh, San Marino fifth and Sweden fourth. By the end of the season we had claimed eighth in the World Championship. These were pretty good results considering the undeveloped state of the KR500 and the fact that the opposition had the jump on us by a good few years. The motor was very impressive. I felt that without the extra weight the bike would have accelerated quicker all the way up to top speed and would have been up with the leaders in a straight line which would have put me in a position to have a go at winning.

At the Yugoslavian GP, during practice I had the closest shave with certain death that I am aware of. During a practice session the front tyre tread came apart and hit and bent a bracket which was a part of the anti-dive mechanism that fitted very close to the tyre. As the bracket bent it got closer until it was grabbed by the tyre, locking the front wheel solid. Unfortunately it happened on a very fast corner with no run-off area. I had designated it as a nine/tenths maximum effort corner so I was dumped at about 175 kph with about two metres of grass on the outside edge of the track with two layers of straw bales protecting the steel barrier. I had no time to position myself for the impact and by pure luck I went in feet first at about 130 kph. Nothing broke, but my ankles were so severely crushed from the impact that I could not walk for two weeks. I still suffer stiffness in both ankles on occasions. Had I gone in head first I doubt if I would have survived the impact. I would have broken my neck or back or both plus a lot of other parts!

In July a parcel arrived from Japan. It contained a special swinging arm designed to our specifications. For the next race, the British GP at Silverstone, we eagerly fitted the short swinging arm and It proved to be a big step in the right direction. The bike came alive, no longer feeling like a log. The front end twitched as I predicted, with the weight bias now favouring the rear more than I would have liked, but on the relatively smooth Silverstone

A nice shot of Dozy, Stuart and me with the 1981 KR500.

Private testing at speed on the 1981 KR500.

circuit it was not a problem. The biggest benefit was that the rear tyre stopped losing grip after two or three hard laps because the short bike was no longer drifting as much as the long one. This was having a significant effect on tyre temperature, reducing it dramatically. When pushed over the limit, the short bike's rear tyre would start sliding more suddenly than the longer bike, but at a higher cornering speed which made it possible to do better lap times. Later in Finland, Peter Ingley and I conducted an experiment. He waited at the end of Imatra's main straight with his tyre temperature measuring apparatus. I did four fast laps on the standard long bike to get the tyre to the state where it started losing grip, then stopped so Peter could record the temperature. I then changed to the short bike and did four fast laps. The rear tyre temperature difference was significant, with the longer bike the higher by far. The front tyre temperatures were almost identical.

The extra weight of the KR500 was not as big a disadvantage at circuits like Silverstone where there were no chicanes and only one second gear corner. The rest of the track was third, fourth and fifth gear, high speed corners where weight would not affect acceleration as much as on slower bends. Best of all, the rear tyre was gripping so much better than before. In the 500 race I got a bad start and set the joint fastest lap of the race on about my third lap to close on the leaders, while going through traffic. Once on the pace of the leaders I simply settled in behind them to watch, wait and learn. On about lap four, Crosby, who was leading, fell at Stowe taking Lucchinelli and Sheene out of

1981 KR500 action.

A wet outing in 1981.

the race with him. This left Roberts in the lead with Mamola, Middleburg and me in hot pursuit. We swapped places for the lead a few times and I was beginning to get excited about the way the race was progressing. It was strange on occasions such as this, when I sensed potential victory my focus and concentration would go into a kind of overdrive zone in which things went into slow motion and it became easier to judge the braking points to the millimetre, lean over to the limit easier, accelerate out of the corners perfectly, and judge and second guess what the opponents were up to or about to do. I was still maintaining the pace without effort, indeed as the other guys might also have been doing, but the biggest encouragement came from the fact that I was not at a power disadvantage between the fast, sweeping bends. My rear tyre was showing no signs of strain. The bike, in fact, appeared more stable on the faster bends than the Yamaha of Roberts and Suzukis of Mamola and Middleburg, particularly on Abbey Curve, an almost flat out fifth gear curve, taken at about 240 kph. Abbey was important because it was the second from last corner before the flag so could be vital in any last lap action. I thought the extra weight of the KR500 was actually helping me take the slightly bumpy, high speed corner very comfortably. However, I did not get a chance to formulate any last lap plans because on lap eighteen of the twenty-eight lap race my motor popped a rotary valve and ran onto three cylinders, forcing me out of the race. In the pits we were all bitterly disappointed by the breakdown, yet encouraged by the excellent performance and the progress we had made towards becoming more competitive. At least Japan would now take notice of what we were trying to tell them, or so I thought.

During the year we raced in about twenty British International races, specifically as test events for development of the KR500. I won the MCN Superbike Championship round at Snetterton and although I only raced in about half the races in the series, finished second in the championship to Ron Haslam, with the up and coming Wayne Gardener third. We did about eight rounds of the Shell 500cc Championship and finished second to Graeme Crosby on the factory Suzuki in the Championship. At the Mallory Park round, Croz and I had a good battle on the amazing little 2.173km circuit, sharing fastest lap at 159.94kph, almost over the magic 160kph barrier that had not yet been breached. A lap of Mallory in 48.9 seconds is an experience, the average speed incredible considering Mallory has the tightest of first gear hairpin corners at which you almost come to a stop and two very short straight sections. In nine other internationals I had a string of seconds and thirds, most of the time against GP rivals such as Sheene, Mamola, and Croz. From a development point of view it was frustrating because we could do very little except play with carburation and suspension, having to wait for Japan to do the major changes to the bike during winter. My crash record was still good. I recall crashing only at Yugoslavia with the faulty front tyre, and at Donington when I overdid it on cold tyres and the front let go.

It was a bad year for loss of life. Good friend, very popular and highly skilled competitor, Dave Potter died after injuries sustained

Leading Randy Mamola on the 1981 KR500 in an International Event.

in a crash in an MCN Superbike race at Oulton Park. I was behind Dave when he went down, braking for the second turn of the track. He hit unprotected armco at speed and I could tell by the impact and body language that he was seriously injured. The Isle of Man claimed cheerful Aussie, Kenny 'Skippy' Blake in the Senior TT. Imola took Italian Sauro Pazzaglia. Seasoned GP campaigner, Michel Rougerie was killed at Rijeka when after falling off and standing up unhurt, was struck by another competitor and fatally injured.

At the end of the season we had our annual sit down with the Japanese engineers to discuss requirements for 1982. Most importantly we had proved that the shorter wheelbase was the way to go. We had the Kayaba suspension working very well indeed and felt it needed no major changes for the next year. The weight would have to be addressed if we were to get anywhere and this would take care of most of our problems by making life a lot easier for the suspension shock absorber units and tyres. The motor needed a lot more bottom power to help acceleration. Again, weight reduction would help here and it also needed a peak power increase to keep pace with the normal annual power increase that would happen in all factories. During 1981 the tyre manufacturers brought out 16 inch front tyres to try against the usual 18 inch ones we were all using. The idea of the experimental smaller diameter front tyre was mainly that, with less inertia generated when rotating, it would make it easier for the rider to change direction in chicanes, a requirement brought about by the addition of chicanes to a lot of the circuits. I raced with it on occasion and it did help the turning ability of the bike, but was a bit unpredictable and sometimes slid away without warning. When discussing chassis requirements I was alarmed to hear from chassis designer, Cowboy Hiramatsu that he intended to design the 1982 KR500 to take the 16 inch wheel only. He wanted to save frontal area for aerodynamic reasons. I knew through constant communication with Peter Ingley that Dunlop had 17 inch tyres on the drawing board which they thought would be the size of the future. It was imperative that the 1982 bike be able to take the incoming 17 inch and the old 18 inch sizes, so we could choose the best option when we needed it. I arranged a meeting between Cowboy and Peter so Cowboy could hear Dunlop's pessimistic view on the future of 16 inch front tyres. He certainly understood what was happening, and went back to Japan to set about designing the chassis.

The front end with mechanical anti-dive mechanism on the 1981 KR500.

The 1982 KR500 takes shape.

Posing for a photo shoot at Donington

Dozy working on the technically amazing 1982 KR500. It sported titanium, magnesuim and carbon fibre bits.

Two steps back

Lo and behold! what we wanted and needed was a far cry from what was delivered. On the plus front, the wheelbase and weight distribution was now in the ballpark but the list of no-nos again outstripped the good stuff. Cowboy had decided that aerodynamics were more important than tyre size and had the frontal area so compact that there was no way anything other than a 16 inch front wheel would fit. The monocoque was redesigned into a slim rectangular box section running from the steering head to behind the motor. The design and engineering were absolutely superb, more like aircraft standard... but... the new, slim monocoque could not carry enough fuel so a regular fuel tank was added. This partly defeated the object of the monocoque which is supposed to double as frame and fuel tank and it helped increase the weight of the bike to heavier than the 1981 version! To crown the depressing picture Kawasaki had changed from Kayaba to Showa shock absorbing systems. This was like going back two years because, like the original Kayaba, the Showa system was too weak at full hard settings. No one could tell us why this unwarranted change was made and I am convinced that no testing at all would have taken place in Japan judging by the ineffectiveness of the front and rear damping systems. The worst part was that we could not enlist the help of the Showa technicians as Showa was contracted to the Honda Racing Corporation and therefore unable to help. Employing independent suspension experts to make up special units was out of the question so we were in a fix on the suspension front. Suspension damping systems had become so technical that we could not tackle it ourselves during a rigorous GP schedule without time for private testing.

The first ride proved that we were going to spend a lot of the season battling to get the chassis and front tyre working in a satisfactory manner. On the motor front, despite the factory technicians' claim that the motor was better on the dyno than the production Grand Prix Suzuki both on bottom and top end power, it was no match for the opposition out of the corners. Half way through the season the guys would discover a simple wiring fault which proved the motor technicians were right about the power, both bottom and top end. When the team got it working properly in the later part of the season, I believe the motor was more powerful than the factory Yamahas and Suzukis.

The first 500 GP was at a new venue at the Autodromo Municipal de la Cuidad near Buenos Aires. We qualified a bad eleventh and finished a frustrating eighth in the race. In year three of the KR500 project we could have and should have been challenging for rostrum positions. Most frustrating of all, we had made huge progress during 1981 and supplied priceless feedback to Japan about what would be required to race at the front in 1982, but KHI, at great expense, had chosen to build what they thought was a GP winner. Being stuck with the 16 inch front wheel was a problem, and as in the previous year it was unpredictable. The Showa suspension, as in 1980 with the Kyaba system, was poor, probably more suitable for road use. Combined with the poor bottom end power and the heavy weight, the bike was a frustrating, depressing and disappointing non-event at the beginning of the season.

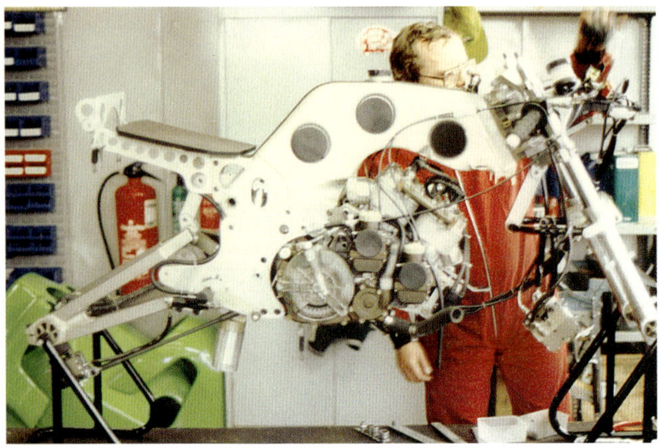

The 1982 monocoque was very different to '80 - '81 and beautifully constructed.

The 1982 KR500, notably shorter than the 1980 and 1981 prototypes.

Buenos Aires was far more exciting than the racing. At some stage in its past it must have been a magnificent city. The architecture was very Southern European but by and large was suffering from neglect. Most buildings were desperately in need of repair. There seemed little order to the traffic, with taxis dominating by sheer numbers and exuberance. The night after the race we got into big trouble in a night-club in the city. Aussie Jeff Sayle and I were having a drink and watching the cabaret, behaving like gentlemen, when we spied one of Yamaha's managerial personnel at a table drinking bubbly. He was being made a big fuss of by the waitresses. Kenny had won the 500 race that day and naturally he was celebrating. He had already got through a couple of bottles of very expensive Champagne and invited Jeff and me to have a drink so we sat down at his table to share his celebration. After a while the waiter brought a bill and handed it to him. He sobered up immediately when he saw the price of the sparkling wine. It was way more than he had in his pocket, in fact it was probably way more than he earned per month. At this stage Jeff and I wanted to disappear but felt we could not desert him, now in heated argument with management who had arrived on the scene. They asked us all to accompany them to an office where we could sort the problem out. We were ushered into the office, the door was shut and locked behind us and the next moment a big pistol was taken out from under the jacket of a large bouncer. It might have been small, but when it's being pointed at you, it seemed very large. The manager was short and to the point. If we did not pay, they would kill us! We enthusiastically put all our money together but it was not nearly enough. They then demanded a credit card. I turned out to be the only sucker to have one, so we settled the bill with it. Once settled, it was all smiles again and we were graciously ushered back to the club as if nothing had happened. I figured it would be a waste of time to go to the cops or anybody else to report the matter because like Venezuela, I sensed that the whole place was corrupt at all levels and we would not have got anywhere.

We did not get away from Argentina without more drama. On the weekend of the GP, Britain and Argentina declared war on each other. The row over ownership of the Falkland Islands as the British called them or Malvinas to the Argentines, finally erupted. The Argentines claimed the islands were theirs and the British would have none of it. At check-in British passport holders were treated very curtly and informed that the Aerolineas Argentinas flight, bound for London would only go as far as Madrid where we would have to disembark and make our own arrangements for onward travel. That was a small penalty for being caught in enemy territory during wartime. The way things work down there, we could have been at the mercy of that unpredictable South American temperament and have become prisoners of war! Back in England I had no joy with American Express over what I considered to be extortion. Then to crown it all, my bank would not take my excess Argentine currency. I hawked it up and down the High Street until I found a foreign exchange department that hadn't been briefed yet to boycott the peso and managed to

The 1982 team at Donington; Dozy, Stuart, Nick, Ken and Kato.

1980 Austrian GP, Mamola's motorhome expolded from a gas leak.

change mine into sterling. A few days later I got a letter from that bank instructing me to call in and collect my pesos and return their pounds to them! After a few letters they gave up.

Back in Europe, conditions at the Salzburgring for the next round were atrocious with snow, sleet and rain each getting a turn during the three official practice days. It was plain stupid that the FIM did not insist on re-arranging the calendar and start the season in southern Europe where the weather was generally good in May. The 1980 Austrian GP was cancelled due to heavy snow and here we were, back at the same venue in early May with the promoters chancing another failure caused by the elements. All official practice was in the wet and there were spills aplenty including a rare one from myself. Like in Finland it was a high speed end of straight front wheel lock up. I slipped and slid for at least one hundred and fifty metres into the catch fences, almost into the arms of a smiling Jack Middleburg who had done the same thing the previous lap and was sitting on a straw bale waiting for the session to end. When I fell I was building up to good lap times. As it was, although only eleventh on the grid, I was on the pace just behind Uncini and ahead of Spencer. Later I learnt that I was not on the top grade wets from Dunlop which were in short supply. This left me feeling let down after having been through such a lot of good times together and after having helped develop the tyres which put Dunlop ahead of Michelin in the last few years. This is an example of the harsh realities of Grand Prix racing. We were no longer in the winner's circle.

We moved from one dramatic event to another at the next

Clowning with Mamola and Crosby at the snowed-out 1980 Austrian GP.

The 1982 Austrian was beset by foul weather again. Craig and I inspect the snow.

round, the French GP at Nogaro. The weather was great but the organisation, circuit and paddock facilities were not. The circuit, like Karlskoga, was too tight and bumpy for 500s and after first practice sounds of dissent were gaining volume as the factory Yamaha, Suzuki and Honda riders complained that the bumps were making their lightweight bikes unmanageable and that it was not suitable for serious racing. Frames were cracking and the steering damper of one of the factory Suzukis was ripped off its mounting. I did not have it as bad because the KR was too solid and its heaviness was effectively reducing the disruptive effect the bumps were having on the bike. I think at the end of the day, if the circuit was the only problem, we probably would have got on with racing. What fuelled the flames of dissent was the fact that the organisers had accepted more entries than the paddock could hold, more than the toilet facilities and power supply could cope with. They made no attempt to upgrade the facilities prior to the event, knowing the paddock would be overcrowded. It was again a case of to hell with the riders and their teams, the guys who were supplying this spectacular show, simply squash them in and to hell with their safety and comfort. By the time everyone was parked and set up, there was only enough space to squeeze the bikes between the different team camps. Had a fire broken out it could have raged through the entire paddock unchecked. By the end of the second day's official practice all the top riders packed up and left. We addressed a statement to the organisers.

The Organisers, French Grand Prix. We the undersigned have unanimously agreed that for the reasons listed below will not compete in the French GP at Nogaro.

1. The overall condition of the circuit and paddock fall well short of civilised standards.

2. The track surface is too bumpy and presents serious safety hazards for both riders and machines.

3. The toilets, used daily by more than 250 people, are a disgrace and a serious health hazard.

4. Although there are some electric power points, they are totally inadequate.

5. The overcrowded paddock is a fire risk, magnified by the problems of the electricity supply. A fire would be totally uncontrollable and due to the confined area and the notable lack of firefighting equipment would cause wholesale loss of property and perhaps even loss of life. We are particularly disappointed to have to make this decision at this stage, but would point out that the FIM was told of our serious concern about the suitability of Nogaro for the French GP at a meeting with the riders at the British GP at Silverstone last year.

All smiles in foul Austrian Grand Prix weather.

My right hand man, Craig hands out stickers while I do autographs.

Craig's second birthday at Nogaro in 1982. Front; Graeme and Brenda Crosby, back left, good friend, journalist, John Brown.

Interesting rear shot.

The Grand Prix did take place, however, without the factory teams participating, was an event of less significance.The early departure left us en route to Spain for the next round, at Jarama. A few of us motorhome dwellers decided to meet just south of Barcelona at La Balena Allegra, a popular camp site on the beach where we could relax for a few days before the long haul across to Madrid.

As in the previous two years with the first and second KR prototypes, Jarama magnified the suspension faults. Ironically we went there knowing what we were in for, yet powerless to do anything about it and by the end of the first day we sat in the workshop scratching our heads for an answer to the problem of inadequate damping systems front and rear. The bike became a bucking bronco as soon as I tried to attack the corners at pace. As I said before, compression and rebound damping and the control thereof had become too high tech for even the Boers to make a plan. We needed special equipment and information, not to mention time, before we could attempt a home repair job. We

I chase Kenny Roberts and Franco Uncini at the Dutch TT, Assen 1982.

were helped out in the most amazing way. The two Showa technicians working for HRC sent us instructions to remove the rear unit and the internals of the front forks. They would collect the parts and modify them that night at their hotel. 'But please be secret!' They had noticed the diabolical handling of the KR and could not bear to watch me, complete with Showa stickers on the fairing, wobbling and sliding around the bends. The next morning the modified bits were delivered and installed. It made a huge difference and my lap times were immediately better, the bike far easier to ride. When we eventually managed to speak to the Showa guys they said the internals of the Showa units we had been supplied were not suitable for racing! I had a great ride in the race, taking ninth, which was not a true reflection of the improvements in the handling of the bike. We really appreciated the generosity of those Showa technicians.

The following weekend at Misano I had an encouraging sixth just ahead of Katayama. Unfortunately for us, 1982 was a harder year with the competition fiercer. Spencer and Katayama were additions to the grid on rapid three cylinder NSR Hondas, with reigning champion, Lucchinelli, drafted into the Honda line up. Franco Uncini on the Team Gallina Suzuki was having a superb year, Fontan and Sarron, French Yamaha, had very good equipment, were riding well and the Yamahas seemed much better than the '81 bikes. The result was that I never made it to the rostrum, despite improved lap times.

In the next three GPs, the Dutch, Belgian and Yugoslavian I had good competitive rides, for example at Spa, I got eighth, less than five seconds behind Mamola in fifth with Lucchinelli and Van Dulmen sandwiched in between us. At Silverstone, where the weight of the bike did not have such an adverse effect on its straight line performance, I was heading for my best show of the year. I was dicing for second with Spencer, Katayama and Reggiani early in the race, until the brakes faded and I had to ease up on them allowing Crosby, Mamola and Ferrari to get by, which left me in seventh at the flag, just four seconds off the elusive third place rostrum position!

At this stage in the season I had learned to ride with the inferior 16 inch front tyre. By going into corners with a little less rolling speed and not braking as hard as I would have liked while leaned over, I avoided stressing out the front tyre. By going in a little slower I could get on the power earlier which although worked the rear tyre harder, reduced the work load on the 'less than ideal' front tyre. The two drawbacks were that it cost fractions of a second and it worked the rear tyre harder, causing the grip to deteriorate progressively during the race. However it is easier to control a sliding rear tyre than a front one. It also left me in the situation whereby I was unable to ride aggressively and could not attack if I was close to other competitors. The British GP was a prime example. I was at the back of a five way dice for third with four seconds covering us and could not have a go because I was having to enter the corners conservatively. It was very frustrating that we could be so near to the rostrum, yet so far. Such simple design oversights, which should not have happened and would not have happened had our requests been

1982 at picturesque Assen, leading Middleburg, Sheene, Mamola and Spencer in the early stages of the race.

1982 KR500 action.

heeded at the end of 1981, were preventing us from great performances in the greatest spectacle on earth, which is motorcycle Grand Prix racing.

At the Swedish and San Marino GPs, I got sixth and seventh respectively. There was no 500 race in Finland, the FIM finally dropping it from the 500 calendar. It is ironic that it usually takes the tragic death of a competitor to stimulate the boycott of a controversial circuit. For many years Imatra had been shrouded in controversy and finally some sense had prevailed as the 1982 Finnish 500 GP was dropped. However the other classes still had FIM sanctioned races to compete in, so they were still under pressure to go there. It was to be the last Finnish GP at Imatra but unfortunately it would take the loss of 1980 sidecar World Champion, Jock Taylor to close the chapter on Imatra. The popular Scot and his equally popular passenger, Swede, Benga Johansson, crashed during the wet race and Jock was fatally injured. It is a tough deal to imagine that had the use of Imatra as a GP circuit been stopped as requested by the riders, Jock would still be with us. The other sad death during the season was that of my friend and 'ambulance driver', John Newbold, killed racing at the infamous North West 200 in Ireland which had also claimed Tom Herron in 1979.

After San Marino one of our Japanese technicians was returning to Japan. While clearing his desk out at race headquarters in Slough, Stuart found an interesting looking ignition system in one of his drawers. Stuart immediately fitted it to the bike for testing and it was a distinct improvement. This made the guys suspect that there was something wrong with the system we had been using all season so they re-fitted the '82 system and re-routed certain wires. At our first test session I could not believe that I was riding the same bike. It pulled from low down like a four-stroke, with smooth strong torque and

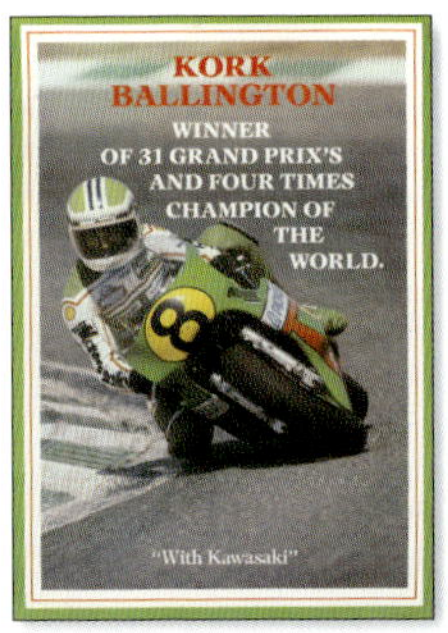

My first beard.

Look Ma, no moustache!

Paddock party. Left; Graeme and Brenda Crosby, back, Lucy Randle, Dozy. Front; Kerry Carruthers and Zita Sayle, Donna Gardiner, Bronwyn, Kel Carruthers and Haley Hatton.

easily revved 500rpm higher to 13,000. It was an abso-bloody-lute rocket and I rushed around popping wheelies whenever I felt like it. Before it had been a mission to get the front wheel off the deck! Dozy, 'The 1982 bike was fitted with a battery powered ignition system. Stuart fitted the ignition system left by the Japanese technician, which was a non-battery system like the 1980 and 1981 bikes used, and as it turned out the bike went better with it. This proved that the battery ignition system had a problem and as an experiment we re-fitted it, separating the coil wires from the trigger wires and re-routed them, suspecting the signals were being scrambled when the wires were in a tight loom. This made the bike run much better but, alas, the discovery came too late in the season.'

One of my first rides on the 'new' rocket was at Oulton Park in a Shell 500 race. I won, going away and easily broke Randy Mamola's 500cc lap record set earlier in the year. The motor's performance throughout the power range was now simply superb.

It was around the time we discovered the ignition problem that Dunlop unveiled an experimental huge rear slick. It was designated the RM and It turned out to be the tyre that we were looking for to cope with the weight of the bike. It had more grip than the regular rear, and did not suffer from rapid temperature build up, but the penalty for all the grip was substantial. It made the bike a far more difficult ride than it already was. Turning the bike into corners and trying to stay on line became a mission. Rear tyres are always bigger than front tyres and the basic rule is the bigger the differential, the stranger the handling becomes. In a straight line the tracks left by the front and rear tyres is on the same line. As the bike starts leaning over, the larger rear tyre causes the track made between the front and rear tyres to move

Our base at Camberley.

apart, the rear track moving inside the front. The larger the rear tyre, the further apart the track and the stranger the steering becomes. The RM measured about 200mm across, far more than the preferred tyre of the time and the average 16 inch front measured about 130mm. Theoretically we should have needed to have a larger front tyre to balance with the rear, but no doubt this would have created new and different problems. I don't think any of the other top Dunlop users ever raced with the RM because of the steering problems it created.

To make the RM work I had to scrap classical smooth lines, already difficult on the overweight KR with the undesirable 16 inch front wheel. To get the best out of the bike with the RM on, I would have to peel earlier than normal towards the apex of the turn when entering the corners, and when near the apex pull the bike over and I mean, using lots of energy to roll over onto the edge of the giant rear slick, pull the bike over as far as possible and get right back hard onto the power to transfer the weight of the bike to the huge rear slick and accelerate as hard as possible from the apex. It was imperative to avoid putting too much work on the front tyre by taking classical lines into corners as it would tend to be 'pushed' by the rear which made staying on line difficult. The new style of 'steering with the throttle' was helped by the new-found torque of the motor, the better response at the lower end of the power range making it that bit easier to implement.

I believe that at this stage we were getting the best we would get out of the 1982 KR500 in its then current state using the RM. This showed in the results in the late part of the season. At the last GP of the season at Hockenheim I made a point of getting alongside new World Champion, Franco Uncini, during practice, to compare straight line performance of his Factory RG500 Suzuki and our KR500. The best section to do this was from the first turn at the end of Hockenheim's pit straight, a tight second gear right hander, to the first chicane at the end of the approximately 1.6km straight, which was at the time one of the longest hauls in GP racing. From turn one Franco's fast title-winning Suzuki did not pull away at all. As we got rolling down the straight I got out of his slipstream so I would not be towed. Our speeds were identical all the way down the long straight to the first chicane. It was at the chicane that Franco flipped the lightweight Suzuki through and pulled a couple of metres on me at the exit. This kind of test proved that the KR500 motor was among the most powerful of the top 500s, hampered only by its

My last event for Team Kawasaki: Leading Franco Uncini in the final round of the Shell Oil 500cc Championship at Brands Hatch. I went on to win the race by 1.6 seconds with fastest lap.

weight and the 16 inch front wheel. An interesting point was that the motor was basic, without innovations such as the power valves of the Yamahas and Suzukis and the ATAC system on the Hondas, yet now that we had finally got it producing the power that our Japanese at Akashi said it produced, it was a match for them in a straight line. All along the Japanese said that it had the same torque and power as the RG500 yet to start with on the track it was not as fast. Perhaps on the motor dyno, the wiring system was spread out and not in a tight loom as on the bike and thus produced the desired bhp figures? If only that bike had have been of a comparable weight to the opposition, it would have been a world beater. At one of our next major races, the John Player 500cc World Cup, I chased and nearly beat Mamola in the second of the two leg series and scored fastest lap of the day at 1min 14.8 secs, beating both Uncini and Lucchinelli into the bargain.

Although I only finished ninth in the World Championship, one position less than the previous year, I had a lot of success in England, winning the ITV Superbike Championship and Shell 500 Championship with six wins and three lap records. I also won the Race of Aces at Snetterton, my old stomping ground from the earlier days with the Aldridges.

The end of an era.

Near the end of the season KHI announced that due to the recession which had adversely affected global sales, they would withdraw from all motorsport activities world-wide. Ken Suzuki; 'The decision to quit the World Grand Prix had nothing to do with the KR500's problems or the team. It was a company decision as a motorcycle business to quit the World Grand Prix. In my racing career it was a little disappointing to me but I think considering low budgets and the smaller number of team staff (racing and development) to other teams (Honda, Yamaha and Suzuki), we had no choice....But maybe if we had won at the 1981 Silverstone British GP. Just maybe.....'

On my last ride for Kawasaki Racing Team at Brands Hatch on October 24th 1982, I set the outright lap record for the Grand Prix circuit and won the Shell 500cc race. It marked the end of five wonderful, tough and trying years as the number one factory Grand Prix rider for Kawasaki Heavy Industries Motorcycle Division, Racing Department, Akashi, Japan, and I was ready for a break.

The final curtain. Brands Hatch at the end of 1982 with Ken Suzuki.

Part 5: After GP Racing

The pocket rocket, a limited edition Porsche Carrera Le Mans homologation model. 0 to 100kph in 5.6sec with a top speed of 240kph, incredible from 2 litres.

Back to Pinetown, where it all started

At the time Kawasaki's withdrawal was announced, Bronnie and I were in need of some 'time out' from racing. I had no aspirations to stay in Grand Prix racing in a managerial or administrative position, so we decided to sell up in the UK and return to South Africa. Financially I had done very well from my years with Kawasaki and Ludwig's investments were thriving so there were no financial worries. We could kick back and take stock of our lives after such an exciting decade.

With the disbanding of the team, Dozy stepped into a top job with Honda Racing Corporation as Chief Technician to Ron Haslam's NSR 500 three cylinder bikes. Dozy recalls; 'I did two years with Honda but by the end of the second season I was worn out and happy to retire! Working with Kawasaki on the 250 and 350 was an incredibly interesting challenge, a mixture of research and development on the relative GP newcomers, but with the Kawasaki KR500 the work was much more labour-intensive which left no time for tinkering. The KR500 had so many changes each year that it was a nightmare to get to grips with. The Honda NSR500 was well-developed and generally only gearbox changes and suspension setting adjustments were necessary. The biggest problem with 500s seems to have been tyres. A tyre may suit one bike and be lethal on another and likewise the rider's style may not be to the tyre's liking!'

Stuart Shenton also went to HRC to work on the NSR500s assigned to Takazumi Katayama, which he describes as 'an interesting experience'. In 1985 Stuart was drafted into the Irv Kanemoto/Honda team to look after Freddie Spencer's NSR250 and they won the championship. Stuart was drafted back into the HRC team to work on the NSR500s assigned to Wayne Gardner and in 1987 Wayne won the championship. At the end of 1991 Stuart was approached by Suzuki to help sort out the troublesome RG500, ridden by Kevin Schwantz. Kevin and Team Suzuki won the championship in 1993. Stuart's Gand Prix career had seen him closely involved with a total of seven World Championship titles, a remarkable record.

Ken Suzuki returned to Japan where he bought land in the

Craig and Mom next to the Bullet Train speedo.

Craig gets a lesson on the pit bike.

With Johnno and Sheila at Cowies Hill.

beautiful resort town of Karazuiwa and built a guest house which he called Pensione Silverstone. To this day he entertains racing enthusiasts from all over Japan who go there to see his Grand Prix memorabilia and chat about Kawasaki's glorious Grand Prix years. Bronnie, Craig and I had the good fortune to visit him many years later and experience the hospitality for which the Japanese have no peers.

We bought a house in the green hills of Cowies Hill near Pinetown, within a kilometre of my mother and father's old house where I first did laps on the Maz and rolled down the dirt roads in my soap-box cart. Everything had changed, gone were the dirt roads and the old shop where Dozy and I used to sleep on the veranda. Gone too was the old house surrounded by acres of bush, where I learnt to ride on the 'Circuit del la Casa'. In its place was a four lane road rudely running right over where some my most nostalgic memories lingered like spirits. The recognition that we enjoyed in my old town was touching. I was invited to talk at functions on the odd occasion, which I dreaded, but by

© CRETE

Pensione Silverstone many years later at a gathering of the enthusiastic Kawasaki KR250 Owners Group (KROG). Ken and Noriko are on the right.

and large we were left to ourselves, which suited us. I had imported my blood red limited edition Porsche Carrera, which became known and admired in town. Perhaps some young barefoot, ragass kid sitting on his bicycle at the side of the road, admired it just as I had admired Dr. Savage's beautiful red Alfa Sprint Veloce and Mrs Mac Donald's E-Type Jag. Perhaps he was inspired to dream that one day he would drive such a car!

I built an excellent bar and trophy room and put my three hundred odd trophies on display for the first time. We saw lots of old friends, but found we had drifted away from many of them, our life's journey having taken us so far from home. At least we could spend time with Johnno and Bronnie's mother, Sheila, which was wonderful. Sadly, Bronnie's father had passed away in 1979 and my mother in 1982.

Generally life was very comfortable and it was nice to be away from Grand Prix racing. I went to a few local races as a guest of Kawasaki South Africa but I just didn't feel comfortable or relaxed. The meetings were a mixture of bikes and cars, but still dominated by the car fraternity. The classes for racing motorcycles were poorly supported and the standard of competition seemed to have deteriorated in the last ten years, possibly having suffered from lack of international competition. Being fresh from the immaculate preparation and high standards of professionalism of the Grand Prix scene, I did not enjoy being at the local races. I had never been a good spectator so I fulfilled my commitment to Kawasaki South Africa in 1983, and seldom went to any local races thereafter.

The trophy room.

Our home at Cowies Hill had a wonderful ambiance.

I prepare to run to the bike at the start of the Suzuka Eight Hour.

An invitation to Japan

In April 1984, Japanese racing enthusiast and businessman, Hiro Tsukigi, invited me to race for his private team on a tuned GPZ750 Kawasaki with a Moriwaki frame in the prestigious Suzuka Eight Hour World Championship Endurance Race. The timing was good. I felt ready to do some competitive riding again and had never raced in Japan. I named my price and set off to race in the Suzuka 200Km, an international event taking place a few weeks before the eight hour race, as a shakedown for the big event. The 200km race was run in torrential rain and because Tsukigi's home-tuned GPZ750 motor was not very powerful, it was very easy to ride in the wet. I did well and was in third place until our fuel stop near the end of the race when the tank took on some water and the bike ran onto two cylinders. My old pal, Crosby, riding a Yoshimura Suzuki snuck in and beat me on the last lap.

I had arrived in Japan two weeks before the 200km race to test and set up Hiro's bike. Hiro invited me to stay with his family in the mountainous countryside a fair way out of Osaka. It was an experience staying in a wood and paper Japanese home, eating home-cooked Japanese food and experiencing the Japanese way of life. Bathing Japanese fashion, which I had already experienced on my first trip, is the best. A Japanese bathroom consists of a shower that has no cubicle around it, a large tub full of extremely hot water, a stool to sit on and a hand held shower which also attaches to the wall. After an intense shower and shampoo, and only when totally clean and free of soap and shampoo can you enter the hot tub. The Japanese do it together, although Hiro and his wife Satchko would not join me! The temperature of the water in the tub is very high, almost unbearable, but once I had eased into it and my body had adjusted to accept the extreme heat, it was a totally invigorating experience. Hiro and Satchko's hospitality and thoughtfulness was touching to say the least.

For the eight hour race, which was about six weeks later, Tsukigi planned to have his 'dream' frame complete so we would be more competitive. I flew into Osaka about two weeks before the event to test and set up the new bike. Immediately I felt something was wrong. Tsukigi's race manager, a serious-faced Buddhist monk by the name of Kasumi-san met me at the airport and he looked like the sky had fallen on him. The fine new chassis had been completed a few days before and was on the floor in the middle of their warehouse with the new paint drying, when

Tsukigi Racing Team at Suzuka.

Tsukigi-san's brother reversed his truck over it and destroyed it.

At the eight hour race, each team has two riders per bike. Tsukigi-san invited Australian Superbike Champion, Rob Phillis to ride with me. Rob had agreed to race in the team under the assumption that, if I was riding for this team, it must be very good. We ended up on the same bike I had raced six weeks earlier. It was not competitive against the world's top endurance teams and broke down irreparably within a few laps, forcing us to retire.

What the racing lacked, the social life more than made up for. The most entertaining place was Mama's bar in Suzuka town. I was introduced to it by Graeme Crosby, we were both in the Suzuka Grand Hotel which is over the road from the infamous bar. Croz had done many races at Suzuka over the years and, as far as can be deduced, was the first gaijin to enter Mama's. Mama, a Japanese lady and owner of the tiny Karaoke bar, was a live wire and character of note. When Croz and I entered on my first visit, Mama shrieked in her shrill gravely voice, 'Ah Closbeee, konichiwaaa!' She was very happy to see her favourite son. She spied me and came rushing from behind the counter to greet the new 'flend of Cloz'. She put her hand out as she came towards me but instead of shaking my outstretched hand grabbed me in the crotch and had a good feel, giving me a hell of a fright and said, 'How do you do'! What happened next was so funny that I still laugh when I think about it. Croz chased her around the back of the bar and disappeared from sight below the counter. Mama stood there with a huge smile on her face, giggling and twitching while the other patrons and I were left wondering what on earth was going on. A few seconds later Croz surfaced next to the beaming Mama... wearing her panties on his head. It was a slick operation and it took place every time we entered Mama's regardless of who or how many people were in there. Evenings in Mama's bar were hilarious, particularly the night after the race when the little bar was jammed with riders from all corners of the globe, all ready to let off steam after a hard week's work. There, as

ZX10 launch at Jerez in Spain.

Mike, Croz and I getting into serious stuff at Mama's.

Bronnie and Carol Phillis getting rowdy at Mama's!

usual, the only gaijin allowed behind the bar, Croz served drinks and Sashimi, drank, sang and joked with Mama's knickers on his head with his ears sticking out of the leg holes,

At the end of '84 Kenny Roberts and I secretly negotiated and agreed terms for me to ride in his Marlboro Yamaha 250 GP team in 1985. Unfortunately the team's sponsorship fell through so it never came to pass. I never tried to secure any other rides during 1985. It was a case of, if something came along I would consider it. I had racing miles left in me but in true phlegmatic style, was not concerned if nothing materialised.

My trip to Japan for Tsukigi had re-kindled the association with Kawasaki and in 1985, Iwasaki-san, who was by then World Sales Promotion Manager, invited me to the world press launches of three sport superbikes, the GPZ600 at Jarama, the GPZ1000 at Salzburgring the ZX10 at Jerez and the lightweight KR250 at Fuji Raceway. Of course it was nothing but the best for Kawasaki staff, and the invited press and Kawasaki would take over the very best restaurants at each venue and arrange the most lavish and impressive entertainment. Iwasaki was at each venue and we shared a lot of time together reminiscing and drinking a lot of 'campais'.

Good friend, Mike Cline from Inter-Image interviews me at the KR250 launch at Fuji Raceway.

The KR250 streetbike launch was a big occasion. Here, the Tokyo Press Conference.

Leading Randy Renfrew, both on on NS500s.

Racing in the USA and Japan. Kawasaki comeback

At the end of 1985 an interesting proposition came along from the USA. Bob MacLean, sponsor of the top private team in the USA invited me to ride a season in the AMA GP500cc US National Championship. This offer interested me. The US racing scene was a total unknown to me, except that they had produced superb riders in the past few years. Most interesting though, was the opportunity to race a proven 500cc Grand Prix bike. MacLean had a 1985 NS500 three cylinder Honda, a bike very similar, if not the same as that used by Randy Mamola when he finished second in the 1984 500cc World Championship. This would be an interesting exercise. We agreed on a contract and I tested the MacLean Honda at Laguna Seca early April '86. Wayne Rainey had ridden the bike for MacLean in 1985 and had won a few of the AMA races on it, so we had good lap times to chase. I had not ridden a GP500 for over three years and had never used radial tyres before. After a few laps it felt like I'd never taken a break from racing. The radial Dunlops, Jim Allen, chief of Dunlop USA Racing, assured me, were almost up to current GP specification tyres. They were really fantastic. They were so predictable it seemed impossible to fall off. When you pushed them hard they simply started drifting controllably and they did not lose grip after a few laps like the old cross-ply tyres I had last ridden hard with. The bike was small and light and ever so rideable. All of this plus good low down pulling power, made a great package. In our first test at Laguna Seca, after about seventy laps of simply adjusting to the bike's requirements, I had apparently done laps comparable to Rainey's on the same bike. I was pumped as we left to head for Sears Point, North of San Francisco for our first race. MacLean's team was very well set up with two NS500s and a fully fitted-out transporter, almost the equal of some of the smaller GP set-ups. Dozy had joined the team for the season and ex Freddie Spencer technician, Stuart Toomey was under MacLean's employ to oversee the whole operation.

Sears Point turned out to be a fairy tale. After a race long dice with Rainey and Randy Renfrew, I squeaked through on the last lap to win the race. It was as hard as any race I had ridden anywhere and it was pure magic to win, beating the Americans on their own circuit in their own back yard. The American riders were great fun, and racing in the States was a ball. We rode hard and played hard. Almost everyone took their golf clubs around with them and as soon as practice was over, we would all go golfing, hire golf carts and race around the courses like lunatics. I became good buddies with Bubba Shobert, one of the best guys I ever met. Bubba was at the time the USA's number one dirt tracker and had just turned to road racing. He and Wayne Rainey were great guys, both of whom had their careers cut short by terrible accidents which put them out of racing for good. In 1989, on the slow down lap of the US GP at Laguna Seca, Bubba rode into the back of a stationary Kevin Magee, who had stopped on the circuit to do a burn out, a rather pointless exercise. Bubba was having his first race on a NSR500 Honda before embarking on a fully-sponsored tour of the GPs. He had enjoyed a race-long dice with Eddie Lawson and they were riding side by side down the main straight shaking hands

Team MacLean 1986. Left to right, Bob, Martin, me, Tim, Dozy and Stuart at Road Atlanta.

On a race-ready 500 at last and on my way to victory at Sears Point.

and nodding approval at each other. Unfortunately Bubba was unaware of Magee's antics and looked up too late. Travelling at up to 160 kph, Bubba rode straight into the back of Magee, sustaining awful injuries and spending weeks in a coma.

When he rejoined the planet, he had serious injuries and would never recover enough of his reflexes to race again. Bubba had the capabilities and backing to become another of the American World Champions, but had his opportunity and dreams dashed in a split second. Magee, although injured, made a full recovery. Wayne Rainey had a relatively straightforward crash at Misano in 1993 but was very unlucky to have been spiked in the back by a foot peg, handlebar or some other part of his bike. The injury paralysed him permanently from the waist down, ending a superb career which included two World Titles in the 500 class.

One thing that amazed me about racing in the States was the amateur way in which the races were organized and run and the 'like it or lump it' attitude of the officials toward the riders. As an experienced GP campaigner, I had a lot to offer towards improving the situation at the tracks, especially in the area of circuit safety, which was very retarded at most circuits. Any attempt at voicing an opinion was met with the 'if you don't like it here, go back to Europe' attitude! After a season in the States, racing on some of the more dangerous circuits that I have ever ridden on, I was amazed that Kenny Roberts raced on these tracks then came to Europe and found certain GP tracks which were safer than most US tracks, to be too dangerous. However, at the end of the day his presence and motivation to reform safety in Europe was Europe's gain and the AMA's loss. There was so much potential to create a superb professional show in the USA which was stifled by lack of progressive thinking by the AMA whose way of thinking was much like that of the FIM.

1986, NS500 MacLean Honda at Saguna Seca.

I rode for Suzuki GB at Daytona in 1985 in the 200 mile event on a Yoshimura GSXR750. The bike stopped after about 100 miles.

Bronnie, Craig and I drove across the States in luxury.

Yoko Ogawa's (lady on my right) Honda team in 1986. Matin Carney, Bronwyn plus Honda personnel.

For the rest of the season I duked it out mainly with Renfrew and won a couple of races on the safer circuits. Generally, I was not prepared to stick my neck out on the poorer circuits, opting for safe seconds or thirds. I was on track to challenge Renfrew for the title, but a stupid mistake at Mid Ohio circuit, while I was leading by seventeen seconds, led to a crash. I had just decided to ease the pace, feeling secure that a win was in hand. This led to an unforgivable momentary easing of concentration, and on the tricky left hand bend coming onto the pit straight, the front tyre let go on the ripples in the middle of the corner and down I went. The lack of points effectively ruined my chance of becoming USA 500cc Champion and I finished runner-up.

It was a busy year. I was flying between South Africa and the States about every two weeks to fulfil both my racing and family commitments. In July, Bronnie and Craig, then a whopping six years old, flew out and joined me after a race event at Loudon in New Hampshire. We hired a luxury motorhome in Boston and drove from there across the States to Los Angeles, a mammoth trip of about 4500km, depending on your route. I firmly believe the US Interstate road system should be listed as the eighth wonder of the world. No matter where you want to go in the States, you can do most of the journey on a good dual highway. We toured California which has some of the world's most fabulous natural scenery; Sequoia, Yosemite, Tahoe and plenty more. Even the deserts have a certain beauty. Death Valley, where the bottom of the valley is below sea level, is awesome. It was hot, desolate and enormous. It was a humbling experience, as was the Grand Canyon in nearby Arizona which is the largest, most spectacular natural wonder I have seen.

During 1986 a Japanese friend of mine, Yoko Ogawa, a skilled entrepreneur, put together a sponsorship deal and arranged a ride for me with Honda Racing Corporation in an international 250 race at Suzuka and another at Fuji Raceway on their prototype 1987 RS250. It was a lemon, and at Suzuka, despite poor handling and ineffective front brakes I finished sixth in a very tough field. It was interesting to see how desperate the pace was in Japanese national 250 racing. In practice at Suzuka, I could only manage to qualify sixteenth but in the race I managed to cut through to fifth from about fifteenth on the first lap ...almost without overtaking anyone! It involved some of the most skilful avoidance of crashed and crashing riders I have ever had to contend with. The first few laps were carnage as the desperadoes who managed to stay on for their one fast lap in practice, were dropping at every corner. There was so much yellow flag waving that it looked more like a carnival than a race. At the end I was involved in a four bike dice for third but with a serious front brake problem had to settle for sixth with third a few metres ahead. Third would have been a satisfying result as I would have got onto the rostrum with old friends and rivals, Anton Mang who was second on a factory NSR250 Honda and winner, Carlos Lavado on a factory YZR250 Yamaha.

At Fuji raceway, by the end of practice the Honda technicians still could not get the brakes working, so I started in the first of two heat races still experimenting with remedies. The brakes were no

Yoko, Bronnie and I catch up with Stuart at Fuji.

Martin works on the troublesome prototype RS250.

better, so I pulled in after five laps and refused to ride in the second heat race. This prompted Honda to wheel 1985 250cc World Champion, Freddie Spencer's NSR250 out of the van for me to use in the second heat. The RS250 was on non-special cross ply Dunlops and Spencer's NSR on the best GP Michelin Radials. My first lap on both bike and tyres would be the warm-up lap. Grid positions were determined on finishing positions from heat one so I would have to start on the second from the back row! To crown it all it rained before the race so I set off on the warm-up lap on a strange bike on strange tyres on a wet but drying race track.

When the flag dropped, Carlos Lavado, the newly crowned 250 World Champion, sped off on his Yamaha followed by Sito Pons, also on an NSR250. I set off cautiously and cut through the field of forty riders to about fifteenth on the first lap. As my confidence grew I started piling on the coals and began to match the pace of Lavado and gain on Pons. At the flag I was alongside Pons who was judged to be second by one hundredth of a second, both of us just under six seconds down on Lavado.

Carlos Lavado (first) and Sito Pons (second) at Fuji Raceway, 1986.

In action on the RS250.

The NSR250 Honda was superb, much like my championship-winning KR250 Kawasaki, and far more refined than the 'over the counter' RS250. I impressed myself with my ride, especially with the fact that I did not stress out to stay with the current GP champions, on a strange mount, on strange tyres in tricky conditions! Being in Japan as a guest of Yoko was fun and we were cared for like royalty. Bronnie, myself and Martin Carney, along as my personal choice of mechanic, were put into the best hotels with no expense spared.

The AMA GP500cc Class or Formula 1, as they called it, was to be scrapped at the end of 1986. Bob asked if I wanted to race in the GP250cc, or F2 class in 1987 on an NS250 Honda.

I was having a lot of fun racing and seeing the USA so I agreed. We kicked off the season with a win at Daytona in the long 100km F2 event. It was a good win, despite hairy last lap antics. During the race Randy Renfrew and I were having a classic battle, going at it hammer and tongs, never more than inches apart. As we came out of the horseshoe bend in the middle of the infield on the last lap I was just behind Randy. He suddenly picked his bike up and slowed down, so I was forced to take the lead. My first thought was that he was trying to trick me, because usually if you went onto the final banking of the ultra high speed circuit in the lead with someone in your slipstream, you would not get to the flag first because the following rider would get such a tow that it was easy to pull out and slingshot past on the final dash to the line. I had not anticipated such a move at the horseshoe bend. I decided that I would just keep my head down, go hard and try to pull enough of a gap to hopefully reach the flag first. Going down the back straight to the last chicane before the final dash to the line I was still in the lead, but dared not look back to see where Randy was and in the process lose some speed. On this section, to look back at about 240kph would interfere with the aerodynamics and slow the bike a few kph. Approaching the last chicane I was catching a slower rider. I could see that I would catch him as we braked for the chicane. He could balk me, thus allowing Randy a shot at taking the lead. I decided that if I was to have a chance to win I would have to take him on the entrance to the first chicane and put him between Randy and me. Bad decision! I went in much too fast. I felt the back break away and slide right out. I could not let the brakes go, so carried on braking hard while leaning right over to the left with the back wheel now around by my

Taking a communal shower at Mid Ohio.

right ear. I reached the spot where you need to flick over to the right in the middle of the chicane, still going too fast. I flicked it over and laid it down onto the right footpeg. The rear tyre now broke away to the left and I sailed through the middle of the chicane in a huge broadslide. It looked like I might get away with it, but I drifted a little wide off line onto the marbles or loose dirt and bits of rubber on the edge of the track. The rear tyre said 'no more grip' and dumped me. I was still not through trying though, and although skidding down the grass on my side, I did not let the handle bars go. As the bike and I spun around on the grass I fought to keep the motor running. When we came to a stop I hauled the barely damaged bike up, set off back onto the track and buzzed it up through the gears for the final one mile dash to the line. I was really pissed off with myself and thought that perhaps I could still get third. I crossed the line and coasted around back to the pits where I was greeted by huge smiles and pats on the back. I had won the race! As it turned out Randy had run out of petrol in the infield and when I crashed was so far ahead of Kocinski that he did not overtake me during my excursion.

However, the whole season did not go as planned. Although always running at the front, I had made the error of changing to Michelin tyres. This decision was based on my experience in Japan on the NSR250 Honda and the fact they were in the front in the GP, plus Michelin USA said they would be able to get the GP tyres for us. They never materialised, and I was left slipping and sliding on production tyres, trying to stay with the Dunlop-clad opposition. The '87 Yam 250 was also a jet so we had double trouble. Dozy managed to extract more power from the NS250, but without the right kind of grip, the going was tough. At the end of the season Renfrew was again the champ. During the season a young freckle-faced guy by the name of John Kocinski, riding a fast Bud Aksland tuned Yamaha, started making an impression. He beat us a couple of times. His riding style reminded me a little of Saarinen and I went on record as saying that given the right break he could be a world champion, which he was in 1990 with Kenny Robert's Marlboro 250 GP team.

Team MacLean 1987 for the 250 AMA championship. Left to right, Creighton, me, Jane, Bruce, Tim and Bob.

Leading the pack (RS250 Honda) in the 1987 AMA 250cc National Championship.

Earlier in the year I had a fax from Iwasaki-san. Kawasaki were officially coming back into racing at the Suzuka Eight Hour World Endurance Championship event and wanted me to join the team on this important occasion. It was to be my first taste of racing big four strokes at factory level and an experience that appealed to me. The fabulous ZXR-7 Kawasaki we were to race used an in-line, four cylinder, water-cooled motor based on that used in their acclaimed 750cc sports road bike. The chassis was 'state of the art' latest generation, all aluminium twin-spar construction. At first I thought I would not enjoy racing the F1 750 so much because it was wide and high, but as I got used to the package I fell in love with the way the big four stroke went and what fun it was to use the immense torque the approximately 140bhp motor produced. Out on the circuit during practice I was amazed at the way the faster bikes laid black stripes out of the slower corners as the Radial rear tyre spun under acceleration. The last time I had raced the KR500, in 1982, this was barely possible on the cross-ply tyres of the day. Radials were so much better. At the exit of the hairpin, a slow first gear corner, I could get the bike drifting sideways with the rear wheel spinning and keep it drifting until we gained enough momentum for the back wheel to hook up and stop spinning. As the tyre hooked up it would cause the front wheel to lift into the air, only coming down when the next gear was selected. Riding this category of bike on such tyres was a new art form which I enjoyed immensely. The sound of the four stroke engine with valves and cams at work reminded me of the C110 50cc Honda on which I had started racing. The big difference was that on the 50 I had a long time to listen to the beat between corners, whereas the 750 propelled me from bend to bend like a slingshot dragster, with barely time to think!

Kawasaki fielded three bikes with two riders on each. I again shared with Rob Phillis who was then contracted to Kawasaki Australia for superbike racing. By the end of practice I had the fastest time of our teams which put us sixth on the grid, a very good result for Kawasaki's debut against established F1 teams such as Suzuki, Honda and Yamaha. The field was a who's who of racing with such names as Gardner, Crosby and Schwantz competing. In the race, Rob and I were in a very comfortable fourth after four hours and were starting to gain time on the third place factory Yamaha team of Martin Wimmer and Kevin Magee on the YZF750. But then the clutch on our bike disintegrated, putting us out of the race. That night in true eight hour tradition, at Mama's we all celebrated life, watched the Graeme Crosby floor show and drank countless 'campais'!

Eight Hour pit action.

I managed to acquire two sets of the 'right' Michelins for the NS250 and carried them back to the US for our next race, which was to be in Memphis. The difference was astounding, but unfortunately I was knocked off on a fast section of the circuit in practice and hurt to the extent that I was unable to give my best in the race. Despite this, I finished in fourth position, got the fastest lap of the race and if healthy I would have been in a position to race at the front. The front tyre in particular was so much better, enabling me to push the bike much harder into the bends. By the next race they were worn out, so we had to revert to the standard low grip tyres.

My presence in the 250 class in the States raised the pace of the class, and the 250cc lap records were broken at most circuits by a larger than normal margin, at some circuits by up to three seconds. The local riders took up the challenge of having a foreigner in their midst and went faster, much like having Agostini and the other fast Europeans come to Roy Hesketh when I was a kid, inspiring us locals to go faster.

Our Californian home.

The final furlong

By the end of 1987, racing in the States was drifting into the doldrums. A lot of the sponsors were planning to cut back on their financial involvement for the next year, prize money was being reduced and generally things were not looking good. Bob decided to reduce his involvement for 1988. I decided to do one more season of racing before stopping for good. I teamed up with my old 250 Kawasaki mechanic, Martin Carney as Dozy had decided to hang up his full time spanners. By then Bronnie, Craig and I had moved away from South Africa and settled in California.

By that time I had lost the intense desire to race and probably should have hung up my travel bag at the end of '87. One reason that I wanted to keep on racing was that I was due to race for Kawasaki again at Suzuka in July so I wanted to stay in form. Hopefully their next F1 would be more competitive, and Rob and I could have a crack at winning the event.

1988 would turn out to be Kocinski's year in the AMA 250 class. Martin and I had a great time driving around the immense country, reliving old days of GP glory, drinking a few ales and playing a lot of pool. The most memorable occasion during the year was at Road America in Wisconsin. Most of the teams were at a very pleasant hotel in Elkhart Lake near the circuit. It had an excellent Saloon Bar in the American tradition and the night after the race everybody gathered there to celebrate. Later in the evening, Bubba, Randy, myself and Jim Allen, tanked on Dutch courage, decided to do an old fashioned streak through the bar. We planned to strip around the side of the building, enter at the main entrance and run through the saloon to the exit at the rear. We did so and entered in a line as planned in all our naked glory. We were running in a tight group through the saloon towards the rear exit when Randy skidded and fell down. Jim, right in his slipstream tripped over him and went sprawling, Bubba ended up on top of them both and me on top of Bubba. By now of course there was much commotion in the place and we had obviously become a point of interest to the entire clientele. We untangled and scrambled to our feet amidst much hilarity. All we wanted was to get to the escape door as quickly as possible because we had not planned to expose ourselves for so long... but there was worse to come. We got to the back door, the escape route for our prank, only to find that some joker had locked it! We were now stacked up against the locked door starting to feel self-conscious. The only way out was the main entrance by which we had entered!

By the Loudon National race in New Hampshire we had our bike going nicely. Dozy had done some part-time work on it and it was fast. In practice I was doing great lap times and was set for a good ride. In the race I was chasing Kocinski and Jim Felice when the front tyre let go in turn two and I fell. It was not a particularly spectacular crash but when I came to a halt in the dust I knew that I had done an injury to my right wrist. It turned out to be another broken scaphoid to match the left one, broken back in 1977 at Jarama!

I was due to ride at Suzuka for Kawasaki in three weeks, an event that I was determined not to miss. So I would have to work hard on the wrist to get it useable by then. With the benefit of the experience of 1977, I knew it would be possible to condition the wrist enough to race at Suzuka. I decided to try a new approach. My left wrist had, over time, regained normal strength. The loss of about half of its regular movement and the occasional stabbing pain were the only after-effects. I would have to try and accelerate the time a broken wrist takes to regain enough strength to race a large, powerful motorcycle. In attempting to do this, I borrowed a GPZ600 sports road bike from Kawasaki USA and for the next two weeks I set out to ride around the twisty bumpy roads in the quiet hills near our home near San Diego in southern California to work on the broken wrist. On the first day I could only manage about 100km. As the days went by I increased my distance, pace and severity of load on the wrist. It was a real battle, more difficult in many ways

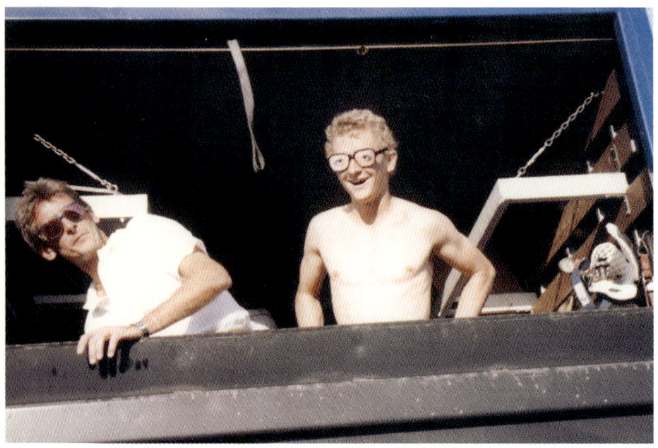

Kevin Schwantz looks better with the glasses on.

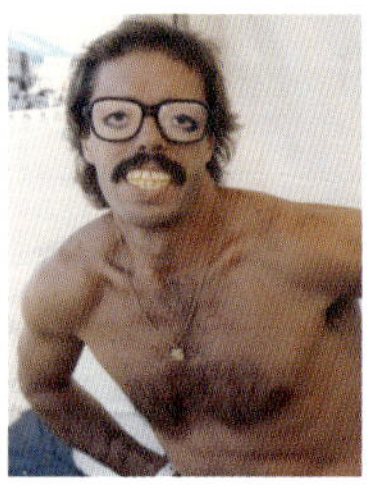

Not a pretty sight.

Rob and I make the results at last. We get sixth at the 1988 eight hour.

The part of Japan I miss the most; great friends, hospitality and food. This is one of many memorable occasions, here with Scott, Kawasaki san and Seth Nagatomo.

than when I broke the left one, because the right hand of a motorcyclist has to open and close the twistgrip with a rotating motion to control power supply to the rear wheel. A broken scaphoid makes it very difficult, almost impossible to do this properly. I could roll the throttle normally for the first half of the distance between closed and fully open, but then had to roll it with a flat palm for the last half. I figured I would manage this way because the important part of feeding power to the rear wheel happens in the early stages of the throttle openings where the broken wrist was working okay. I did as much as I could, and packed for Japan. I was determined to have a go.

I admit it was tough riding the heavy and powerful 750 Kawasaki this way. Really I should not have even tried but in the eight hour race I was managing, turning competitive lap times. Rob and I were going well and lying a superb fourth after five hours, behind leaders Kevin Magee/Wayne Rainey, second place team, Tadahiko Taira/Mick Doohan, and third place stars Kevin Schwantz/Doug Polen. The format at Suzuka was roughly one hour between fuel stops and rider changes. It was during my stint in the fifth hour that I made a silly mistake at the Degner Curve, ran off the track and got stuck in the sand trap. By the time I had extricated myself and the bike and rejoined the race we had dropped to sixth place, which we maintained to the flag. Rob and I were doomed as partners always to be bridesmaids at Suzuka. This was to be my last ride at one of my favourite venues.

Back in the States, to fulfil contractual obligations, Martin and I went to Mid Ohio for the last race of the season and of my career, spanning twenty-two fun and action packed years. There I raced a motorcycle in serious competition for the last time. It was a nostalgic moment but I felt content that I had done enough and given it my best shot.

For me, riding motorcycles has been an exhilarating and addictive experience. Riding gives one the feeling of total freedom, exposed to the elements, pushing into the air feeling the resistance created by the atmosphere. The sensations of banking over steeply, the rapid acceleration which the more powerful bikes are capable of and basically pushing the limits is addictive. As a teenager when I first started riding a motorcycle I got hooked and my mission became to go as fast as possible and to lean over as far as possible whenever possible as any addict wants more of whatever they are addicted to. Feeding the riding addiction is hazardous on the road and can only lead to trouble and serious injury. The race track became the 'shooting gallery' where I could feed my addiction to speed and push the limits in relative safety. As skill level increases, the addiction hungers for the optimum lap time. This involves getting the most out of the engine, braking as late as possible and as far as possible into the bends, leaning over to the limit and re-applying power without breaking adhesion at the rear tyre in order to enter the straight at the highest possible speed. The lap record is the yardstick by which to measure one's performance. Breaking lap records and winning races are the two incredible highs and last for days and even months. Winning titles has been my ultimate high and is a high that lasts forever.

I am eternally grateful, particularly to my parents, Johnno and Joan for their unwavering, unconditional support and Lynn and Berry for their help in the early days. I owe a great deal to Dozy for his huge effort and ingenuity, and to gorgeous Bronnie for being there the whole trip. We were a great team, something special, I will always remember the satisfaction of close teamwork and the challenges of problem-solving 'on the hoof'.

Sincere thanks must go to the Aldridge family for their support during the toughest time of the adventure. Without their help we would not have been able to continue. Also, gratitude to Sid Griffiths for setting me up with competitive machinery which enabled me to prove my talents, Stan Shenton for recognising that talent and convincing Kawasaki to offer me the contract and Ken Suzuki for his support and faith in me during the Kawasaki years.

All of my friends at Kawasaki Heavy Industries Motorcycle Division I thank for the opportunity to make full use of the talent that nature bestowed upon me, as well as the many unforgettable experiences and tremendous hospitality shown to me throughout my association with Kawasaki. Doumo arigatougozaimasu.

In 1998 we settled in Australia near Brisbane. Life certainly is nowhere near as exciting as in those heady days of my racing career but I am totally as ease about it. We are very comfortable, have a close family unit and are all very healthy. One of the first things I did when we got to Australia was to begin writing this autobiography. My aim was to get the story of our amazing adventure on paper for our kids and their kids before the memory faded.

The question has often been asked since I gave up racing. 'Do you miss it?' The answer is very easy, I miss everything about it. I had my last competitive ride eighteen years ago and not a moment goes by when I do not reflect on the amazing times I had during my twenty-two year career. Only a handful of people succeed to the degree that I did. Since Grand Prix racing came into being in 1949, there have been two hundred and twenty-four world champions in the various classes. To be a part of this elite group is amazing. I am thirteenth in a list of only eighteen riders during this forty-eight year period to achieve multiple world titles and sixth of only fourteen riders to win a double title in the same year. It would be impossible not to miss a career that culminated in such results.

I miss the actual racing, the qualifying, setting up to get the most out of the bike to try and qualify on pole position, the electrifying atmosphere on race day and the incredible tension on the start line minutes before doing battle. When the flag drops the tension would disappear and concentration and focus take over. It would take over to the degree that all else is blocked out and I became as one with the motorcycle forming the bond that enables riders to ride on the fine edge. After a successful day there is the intense elation of a win combined with the adoration of many thousands of fans. The moment on the rostrum in front of a multitude of cheering and clapping spectators is mind blowing. As I said earlier, it is a powerful drug, a powerful addiction.

I miss the parties after events where we could celebrate with the team and mates and relive the weekend's trials and tribulations. In life after motorcycle racing I have not experienced anything close to the total feeling of fulfilment, the absolute elation at the end of a successful weekend's competition.

I miss the amazing people from every corner of the globe with whom we shared the journey, both riders and technicians. They were a unique group of people of immense courage, drive and determination.

I miss the involvement with a Japanese factory. To be taken into the heart of operations at the factory in Japan, to be entrusted to the innermost secrets of the racing department and to meet the Japanese technicians and administrators behind the effort was an absolute honour and a total privilege. As a kid when Dozy and I fitted our first factory racing kit bits from Japan into our 50cc racer it was a dream come true and made me feel in some way connected to that mystical land but I never thought for one second that I would some day be a part of it.

Although I miss all these things, at the same time I feel deeply content that I experienced and achieved so much in the toughest sport in the world, Motorcycle Grand Prix Racing.

From the left, Craig's wife Samara, Craig, Jake, me and Bronnie. September 2007 at our home in Queensland.

Career Highlights. Major titles and awards.

Twice Natal production motorcycle champion.
1968: CB175 Honda.
1970: Kawasaki H1 500.

Three times Natal 50cc champion.
1968: Yamaha YF1 and Suzuki AS50
1969: Yamaha YF1
1971: Yamaha YF1

Natal Colours awarded 1970

South African unlimited (500 -1000cc) champion.
1972: Kawasaki H1R 500

Natal Motorcycle and Car Club honours awarded 1972

Springbok Colours awarded in 1974 for success in Europe.

Ken Lee Memorial Trophy awarded in 1978 by the Sports Car Club of South Africa for outstanding achievements.

Four World Championships.
1978: 250 and 350cc (Kawasaki KR250 and KR350.)
1979: 250 and 350cc (Kawasaki KR250 and KR350.)

Twice awarded the State Presidents Award.
(The highest accolade a South African can receive.)
1978 and 1979.

British Shellsport 500cc Champion.
1982: Kawasaki KR500.

British ITV Superbike Champion.
1982: Kawasaki KR500.

17 250cc and 14 350cc Grand Prix wins.
(1976-1980).

6 British GP wins at Silverstone.
1977: 250cc. TZ250D Yamaha. (Sid Griffiths Racing.)
1977: 350cc. TZ350C Yamaha. (Sid Griffiths Racing.)
Possibly the only Privateer in history to do the 250/350cc double GP win on production machinery.
1978: 350cc. Kawasaki KR350.
1979: 250cc. Kawasaki KR250.
1979: 350cc. Kawasaki KR350.
1980: 250cc. Kawasaki KR250.

4 Spanish GP wins.
1976: 350cc at Montjuich Park, Barcelona.
TZ350C Yamaha. (Sid Griffiths Racing.)
1979: 250cc at Jarama. Kawasaki KR250.
1979: 350cc at Jarama. Kawasaki KR350.
1980: 250cc at Jarama Kawasaki KR250.

4 Finnish GP wins at Imatra.
1978: 250cc. Kawasaki KR250.
1978: 350cc. Kawasaki KR350.
1979: 250cc. Kawasaki KR250.
1980: 250cc. Kawasaki KR250.

4 Czechoslovakian GP wins at Brno.
1978: 250cc. Kawasaki KR250.
1978: 350cc. Kawasaki KR250.
1979: 250cc. Kawasaki KR250.
1979: 350cc. Kawasaki KR350.

3 Italian GP wins.
1978: 250cc. Kawasaki KR250 at Mugello.
1978: 350cc. Kawasaki KR350 at Mugello.
1979: 250cc. Kawasaki KR250 at Imola.

3 West German GP wins.
1978: 250cc at the Nurburgring. Kawasaki KR250.
1979: 250cc at Hockenheim. Kawasaki KR250.
1980: 250cc at the Nurburgring. Kawasaki KR250.

2 Dutch TT wins at Assen.
1977: 350cc. TZ350 Yamaha. (Sid Griffiths Racing).
1978: 350cc. Kawasaki KR350.

2 Austrian GP wins at the Salzburgring.
1978: 350cc. Kawasaki KR350.
1979: 350cc. Kawasaki KR350.

2 French GP wins.
1978: 250cc at Le Mans. Kawasaki KR250.
1980: 250cc at Paul Ricard. Kawasaki KR250.

1 Yugoslavian win at Rijeka.
1979: 350cc. Kawasaki KR350.

Total of 47 podium finishes in GPs from 109 starts:
1973: 0 from 2 starts.
1976: 3 from 6 starts.
1977: 5 from 19 starts.
1978: 17 from 23 starts.
1979: 14 from 23 starts.
1980: 6 from 13 starts.
1981: 2 from 11 starts.
1982: 0 from 12 starts.

Total of 54 International race wins at the following circuits:

South Africa:
Roy Hesketh.
Kyalami.

England:
Mallory Park.
Oulton Park.
Brands Hatch.
Snetterton.
Thruxton.
Donnington Park.

France:
Rouen.
Nogaro.
Cognac.

Austria:
Schwannenstadt.

Italy:
Imola.
Misano.

Holland:
Raalte.

Belgium:
Mettet.
Chimay.

USA:
Daytona.

Career win total of 172 races (1967-1988)

Circuits raced on:

South Africa:
Roy Hesketh.
Westmead.
Richmond.
Eshowe.
Estcourt.
Isando.
Kyalami.
East London.
Killarney.
Bloemfontein.
Welkom.
Tempe.
Margate.
Greytown.
Umhlanga Rocks.

Zimbabwe:
Bulawayo.

Finland:
Imatra.

Austria:
Salzburgring
Oesterreichring.
Schwannenstadt.

Yugoslavia:
Opatija
Rijeka.

Czechoslovakia:
Brno.

England:
Brands Hatch.
Snetterton.
Mallory Park.
Cadwell Park.
Croft.
Thruxton.
Silverstone.
Oulton Park.
Donnington Park.
Darley Moor.
Scarborough.

France:
Rouen.
Le Mans.
Paul Ricard.
Cognac.
Nogaro.

Sweden:
Anderstorp
Karlskoga

Germany:
Hockenheim.
Nurburgring.
Norisring

Spain:
Jarama.
Montjuich Park.
Jerez. (Original street circuit.)

Italy:
Misano.
Mugello.
Imola.
Monza.

Belgium:
Zolder.
Chimay.
Mettet.
Spa-Francorchamps

Holland:
Assen.
Zandvoort.
Tilburg.
Raalte.
Venezuela:
San Carlos.

Argentina:
Buenos Aires.

Japan:
Suzuka.
Fuji.

USA:
Sears Point.
Brainerd.
Road America.
Road Atlanta.
Laguna Seca.
Loudon.
Mid Ohio.
Daytona.
Memphis.

Motorcycles raced:

Honda:
C110 50
SS50.
CB175.
NSR250
NR250.
CR350.
VFR750.

Suzuki:
AS50
GSX750.
GSXR750.

Yamaha:
YF1 50.
TD2B 250.
TZ250.
TZ350.
TZ700.
TZ750.

Ducati:
250cc (Can't remember model!)

Kawasaki:
H1.
H1R.
H2R
ZXR750.
JR1000. (Special homologation model for production racing in South Africa.)
1000J.
KR250
KR350.
KR500.

History of races:

First race at age 16 years:

1967:

50cc Racing class. Honda C110. (Team Ballington)

7 May. Roy Hesketh circuit. Pietermaritzburg.
3rd, 5th.

28 May. Westmead go kart track.(Retired from both races with engine trouble while leading.)

5 August. BP Bend Link. (A section of Roy Hesketh)
1st, 1st, 2nd, 4th.

20 August. Westmead go kart track.
2nd, 3rd, 6th.

3 September. Richmond go kart track.
2nd, 2nd, 2nd, 2nd, 1st.
1 October. Westmead go kart track.
3rd, 2nd, 1st, 2nd.

10 October. Eshowe street course.
3rd, 3rd.

50cc Honda SS50 (overhead cam)

12 November. BP Link.
3rd, 3rd, DNF (engine trouble)

3 December. Westmead go kart track.
3rd, 4th, 2nd, 1st.

1968:

50cc Racing class. Honda C110 and Yamaha YF1. (Team Ballington.)
Suzuki AS50. (Full factory race kit.)
(Sponsored and prepared by Alpet Motors.)

7 January. Westmead go kart track.
2nd, 1st, 5th, 1st, 1st. (Honda)

11 February. BP Link.
1st. (Honda)

3 March. Roy Hestketh long circuit.
DNF. (crash) (Honda)

10 March. Westmead go kart track.
2nd, 2nd, DNF (crash), 1st. (Last ride on Honda)
Note: 2 Strokes started winning the power race.

Changed to 50cc Yamaha YF1 (2 stroke)

7 April. Westmead go kart track.
1st, DNF (crash).

5 May. Roy Hesketh long circuit.
1st, 1st.

2 June. Westmead go kart track.
1st, 1st, 4th, 3rd.

14 July. Roy Hesketh long circuit.
5th, DNF (exhaust fell off!)
4 August. Westmead go kart track.
1st,1st,1st, DNF(engine trouble), 3rd (h/cap race)
First use of factory specs given to me by Yamaha (Japan).
I smashed the lap record (40.2secs) to 39.4secs)

50cc Suzuki AS50. (2 stroke with factory kit)

2 September. Eshowe street course.
2nd, 3rd (h/cap race).

22 September. Richmond go kart track.
1st, 1st (h/cap race).

20 October. Drakensberg Gardens Hotel go kart track.
1st, 2nd, DNF (crash)

17 November. BP Link.
2nd,1st, 2nd (h/cap), 4th (h/cap)

1 December. Westmead go kart track.
DNF (blocked fuel tap), 1st, 2nd, 2nd (h/cap)

Won Natal 50cc Championship.

1969:

50cc. Racing class. Yamaha YF1. (Team Ballington.)
50cc. Racing class. Suzuki AS50.
(Sponsored and prepared by Alpet Motors.)
175cc Production class. Honda CB175.
(Sponsored by Shimwells Motorcycles and prepared by Syd Stacey.)
250cc Racing class. Ducati.
(Sponsored and prepared by Syd Stacey.)

5 January. Westmead go kart track.
50cc. 2nd, 3rd. DNF (flat battery) 1st (h/cap). (Yamaha)

2 February. BP Link.
1st, 1st, 2nd (h/cap). (Suzuki.)

16 February. Roy Hesketh long circuit.
50cc. DNF (crash). (Suzuki.)
250cc. 4th, 6th (allcomers race).
175cc. 1st.

22 February. Westmead go kart track.
50cc. 1st, 4th (h/cap), 4th (h/cap). (Suzuki)

30 March. Westmead go kart track.
50cc.1st. (Last ride on Alpet Suzuki).
4 April. Roy Hesketh long circuit.
175cc Production class. 1st.

50cc Yamaha YF1. (back to old faithful!)

20 April. Richmond go kart track.
50cc. 1st, DNF, DNF, (both engine trouble). 4th (h/cap}.

4 May. Roy Hesketh long circuit.
175cc: 1st. (Fell off at BP Bend breaking my left collarbone but continued!)

22 June. Westmead go kart track.
50cc. 1st, 3rd (leading but fell off).

29 June. Roy Hesketh long circuit.
175cc. 1st.

20 July. Roy Hesketh long circuit.
175cc. 1st.

16 August. Tempe circuit. Bloemfontein.
175cc. 2nd.

24 August. BP link circuit.
50cc. 2nd, DNF (crash). DNF (crash).
7th September. Roy Hesketh long circuit.
175cc. 1st.
250cc. 6th. (Ducati)

19 October. Roy Hesketh long circuit.
50cc. 3rd, 3rd.
175cc. 1st.

26th October. BP link circuit.
50cc. 2nd, 1st, 1st. 1st (h/cap) 1st, (h/cap).

9 November. Westmead go kart track.
50cc. 1st, 2nd, 3rd (h/cap)

23 November. BP link circuit.
50cc. 1st, 1st, 1st, 3rd (h/cap)
Clinched Natal 50cc Championship for 2nd time.

14 December. Westmead go kart track.
50cc. DNF (chain off), 1st, 3rd, 2nd (h/cap),
Won Natal 175cc Production Championship.
Won Natal 50cc Championship.

1970:

1000cc Racing class. Kawasaki H1. (Team Ballington)
500cc Production class. Kawasaki H1. (Team Ballington)
50cc Racing class. Yamaha YF1. (Team Ballington)
350cc Racing class. Honda CB350.
(Sponsored by Shimwells and prepared by Syd Stacey) and CR350. (Sponsored by Midmacor and prepared by Syd Stacey.)

3. January. East London Grand Prix circuit.
1000cc Racing class. 3rd. (my first National).

10 January. Killarney long circuit. Cape Town.
1000cc Racing class. 3rd. DNF (out of fuel).

1 February. BP Link circuit.
50cc. 1st, 1st, DNF (h/cap) (water in fuel).

22 February. Roy Hesketh long circuit.
50cc. 1st, 1st (h/cap).
500cc Production Class.1st, 2nd.

28 March. Roy Hesketh long circuit.
350cc Racing class. DNF. (motor trouble while 3rd)
1000cc Racing class. 6th.
500cc Production class. 1st.

3 May. Roy Hesketh long circuit.
500cc Production class. 1st.
50cc. 1st. (Record lap 1m 45s.)
The first 3 bikes were stripped. Mine and 2nd place Alan North's came in at a legal 51.2cc. The third place bike was 58cc and was disqualified.

9 May. East London Grand Prix circuit.
1000cc Racing class. 2nd, 3rd.
50cc. 1st.

7 June. Roy Hesketh long circuit.
500cc Production Class. 1st.

July: Started 11 months of military training. Racing activities curtailed.

26 July. Roy Hesketh long circuit. (I went awol to race!)
Castrol 2 hour Endurance event for Production Bikes.
1st Overall.
50cc. 1st.

11 October. Roy Hesketh long circuit.
500cc Production class. 1st.
350cc Racing class. No record of position.
50cc. 1st (h/cap).

11 December. Kylami Grand Prix circuit.
100 Min Production race. 1st in 500cc class and 2nd overall.

27th December. Roy Hesketh long circuit.
1000cc Racing class. 3rd.
Won Natal 500cc Production Championship.
Awarded Natal Colours.

1971:

500cc Production class. Kawasaki H1. (Team Ballington)
1000cc Racing class. Kawasaki H1R. (Team Ballington)
50cc Racing class. Yamaha YF1. (Team Ballington)
250cc Racing class. Yamaha TD2B. (Team Ballington)

24 January. Roy Hesketh long circuit.
500cc Production class. 1st.

7 February. BP Link circuit.
50cc. 1st, 2nd.

21 February. Roy Hesketh long circuit.
50cc. DNF (seized). 2nd (h/cap)
500cc Production class. 1st.
1000cc racing class. DNF (leading when chain broke on last lap)

14 March. BP Link circuit.
50cc. 2nd, 1st,

12 April. Roy Hesketh long circuit.
1000cc Racing class. 1st.
500cc Production class. 1st.

1 May. Welkom circuit.
1000cc racing class. 3rd.

5 June. Kyalami Grand Prix circuit.
1000cc Racing class. DNF (puncture).

13 June. Roy Hesketh long circuit.
1000cc racing class. 1st.
500cc Production class. DNF (crash).

8 August. Roy Hesketh long circuit.
1000cc Racing class. 2nd, DNF (bearing failure).
500cc Production class. 1st.

2 October. Kyalami Grand Prix circuit.
1000cc Racing class. 1st.
250cc Racing class. 6th.

24 October. BP Link circuit.
50cc. 1st, 2nd, DNF (crash).

Won Natal 50cc Championship.

1972:

1000cc Racing class. Kawasaki H1R. (Team Ballington)
250cc Racing class. Yamaha TD2B. (Team Ballington)
50cc Racing class. Yamaha YF1. (Team Ballington)
500cc Production class. Kawasaki H1. (Team Ballington)

8 January. Killarney long circuit.
1000cc Racing class. 1st.
250cc Racing class. 6th.

23 January. Roy Hesketh long circuit International event.
1000cc Racing class. 1st, 3rd.

29 January. Kyalami Grand Prix circuit. International event.
1000cc Racing class. 3rd.
27 February. Roy Hesketh long circuit.
350/1000cc Racing class. 3rd, 3rd.
50cc. DNF (engine trouble).

12 March. Estcourt street circuit.
50cc. 3rd, 2nd.

1 April. Roy Hesketh long circuit.
250cc Racing class. 3rd, 3rd.
1000cc Racing class. 1st, 1st.

9 April. BP Link circuit.
50cc. 1st, 1st, 4th (h/cap).

22 April. Goldfields Raceway. Welkom.
1000cc Racing class. DNF (engine trouble).
250cc Racing class. 5th.

23 April. Roy Hesketh go kart track. (new)
50cc. 2nd.

30 April. Roy Hesketh long circuit.
50cc. DNF. (engine trouble).
250cc. 3rd.
1000cc 1st.
500cc Production. DNF (Handle bar broke off).

14 May. Bulawayo National Circuit.
250cc. 4th
1000cc. 2nd.

21 May. Roy Hesketh go kart track.
50cc. 1st, 1st, 1st (h/cap), 1st (h/cap).

3 June. Kyalami Grand Prix circuit.
1000cc. 1st.
250cc. 6th.
11 June. Roy Hesketh long circuit.
50cc. DNF (melted piston) new lap record 1m 40.8.
250cc. 3rd.

25 June. Roy Hesketh go kart track.
50cc. 1st. 1st, 1st (h/cap), 3rd (h/cap).

2 July. Roy Hesketh long circuit.
250cc. 6th.
1000cc. 1st.
500cc Production. DNF (piston broke).

5 August. Kyalami Grand Prix circuit.
1000cc. DNF (broken crankshaft).

6 August. Roy Hesketh go kart track.
50cc. 1st, 1st, 1st (h/cap).

26 August. Killarney long circuit.
1000cc. DNF (hole in piston).

27 August. Roy Hesketh go kart track.
1st, 1st.

10 September. Roy Hesketh long circuit.
250cc. 3rd.
1000cc. DNF (seized piston).

17 September. Margate street course.
50cc. 1st, 1st.

23 September. Brandkop circuit. Bloemfontein.
1000cc. 3rd.

30 September. Kyalami Grand Prix circuit.
1000cc. 1st.
21 October. Goldfields Raceway. Welkom.
1000cc. 2nd.

Clinched South African Unlimited Championship.

29 October. Roy Hesketh long circuit.
50cc. 1st.
1000cc. 1st.

26 November. Roy Hesketh long circuit.
1000cc. DNF (engine trouble)

3 December. Umhlanga Rocks Drive-in circuit.
50cc. 2nd, 2nd, 3rd.

10 December. Roy Hesketh.

Race of Champions.

(The winner receives sponsored trip to Europe to race.)
Allcomers race. H1R/Seeley. 1st.
Won South African Unlimited Championship.
Awarded Natal Motorcycle and Car Club honours.

1973. Tour of Europe:

500cc Racing class. Seeley Kawasaki H1R.
(Team Ballington)
250cc Racing class. Yamaha TD2B.
(Team Ballington)
750cc Racing Class. Seeley Kawasaki H2.
(Team Ballington)

12 April. Mettet, Belgium.
500cc Racing Class. DNF. (motor very sick.)

19 April. Paul Ricard. French Grand Prix.
500cc. DNF. (bad oil leak).

27 April. Nurburgring. Germany.
250cc. 26st.
500cc. 21st.

3 May. Salzburgring. Austrian Grand Prix.
250cc. 23rd.
500cc. DNF. (Motor sick.)

22 May. Misano. Italy.
250cc. 2nd. (new sticky compound tyres and Krober ignition.) (Qualified 3rd.)
500cc. DNF (seized)

8 June. Chimay. Belgium.
250cc. 12th.

7 July. Snetterton. England.
250cc.1st.
350cc. (on 250). 2nd, 2nd.

4 August. Hutchinson 100. Brands Hatch. England.
250cc. 3rd.
750cc. 10th.

11 August. Silverstone. England.
F750 European Championship. (Two 100 mile legs.)
Leg 1. 20th.
Leg 2. DNF.
750cc. DNF. (tyre problem).
250cc. 9th.

9 September. Scarborough. England.
250cc. 14th. (continued after falling off).
750cc. 10th.

16 September. Mallory Park. England.
750 MCN Superbikes. 7th.
Race of the Year. (Open to all classes.) 11th.
250cc. 6th.
23 September. Cadwell Park. England.
250cc. 2nd.
750cc. 17th. (ran onto 2 cylinders)

30 September. Hockenheim. Germany.
FIM F750. (Two 100 mile legs.)
Leg 1. 15th.
Leg 2. 5th.

28 October. Brands Hatch. Race of the South.
250cc. British Championship. DNF.
(leading with new lap record until crank broke)
750cc MCN Superbikes. 12th.
Race of the South. (Open to all classes.) 7th.

1974. (Restricted by finances to England.)

250cc Racing class: Yamaha TD2B.
(Team Ballington)
750cc Racing class: Seeley/Kawasaki H2.
(Team Ballington)

24 March. Brands Hatch.
250cc. 5th.
750cc. 10th, DNF (crash)

12 April. Brands Hatch.
250cc. DNF (engine trouble).
750cc MCN Superbikes. 10th.
1000cc. 3rd. (joint fastest lap).

14 April. Mallory Park.
250cc. DNF (engine trouble).
1000cc. 9th.

15 April. Oulton Park.
250cc. DNF (engine trouble).
750cc Superbikes. 7th.

12 May. Cadwell Park.
250cc. DNF again! (crash)
750cc Superbikes. DNF (ignition failure).
1000cc. Heat race. 3rd (fastest lap)
1000cc. Final. DNF (crash and KO'd!)

26 May. Mallory Park.
250cc. 5th.
750cc. 4th.

27 May. Brands Hatch.
250cc. 2nd.
750cc. 4th.
750cc. 5th.
9 June. Mallory Park. Post T.T. event.
750cc Superbikes. 6th.
28 September. Thruxton.
400 Mile Endurance race. 1st.
(Factory ride with Kawasaki UK. Partner: Barry Ditchburn)

21 June. Croft.
250cc. 3rd.
750cc. 1st. (lap record)
1000cc. 1st. (lap record)

7 July. Scarborough.
750cc MCN Superbikes. DNF.

14 July. Darley Moor.
1000cc. 10th, 5th.

4 August. Brands Hatch Hutchinson 100 (Reverse direction)
250cc. DNF. (ignition failure), 12th
750cc Superbikes. 7th.
Hutch 100. 8th.

10 August. John Player Grand Prix. Silverstone.
FIM F750. (Two 100 mile legs.)
Leg 1. DNF (ignition failure)
Leg 2. 7th.
250cc. 14th.

25 August. Snetterton. Race of Aces.
250cc. 7th.
1000cc Race of Aces. 3rd.
1000cc. 5th.

26 August. Oulton Park.
250cc. 5th. (last ride on TD2B after 3 years of good service: No longer competitive).
750cc Suberbikes. 3rd (fastest lap)

8 September. Scarborough.
750cc Superbikes. 5th.

14 September. Mallory Park Race of the Year.
Race of the Year. 12th.
750cc Superbikes. 4th.

21 September. Croft.
1000cc. Ken Redfern Trophy. 1st.

22 September. Cadwell Park.
1000cc. 7th, 9th.

20 October. Snetterton. British Championships.
1000cc. 3rd.
27 October. Brands Hatch. Race of the South.
1000cc Bill Ivy Race. 2nd. (lap record.)
750cc Superbikes. 13th (pulled in to wipe misted visor).
Race of the South. DNF (chain broke).

1975:

Kawasaki H2R (on loan from Kawasaki U.K.)
Yamaha TZ250B (Sid Griffiths Racing).
Yamaha TZ350B (Sid Griffiths Racing).
Yamaha TZ700 (Sid Griffiths Racing).

2 March. Mallory Park. Leics.
750cc. 2nd.

9 March. Cadwell Park. Lincs.
750cc. 2nd, 1st.

14 March. Rouen. France.
750cc. (Two 40 minute legs.)
Leg 1. 10th
Leg 2. 1st.

31 March. Oulton Park. Cheshire.
750cc. DNF (crash).

4 April. Imola. Italy.
FIM F750. (Two 100 mile legs.)
Leg 1. 10th.
Leg 2. DNF (ignition problem).

27 April. Cadwell Park. Lincs.
750cc Suberbikes.9th.

18 May. Cadwell Park. Lincs.
750cc. DNF (crash at Barn Corner!)
(Last ride on a Kawasaki until 1978.)
250cc. 4th. (first ride for Sid Griffiths).

8 June Mallory Park Post TT. International. Leics.
750cc Suberbikes. (TZ700)
DNF. (Stopped after hitting a marshall running across the track at Gerard's).
350cc. 1st. (Fastest lap).
1000cc. 6th.

15 June. Mettet. Belgium.
FIM F750. (Two 100 mile legs.)
Leg 1.DNF. (Hole in radiator. Retired while 4th.)
Leg 2. 5th.
250cc. 13th.

21 June. Croft. Durham.
1000cc. 4th.
350cc. 1st.
250cc. 3rd. (Lap record).
1000cc. 1st. (Lap record).

July. Snetterton.
1000cc. British. Championship 2nd (fastest lap).
1000cc. 1st (fastest lap).
1000cc. 2nd (outright lap record).
350cc. 2nd (fastest lap).

3 August. Brands Hatch. Hutchinson 100.
(Reverse direction!)
250cc. 2nd.
750 Superbikes, 6th.
Hutch 100. 8th.
1000cc. 4th.
350cc. 1st.

9 August. John Player Grand Prix. Silverstone.
FIM F750. (Two 100 mile legs.)
Leg 1. 6th.
Leg 2. 6th.
250cc. 10th.
350cc. DNF (engine trouble)

24 August. Snetterton. Race of Aces.
250cc. 2nd.
Race of Aces. 5th.
1000cc. 3rd.

25 August. Oulton Park International.
250cc. 4th.
350cc. 6th.

13 September. Race of the Year. Mallory Park.
(NO RECORDS.)

20 September. Croft. Durham.
1000cc Ken Redfern Trophy. 1st.
350cc. 2st (lap record).
250cc. 1st (fastest lap).

11 October. Race of the North. Oulton Park. Cheshire.
1000cc. 1st.

26 October. Brands Hatch. Kent.
750cc. MCN Superbike. DNF (crash).
1000cc. 7th.
350cc. 6th.
1000cc Powerbike International. 4th.

1976: (Sid Griffiths Racing.)

Yamaha TZ250C.
Yamaha TZ350 B.
Yamaha TZ750.
7 March. Mallory Park.
750cc. 8th.

21 March. Cadwell Park.
250cc. 4th.

28 March. Rouen. France.
1000cc. Leg 1. 2nd (fastest lap).
Leg 2. 3rd.
Overall. 3rd.
250cc. 1st.

31 March. Imola. Italy,
FIM F750. (Two 100 mile legs.)
Leg 1. DNF. (water pump gear stripped while 8th).
Did not start leg 2.

11 April. Paul Ricard. France
750cc. 6th.
250cc. DNF. (crash).

23 April. Le Mans. French Grand Prix.
250cc. DNF. (crash.)
350cc. DNF. (seized).

9 May. Mettet. Belgium.
1300cc. Leg 1. DNF (ignition problem).
Leg 2. 4th.
250cc. 2nd.

16 May. Mugello. Italian Grand Prix.
250cc. DNF. (crash while 3rd).
350cc. 6th.

23 May. Oestereichring. Austria.
750cc. 2nd.
250cc. 2nd.

27 May. Nogaro. France.
FIM F750. (Two 100 mile legs.)
Leg 1. 8th.
Leg 2. DNF (engine trouble).
250cc. 1st.

6 June. Chimay. Belgium.
250cc. DNF. (engine trouble while 2nd).
750cc. DNF. (engine trouble).

13 June. Mallory Park Post TT.
750 Superbikes. DNF.
350. 3rd.
1000cc. DNF.

19 June. Norisring. Germany.
350cc. 2nd.
750cc. DNF.

11 July. Zandvoort. Holland.
250cc. 3rd.
350cc. 3rd.

7 August. Hutchinson 100. Brands Hatch.
250cc. 14th.
350cc. 2nd (fastest lap).
750cc Superbikes. 7th.
1000cc. DNF (crash).

15 August. Silverstone.
FIM F750. (Two 100 mile legs.)
Leg 1. 12th.
Leg 2. 9th.
Overall. 5th.
1000cc. 5th.
350cc. 3rd.
250cc. 4th.

29 August. Nurburgring. West German Grand Prix.
350cc. 12th.
250. 2nd. (First Grand Prix rostrum position.)

7 September. Assen.
FIM F750. (Two 100 mile legs.)
Leg 1. 9th.
Leg 2. 2nd.
12 September. Race of the Year. Mallory Park.
750cc Superbikes. 11th.
1000cc. DNF. (crash while 4th.)
350cc. 1st.

19 September. Monjuich Park. Spanish Grand Prix.
250cc. 8th.
350cc. 1st. (First Grand Prix win.)

26 September. Cognac. France.
250cc. 1st. (fastest lap).

17. October. Jerez. Spain.
250cc. 4th.
350cc. 5th.

31 October. The Race of the South. Brands Hatch.
750cc Superbikes. 14th.
1000cc. 5th.

1977. (Sid Griffiths Racing.)

Yamaha TZ250C.
Yamaha TZ 350D.
Yamaha TZ 750/Nico Bakker Chassis.

19 March. San Carlos. Venezuelan Grand Prix.
250cc. 5th.
350cc. DNF. (crash).

27 March. Tilburg. Holland.
350cc. DNF. (engine trouble).
750cc. 7th.

3 April. Imola. Italy.
FIM F750. (Two 100 mile legs.)
Leg 1. 12th.
Leg 2. 9th.
250cc. 100 mile. 1st.

10 April. Misano Italy.
250cc. 5th.
17 April. Paul Ricard. France.
250cc. 3rd.
750cc. DNF (seized).

23 April. Mettet. Belgium.
250cc. 5th.
750cc.DNF.

29 April. Austrian Grand Prix. Salzburgring.
350cc. DNF (crash).

6 May. West German Grand Prix. Hockenheim.
250cc. 7th.

13 May. Italian Grand Prix. Imola.
250cc. DNF (engine trouble).
350cc. DNF. (ran out of fuel 2 laps from end of race while 3rd)

22 May. Spanish Grand Prix. Jarama.
250cc. 11th.
350cc. DNF (crash resulting in broken scaffoid).

12 June. Raalte. Holland.
250cc. 3rd.
350cc. 2nd. (fastest lap).

18 June. Yugoslavian Grand Prix. Opatija.
250cc. DNF.
350cc. DNF.

25 June. Dutch T.T. Assen.
250cc. DNF.
350cc. 1st.

3 July. Belgian Grand prix. Spa-Francorchamps.
250cc. 6th. (average speed: 199 kph!)

10 July. Zandvoort. Holland.
350cc & 500cc combined. Points from 2 legs to count.
Leg 1. 4th
Leg 2. DNF. (crash).
Leg 3. 10th.
Overall. 8th.

24 July. Swedish Grand Prix. Anderstorp.
250cc. DNF.
350cc. 2nd. (lap record).

31 July. Finnish Grand Prix. Imatra.
250cc. 3rd.
350cc. 13th.

7 August. Czechoslavakian Grand Prix. Brno.
250cc. 4th.
350cc. 7th.

14 August. British Grand Prix. Silverstone.
250cc. 1st.
350cc. 1st. (lap record).

21 August. Salzburgring. Austria.
FIM F750. 11th. (Only one 100 mile leg run due to rain.)

4 September. Assen. Holland.
FIM F750.
1st leg. 5th.
2nd leg. 9th.
Overall position. 6th.

18 September. Imola. Italy.
350cc. 3rd.

25 September. Schwannenstadt. Austria.
350cc. 5th.
250cc. 1st. (fastest lap).

9 October. Mallory Park. Race of the Year.
Race of the Year. DNF (crash).
350cc. 1st. (fastest lap).

1978: Kawasaki Heavy Industries Motorcycle Division. Team Kawasaki U.K.
KR250.
KR350.

Grands Prix:

19 March. Venezuelan Grand Prix. San Carlos.
250cc. 5th.
350cc. 4th.

16 April. Spanish Grand Prix. Jarama.
250cc. 4th.

30 April. Austrian Grand Prix. Salzburgring.
350cc. 1st.(lap record).

7 May. French Grand Prix. Nogaro.
250cc. 3rd.
350cc. 2nd.

14 May. Italian Grand Prix. Mugello.
250cc. 1st. (lap record).
350cc. 1st.

24 June. Dutch TT. Assen.
250cc. 2nd.
350cc. 1st.

2 July. Belgian Grand Prix. Spa-Francorchamps.
250cc. 5th.
23 July. Swedish Grand Prix. Karlskoga.
250cc. 2nd.
350cc. 2nd.
30 July. Finnish Grand Prix. Imatra.
250cc. 1st. (fastest lap).
350cc. 1st.

6 August. British Grand Prix. Silverstone.
250cc. DNF. (crank failure).
350cc. 1st. **Clinched 350cc World Championship.**

20 August. West German Grand Prix. Nurburgring.
250cc. 1st.
350cc. 2nd.

27 August. Czechoslovakian Grand Prix. Brno.
250cc. 1st. (fastest lap).
350cc. 1st. (fastest lap).

Yugoslavian Grand Prix. Rijeka.
250cc. 3rd. **Clinched 250cc World Championship.**
350cc. DNF. (engine trouble).

International events:

2 April. Imola. 100 mile 250cc event. Italy.
250cc. 6th.

9 April. Paul Ricard 100 mile 250cc event. France.
250cc.6th.

25 April. Misano.
250cc 1st.

21 May. Mettet. Belgium.
250cc. 1st.
350cc/500cc combined. 2nd.

9 July. Donington Park. Derbyshire.
250cc. 1st. (fastest lap).
350cc. 1st. (fastest lap).

24 September. Donington Park. Derbyshire.
250cc 1st. (fastest lap).
350cc.1st. (fastest lap).
1 October. Mallory Park. Leicestershire.
250cc. (fastest lap).

30 October. Mallory park. Leicestershire.
350cc. 2nd. (fastest lap).
1979: Kawasaki Heavy Industries Motorcycle Division. Team Kawasaki U.K.
KR250.
KR350.

18 March. Venezuelan Grand Prix. San Carlos.
250cc. 2nd.
350cc. 4th.
29 April. Austrian Grand Prix. Salzburgring.
350cc. 1st. (lap record).

6 May. West German Grand Prix. Hockenheim.
250cc. 1st. (lap Record).
350cc. 4th.

13 May. Italian Grand Prix. Imola.
250cc. 1st. (fastest lap).
350cc. DNF. (crank failure) (fastest lap).

20 May. Spanish Grand Prix.
250cc. 1st. (fastest lap).
350cc. 1st.

17 June. Yugoslavian Grand Prix. Rijeka.
250cc. 4th.
350cc. 1st.

23 June. Dutch TT. Assen.
250cc. 3rd. (lap record).
350cc. DNF. (seizure).

1 July. Belgian Grand Prix. Spa-Francorchamps.
Boycotted.

20 July. Swedish Grand Prix. Karlskoga.
250cc. 5th.

28 July. Finnish Grand Prix. Imatra.
250cc. 1st.
350cc. 9th. (crashed but continued).

12 August. British Grand Prix. Silverstone.
250cc. 1st. (lap record).
Clinched 250cc World Championship.
350cc. 1st. (fastest lap).

19 August. Czechoslovakian Grand Prix. Brno.
250cc. 1st. (fastest lap).
350cc. 1st.
Clinched 350cc World Championship.
2 September. French Grand Prix. Le Mans.
250cc. 1st. (fastest lap).
350cc. 5th.

International Events:

January. Roy Hesketh. Pietermaritzburg. South Africa.
250cc. 1st. (lap Record.)

January. Kyalami. South Africa.
250cc. 1st.

8 July. Donington Park. Derbyshire.
250cc. 1st. (fastest lap).
350cc. 1st. (fastest lap).
14 October. Oulton Park. Cheshire.
250cc. 1st. (fastest lap).
350cc. 1st. (fastest lap).

Raalte. Holland.
250cc. 3rd.
350cc. 1st.

Bol d Or 24 hour endurance. Paul Ricard. France.
Kawasaki Z1000. 7th. Partnered with Jean Francois Balde.

1980: Kawasaki Heavy Industries Motrocycle Division. Team Kawasaki U.K.
KR250.
KR500.

11 May. Italian Grand Prix. Misano.
250cc. DNF. (crash) (fastest lap).
500cc. DNF. (ignition problem).

18 May. Spanish Grand Prix. Jarama.
250cc. 1st. (lap record).
500cc. 13th.

25 May. French Grand Prix. Paul Ricard.
250cc. 1st.
500cc. 8th.

15 June. Yugoslavian Grand Prix.
Absent due to stomach operation.

29 June. Dutch TT.
Absent due to stomach operation.

6 July. Belgian Grand Prix.
Absent due to stomach operation.

27 July. Finnish Grand Prix.
250cc. 1st. (fastest lap).
500cc. 5th.
10 August. British Grand Prix.
250cc. 1st.
500cc. 7th.

17 August. Czechoslovakian Grand Prix.
250cc. 2nd.

24 August. West German Grand Prix.
250cc. 1st. (fastest lap).
500cc. 11th.

International events:

13 April. Donington Park. Derbyshire.
250cc. 1st.(fastest lap).
Shell 500. 7th.
21 September. Mallory Park. Leicestershire.
Race of the Year. 5th.

1981: Kawasaki Heavy Industries Motorcycle Division. Team Kawasaki U.K.
KR500.

26 April. Austrian Grand Prix. Salzburgring.
500cc. 6th.

3 May. West German Grand Prix. Hockenheim.
500cc. DNF. (qualified 9th).

10 May. Italian Grand Prix. Monza.
500cc. DNF. (qualified 6th).

17 May. French Grand Prix. Paul Ricard.
500cc 7th.

31 May Yugoslavian Grand Prix. Rijeka.
500cc. Did not start. Injured in practice.

27 June. Dutch TT. Assen.
500cc. 3rd. (fastest lap).

5 July. Belgian Grand Prix. Spa-Francorchamps.
500cc. DNF. (qualified 12th).

12 July San Marino Grand Prix. Imola.
500cc. 5th.

2 August. British Grand Prix. Silverstone.
500cc. DNF. Rotary valve broke while 3rd.
Shared fastest lap with Mamola.

9 August. Finnish Grand Prix. Imatra.
500cc. 3rd.

16 August. Swedish Grand Prix. Anderstorp.
500cc. 4th.

International Events:

12 April. Donington Park. Derbyshire.
ITV Superbike Challenge. 3rd.
17 April. Brands Hatch. Kent.
Shell 500cc. 3rd.

19 April. Mallory Park. Leicestershire.
Shell 500cc. 4th.

20 April. Oulton Park. Cheshire.
Shell 500cc. 2nd. (fastest lap).

24 May. Brands Hatch. Kent.
Shell 500cc. 4th.
1000cc. King of Brands. 2nd.

21 June. Donington Park. Derbyshire.
ITV Superbike Challenge. 4th.
1300cc Superbikes. (2 legs) 3rd & 4th.
19 July. Snetterton.
Race of Aces. 2nd.

30 August. Donington park. Derbyshire.
Shell 500cc. 2nd.

30 August. Donington Park. Derbyshire.
500cc. 4th.
ITV Superbike Challenge. 4th.

31 August. Oulton Park. Cheshire.
Shell 500cc. 2nd.
(Always beaten by that bloody Crosby!)

20 September. Mallory Park. Leicestershire.
Shell 500cc. 3rd.
(Joint fastest lap with Croz at 99.38mph!)
Race of the Year. 3rd.

25 October. Brands Hatch. Kent.
Shell 500. 3rd.

1982: Kawasaki Heavy Industries Motorcycle Division.
Team Kawasaki U.K.
KR500

28 March. Argentinian Grand Prix. Buenos Aires.
500cc. 8th.

2 May. Austrian Grand Prix. Salzburgring.
500cc. DNF. (qualified 11th).

9 May. French Grand Prix. Nogaro.
Boycotted. Unacceptable circuit and paddock conditions.

23 May. Spanish Grand Prix.
500cc. 9th.
30 May. Italian Grand Prix. Misano.
500cc. 6th.

26 June. Dutch TT. Assen.
500cc. 7th.

4 July. Belgian Grand Prix. Spa-Francorchamps.
500cc. 8th.

18 July. Yugoslavian Grand Prix. Rijeka.
500cc.10th.

1 August. British Grand Prix. Silverstone.
500cc. 7th.
8 August. Swedish Grand Prix. Anderstorp.
500cc. 6th.

5 September. San Marino Grand Prix. Mugello.
500cc. 7th.
26 September. West German Grand Prix. Hockenheim.
500cc. DNF.

International Events:

9 April. Brands Hatch. Kent.
Shell 500cc. 3rd. (shared fastest lap).

11 April. Mallory Park. Leicestershire.
Shell 500cc. 1st.

12 April. Oulton Park. Cheshire.
Shell 500cc. 1st.

18 April. Donington Park. Derbyshire.
500cc Gold Cup. Leg 1. 6th.
Leg 2. DNF.

19/20 June. Donington Park.
ITV Superbike. 2nd.
500cc Trophy race. Leg 1. 5th.
Leg 2. 4th. (4th Overall.)

25 July. Snetterton.
Shell 500cc. 1st. (lap record at 99.87mph).
Race of Aces. 1st. (lap record at 100.01mph).

28/29 August. Donington Park.
ITV Superbike Challenge. 1st. (shared fastest lap).
Shell 500cc. 1st. (shared fastest lap).

3 October. Donington Park.
500cc Workd Cup. Leg 1. 4th.

Leg 2. 2nd. (fastest lap).
10 October. Oulton Park.
Shell 500cc. 1st (lap record).

24 October. Brands Hatch.
Powerbike International. DNF. (outright lap record).
Shell 500cc. 1st. (fastest lap).

1983: No racing activities.

1984: Two appearances.

Tsukigi Racing.
Moriwaki Kawasaki GPZ750.

June. Suzuka. Japan.
100km of Suzuka. 4th.
July. Suzuka. Japan.
World Endurance Championship event.
Suzuka 8 Hr. DNF. (engine failure) (Partner: Rob Phillis).

1985: No racing activities:
1986:

Suzuki Great Britain.
Suzuki GSXR750.

9 March. Daytona. Florida. USA.
200 Mile. DNF. (broken conrod).

Privately entered. Japan.
Honda VFR750.

27 July. Suzuka. Japan.
World Endurance Championship event.
Suzuka 8 Hour. 8th. (Partner: Rob Phillis.)

Ogawa Racing. Japan.
Honda RS250
Honda NSR250

13 September. Suzuka. Japan.
250cc. 6th. (Honda RS250.)

20 September. Fuji. Japan.
250cc. Leg 1. DNF (Honda RS250. Front brake problem.)
Leg 2. 3rd. (Honda NSR250.)
MacLean Racing. AMA National Series.
Honda NS500.

18 May. Sears Point. California.
500cc. 1st.
1 June. Brainerd. Minnesota.
500cc. 2nd.

8 June. Road America. Wisconsin.
500cc. 3rd.

14 June. Loudon. New Hampshire.
500cc. 2nd.

22 June. Pocono. Pennsylvania.
500cc. 3rd

13 July. Laguna Seca.
500cc. 4th.

3 August. Mid Ohio. Ohio.
500cc. DNF. (crash while leading).
10 August. Road Atlanta. Atlanta.
500cc. 1st.

1987:

MacLean Racing.
(Some finishing positions not on record.)
Honda NS250.

8 March. Daytona. Florida.
250cc 100 Mile. 1st.

17 May. Road Atlanta. Georgia.
250cc (Not on record.)

7 June. Brainerd. Minnesota.
250cc. 1st.

21 June. Loudon
250cc (Not on record.)

28 June. Road America. Wisconsin.
250cc (Not on record.)

12 July. Laguna Seca. California.
250cc. 2nd.

2 August. Mid Ohio. Ohio.
250cc (Not on record.)

9 August. Memphis. Tenesee.
250cc. 2nd. (fastest Lap).
30 August. Sears Point.
250cc. 2nd.

Kawasaki Heavy Industries Motorcycle Division.
Akashi Japan. Kawasaki ZX750R.

25 July. Suzuka. Japan. (Partner: Rob Phillis.)
World Endurance Championship event.
Suzuka 8 hour. DNF. (Clutch failure at 4 hours while 4th.)
1988: MacLean/Buggy Tamai Racing.
(Some finishing positions not on record.)
Honda NS250.

6 March. Daytona.
250cc (Not on record.)

17 May. Road Atlanta. Georgia.
250cc (Not on record.)

19 June. Loudon. New Hampshire.
250cc. DNF (crash).

7 August. Mid Ohio. Ohio.
250cc (Not on record.)

Kawasaki Heavy Industries Motorcycle Division.
Akashi. Japan.
Kawasaki ZX750R.

31 July. Suzuka. Japan.
World Endurance Championship event. (Partner: Rob Phillis.)
Suzuka 8 Hour. 6th.

Index

REDLINE BOOKS
Designed and published by Redline Books. **www.redlinebooks.co.uk**

Other titles from Redline Books - www.redlinebooks.co.uk

Mick Walker's British Racing Motorcycles
ISBN 09531311 0 6
£20

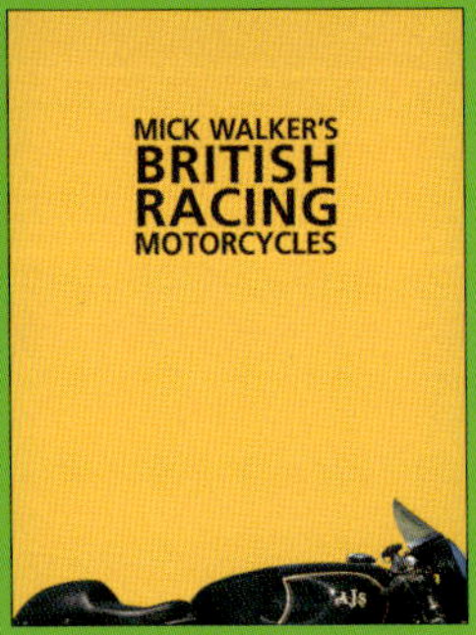

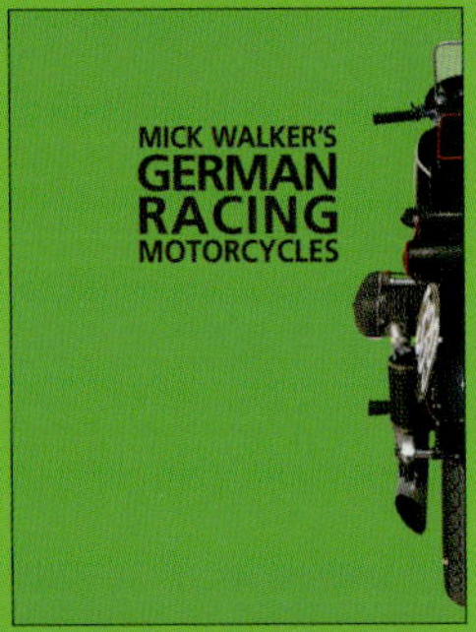

Mick Walker's German Racing Motorcycles
ISBN 09531311 2 2
£20

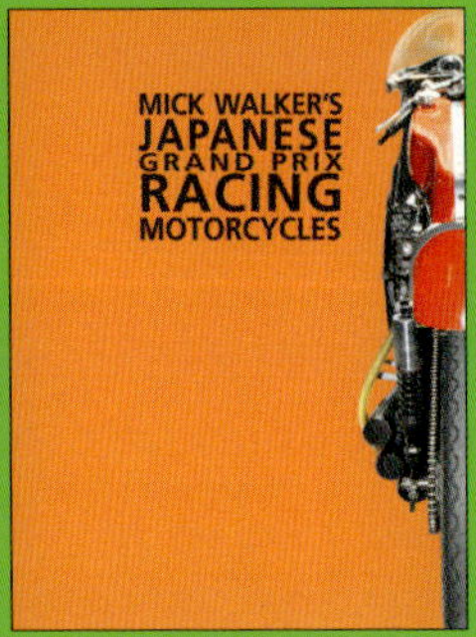

Mick Walker's Japanese Grand Prix Racing Motorcycles
ISBN 09531311 8 1
£20

Moto Morini
ISBN 09544357 2 9
£17.95

Mick Walker's Italian Racing Motorcycles
ISBN 09531311 1 4
£20

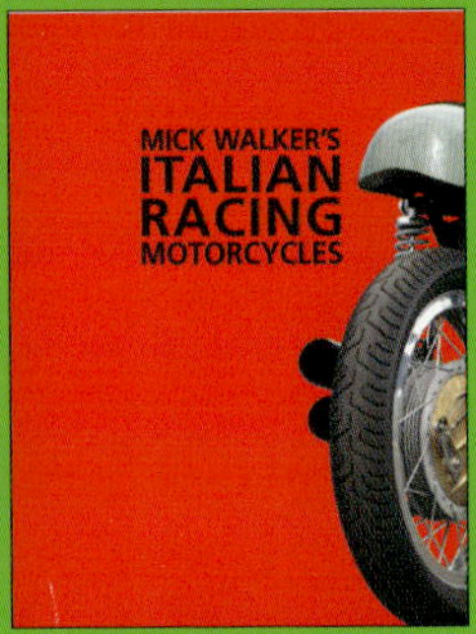

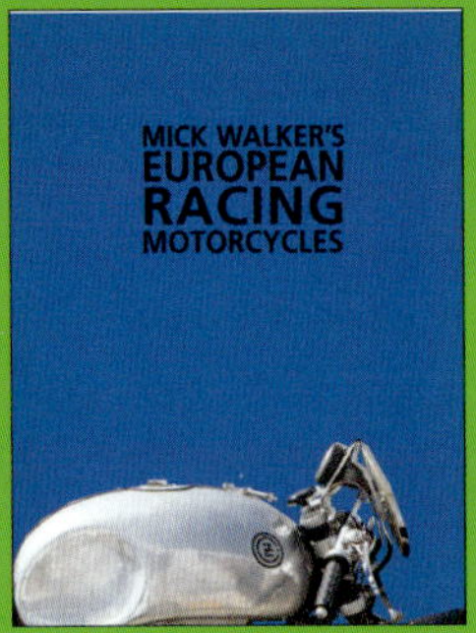

Mick Walker's European Racing Motorcycles
ISBN 09531311 3 0
£20

Mick Walker's Japanese Production Racing Motorcycles
ISBN 09544357 0 2
£25

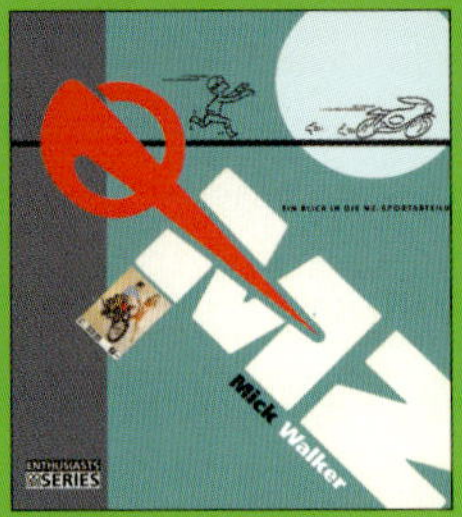

MZ
ISBN 09544357 4 5
£17.95

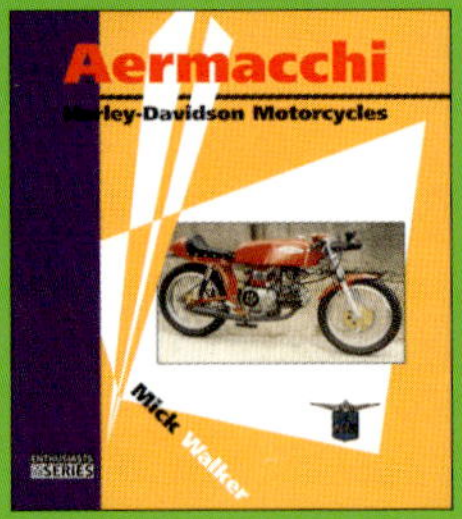

Aermacchi Harley-Davidson Motorcycles
ISBN 09544357 6 1
£19.95

Manx Norton
ISBN 09544357 9 6
£29.95

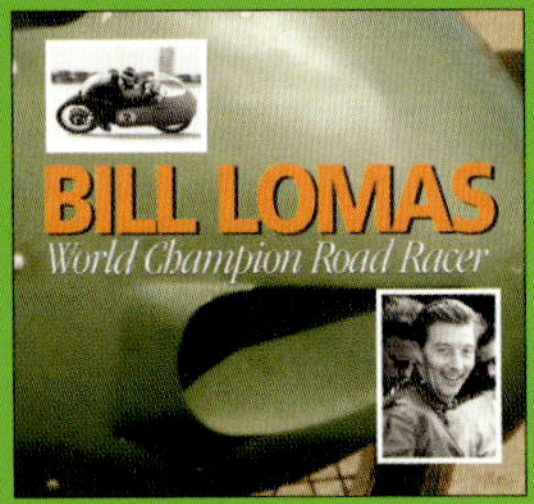

BILL LOMAS
ISBN 09531311 9 X.
£30

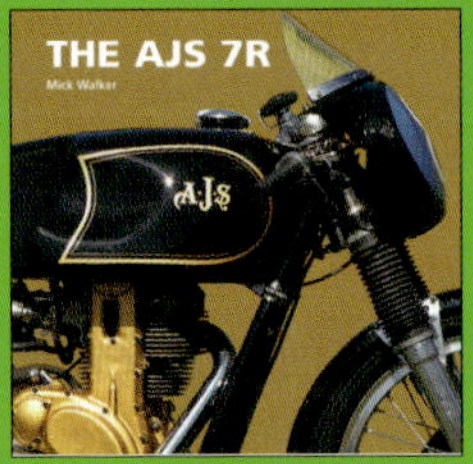

The AJS 7R
ISBN 09531311 7 3
Hardback
£29
ISBN 09531311 6 5
Softback
£20

BSA Gold Star
ISBN 09544357 3 7
£29.95.

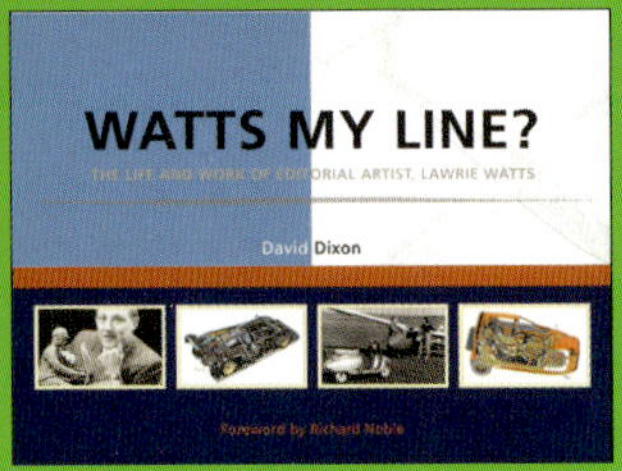

WATTS MY LINE?
ISBN 978 0 9544357 7 6
£19.95

COLIN SEELEY
ISBN 978 0 9544357 1 4
£29.95

JET BLAST
ISBN 978 0 9544357 8 3
£29.95